ZEAL FOR ZION

Shalom Goldman

ZEAL FOR ZION
Christians, Jews, & the Idea of
THE PROMISED LAND

The University of North Carolina Press
Chapel Hill

For Jen
From Shalom Goldman

Designed by Heidi Perov

Set in Dante by Keystone Typesetting, Inc.

The publication of this book was supported by a subvention
from Emory College and the Graduate School of Arts and
Sciences of Emory University.

The paper in this book meets the guidelines for permanence
and durability of the Committee on Production Guidelines for
Book Longevity of the Council on Library Resources.

The University of North Carolina Press has been a member of
the Green Press Initiative since 2003.

Library of Congress Cataloging-in-Publication Data

Goldman, Shalom.

Zeal for Zion : Christians, Jews, and the idea of the Promised Land /
Shalom Goldman.

p. cm.

Includes bibliographical references and index.

ISBN 978-0-8078-3344-5 (cloth : alk. paper)

1. Christian Zionism—History. 2. Zionism—History. 3. Jews—Restoration.
4. Israel—History—Religious aspects—Christianity. I. Title.

DS150.5.G65 2009

320.54095496—dc22

2009030686

cloth   13 12 11 10 09   5 4 3 2 1

In memory of

Professor Eliezer Goldman

(1918–2002),

whose zeal for Zion was

shaped by wisdom

And it came to pass, that, when the sun went down, and it was dark, behold
a smoking furnace, and a burning lamp that passed between those pieces. In the
same day, the Lord made a covenant with Abram, saying, Unto thy seed have I given
this land, from the river of Egypt unto the great river, the river Euphrates.

GENESIS 15:17–18

~

So then the mystery of this restitution of all things is to be found in
all the Prophets: which makes me wonder with great admiration that so few
Christians of our age can find it there. For they understand not that the final return
of the Jews' captivity and their conquering the nations of the four Monarchies and setting up a righteous and flourishing Kingdom at the day of Judgment is this mystery.

SIR ISAAC NEWTON, 1701

~

Oh! Weep for Those

Oh! Weep for those that wept by Babel's stream,
Whose shrines are desolate, whose land a dream,
Weep for the harp of Judah's broken shell—
Mourn—where their God that dwelt—the Godless dwell!

And where shall Israel lave her bleeding feet?
And when shall Zion's songs again seem sweet?
And Judah's melody once more rejoice
The hearts that leap'd before its heavenly voice?

Tribes of the wandering foot and weary breast!
How shall ye flee away and be at rest!
The wild-dove hath her nest—the fox his cave—
Mankind their Country—Israel but the grave.

LORD BYRON, 1815

~

The word Palestine always brought to my mind a vague suggestion of a country as
large as the United States. I do not know why, but such was the case. I suppose it was
because I could not conceive of a small country having so large a history.

MARK TWAIN, 1869

~

[In 1948] beyond the so-called "Jewish vote" there was the country at large,
where popular support for a Jewish homeland was overwhelming. As would sometimes be forgotten, it was not just American Jews who where stirred by the
prospect of a new nation for the Jewish people, it was most of America.

DAVID MCCULLOUGH, 1993

Contents

Illustrations

Acknowledgments

The manuscript of *Zeal for Zion* benefited from careful readings by a dedicated group of colleagues, students, and friends. Among them are Patrick Allitt, Oded Borowski, Michael Dak, Yishai Elder, David Finkelstein, Shlomit Finkelstein, Michael Galchinsky, Ari Goldman, Daniel Goldman, Dov Goldman, Robert Greeley, John Harrison, Susannah Heschel, Tom Jenkins, Uri Katz, Ruby Lal, Julie Lascar, Jeffrey Lesser, Brian Mahan, Gordon Newby, Gyan Pandey, Laurie Patton, Bruce Rodgers, David Tal, Alan Tansman, and Ofra Yeglin.

Thanks are due to the staff of the libraries at these institutions: Columbia University, Emory University, The Jewish Theological Seminary, Tel Aviv University, and the Hebrew University of Jerusalem.

The owners and staff of cafes that provided me a quiet place to work are also due a note of appreciation. Among them are: Emory Starbucks, Sweetwater Café of Sautee, and T'Mol Shilshom of Jerusalem.

To my colleagues at Emory's Department of Middle Eastern and South Asian Studies, to department chair Gordon Newby, and to Emory deans Robert Paul and Lisa Tedesco, thanks are due for support both intellectual and financial.

For editorial and technical assistance, many thanks to Nick Fabian of Emory. Loretta Anderson brought her typing and organizational skills to the project.

To Laurie Patton, partner and first reader, *todah mikerev halev*.

ZEAL FOR ZION

Introduction
The Two Zionisms

We think of Zionism as a Jewish political cause, one to which an occasional "Righteous Gentile" might have lent support. The standard presentations of Zionism, whether written by its proponents or opponents, serve to reinforce this view. They enumerate and describe the movement's Jewish founders, supporters, and adversaries. If there is diversity in these descriptions, it is in the descriptions of the variety of opinions held by Jewish Zionists, and Jewish non-Zionists, in the late nineteenth and early twentieth centuries. For the most part, Christians do not feature in this narrative except as antagonists. For it was implicit in Zionism's self-understanding that Christian anti-Semitism generated the need for a Jewish state as a refuge from persecution. Once that state comes into being, Jews, separated from Christians, could live free and independent lives. Histories of Zionism therefore focus on the Jewish proponents of Jewish territorial nationalism and the unity that Jews achieved through support of Zionism. *Zeal for Zion*, in contrast, makes the case for a wider and more inclusive history, one that takes the Christian involvement with Zionism into account.

Zeal for Zion tells the story of Christian engagement with Zionism through six narratives set in the nineteenth and twentieth centuries. Each narrative is framed around political, cultural, and religious interactions between Christian Zionists and Jewish Zionists. The first three chapters, set before the 1948 establishment of the State of Israel, relate the stories of three personal and political relationships: poet Naphtali Herz Imber and British diplomat and journalist Laurence Oliphant, Zionist leader Theodor Herzl and Anglican cleric Rev. William Hechler, and Hebrew University professor Joseph Klausner and Hebraist Rev. Herbert Danby. The next three chapters, set in the second half of the twentieth century, widen the focus from the individual to the organizational level. Chapter 4 relates the remarkable story of the Vatican's engagement with the State of Israel. In that chapter I demonstrate that despite the Vatican's initial hostility to political Zionism, individual Catholics, among both the clergy and the laity, were supportive of Zionist aims. Their advocacy for Zionism played a part in the church's eventual acceptance of the State of Israel. Chapter 5 tells of three modern literary masters, Jorge Luis Borges, Robert Graves, and Vladimir Nabokov, and their enthusiastic support of the State of Israel. The final chapter chronicles a recent political alliance that some observers of current Middle East affairs praise as "a match made in heaven" and others fear as "the road map to Armageddon." In this chapter I focus on the group that is now popularly designated as "Christian Zionist," the members of conservative evangelical churches who are influenced by fundamentalist views. But as the reader will discover, the term "Christian Zionist" has a much longer history and a much wider connotation. Over the past century, it has been used to describe Catholics and Protestants, liberals and conservatives, reformers and traditionalists. Theodor Herzl, the founder of political Zionism, used the term to describe Christian associates who supported the cause. In each of the book's chapters, we encounter different and changing forms of Christian Zionism and Jewish Zionism, and different and changing forms of Judaism and Christianity. Like the religious and cultural movements from which it emerged, the Zionist movement was in a constant dynamic flux, and this makes the story of Zionism's encounter with the Jewish and Christian religious traditions all the more rich and complex.

Between the 1950s and the 1970s, the number of books on Israel and Zionism increased dramatically. The extensive bibliography of Walter Laqueur's *History of Zionism*, published in 1972, opens with the observation that "there are many thousands of books and pamphlets on Zionism." By 2008, the bibliography of Zionism had grown exponentially, and today there are large libraries and archives devoted to the topic. Why, then, this, another book on Zionism? Because in that vast list of books, there was, until recently, comparatively little on Christians and Zionism. The focus of most broad histories and detailed studies of Zionism has been on its Jewish leaders and their Jewish followers, and for the most part the books were directed toward a Jewish audience. This emerging literature emphasized the persistent Jewish millennial hope for a return to the Land of Israel. The focus in this emerging "official" presentation of Zionism was on the continuity of Jewish aspirations for a renewed Jewish commonwealth. The website of the Israel Ministry of Foreign Affairs presents this long complex history in capsule form that seamlessly joins Jewish history to Zionism: "Yearning for Zion and Jewish immigration continued throughout the long period of exile, following the Roman conquest and the destruction of the Temple in A.D. 70. This yearning took on a new form in the nineteenth century, when modern nationalism, liberalism and emancipation forced the Jews to contend with new questions, which the Zionist movement tried to answer."[1] There is, of course, no denying the power and continuity of the aspiration to return to Zion; it is emphasized in the daily and holiday prayers of the Jewish tradition. But, as historian of ideas Richard Popkin has pointed out, "one has to distinguish between two views: one, the hope of the Jewish people to return some day to their homeland; and the other, setting forth a program to accomplish this end."[2] For two thousand years the hope for a return to Zion was Jewish. But this hope was neither political nor military. Jews in the dispersion were powerless, and they did not come to any consensus about the need for a homeland. Rising anti-Semitism in nineteenth-century Europe, particularly in Russia and Romania, as well as in France and Germany, helped shape a nationalist consensus to which many Jews soon subscribed. Until the late nineteenth century, most plans for a Jewish entity in Palestine were Christian. These plans were predicated on the perception that geographical Palestine was the ancient homeland that "belonged" to Jews. This perception, rooted in a biblical worldview, influenced wide sectors of Christendom. It was a pre-modern perception that persists into modernity, and it continues to influence many Christians to this day, especially, but not exclusively, in the United States.

A related perception, that Jews are a religiously observant people, was equally influential in the formation and growth of Christian Zionism. Here, too, American Christians led the way. This presumption clashed with the realities of Jewish Zionism—that political Zionism was founded and led by secular Jews, and that Israel's ruling elites are to this day secular. If one seeks a measure of "religiosity"—one measure might be the frequency with which citizens attend weekly worship services—the United States is today the most "religious" nation in the Western world. Over 40 percent of Americans attend weekly services. In contrast, only 20 percent of Israeli Jews report that they attend a synagogue weekly. Furthermore, with a flourish uniquely Israeli, 20 percent told pollsters that they would never attend religious services, so assertive is their right to a secular Israeli Jewish identity.

From the seventeenth century onward, programs for the restoration of the Jews to their land were suggested and publicized by Christians, many of them American Protestants. Jews of the pre-modern period did not have the ability to influence international public affairs and were in no position to work for the establishment of a Jewish homeland. From the eighteenth century onward, small groups of European and Middle Eastern Jews began emigrating to Ottoman Palestine. Their motives were religious, and not political. They did not seek to establish a Jewish state. Rather, they wished to fulfill their religious obligations in the land of their fathers. When Jewish political Zionism emerged in the late nineteenth century, an emergence heralded, though not originated, by the publication of Theodor Herzl's *The Jewish State* in 1896, that new political movement quickly forged alliances with Christian proponents of Zionism. Herzl, once he became aware of potential Christian allies, was particularly prescient and active in garnering Christian support for his cause. His successors continued to cultivate that support. They understood, as did Herzl, that assistance was most likely to come from Protestants, and that it was essential to the success of Zionist political aspirations that Christians join Jews in the international campaign to establish a Jewish state in Palestine.

The Promised Land

Central to all forms of Zionism, both Jewish and Christian, is the idea of the Promised Land. Within the narratives of the Hebrew Bible, God's promise to Abraham that his seed will inherit Canaan is fulfilled in the settlement and conquest of Canaan by the tribes of Israel. The scholarly consensus is that the Israelites entered Canaan about 1200 B.C. Israel's long sojourn in the land was interrupted by the Assyrian exile of the inhabitants of the Northern Kingdom ("Israel") in 722 B.C. (these exiles, "the Ten Lost Tribes of Israel" were never to return) and by the Babylonian exile of the people of the Southern Kingdom ("Judah") in 586 B.C. It was during that Babylonian invasion that the First Temple of Jerusalem was destroyed. Under the Persian conquerors of Babylon, some of the Judeans returned in 500 B.C. and built the Second Temple. The prophets of the Hebrew Bible spoke of a future time when all of the exiles, both those of the north ("Israel") and those of the south ("Judah") would be reunited in a rebuilt Zion. With the Roman destruction of the Temple and the city in A.D. 70, the Jews again went into exile. In the rabbinic tradition, this cycle of exile and return was understood as a divinely ordained cycle of reward and punishment. The destructions of Jerusalem and its Temple were therefore read as the consequences of Israel's sins. According to the rabbis, the First Temple was destroyed because the Hebrew people engaged in idolatry, murder, and sexual license. Concerning the Roman destruction of the Second Temple, the Talmud focuses on less dramatic but equally serious infractions of the law. The Jews of the Second Temple period were driven by factionalism and the "hatred of brother for brother." To illustrate this situation, the Talmud tells the story of Kamtza and Bar Kamtza, the Jerusalemites whose bitter feud precipitated the fall of the city. It was their mutual enmity that turned "brother against brother" and brought the Romans to intervene in an ongoing feud between Jewish factions. The dire unexpected consequence was the destruction of Jerusalem and its Temple and the subsequent exile.[3]

The rabbinic tradition, which developed in the aftermath of the Roman sacking of the Holy City and was recorded in the Mishnah (A.D. c. 200) and the Talmud (A.D. c. 600), foresaw a messianic redemption that would recover and restore what had been lost in Jerusalem's destruction. This idea had first been adumbrated in the visions of the Hebrew prophets. The Messiah, "the anointed," descendant of the Davidic line, would preside over the ingathering and restoration of the people of Israel. The Temple of Jerusalem would be restored to its original glory. This concept was based on the biblical prophecies of Isaiah, Jeremiah, Ezekiel, and Micah, and it was amplified and elaborated in the teachings of the rabbis. Jerusalem, in the messianic era, would be a place of prayer for all of the nations. A classical Jewish statement on the universal religious significance of Jerusalem and the Land of Israel is that of Rabbi Judah Halevi, the twelfth-century poet and philosopher, in his book *The Kuzari: An Argument for the Faith of Israel*:

> Moses prayed to see it, and when this was denied to him, he considered it a misfortune. Thereupon it was shown to him from the summit of Pisgah, which was to him an act of grace. Persians, Indians, Greeks, and children of other nations begged to be allowed to offer up sacrifices, and to be prayed for in the holy temple; they spent their wealth at the place, though they believed in other laws not recognized by the Torah. They honor it to this day, although the Shekhinah (the divine presence) no longer appears there. All nations make pilgrimages to it, long for it, excepting we ourselves, because we are punished and in disgrace.[4]

That Jerusalem and its Temple would be restored by divine intervention and not by human endeavor became a tenet of Rabbinic Judaism. Only the Messiah, sent by God, could restore the people of Israel to its land. And it was the Messiah who would rebuild the Temple. The most explicit statement to this effect is the legend of the Three Oaths, recorded in the Babylonian Talmud (Ketubot, 11a): "What are the three oaths? One, that Israel not ascend the wall (to go as one to the Holy Land), one, that they not rebel against the nations of the world, and one that nations swear that they would not oppress Israel too much." This text provided support for early Orthodox Jewish opposition to political Zionism, an opposition that was vociferously expressed in the early decades of the movement. For nineteenth- and early-twentieth-century Zionist leaders, the majority of whom were secularists, the Three Oaths represented a tradition of Jewish passivity that had to be overcome in order for a modern Jewish state to come into being.[5]

For Christians, in contrast, the Roman destruction of Jerusalem was understood as the consequence of the Jewish rejection of Jesus. The Gospels and Letters address this issue early on. The Gospel of Luke tells of Jesus's ascent to Jerusalem in the company of the disciples: "When he came in sight of the city, he wept over it and said, 'If only you had known this day the way that leads to peace! But no; it is hidden from your sight. For a time will come upon you, when your enemies will set up siege-works against you, they will encircle you and hem you in at every point; they will bring you to the ground, you and your children within your walls, and not leave you one stone standing on another, because you did not recognize the time of God's visitation'" (Luke 19:21–24). According to the classical Christian commentators, what the people did not recognize was Jesus's divine mission.

The church fathers Eusebius and Origen make the explicit point that the Temple was destroyed because of the Crucifixion. This point is based on verses in Luke (13:34): "O Jerusalem, Jerusalem, city that murders the prophets and stones the messengers sent to her. How often have I longed to gather your children, as a hen gathers her brood under her wings; but you would not let me. Look! There is your temple, forsaken by God. I tell you, you will not see me until the time comes when you say Blessings on him who comes in the name of the Lord." If the Temple is "forsaken by God," then its fate is destruction. Early Christian ideas of redemption developed within the framework of Jewish messianism. Jesus, the "Christos," or anointed, was presented in the Gospel of Matthew as the descendant of the Davidic kings. A variety of Christian understandings of the Messiah's role were expressed in the books of the New Testament. Some of these understandings were based on new readings of the Hebrew prophets, particularly of Isaiah, Jeremiah, and Ezekiel. Other more visionary ideas about the Messiah were expressed in the New Testament's final and most enigmatic book, Revelation.[6]

Just as the Hebrew Bible underwent what Christians understood as a process of "spiritualization" to become the Christian "Old Testament," the biblical Land of Israel was transformed in the Christian imagination into the Holy Land in which Jesus had lived, died, and was resurrected. Thus, in the first

Christian centuries, while the Jewish tradition continued to express the yearning for Zion in its liturgical and other ritual practices, Christians developed the idea of Palestine as a Christian Holy Land that pilgrims were obligated to protect and visit. Pilgrims to that land could walk in Jesus's footsteps.[7]

That idea is still very much alive today, when more than half of the annual visitors to Israel are Christian. Against the background of the centuries-long transformation of the Land of Israel into the Christian Holy Land, Jewish Zionism offered a considerable challenge to Christian ideas. For it presented a set of political and religious alternatives to Christian understandings of the sanctity of the Holy Land. These understandings were varied and often conflicting. Catholic and Orthodox Christian thinkers were more reluctant than their Protestant counterparts to countenance the possibility of a Jewish state in the Holy Land. The ways in which the challenge of Zionism was met and understood by Christians of different denominations is one of the underlying themes of this book.

~

The Anglican Communion, the Protestant Churches, and the Return to Zion

Since the Reformation, an interest in the restoration of the Jews to their land has been a factor in Anglican and Protestant thought. Among the first English Christian advocates of this restoration were the seventeenth-century theologians Henry Finch and Thomas Brightman. Finch's tract *The Calling of the Jews* predicted that the Jewish people would return en masse to Palestine. Brightman's 1614 commentary on the Book of Daniel was subtitled "The restoring of the Jews and their calling to the faith of Christ after the overthrow of their enemies." Brightman saw Jewish restoration in religious and political terms. Jews would accept Christianity, the Ottoman Turks would be defeated, and Jerusalem would become the new center of a revived Christian faith. Thus, from the early seventeenth century onward, there were English Christian proponents of the Jewish return to Zion. There also were many Christian opponents of the idea. For the proponents, Jewish return was inextricably linked to hopes of the Jews' conversion to Christianity at the end of times. For the opponents, the Jews of their time were not "the true Israel," the beloved of God. The church was "the true Israel"; the Jewish people no longer had a part to play in history. This form of "replacement theology," in which the historical or "carnal" Israel is replaced by the "spiritual" Israel, was articulated forcefully in the Anglican tradition, which, on this point, agreed with Catholic doctrine.

The larger context in which we may situate these restorationist ideas is that of millennialism. Inspired by the vivid visions of the Book of Revelation, or the Apocalypse of John, this belief asserts that God's plan for the End Time is knowable and predictable. The divine plan as described in Revelation predicts a series of catastrophes, but it also promised a thousand-year reign of peace. For much of Christian history, millennialist ideas were tamed, or domesticated, and the predictions of Revelation were understood metaphorically, not historically. From the twelfth century onward, when the Christian mystic Joachim of Fiore offered a literalist reinterpretation of Revelation, many millennialist movements have based their expectations and actions on a more historicized reading of the enigmatic text of the Apocalypse of John. As the text of the Apocalypse is replete with allusions to the Hebrew Bible, the messianic idea, and the city of Jerusalem, the situation and fate of the Jews became a central element in millennialist speculation. Joachim of Fiore wrote of the return of the Jews to Zion as an essential element of the unfolding of the Eschaton, the End Time. He predicted that the events of the End Time would proceed in a well-ordered sequence: the Roman and Eastern Orthodox churches would be reunited, Jews would see the Christian truth, and Christ's eternal reign would commence. Subsequent End Time enthusiasts would offer other scenarios, but common to all Apocalypse-based predictions was the insistence that events would unfold in a very specific and unalterable sequence.

Four centuries later, some Calvinist Reformers also read Revelation in a very literalist manner, most famously in identifying Rome and the papacy with the Antichrist. The English scholar Joseph Mede (1586–1638) went so far as to predict the imminent end of the papacy on the basis of the predictions of Revelation and the Book of Daniel. Prophecy was thus linked powerfully to a new Christian understanding of the unfolding of history according to God's plan.

Interest in the restoration of the Jews was also linked to Luther's concept of "Sola Scriptura" (by scripture alone); the Bible is the primary source of authority. This was one of the theological pillars of the Reformation, and it would have a profound effect in shaping the diverse phenomenon we now refer to as Evangelicalism. The Reformers emphasized the authority of the biblical texts, in contrast to the authority of the pope and the Catholic hierarchy. This shift in emphasis to biblical authority encouraged Anglicans and Protestants to ground their arguments in scripture.

For this reason, many Christian scholars undertook the study of Hebrew. This resulted in the tradition of Christian Hebraism, a tradition that still lives on today. This intellectual endeavor was particularly strong in England; in the seventeenth and eighteenth centuries it took hold in the American colonies. In each of the ten American colleges founded before the American Revolution, biblical Hebrew was an essential part of the curriculum. Hebraism strengthened the American familiarity with—and identification with—the biblical narratives. One quite recognizable vestige of American Hebraism is the presence of Hebrew words on American college seals, most famously on the seals of Yale, Columbia, and Dartmouth.

Among Protestants generally, and American Protestants particularly, a key biblical theme, that "Israel" is a living people to whom "the Promised Land" was granted, was thus given a new emphasis and grounding. For centuries before the Reformation the dominant view in Catholic theology concerning the Jews had been that the church had replaced Israel in God's affections. For the most part, the theologians of the Anglican Church accepted this view. Scriptural references to "Israel" were therefore understood as allegorical references to the church of Christian believers. For some Protestant churches, however, the heretofore abstract idea of "Israel in its Land" took on a concrete meaning. In this new view, Jews, the descendants of the Hebrews of the Bible, should be restored to the Land of Israel. This was particularly true for those Protestants influenced by the dispensationalist ideas of the mid-nineteenth century. Following the teachings articulated most forcefully by John Nelson Darby, these biblical literalists asserted that history was divided into eras or "dispensations," the last of which would soon begin. "Israel" of the Bible was understood by dispensationalists as the actual Jewish people of present times, and the return of "Israel" to their land was a prerequisite of Redemption. As Joel Carpenter has noted, "Premillennialists believe that Jesus Christ will personally and bodily return to earth to defeat the forces of evil and establish the millennium, the age during which, many Christians have affirmed, God's kingdom of holiness, justice, peace and prosperity will prevail on earth for a thousand years."[8] While earlier Christian writers had sought to sunder the ties between biblical Israel and the Jews of their own time, and Reformation theologians struggled with the ramifications of believing in a prophesied restored Israel, Darby and his dispensationalist followers sought to reaffirm the connection between Israel of the Bible and the Jewish people. This effort dovetailed with emerging Jewish Zionist thought, which emphasized the unbroken continuity of the relationship between the people of Israel and the Land of Israel. It also foreshadowed the Zionist call for a renewed emphasis on the Bible, and a decreased emphasis on rabbinic authority.

These historical and theological developments provide the background necessary to understand a fascinating and little-known phenomenon: Between the early seventeenth century and the stirrings of political Zionism in the last decades of the nineteenth century, scores of Christians advanced plans for settlement in Palestine. Not all were obsessed with millennialist speculation. They were driven by a variety of motives, including sympathy for Jews suffering oppression and discrimination. Some Christians actually tried to implement these restorationist plans; among them were British adventurers such as Laurence and Alice Oliphant, American visionaries such as George Washington Adams, and the American Adventist prophetess Clorinda Minor. In the last years of the nineteenth century, as the Ottoman Empire weakened, some leaders of American Protestant denominations were deeply engaged in the question of how the Holy Land would be settled and governed. Their engagement was influenced by their ideas on the unfolding of history and the advent of the millennium. As Kenneth Ray Bain has noted, "Details of the belief varied considerably, but the basic approach centered on the notion that the return of the Jews to power in the Holy Land was a sign from God that time was coming to an end . . . wars and rumors of wars, social turmoil and violence, corruption and growing materialism all combined to convince many that the dire predictions from the Revelation were true."[9]

In a striking parallel to these Christian "yearnings for Zion," Jewish thinkers, beginning in the eighteenth century, were also moved by visions of divine redemption and advocated the "ascent" to Israel of small groups of Jews. Some of these Jewish visionaries embarked on small-scale settlement. For example, three hundred rabbis and their families "ascended" from Europe to Ottoman Palestine in the late eighteenth century. Along with other pious Jewish immigrants, they settled in the four holy cities: Jerusalem, Hebron, Safed, and Tiberias. Among both Jews and Christians these settlement attempts increased at times of intense messianic speculation, such as in the year 1840. In the last decades of the nineteenth century, as political Zionism emerged and Jews were able to actively participate in the public life of the United States and some countries in Western Europe, Jewish plans for Jewish settlement in Palestine were publicized and implemented.

These plans had their opponents. Most, but not all, European Orthodox rabbinical authorities opposed Zionist plans for a Jewish political entity in Palestine. Individual or small group settlements were acceptable to these Orthodox rabbis, but any larger political plans contravened the idea that Jewish redemption would come only through divine intervention. The most religiously conservative of these rabbis invoked the Talmudic legend of the Three Oaths as a way of expressing their opposition to modernity in general and Zionism in particular. Reform rabbis were wary of Jewish nationalism for different reasons. They feared that plans for a Jewish state would undercut the political and social progress Jews had achieved in Western Europe and the United States.

The founders of the Zionist movement were keenly aware of sympathy for Zionism among some influential Catholics and Protestants. Zionist publicists wrote in *Hamaggid* and other Hebrew-language Zionist journals of earlier Christian settlement attempts, and they exhorted Jewish readers to act as bravely and resolutely as Christian Zionists had in their attempts to settle in the Land of Israel. The Adams colony of Jaffa, Clorinda Minor's colony in Artas, and the German Templer colonies of Haifa, Jaffa, and Sarona were held up as examples of courage and industriousness by Zionist writers. The seven Templer colonies, built by German Christian Pietists between 1869 and 1907, were models of efficiency and productivity. As the Israeli historian Yossi Ben-Artzi has noted, these colonies, "as the first truly planned settlements in modern Palestine, were exemplary models that inspired the local Arabs, the Turkish rulers, and most of all the Jews, who in 1882 began reaching Palestine in large numbers with a goal similar to that of the Germans: settlement in agricultural colonies."[10]

The United States and the Restoration of the Jews

American Protestants, from the colonial period onward, had a particular interest in plans to restore the Jews to their Promised Land. The biblical self-image of the early American colonists, a self-image reflected in the over two hundred biblical place names on the map of the United States, had a profound effect on American attitudes toward the Holy Land. By naming their towns and cities Salem, Hebron, Bethlehem, and Pisgah, Americans were declaring the New World a "biblical" area. They were also asserting an American connection to the places where Christianity originated. American scholars, foremost among them nineteenth-century biblical scholar Edward Robinson, were among the pioneers of discovery and archaeology in Palestine. Robinson, professor of sacred literature at New York City's Union Theological Seminary, traveled to Palestine in 1836 and 1852. He was convinced that one could not fully understand the Old and New Testaments without a thorough study of the land of the Bible. Robinson's five-volume opus, *Biblical Researches in Palestine, Mt. Sinai and Arabia Petraea*, was widely read by American and European scholars and laymen. For Robinson and his readers, the Holy Land was a "Third Testament" without which the other Testaments could not be fully understood. Robinson, a tireless "biblical researcher," as he styled himself, articulated an American Christian yearning to study that "Third Testament" firsthand. In the introduction to his book, Robinson wrote, "As in the case of most of my countrymen, especially in New England, the scenes of the Bible had made a deep impression on my mind from the earliest childhood, and afterwards in riper years this feeling had grown into a strong desire to visit in person the places so remarkable in the history of human race."[11]

Among Edward Robinson's discoveries was the site of Masada, the Herodian fortress described by the historian Josephus. That the mountain Robinson saw from Ein Gedi was Masada was suggested to him by his translator and traveling companion, Eli Smith. Smith, a fellow biblical researcher, was a longtime American missionary in the Levant and translator of the New Testament into Arabic. Robinson and Smith did not climb Masada, though. That honor went to another American Christian missionary, S. W. Wolcott, who investigated the site in 1842. In the 1930s, a century after Robinson's first visit to Palestine, Masada was promoted as a site of great importance for the Zionist movement. A key future in that effort was Zionist youth movement leader Shmaria Guttman (1909–96). Guttman climbed Masada in 1933 and became convinced of the site's potential as a signifier of Zionist strength and determination. Masada, the fortress (Hebrew "Metzudah") in which Jewish zealots in rebellion against Rome committed mass suicide rather than surrender to the Tenth Roman legion, became a potent symbol of Zionism both before and after the 1948 establishment of Israel. In 1983, fifty years after Guttman climbed Masada, Israeli defense minister Moshe Dayan wrote, "Today we can point to the fact that Masada has become a symbol of heroism and of liberty for the Jewish people to whom it says: Fight to death rather than surrender; prefer death to bondage and loss of freedom."[12] In June 2008, Masada was one of the Israeli sites visited by President George W. Bush. In his address to the Knesset, the Israeli parliament, Bush quoted the Israeli maxim that "Masada shall not fall again."

Throughout the nineteenth and twentieth centuries, thousands of Americans of various Christian denominations traveled to the Holy Land. Mormons and Catholics were among the most active and enthusiastic of these travelers. In 1836, the prophet and founder of the Mormon Church, Joseph Smith, mentioned the actual physical return of the Jews to Zion in his dedicatory prayer at the Kirtland Temple in Ohio. Smith prayed that "Jerusalem, from this hour, may begin to be redeemed; and the yoke of bondage may begin to be broken off from the house of David." Smith understood "Zion" as both the spiritual designation of a new American sacred space and a reference to the Zion of biblical Israel, a city that would soon be renewed. The East had its Zion, and now the West, in the United States, would have its Zion. Both Zions would experience "the literal gathering of Israel and the restoration of the ten tribes."[13] Mormons were eager to visit Jerusalem, to which Joseph Smith had sent his emissary Orson Hyde. For centuries, Catholics had visited the Jerusalem's Church of the Holy Sepulcher and the many other holy places throughout the Holy Land. Many of the Christian pilgrims kept diaries of their journeys, and hundreds of Palestine travel accounts were published and eagerly read by nineteenth-century audiences.

Especially influential were the nineteenth-century books about Palestine written for North American children. Titles such as Henry Osborn's *The Little Pilgrims in the Holy Land* (1861) and Hester Douglas's *The Land Where Jesus Christ Lived* (1890) were extremely popular, as was Mrs. Annie Johnstone's *Joel: A Boy of Galilee: A Story of the Time of Christ* (1895). In these accounts, entertainment went hand in hand with edification. The geography and history of biblical tales were also taught to schoolchildren in a more straightforward manner. As Edward Robinson's five-volume *Biblical Researches in Palestine* was too daunting for many teachers and students, Robinson published a more accessible work, *A Dictionary of the Holy Bible, for the Use of Schools and Young Persons* (1833).[14] A decade later the biblical scholar and Swedenborgian mystic Professor George Bush of New York University published *Valley of Vision; or, The Dry Bones of Israel Revived: An Attempted Proof of the Restoration and Conversion of the Jews.* Bush, in a polemic against millennialist ideas, argued that the restoration of the Jews to Palestine would occur naturally, as the result of "the affairs of the nations, or the progress of civilization." Restoration would result not from miraculous divine intervention but rather from natural developments within the divine plan. Speaking of Ezekiel's vision of the dry bones of Israel revived, Bush wrote, "Nothing more is implied that it will be so ordered in Providence that motives will be furnished for such a return, appealing it may be to the worldly and selfish principles of the Jewish mind."[15]

The American experience of the Holy Land was not limited to reading travel accounts, whether written for children or adults. After the Civil War, the development of long-range steamship travel enabled large-scale tourism to Europe and the Middle East. Mark Twain's account of one of these early tours, told in his raucous best-selling book *The Innocents Abroad*, both publicized and satirized these "pilgrimages."

Pilgrimage and tourism were joined in grand excursions. In March of 1904, over eight hundred American Sunday school teachers embarked on the North

German Lloyd steamer *Grosser Kurfurst* for a journey to Palestine and other "mission fields" of the Middle East. The high point of the voyage was "The World Sunday School Convention in Jerusalem" held over the Easter holiday. There the American pilgrims met with their counterparts from Europe, from which six hundred delegates came to the convention. This journey left a profound impression on the visitors and on their associates back in the United States, who heard and read detailed accounts of their journey.[16] Many photographs of this pilgrimage were circulated in American churches and Sunday schools.

To this day the American fascination with the Bible and the "Bible Lands" continues in many forms. Americans unable or unwilling to travel to Israel can visit the Holy Land Experience theme park in Orlando, Florida, or they can visit other Holy Land models throughout the United States. The first of these American Holy Land substitutes was built in Chautauqua, New York, in 1874. Known as Palestine Park, it drew visitors from all over the United States. Thirty years later, at the Louisiana Purchase Exposition, the St. Louis World's Fair of 1904, a model of Jerusalem's Old City was constructed on the fairgrounds. To lend the exhibit an air of authenticity, hundreds of craftsmen and guides from Jerusalem were brought to St. Louis to staff the Old City replica. The model of the Church of the Holy Sepulcher was among the most popular of the fair's exhibits.[17] Today, at the beginning of the twenty-first century, hundreds of thousands of American evangelicals visit Israel annually. American Christian tourism accounts for a large part of Israel's "pilgrimage economy" (in 2007, it accounted for half of Israel's tourism), and American evangelical Christian political support is highly prized by the Israeli government.

~

Earlier Scholarship on Christians and Zionism

What has been the scholarly understanding of the relationship between these seemingly distinct movements, Christian Zionism and Jewish Zionism? In the mid-twentieth century a few scholars began to grapple with this question. In 1953, English historian Christopher Sykes, in examining the religious background of the Balfour Declaration, noted that "so much has been written on Zionism within the last thirty years that, when producing a new essay, some apology may be thought necessary." Sykes's essay, in *Two Studies in Virtue*, was "primarily addressed to Gentile readers," for, in his words, "a very high proportion of the best Zionist books in Great Britain and America are addressed to Jewish audiences and assume a knowledge of Jewish history rare among

Gentiles who have not made detailed studies."[18] From Sykes's essay we learn how deeply British foreign secretary Lord Balfour's religious beliefs influenced his political decisions, particularly on the question of a Jewish return to Palestine, which he felt would be the fulfillment of biblical prophecy. Many of Zionism's supporters expressed similar sentiments. For when the Balfour Declaration was issued, Jews and Christians in large numbers responded to its support for a "Jewish national home" in Palestine with modern forms of messianic expectation. Sykes thus opened up the question of the relationships between the two Zionisms, Christian and Jewish, but in the decades that followed, the trajectory of scholarship on Zionism was in the opposite direction. It focused on Jewish Zionism. When Christian Zionism was mentioned in the emerging large body of literature on Zionism, it was assigned a peripheral role.

Two early and important exceptions to the initial scholarly neglect of Christian Zionism were the opening chapters of Nahum Sokolow's *The History of Zionism, 1600–1918*, published in 1919, and N. M. Gelber's *Zur Vorgeschichte des Zionismus* (On the prehistory of Zionism), published in 1927. Both Sokolow and Gelber were ardent Zionists who devoted their professional lives to the cause. Sokolow, and following him Gelber, lauded and described the many Christian "precursors of Zionism" who advocated the restoration of the Jews to their land. Three decades later, Franz Kobler's *The Vision Was There: A History of the British Movement for the Restoration of the Jews to Palestine* was published. But while Kobler gathered much information, he supplied little analysis. In 1978 Israeli scholar Yona Malachy published *American Fundamentalism and Israel: The Relation of Fundamentalist Churches to Zionism and the State of Israel*. Malachy's introduction notes, "No one has so far dealt with the history of Christian Zionism in a comprehensive manner."[19] This was framed as the rationale for his short book, but it was a mandate his book did not fulfill, for he focused on one particular subset of fundamentalist evangelical Protestants. Among specialized studies of Protestant denominational aspects of American Christian Zionism are *American Protestantism and a Jewish State*, Hertzel Fishman's 1973 study, and Yaakov Ariel's 1991 authoritative work on dispensationalism, *On Behalf of Israel: American Fundamentalist Attitudes toward Jews, Judaism, and Zionism, 1865–1945*. Today a comprehensive study of the topic is more important than ever, especially as Christian Zionism in its various forms is now a major force in American political life.

The most detailed description of English Christian "proto-Zionism" was Barbara Tuchman's *Bible and Sword: England and Palestine from the Bronze Age to Balfour*, published in 1956. Tuchman's highly influential book left its many readers with the impression that the majority of pre-modern English church-men were supporters of restoring the Jews to Palestine. We read little in Tuchman of opposition to such plans. But there was considerable opposition, especially in High Church circles. Among church missionaries to the Jews there was considerable opposition to a "national restoration." In 1849 the Reverend William Withers Ewbank addressed the annual meeting of the Society for Promoting Christianity Among the Jews. In a speech titled "The National Restoration of the Jews to Palestine Repugnant to the Word of God," Ewbank descried any tendency within the church to distinguish between Jew and Gentile. True restoration, said Ewbank, was "to restore the Jews to the true Church of God, to their own olive tree. For God's Church was once their Church. . . . It pleased Him, in his great goodness, to abolish its old Covenant by giving it a new and better one." In Ewbank's view, a national home for Jews would only encourage their resistance to the Christian message: "Let us rather beseech him . . . to restore himself to that Church which may again be his own as well as ours. We will all welcome him as a brother in Christ."[20] Tuchman's book, published during Israel's first decade, was itself a work of advocacy for Zionism and as such left students of the topic with the impression that advocates of Jewish restoration represented a majority opinion within what would later be known as "the chattering classes" of the English-speaking world.

Arthur Hertzberg's influential 1959 anthology *The Zionist Idea* makes no mention of Christian precursors of the Zionist idea. His "precursors" are the nineteenth-century Jewish thinkers Alkalai, Kalischer, and Hess. In his 1969 introduction to a reprinting of Sokolow's *History of Zionism*, Hertzberg pointed out that Sokolow, a representative of the Zionist movement who was hopeful of fulfilling Zionist aspirations with British imperial assistance, "set out to prove that there had been a long and previously little known tradition of British, and to some degree, of French interest in the restoration of a Jewish state in Palestine. He thus presented the Zionist demands from the Jewish side as no new idea, but rather, as a response to earlier religious and political thinking by Christians."[21] Hertzberg thus implies that there were no actual Christian precursors; Sokolow was overstating their importance. Zionism, for Hertzberg, and most other twentieth-century historians, was a thoroughly Jewish movement, and it should be studied and analyzed as such.

This insistence on the exclusively Jewish origins of Zionism is related to the dominant trends in Zionist historiography. In an 1897 diary entry Herzl predicted that a Jewish state would come into being, "perhaps in fifty years." Herzl's startling prediction of 1897 was fulfilled, and a Jewish state was

THE

NATIONAL RESTORATION OF THE JEWS

TO

PALESTINE

REPUGNANT TO THE WORD OF GOD;

A SPEECH,

DELIVERED IN THE LECTURE HALL OF THE COLLEGIATE

INSTITUTION, IN LIVERPOOL, AT THE

ANNIVERSARY MEETING OF THE AUXILIARY SOCIETY FOR PROMOTING

CHRISTIANITY AMONGST THE JEWS, OCT. 21, 1849,

The Lord Bishop of Chester

IN THE CHAIR:

BY WILLIAM WITHERS EWBANK, M.A.

MINISTER OF ST. GEORGE'S CHURCH, IN EVERTON.

———

Ὁ ποιήσας τὰ ἀμφότερα ῞ΕΝ.
Who hath made both ONE.—Eph. ii. 14.

———

LIVERPOOL: DEIGHTON AND LAUGHTON.
LONDON: F. AND J. RIVINGTON.
CAMBRIDGE: JOHN DEIGHTON.
1849.

Title page of William Withers Ewbank's speech "The National Restoration of the Jews to Palestine Repugnant to the Word of God" (Emory University Libraries) established within fifty-one years of his envisioning it. In telling the story of the establishment of the state, Israeli historians, politicians, and educational leaders have for the most part reinforced a sense of Jewish accomplishment and separateness. That ubiquitous Israeli phrase, "After two thousand years," conveys the idea that, with a state of their own, Jews had separated from the European and Middle Eastern cultures in which they had originated and were now free to develop institutions that reflected their newfound independent Jewish identity. For this reason Zionist educators found it imperative to emphasize that the separation from "exile" and the creation of a "national home" were solely Jewish accomplishments. Furthermore, for Zionists, the State of Israel was seen as the culmination of Jewish accomplishment; it was the goal toward which Jewish history had been marching for two millennia. Separation from Christians and Christianity was the only way to insure Jewish survival. Therefore, in the prevailing ideology of the first decades of Israeli culture, Gentiles were actors in the history of Zionism only insofar as they had persecuted Jews and thereby generated the need for a Jewish state. If some Gentiles had helped pave the way, they were marginalized as rare exceptions. Their contributions were seldom mentioned and less often praised.

Overlooked in this analysis was the fact that Bible-reading Christians all over the world had for centuries thought of Palestine as the Land of Israel, as had Jews throughout the Diaspora. It was this identification that had enabled Jewish Zionists, with the help of some Christians, to turn that perception into a political reality in the half century between the First Zionist Congress and the establishment of the State of Israel in 1948.

⁓

Zionism and the Jewish-Christian Relationship

Some scholars would agree with the opinion expressed by historian Evyatar Friesel in a 2006 essay titled "Zionism and Jewish Nationalism": "The author is aware of the historical interest in certain non-Jewish quarters, especially in nineteenth-century England, toward the restoration of the Jews to the Holy Land. An examination—admittedly not systematic enough—regarding the relationship between these ideas and the emergence of Zionism suggests only a very marginal and indirect influence."[22] Other scholars, myself among them, have found a more direct and powerful connection between Christian Zionism and Jewish Zionism. As historian of ideas Richard Popkin noted in the early 1990s, "Much of Zionism has its roots in Christian rather than Jewish doctrine."[23] Among those doctrines is the tendency in the Protestant churches to read biblical narrative and prophecy in a more literal and historical manner than had been the tradition in either Rabbinic Judaism or in the Orthodox or Catholic Churches. Equally relevant is the millennialist trend in Protestant history. By the mid-twentieth century, three centuries of Christian enthusiasm for a return of the Jews to their land created an atmosphere in the West in which previously inchoate and unrealizable Jewish aspirations for a revived national home could take shape and find direction.

Gideon Shimoni's 1995 study *The Zionist Ideology* briefly surveys "Christian Ideas of Jewish Restoration." Shimoni points out, "No doubt, the cumulative weight of Christian restorationist ideas, particularly those appealing to the political interests of European powers, contributed to the intellectual and political atmosphere that accorded a degree of credibility to various 'proto-Zionist' proposals by Jews in the course of the nineteenth century. By the same token, they had a bearing on the history of Zionism as a movement, for they endowed some leading statesmen—Arthur James Balfour is the most famous example—with a predisposition favorable to Zionism." Shimoni's summation ends with a note of caution about overall conclusions on the significance of Christian restorationist ideas in the implementation of Zionist aims. "This is a subject," writes Shimoni, "that still awaits definitive research."[24]

In the late nineteenth century, Theodor Herzl's vision of "a state for Jews" resonated powerfully with Christian scholars, churchmen, and diplomats. Through the good offices of Rev. William Hechler, Anglican chaplain of the British embassy in Vienna, Herzl made his first diplomatic contacts with Kaiser Wilhelm and other European rulers. Through the intervention of another prominent Christian, Professor Arminius Vambery of Budapest, Herzl met with the Turkish sultan Abdul Hamid II. On the 1997 centenary anniversary of the First Zionist Congress, Israeli historian Alex Carmel called for the reinstatement of Hechler and other Christian Zionists into Zionist history. Carmel described the absence of William Hechler from standard Zionist histories as "astonishing."[25]

What, we might ask, was so significant about Rev. William Hechler's philo-Semitic and Zionist activities, and why are they worth recovering and recounting? In 1881 he joined Laurence Oliphant and other British notables in collecting and distributing funds for Russian and Romanian Jews victimized by the pogroms. In 1883 Hechler wrote a one-page broadside titled "The Restoration of the Jews to Palestine." He had hundreds of copies of this tract distributed in the churches and streets of London. This was over a decade before Herzl wrote *The Jewish State*. Accompanying his friend Theodor Herzl, William Hechler attended each of the early Zionist Congresses, and Hechler continued to serve the movement for twenty-five years after Herzl's death. As Alex Carmel has suggested, "One hundred years after the First Zionist Congress, the time has come to honor all of Herzl's numerous Christian friends, especially Hechler."[26] Through the stories of Laurence Oliphant, William Hechler, Herbert Danby, and other Christian "lovers of Zion," *Zeal for Zion* chronicles and analyzes the relationship between "the two Zionisms," Jewish and Christian, and makes the case that they have always been inextricably bound.

Many nineteenth- and early-twentieth-century English and American literary figures expressed sympathy for the rebirth of Jewish life in Palestine. Perhaps the most influential of them was George Eliot, whose novel *Daniel Deronda* had an enormous effect on British and American public opinion. When Eliot's novel was published in the United States—and soon afterward translated into Russian, German, French, Yiddish, and Hebrew—it influenced Christian and Jewish readers throughout the world. In the novel, Mordecai, Daniel Deronda's teacher, says that when Jews have a state, "our race shall have an organic center, a heart and brain to watch and guide and execute; the outraged Jew shall have a defense in the court of the nations, as the outraged Englishman or American. And the world will gain, as Israel gains. . . . Difficulties? I know there are difficulties. But let the spirit of sublime achievement move the great among our people, and the work will begin."[27] Among the young European Jews who were deeply influenced by *Daniel Deronda* were Eliezer Perlman (later Eliezer Ben-Yehuda), pioneer of the revival of the Hebrew language, and David Green (later David Ben-Gurion), Israel's first prime minister. Eliezer Ben-Yehuda, in his autobiography, *A Dream Come True*, tells of the rabbinic education he rejected and of the secular Jewish nationalist vision that replaced it. His life task, as he saw it, would be "the restoration of Israel and its language on the land of its ancestors." To his dismay, Perlman/Ben-Yehuda's Orthodox yeshiva teachers and fellow students rejected his Zionist ideas. One yeshiva friend, though, did not reject him. Rather, he told Perlman of "an English story he had read in the monthly Russian journal 'Vestnik Evropi' in which a man was described who had a vision similar to [Perlman's] own. . . . It was the novel *Daniel Deronda*, by George Eliot." "After I read the story a few times," Perlman wrote, "I made up my mind and I acted: I went to Paris, to the source of light and the center of international politics, in order to learn and equip myself there with the information needed for my work in the Land of Israel."[28] George Eliot's "Zionist novel" was enthusiastically received in the small Jewish agricultural colonies in Palestine. Avshalom Feinberg, born in Gedera in 1889, read *Daniel Deronda* as a boy. It

THE RESTORATION OF THE JEWS
TO PALESTINE.

שַׁאֲלוּ שְׁלוֹם יְרוּשָׁלָ͏ם

Pray for the peace of Jerusalem.

"They forget a main part of the Church's glory, who pray not daily for the Jew."—Archbishop Leighton.

Some points to be remembered in connection with this most important question.

I. Precursory Signs.

1. When we speak of the Restoration of *Israel*, we mean
an event which is *still in the future*,
when the *Jews* will confess and receive *Jesus as their true Messiah*,
and be again in their own land.
And we believe the time is *close at hand*, when
God will restore *His ancient people* to their own land, Palestine;
because :—(a) there are *many signs* gathering quickly around us,
which lead to the belief that
the Lord's coming is near;   Heb. x. 25.

". " There shall be.........distress of nations, with perplexity ; ....
Men's hearts failing them for fear, and for looking after
those things which are coming on the earth." Luke xxi. 25, 26.
and our Lord added,
" When ye see these things come to pass,
know ye that the kingdom of God is at hand." Luke xxi. 31.

(b) specially there is an increasing interest shown on the part
of Christians and others in the
land, the *prospects*, and *hopes* of the Jewish people.
Palestine was *a land that no man cared for ;* but it is not so now.
" Thou shalt arise, and have mercy on Zion,
for the time to favour her, yea, the set time, is come,
For thy servants take pleasure in her stones,.........
When the Lord shall build up Zion,
He shall appear in His glory." Ps. cii. 13, 14, 16.

II. Dispersion Fulfilled.

2. The present *dispersion* of the Jews among all nations, and
the *desolation* of their land Palestine,
are *distinctly foretold* in the Bible by Moses and the prophets.
(Compare Lev. xxvi. 33.) Deut. xxviii. 62, 64. Jer. ix. 11, 15, 16. Amos ix. 9. Luke xxi. 24.
3. Now, these prophecies have been *literally fulfilled*, for the Jews
have been *dispersed* ever since the destruction of Jerusalem
and the temple by the Romans under Titus.
4. It is most remarkable that to this day the Jews have remained,
although scattered among all the *nations* of the earth,
a *distinct and separate people*, as foretold in the Old Testament.
"The people shall dwell alone, and shall not be reckoned among the nations." Num. xxiii. 9.

But as the dispersion of the Jews has been literally fulfilled,
so also must be their restoration.

III. Restoration Foretold.

5. Accordingly the *future restoration* of the Jews is *also foretold* by the
prophets.
Remember, *prophecy* is *history* written beforehand by inspiration.
(Lev. xxvi. 44, 45.) Is. xl. 11, 12 ; xxvii. 13 ; xliii. 5–7 ; lx. 8–10. Jer. xvi. 14, 15 ; xxiii. 5–8 ;
xxvi. 19 ; xxxii. 37–43 ; xlvi. 27, 28. Ezek. xxxiv. 11–16, 25–31 ; xxxvi. 8–38 ; xxxvii. 21 ;
xxxix. 25. Hosea ii. 19 ; iii. 4, 5. Micah ii. 12 ; iv. 6, 7. Zech. viii. 1–8 ; x. 6–11. Rom. xi. 25, 26.

These prophecies must have a literal fulfilment ;
just as those of their dispersion.
6. After the Babylonish Captivity
portions only of the *two* tribes of *Judah* and *Benjamin*, and a great
number of *Levites* returned to the Holy Land.
Ezra ii. 1, 70 ; iv. 1, 12 ; v. 1 ; x. 5. Zeph. iii. 20. Zech. xii. 6, 7.
The other *ten* tribes remained in the land of their captivity,
and *have not yet returned.* Is. xxvii. 12, 13. Jer. 30, 4, 5.
7. The passages, which refer to the restoration of the *whole nation*
cannot be applied to their *partial return* from Babylon ;
because :—(a) in that day *all the twelve tribes* are to be gathered in ;
not two tribes only ; (See 6) Is. xi. 11, 12. Hos. i. 11.
(b) the future restoration of the Jews
is to be from *all lands ;*
not from *one land* only, as then, from Babylon ;
Is. xi. 11, 12 ; xliii. 5, 6. Jer. xvi. 14, 15.
(c) when finally restored   Amos ix. 14, 15.
the Jews are *never again to be scattered* among all nations ;
hence their last restoration cannot have taken place.
8. Many books of the Jews abound in confident expressions of hope,
and *petitions for restoration* to their own land,
and *confess*, that they have been scattered because of their sins.
We believe their great sins since their return from Babylon have
been :——
(a) the crucifixion of Jesus, their Messiah ; Zech. xii. 10. Rev. i. 7.
(b) their rejection of the witness of the Holy Ghost in the
Christian Church.   Acts vii. 51. 1 Thess. ii. 15, 16.
9. With reference to the *conversion* of the Jews,
(a) some passages speak of their conversion *before restoration*,
(Compare Lev. xxvi. 40–43.) Deut. xxx. 1, 3, &c. Jer. 50, 4, 5. Rom. xi. 23.
(b) other passages, however, state that
their conversion will follow *after their restoration.*
Ezek. xxxiv. 22–31 ; xxxvi. 21–33. Zech. xii. 6–14.
10. From these passages we conclude, that
some will return, believing in Jesus, their Messiah ;
whilst *others will see their error* only at the sight of the Messiah.

IV. Concurrent Events.

11. The restoration of the Jews will *result in good* to the other
nations of the earth ;
for they are to be a source of great spiritual blessing.
Ps. lxvii. 1, 2 ; xcvii. 3 ; cii. 13–15. Is. ii. 1–4.
Ezek. xvi. 60 (see Hebrew). Micah iv. 1–3 ; v. 7.
Zech. viii. 13, 20, to end. Rom. xi. 12–15.

But the Jews will *first* undergo great *affliction* and *persecution ;*
has this already begun ?
" And when these things begin to come to pass, then look up,.........
for your redemption draweth nigh." Luke xxi. 28. Micah iv. 6.
Jer. xvi. 16, &c ; xxx. 7. Ezek. xx. 25–37 ; xxii. 17–22.
Dan. xii. 1. Zech. xiii. 8, 9 ; xiv. 1–3. Mal. iii. 5.
12. A most important event is also foretold in immediate connection
with their restoration and conversion.
The Second Advent of our Lord.
" He is near, even at the doors." Matt. xxiv. 33.
Ps. cii. 16. Is. xxiv. 23. Jer. xxiii. 5–8. Zeph. iii. 15–18. Zech. xiv. 4. Matt. xxiii. 39, 40.
13. Then will be fulfilled the prophecies, which speak of the Lord Jesus
Christ as being King of the Jews,
and as reigning in Jerusalem, " in Mount Zion." Is. xxiv. 23.
Luke i. 32, 33.
14. Jesus will then be not only King of the Jews, Ps. xlvii. 2 ; lxxii. 8.
but also King *over all the earth.*   Zech. xiv. 9.

V. Our Duty.

15. The *duty* of every Christian is
to *pray earnestly* and to long for the restoration of *God's chosen race,*
and to *love the Jews*;   Rom. xi. 28.
for they are *still beloved for their fathers' sakes.*
" *Pray for* the peace of Jerusalem ; they shall prosper that love thee." Ps. cxxii. 6.
" Ye that make mention of the Lord, keep not silence and give Him no rest, till He establish
and till He make Jerusalem a praise in the earth." Is. lxii. 6, 7.
Remember, *Christ*, the Lion of the tribe of Judah, the Prince of Peace,
The Saviour of mankind, was the Son of David and a Jew,
" for salvation is from the Jews." John iv. 22.
God will, in His own good time, and by His own means,
graft the broken branches into His olive tree ;
for God has not cast away His people. Rom. xi. 1.
Blessed shall that nation be, which *loves the Jews ;*
for God promised to Abraham and his children,
" I will bless them that bless thee." Gen. xii. 3 ; xxvii. 29.
And let us not forget the *terrible punishments*, which await those
who " *hate* " and " *persecute* " the Jews.
" The Lord thy God will put all these curses upon thine enemies,
and on them that hate thee, which persecuted thee." Deut. xxx. 7.
" I will.....curse him that curseth thee." Gen. xii. 3.
16. The *practical effect* which this solemn subject
should produce in our lives and conduct is,
(a) Confidence in the truth of God, that
He will, notwithstanding abounding wickedness,
gather out *His elect people.*
Is. iv. 10, 11. John vi. 37 ; x. 27, 28. Acts xv. 14, &c.
(b) Earnest watchfulness and looking for the Advent
and appearing of our Lord Jesus Christ.
Luke xii. 35, 36. 2 Peter iii. 12. Rev. xxii. 20.
(c) Separation in heart and affection from the world, with a view
to being ready ourselves.
2 Cor. vi. 17. 2 Peter iii. 11. 1 John ii. 15.
(d) Diligence in making known the way of salvation
while it is called to-day.   Is. lxii. 11. John ix. 4.
17. In *studying* this momentous question
we shall be *refreshed* and cheered as we prayerfully and
patiently pursue our investigation. Acts iii. 19, 20.
We may make mistakes, and
may now and then have to give up preconceived views and ideas;
but if we proceed in dependence on the teaching of the Holy Spirit,
we shall make gradual and sure progress,
and find that this study is most profitable, instructive, and
helpful to our soul's life.
And by our mistakes, let us be *humbled,* and
thus led more earnestly to seek the teaching of the Spirit of God.
Come, Lord Jesus ! Come !
Pour out Thy Holy Spirit upon us ; may He guide us into *all the truth,*
and give us grace to *occupy* us and to work diligently and faithfully until
Thou comest in power and glory. Amen.
At the longest, it can be but
" A very little while, and He that cometh, shall come and not tarry." Heb. x. 37.
" Ye, brethren, are not in darkness, that that day should overtake you as a thief." 1 Thess. v. 4.
" I come quickly."
Rev. xxii. 17–20.

*Every suggestion, either by way of addition, or improvement of the above
will be most thankfully received by a " Lover of God's Ancient People."
Please address to Rev. WILLIAM H. HECHLER, Temple Chambers,
32, Fleet Street, London, E.C.*

was one of the books, along with Laurence Oliphant's *Land of Gilead*, that fired his young imagination and convinced him of the need for an independent and self-sufficient Jewish state. Feinberg, as a young man, was one of the heroes of NILI, the Jewish spy network that worked against the Turks during the First World War.

The influence of *Daniel Deronda* was not limited to Christian Zionists and Jewish secularists. When Theodor Herzl visited the Jewish community of London he was introduced to the British chief rabbi, Nathan Adler. After Herzl presented his political program to Rabbi Adler, the rabbi said to him, "That is the fundamental idea of the novel *Daniel Deronda*." Herzl said in reply, "The idea is two thousand years old, but I shall bring about its realization."[29] Seventy years later, Rabbi Zvi Yehuda Kook, the ideological founder of Gush Emunim, the religious Zionist settler movement, told an interviewer that George Eliot was one of the few Christians who understood the religious roots of Zionism.[30]

In the United States *Daniel Deronda* was enthusiastically received by Jews and Christians. Prestigious literary journals reviewed the novel and *Harper's* magazine serialized sections of the novel in its pages. These many examples from the nineteenth and early twentieth centuries show that there was strong sympathy among American Christians (primarily, but not exclusively, among Protestants) for the Zionist cause. The grounds for this sympathy was the biblically influenced perception that Palestine "belonged" to the Jewish people, even if another people, the Arabs of Palestine, were living in the land. In the United States, *The Fundamentals*, a series of essays published between 1910 and 1915 by conservative evangelical theologians, emphasized the necessity to believe in the literal truth of scripture. This helped reify the relationship between the Jews of the present and the Israelites of old. In the view of many in the Christian West, Palestine was understood to be "empty," and this emptiness should be filled by Jews, the descendants of the land's ancient biblical inhabitants. The phrase "a land without a people for a people without a land" conveyed this view in a very concise and pithy manner. The idea was first promoted by Christians. In 1853 Lord Shaftesbury (Anthony Ashley-Cooper) wrote that Palestine was "a country without a nation" in search of "a nation without a country." He made this observation during the Crimean War, when the continued viability of the Ottoman Empire came into question. With the weakening of the Ottoman Empire, continued Turkish rule in Palestine came into question. In Shaftesbury's view, first expressed two decades before the Crimean War, Christians needed to support a Jewish restoration so as to prepare the stage for the Second Coming. As Shaftesbury was a friend and relative of Henry John Temple Palmerston, the British foreign minister, his views had considerable weight. Palmerston opened a British consulate in Jerusalem in 1838. Two years later, Shaftesbury wrote that "Palmerston has already been chosen by God to be an instrument of good to His ancient people." A half century later, the phrase "a land without a people for a people without a land" was popularized by Anglo-Jewish novelist Israel Zangwill.[31] From Zangwill's writings the phrase, translated into many languages, became a mainstay of Zionist polemics. The phrase was utilized in a number of ways, some more sophisticated than others. While some advocates of Zionism used it to imply that Palestine was empty of people, that suggestion was contradicted by the reports of many Western visitors. The phrase was most pointedly used to claim that the Arabs of Palestine had no distinct Palestinian identity. They were "Arabs," not a cohesive national group. That Palestine was not "empty" (in either the demographic or political sense) soon became clear to some Jewish observers. This was ruefully acknowledged in the telegram sent home by two rabbis from Vienna who visited Palestine in 1898, the year after the First Zionist Congress: "The bride is beautiful, but she is married to another man."[32]

More explicit Jewish warnings about the presence of the Arabs of Palestine were offered by the Zionist philosopher Ahad Ha'am (Asher Ginzburg) and his disciple Isaac Epstein. In his Hebrew-language essay "The Truth from the Land of Israel," Ginzburg wrote that "we tend to believe that Palestine is nowadays almost completely deserted, an uncultivated wilderness, and anyone can come there and buy as much land as his heart desires. But in reality this is not the case. It is difficult to find anywhere in the country Arab land which lies fallow." Isaac Epstein, in a 1907 article in the Hebrew-language periodical *Hashiloah*, called the Arab presence in Palestine "The Hidden Question." Epstein had settled in Palestine in 1886. After twenty years in Palestine he warned his fellow Zionists that they would have to confront a painful reality: "There resides in our treasured land an entire people which has clung to it for hundreds of years . . . the Arab, like all other men, is strongly attached to his homeland." But Epstein's project was not to assign blame. He wrote, "The Zionists' lack of attention to an issue so basic to their settlement is not intentional; it went unnoticed because they were not familiar with the country and its inhabitants, and furthermore, had no national or political awareness." Now that Zionist settlement had grown (in the twenty-five years preceding his 1907 essay), Epstein called on the movement to "distance itself from every deed tainted with plunder. . . . When we come to our homeland, we must uproot all thoughts of conquest or appropriation. Our motto must be:

Live and let live! Let us not cause harm to any nation, and certainly not to a numerous people, whose enmity is very dangerous."[33]

These expressions of concern for the future of Jewish-Arab relations did not have much resonance at the time, either among Jews or among Christians. Jewish Zionists were for the most part refugees from persecution who were engaged in building the infrastructure of a future state. Few of them paid attention to the claims of the majority population. Christian Zionists, whose motivations were more theological than practical, did not address the "Arab Question." For the more politically and religiously conservative among these Christians, the Arabs were the interlopers in Palestine, even if they were Christian Arabs. They had no part to play in God's plan for the Holy Land and should therefore be encouraged to emigrate. The perception that Palestine belonged to the Jewish people outweighed the reality of an Arab presence. At the beginning of the twentieth century less than 10 percent of Palestine's population was Jewish, but many Christians, especially in the United States, thought of it as a Jewish land.

A remarkable expression of American Christian Zionist sentiment was the Blackstone Memorial, a petition sent to President Benjamin Harrison in March of 1891. Its organizer, evangelical missionary William Blackstone, was a wealthy Chicago businessman with a passion for organizing missions to Jews of his native city. Blackstone had visited Palestine in 1888 and was there convinced that the return of the Jews to Zion was ordained in God's plan. In his understanding, it was only after the return of Jews to Zion that the stage would be set for the Second Coming. Blackstone called the Jewish people "God's sun-dial." "If anyone desires to know our place in God's chronology, our position in the march of events, look at Israel."[34] Signed by 413 American clergymen, business leaders, politicians, and newspaper editors, Blackstone's petition called on President Harrison to convene an international conference in support of Jewish claims to Palestine. It called on the president to act as "a modern Cyrus to help restore the Jews to Zion." Like the Persian king who enabled Jews to return to Jerusalem and rebuild the Temple in 500 B.C., the American president should act as God's instrument to redeem the people of Israel. The Blackstone Memorial asked: "Why not give Palestine back to them again? According to God's distribution of nations, it is their home, an inalienable possession from which they were expelled by force."[35] Among the signatories were the chief justice of the Supreme Court, Melville Fuller; the heads of many major American corporations and banks (including J. P. Morgan and John D. Rockefeller); and the editors of the *Chicago Tribune* and the *New York Times*.

A group of fifteen rabbinic and Jewish lay leaders from Chicago (where the petition was organized) asked Blackstone to add this note above their names. "Several petitioners wish it stated that the Jews have not become agriculturists because for centuries they were almost universally prohibited from owning or tilling land in the countries of their dispersion."[36] Some Reform rabbis, uneasy with Zionist claims, not only refused to sign the petition but called on their coreligionists to boycott the effort. Led by Rabbi Emil Hirsch of Chicago, these rabbis felt that Zionism might weaken the claims of recently arrived Jewish immigrants to full participation in America public life. In this spirit, one Reform rabbi declared, "American is our Zion." Rabbi Hirsch wrote, "We modern Jews do not wish to be restored to Palestine. We have given up hope in the coming of a political personal Messiah. We say, 'the country wherein we live is our Palestine and the city wherein we dwell is our Jerusalem.' "[37] Hirsch warned the members of his Chicago congregation that he would brook no opposition on this issue: "As long as I am in this pulpit Sinai Congregation will be unalterably opposed to Zionism. There is no cause for Zionism in America. Let those who favor a return to Jerusalem go there if they will."[38] By the 1940s this Reform unease with Zionism would weaken and for the most part disappear.

One of the most vocal opponents of the Blackstone Memorial was Selah Merrill, the U.S. consul in Jerusalem. In an 1891 report to the assistant secretary of state, Merrill dubbed Blackstone's plan "one of the wildest schemes ever brought before the public." According to Merrill, the memorial's signatories "appear to be ignorant of two great facts, 1) that Palestine is not ready for the Jews and 2) that the Jews are not ready for Palestine."[39]

Five years after he organized the memorial, William Blackstone read Theodor Herzl's *The Jewish State*. In the following year, 1897, Blackstone heard reports of the First Zionist Congress in Basel, Switzerland. Blackstone was very enthusiastic that Jews were organizing a political movement, but he was dismayed that the movement's leadership and ideology was assertively secular. Blackstone's Zionism was based on his reading of biblical prophecy; Herzl's was based on the need to find a refuge for the persecuted Jews of Europe. Blackstone sent Herzl a Bible in which he had underlined the passages that referred to the divine promise of the land to Israel. For many years this Bible was on display at the Herzl Memorial in Jerusalem.

Blackstone, in his criticism of secular Zionism, was expressing an attitude common among many of his conservative Christian Zionist contemporaries and successors. He saw "true Zionism" as rooted in Orthodox Judaism, not in the Conservative or Reform denominations of Judaism, and surely not in

Jewish secularism. As a missionary to the Jews, Blackstone targeted Orthodox Jewish immigrants to Chicago and other large urban centers; he felt that their deeply rooted beliefs in messianic redemption would make Orthodox Jews more open to conversion to Christianity.[40] During World War I, Blackstone joined with American Jewish Zionist leaders, foremost among them Louis Brandeis, to issue a new call for support for a Jewish state in Palestine. The 1916 the Blackstone Memorial was signed by hundreds of prominent Americans and sent to President Wilson. Among the signatories were the heads of the large Baptist, Presbyterian, and Episcopalian ministerial associations. In contrast to the 1891 memorial, of which there were few Jewish signatories, the 1916 memorial included the names of scores of Jewish public figures. In the quarter century since Blackstone first penned his call for international support for a Jewish state, some Jews had entered American public life, and Zionism had moved into the Jewish mainstream. But it would be decades before Zionism actually became that mainstream; that would only happen in the aftermath of World War II and the establishment of the State of Israel.

The gratitude that Zionist leaders felt toward the organizer of the memorial was expressed in a 1916 letter from philanthropist Nathan Straus to William Blackstone. Straus conveyed to Blackstone the thanks of Louis D. Brandeis, Zionist leader and later U.S. Supreme Court justice: "Mr. Brandeis is perfectly infatuated with the work you have done along the lines of Zionism. It would have done your heart good to have heard him assert what a valuable contribution to the cause your document is. In fact he agrees with me that you are the Father of Zionism, as your work antedates Herzl."[41] Blackstone remained active in missionary work—and in Zionist activities—until his death at age ninety-four in 1935. In his writings he continued to criticize Jewish secularism, which he saw as an impediment to both full Zionist success and eventual Jewish conversion to Christianity.

In the 1930s, the Nazi rise to power and the subsequent worsening situation of the Jews of Europe made the implementation of Zionist aims all the more urgent. Protestant groups in the United States reacted in different ways to this threat. The leading Protestant intellectual journal the *Christian Century* was skeptical about reports of German atrocities against Jews. Once the proof of these atrocities was demonstrated in 1943, the journal still withheld its approval for a refuge in Palestine for the Jews of Europe. Among the most eloquent and forceful voices for the establishment of a Jewish state was liberal Protestant theologian Reinhold Niebuhr. Niebuhr argued against the *Christian Century*'s critique of Zionism, a critique endorsed by many of his colleagues in the clergy. Niebuhr was one of the leaders of the American

Christian Palestine Committee, a pro-Zionist group that had hundreds of members. His support for Zionism was couched in decidedly nontheological terms. He wrote, "I belong to a Christian group in this country who believe that the Jews have a right to a homeland. They are a nation, scattered among the nations of the world. They have no place where they are not exposed to the perils of minority status."[42] After World War II and the shocking revelations about the murder of two-thirds of Europe's Jews, there was a great surge of American public support for Zionism, support expressed in the public reaction to the United States' immediate diplomatic recognition of Israel. A 1948 opinion poll concluded that 80 percent of the American public favored the establishment of a Jewish state in Palestine. But the editors and readers of the *Christian Century* were not among that 80 percent. Rather than recognize that there was grassroots American Protestant sympathy for Zionism, the journal attributed President Truman's decision to recognize Israel to "the New York vote"—code for the Jewish vote.[43]

Reading the *Christian Century*'s articles in the light of later developments, it seems that these reservations about creating a Jewish state were the opinions of a small elite. As Truman biographer David McCullough has noted, Truman's motives in granting Israel diplomatic recognition were both political and religious. Writing of the 1948 elections, McCullough noted that "beyond the so-called 'Jewish vote' there was the country at large, where popular support for a Jewish homeland was overwhelming. As would sometimes be forgotten, it was not just American Jews who where stirred by the prospect of a new nation for the Jewish people, it was most of America."[44]

In 1948 President Truman, in keeping with American public opinion, granted Israel diplomatic recognition despite the protestations of many senior officials in the U.S. State Department, Secretary of State George Marshall among them. Though historians are divided on the reasons for Truman's decision, they are agreed that among the deciding factors was Truman's sincere belief in the accuracy and historicity of biblical narrative and prophecy. In 1953, only a year after he left the presidency, Truman affirmed explicitly his biblical understanding of the United States' recognition of Israel. In a conversation at New York City's Jewish Theological Seminary, the rabbinical school of Conservative Judaism, Truman was introduced as "the man who helped create the State of Israel." Truman, visibly moved by that statement, said in response, "What do you mean helped create? I am Cyrus, I am Cyrus."[45]

Truman's response evoked the words of the Blackstone Memorial of 1891, which called on President Harrison to act as "a modern Cyrus to help restore the Jews to Zion." Truman's successor, Dwight D. Eisenhower, was not known as an enthusiastic supporter of the State of Israel, but it is clear that he, too, thought of modern Israel in biblical terms. Both in private conversation and in his diary, Eisenhower referred to Israelis as "Israelites," and it seems that he imagined that these modern Israelites were deeply religious. When an aide explained to the president that the Israeli leadership was assertively secular, he was astonished.[46] This "biblical" reading of modern Israel also surfaced in American popular culture. Ten years after Israel's establishment and five years after Truman's Cyrus comment, Leon Uris published his novel *Exodus*, which became a great American bestseller. Within two years of its publication, *Exodus* was made into a successful Hollywood film by director Otto Preminger. One of the novel's two central protagonists, Kitty Fremont, is an American Christian woman whose Zionist sympathies stemmed from an encounter with Jewish survivors of World War II. She serves as a nurse on the refugee boat *Exodus* and later, in 1948, in British Mandate Palestine. There she falls in love with Zionist leader Ari Ben Canaan. When Kitty meets members of the newly organized Jewish army, she has "an electrifying revelation": "This was no army of mortals. These were the ancient Hebrews! These were the faces of Dan and Reuben and Judah and Ephraim! These were Samsons and Deborahs and Joabs and Sauls. It was the army of Israel, and no force on earth could stop them for the power of God was within them!"[47] This fictional evocation of the idea that Israel's nascent army was the army of biblical Israel reborn had its real-life counterpart in the career of Orde Wingate, a British officer who helped shape the ethos and tactics of the Haganah. This was the Jewish fighting force that would become the formative element in the Israel Defense Forces. Thus Christian Zionism's contribution to the establishment of the State of Israel went beyond "theological support" to encompass concrete, practical contributions, such as military planning and assistance, as well as providing models of successful agricultural settlement and technological innovation.

~

Jewish Self-Defense

Along with the idea of the Promised Land, another essential element of political Zionism was the idea of Jewish self-defense. This idea was shaped by the experience of the victims of the Russian pogroms of the 1880s. A rallying call of the early Zionists was that a Jewish territory in Palestine would enable Jews to defend themselves against their enemies. Herzl, though, did not feature this call in his writings. In his utopian view, the future Jewish state would have no need for a standing army; a police force would suffice. The Arabs of Palestine, benefiting from the Jewish presence in their land, would find no cause for hostility toward Jews. In Herzl's 1902 novel *Old-New Land*, he envisioned the Jewish state as it would be in 1923. In that state, Arabs would be satisfied, prosperous citizens. In the novel, the Arab leader Rechid Bey tells a visiting Englishman that his people are "better off than at any time in the past. They support themselves decently, their children are healthier and are being taught something. Their religion and ancient customs have in no way been interfered with. They have become more prosperous—that is all. . . . The Jews have enriched us. Why should we be angry with them? They dwell among us like brothers. Why should we not love them?"[48]

The actual situation was much harsher. Armed conflict between Arabs and Jews escalated in the first decades of the twentieth century, culminating in large-scale Arab attacks on Jewish colonists in 1921, 1929, and 1936. These attacks were the stimulus for the formation of a succession of Jewish self-defense forces. The rhetoric of Jewish self-defense tied the Arab attackers to the Christian attackers in the Russian and Romanian pogroms. The Kishinev pogrom of 1903, which surfaces in the narratives of *Zeal for Zion* a number of times, was a formative event in the development of the movement for Jewish self-defense. Kishinev's Jews had been helpless in the face of the attacks; Palestine's Jews would not remain helpless, they would fight off their attackers and protect those parts of Palestine that had been "redeemed."

In the late 1930s, Orde Wingate, a charismatic Christian Zionist, catalyzed and modernized the self-defense of the Yishuv, the Jewish community in Palestine. Wingate tied the concept of Jewish self-defense to the biblical narratives of conquest and settlement. Just as Joshua and the Israelites conquered Canaan, and Joshua's successors, the Judges, defended the Israelites against enemies within and without, the modern "Israelites" would take back and then defend their ancestral patrimony. Called "Hayedid," "the friend," by Chaim Weizmann and other Zionist leaders, Orde Wingate is memorialized in a number of Israeli institutions, among them the Wingate Institute for Physical Education and Sports, in Netanya.

In 1936 Wingate was a high-ranking intelligence officer in the British army. His grandfather, William Wingate, had dedicated his life to missions to the Jews. Orde was born in India, where his parents, members of the Plymouth Brethren, were Christian missionaries, and as a youngster he had been imbued with an intense sense of identification with the Hebrews of the Bible. But, as he noted when he was first assigned to British forces in Palestine, he had never met a Jew before arriving there. In the British army, the young

Wingate was an excellent soldier and linguist, mastering Arabic before he was thirty. In contrast to other Arabists in British intelligence, Wingate favored the Jews of Palestine over the Arabs. "Long before I reached Palestine," Wingate said in the early 1940s, "I knew what the Jews were seeking, understood what they needed, sympathized with their aims, and knew they were right."[49] Wingate's training in Arabic enabled him to learn Hebrew quickly. He soon read the Bible, with which he was deeply familiar, in Hebrew. He befriended the Zionist leadership and was introduced to the leaders of its clandestine military wing. Wingate set up a training program for the commando units of the Jewish military force, the Haganah. He trained the force's "night squads." These units developed into the Palmach, a force much feared by Israel's Arab enemies. Wingate addressed his trainees as if they were the warriors of the ancient Israelites. As his biographer noted, at these training sessions for Jewish sergeants, "it is no exaggeration to say that Wingate felt like a soldier of the Old Testament too."[50] Moshe Dayan, defense minister during the 1967 war, was a trainee in Wingate's "Course for Jewish Sergeants" held at Kibbutz Ein-Harod in the late 1930s. In 1954 Dayan said to Wingate's biographer Leonard Mosley, "There were many men who served with him in Ein Harod who later became officers in the Israeli Army which fought and defeated the Arabs, but they were not the only ones who benefited from this training. In some sense, every leader of the Israeli Army, even today, is a disciple of Wingate. He gave us our technique, he was the inspiration of our tactics, he was our dynamic."[51]

THE CHRISTIAN ZIONIST roots of Wingate's commitment to Jewish self-defense were not obscured or forgotten, either by Wingate or by others. Wingate, brought up in a Plymouth Brethren family, attributed these ideas to childhood influences. He said of his mother: "She taught me that I must live by the Bible, and that I must help the prophecies of the Bible to come true. It was she who told me to befriend the Jews, and help them to fulfill the biblical prophecy and return to Palestine."[52]

~

Evangelicals, Fundamentalists, and Israel

Support for Israel is strong among evangelical Christians generally; among churches self-described or described by outsiders as "fundamentalist," that support is often quite passionate and unambivalent. The meanings of both the terms "evangelical" and "fundamentalist" are open to constant reinterpretation and reevaluation. The Institute for the Study of American Evangelicals notes that "the term 'Evangelicalism' is a wide-reaching definitional 'canopy' that covers a diverse number of Protestant groups."[53] One prominent scholar of American religion, while pointing out that "defining evangelicalism has become one of the biggest problems in American religious historiography," goes on to describe those beliefs and practices that bind evangelicals together. "I see Evangelicalism as a movement of spiritual renewal which is grounded in certain theological convictions . . . and a commitment to the basic teachings of the Protestant Reformation: the scriptures are true, Jesus is the Son of God, salvation is rooted in grace (not works), and conversion implies a commitment to a life of holiness. All (are) linked to a spirit of renewal—of the individual, the church and the world."[54]

The first of these commitments, that "the scriptures are true" is the bedrock of evangelical support for the State of Israel. As approximately 30 percent of the American public may be identified as evangelical, one can see how belief in the historical accuracy of scripture might affect perceptions of foreign policy, especially on issues related to the Middle East in general and to Israel and the Palestinians in particular. The influence of these ideas on the American public is suggested in the results of national surveys of religious belief. According to a July 2005 survey by the Pew Research Center for the People and the Press, 78 percent of Americans view the Bible as God's word, while 35 percent say that everything in the Bible is literally true. Over 40 percent of Americans believe that Israel was given to the Jewish people by God. Most significantly for the study of Christian Zionism is that "more than one-in-three Americans (thirty-five percent) say that Israel is part of the fulfillment of biblical prophecy about the second coming of Jesus." That American political attitudes toward the Arab-Israeli conflict are related to this biblical worldview is further suggested by the Pew Center's overall findings concerning support for Israel: "Fifty-two percent said they sympathized more with Israel, compared with eleven percent who sympathized more with the Palestinians."[55]

Thus, while some evangelicals might support Israel out of a worldview influenced by a literal reading of the biblical narratives, the subcategory of fundamentalists, particularly those under the sway of dispensationalism, link the fate of the State of Israel to the unfolding destiny of all humanity, a destiny in which, in their understanding, the State of Israel has a pivotal role to play. Both Evangelicalism, with its origins in the eighteenth century, and its subset, Fundamentalism, with its origins in the early twentieth, were tied in their earliest forms to a belief in the literal fulfillment of biblical prophecy, especially as regards the millennium. The eventual conversion of a remnant of the Jews to Christianity and the reestablishment of a Temple in Jerusalem were essential elements in a wide array of prophecy beliefs.

The term "fundamentalism," first coined in 1920, was borrowed from a twelve-volume set of essays, *The Fundamentals: A Testimony to the Truth*, published between 1910 and 1915. The essays, written by a group of conservative Protestant theologians, represented a reaction against the "threats" of modernity. Among these perceived threats were the teaching of the theory of evolution, the increasing acceptance of biblical criticism, and the rise of liberal theologies in the mainstream Protestant denominations. In response, the writers of *The Fundamentals* "criticized liberal theological beliefs, defended cardinal evangelical doctrines, upheld older models of Protestant spirituality, and reaffirmed evangelism's preeminence among the church's tasks."[56] Copies of each volume were widely distributed throughout the United States.

The Fundamentals called on Christians to accept the historical accuracy of all of scripture:

> [I]t is an essential element in a tenable doctrine of Scripture, in fact the core of the matter, that it contains a record of a true supernatural revelation; and that is what the Bible claims to be—not a development of man's thoughts about God, and not what this man and that one came to think about God, how they came to have the ideas of a Jehovah or Yahveh, who was originally the storm-god of Sinai, and how they manufactured out of this the great universal God of the prophets—but a supernatural revelation of what God revealed Himself in word and deed to men in history.[57]

As Genesis records God's promise of Canaan to the Hebrew people, and as the Hebrew prophets predicted the return of that people to their land, believers were to accept these promises in the most literal fashion. As *The Fundamentals* state, "The Book of Genesis is not authoritative if it is not true. For if it is not history, it is not reliable and if it is not revelation, it is not authoritative."[58] Since the New Testament emphasizes these Old Testament promises of a restored Israel, and links their fulfillment to the Second Coming, believers in a literalist understanding of scripture felt called upon to support Zionism. Evangelicals influenced by this body of fundamentalist ideas saw in the history of the twentieth century the fulfillment of biblical promise and prophecy. In 1917, the Balfour Declaration, stating that the British government "supports the establishment of a Jewish national home in Palestine," and the subsequent conquest of Jerusalem were understood by many

American evangelicals as the fulfillment of biblical prophecy. Thirty years later, the British departure from Palestine in 1947 and the establishment of Israel in 1948 were viewed in a similar light. Twenty years after that, the 1967 war was read in the same circles as the culmination of a series of modern-day "miracles."

The resurgence of European anti-Semitism in the 1930s was understood by fundamentalists as a sign of the imminent End Time. As one astute observer of American fundamentalism has noted, "The most astonishing sign of the times for fundamentalists, and the one which they were most ready to explain in prophetic terms, was the rise of anti-Semitism and the widespread persecution of the Jews."[59] Fundamentalists generally and dispensationalists most particularly read rising anti-Semitism as the sign of "Jacob's Tribulation," a reference to the prophecy of Jeremiah on the reunification of Israel and Judah and their restoration to their land: "I will bring them back to the land that I gave to their ancestors and they shall take possession of it" (Jeremiah 30:3). That return, Jeremiah goes on to prophesy, will entail great suffering. In a vivid image, the Hebrew prophet sees Israel suffering like a woman in labor: "Alas! That day is so great that there is none like it; it is a time of distress for Jacob; yet he shall be rescued from it" (30:7). As we shall see in Chapter 6, Jacob's trouble, or "tribulation," would assume a central place in the Book of Revelation and in End Time predictions and speculation based on that book. In the dispensationalist predictions that stemmed from the teachings of John Nelson Darby and were popularized in the immensely successful *Left Behind* series, a set of twelve novels published in the late twentieth and early twenty-first centuries, "Jacob's Trouble," or the Tribulation, is preceded by the Rapture to heaven of true believers in Jesus. During the seven years of Tribulation, Israel will form an alliance with the Antichrist, the representative of evil. But some Jews will see through the Antichrist's plans, evangelize for Jesus, and facilitate his return. Jesus's return will signal the end of evil and Satan, its representative, and will inaugurate the thousand-year reign of peace.

Particularly devoted to political Zionism were those conservative Protestants influenced by the emergence of fundamentalist ideas in the first decades of the twentieth century. As Alan Wolfe noted in the October 2000 issue of the *Atlantic Monthly*, "The terms 'fundamentalist' and 'evangelical' are sometimes conflated, because the movements have common origins."[60] In 1963 historian of ideas Richard Hofstadter had challenged the leaders of the fundamentalist movement to become more engaged with intellectual pursuits. He wrote of "the intellectual disaster of fundamentalism."[61] In the past half century scholars educated in the conservative evangelical traditions have risen to Hofstadter's challenge and have situated the study of American Evangelicalism within the highest reaches of American academic life. Three generations of scholars have now fully entered into and engaged with American academia, and they have produced an important body of work that represents the diversity and richness of evangelical beliefs. *Zeal for Zion* draws on the best of that scholarship. These scholars describe fundamentalists as a subset of evangelicals, and they caution us against ascribing fundamentalist beliefs to all who are affiliated with the very wide, diverse groupings of American evangelicals, who comprise a third of the American population.

Of the eighty million or so American evangelicals, between nine and ten million adults are fundamentalists influenced by dispensationalism.[62] Dispensationalists understand all of history as a progression of "dispensations," or eras. The Old and New Testaments told the story of the first dispensations. Subsequent world history was mapped by the preachers of this tradition onto an unfolding historical schema that would inaugurate the millennium—the thousand-year reign of Christ. Dispensationalists are premillennialists; they believe that Jesus will return *before* the millennium. Therefore, his return may be expected at any moment. This distinguishes dispensationalists from postmillennialists, who believe that it is humanity's role to bring the millennium through personal and social change and that at the millennium's end, Jesus will return to a world already on the path to redemption. Thus, broadly speaking, we might characterize premillennialists as pessimistic about the perfectibility of human society, while postmillennialists are decidedly optimistic about our capacity to improve ourselves and our societies.

The origins of dispensationalism lie in nineteenth-century English religious history, when a dissenting group, the Plymouth Brethren, sought the key to unfolding historical events in a hyper-literal reading of biblical prophecy. Their most influential preacher was John Nelson Darby (1800–1882). Darby, building on earlier Protestant millennialist ideas, taught that all history was divided into periods or "dispensations" and that in each period Christians had thus far failed to redeem themselves, despite God-given opportunities to do so. According to Darby, humanity was soon to face the final period of history, "the kingdom"; this was its ultimate chance for redemption. The unfolding of history would reveal that God's plan for humanity had two aspects. One plan concerned Christians; the other concerned Jews, who retained a degree of chosen-ness in God's eyes. In the final judgment, the remaining Jews would be "brought to Christ." And they would act as agents of evangelization for all humanity. The parents of Orde Wingate, the British officer who helped shape the future Israeli army, were members of the Plymouth Brethren. In the United States, Darby's ideas were popularized and spread in Cyrus Scofield's *Scofield's Reference Bible*. First published by Oxford University Press in 1909, this Bible, of which millions of copies have been sold, became "the most significant premillennialist publication in the twentieth century."[63] In the early editions of this Bible, each event of the narratives was assigned a precise date. Next to the first verses of Genesis was the date 4004 B.C., the date calculated by Bishop James Ussher in the seventeenth century as the "beginning of the world." Scofield emphasized the importance of the Jewish restoration to Palestine in both his edition of the Bible and his prophetic writings. In the first edition of his *Reference Bible,* Scofield wrote that "Israel regathered from all nations, restored to her own land and converted, is yet to have her greatest earthly exaltation and glory." In his *Addresses on Prophecy* Scofield wrote, "Upon the sacred soil of Palestine God has decreed the reconstitution of the nation of Israel."[64] In editions published since 1948, the *Scofield Reference Bible*'s notes emphasized the connection between biblical prophecy and its "fulfillment" in the State of Israel. Tim LaHaye, coauthor of the *Left Behind* series, has acknowledged Scofield's influence on his own work. The opening paragraph of LaHaye's 1999 *Revelation Unveiled* notes, "Almost one hundred years ago the author of the *Scofield Reference Bible* said in his notes on Revelation, 'Doubtless, much which is designedly obscure to us will be clear to those for whom it was written as the time approaches.' Most prophecy scholars believe that time is at hand, and many things are clearer today than they were in Dr. Scofield's day."[65]

Yaakov Ariel has noted that dispensationalism "meshed well with the fundamentalist view, which criticized the prevailing cultural trend in society and offered an alternative philosophy of history to the liberal postmillennialist notions that prevailed in American Christianity at the time."[66] For dispensationalist Christian "prophecy believers," Zionism was as important to Christians as it was to Jews, for the unfolding events of the End Time were, according to prophecy, linked to the Jewish return to Zion and the rebuilding of the Temple in Jerusalem.

In mid-twentieth-century America, belief in the imminent End Time, a belief that crossed the denominational boundaries between the Protestant churches, was spread by radio and television broadcasts. As Paul Boyer has noted in *When Time Shall Be No More: Prophecy Belief in Modern American Culture,* "Prophetic belief was disseminated in these years by American's omnipresent religious broadcasters, including luminaries such as Jerry Falwell of Virginia, Michigan's Jack van Impe, Oral Roberts of Tulsa, and schools of Southern California electronic preachers."[67] The 1948 establishment of the

State of Israel and the 1967 war (known in Israel as the Six-Day War) were understood by many American evangelical preachers as the fulfillment of prophecy. In the early 1980s, as the American Christian Right gained political influence and power in the halls of government, the leaders of the movement articulated their vigorous support for Israeli government policy. The 1979 founding document of the Moral Majority, established by Jerry Falwell, highlighted support for Israel. For large groups of evangelical Christians, support for Israel was thus framed as a moral and religious cause as much as a policy issue. As *Zeal for Zion* demonstrates, a similar, though surely not identical, process took place in the American Jewish community. The proclamation and consolidation of Israeli statehood was thought of as a "miracle" by many American Jews, though one would be hard-pressed to say that the word "miracle" was used with theological intent or precision. In the second half of the twentieth century, and especially since the 1967 and 1973 wars, a more religious Jewish understanding of Israel's "miracle" has emerged. Among American Jews, support for the State of Israel has long been thought of as a Jewish obligation; more recently that support has taken on a religious aspect.

Within the Jewish population of the State of Israel, the euphoric and religiously inflected response to the 1967 victory brought about a new political-military situation in the Middle East. In the aftermath of the war, the pre-1967 pragmatic approach of Israel's leadership was challenged by a resurgent Jewish messianism. The extended post-1967 stalemate between Israel and its Arab enemies enabled the rapid empowerment of the settler movement. As historian Arye Naor noted in the *Journal of Israeli History*, "The longer the stalemate continued the more difficult it became to detach Israelis from the romantic, mystical experience of reunification with their past as expressed in the holding and settling of biblical lands."[68] Many American Jews, especially those belonging to Orthodox communities, were inspired by these religious ideals and were moved to support or join the activities of the settler movement.

Among evangelical Christians as among American Jews, a religious understanding of current events, and especially of Middle Eastern events, seemed to cross denominational and regional lines. As Paul Boyer has noted, "While prophecy belief may be somewhat more pervasive in the South, in the post–World War Two years and certainly since 1970 it was clearly a national, not a strictly regional phenomenon. . . . These beliefs pervaded the United States culture. As the twentieth century drew to a close, many millions of Americans of all races, regions, and socioeconomic levels embraced them."[69]

Today, early in the twenty-first century, the most widespread expression of dispensationalist ideas is to be found in the books, films, and internet sites of the *Left Behind* series. The series has sold over sixty-five million copies. The appeal of these books is widespread; they speak to a very diverse readership, a readership that extends far beyond the ranks of dispensationalist believers. A survey by the Barna Group found that one in four Americans was aware of the *Left Behind* books and that 9 percent of the American general public had read at least one of the novels in the series.[70] The dispensationalist ideas expressed in these books represent the beliefs of a small group of conservative fundamentalist thinkers. But the appeal of these End Time narratives seems so powerful as to overcome theological differences. In each of the *Left Behind* novels, Israel, Israelis, and American Jews play a pivotal role. In the final chapter of *Zeal for Zion*, we take a closer look at the *Left Behind* novels.

But End Time speculation is only one aspect of Christian Zionism; American Christians, like American Jews, have a wide variety of attitudes toward Israel. The majority of evangelicals do not subscribe to dispensationalism; nevertheless they are moved to support Israel, for they see its establishment as the fulfillment of the biblical promise. The State of Israel is for many Christians of all denominations a proof that God continues to act in history. As *Zeal or Zion* demonstrates, this attitude can also be found among those American Christians who are critical of Israeli government policies. For Christian criticism of Israel is often couched in religious, moralistic terms. While Israeli government policies in the Territories may have earned the criticism they have attracted, the tone of such criticism is markedly different from that used in condemnations of other international policies. For, among Christians, a people representing God's hand in history are expected to act morally. If Israel does not do so, it must be chastised and challenged to improve its political behavior. This sensitive issue has come to the fore in discussions between American Jewish leaders and the heads of the Presbyterian Church (U.S.A.). A June 2008 document published by that church identified the State of Israel as "the oppressive force in the Israeli-Palestinian situation." This led to a statement by the leaders of three Jewish denominations—Conservative, Reform, and Reconstructionist—dubbing the Presbyterian document "a new lowpoint in Presbyterian-Jewish relations."[71]

After 1967 and especially since the outbreaks of the first and second intifadas, the more liberal Protestant denominations became increasingly critical of Israeli policies, and some Protestant denominations have initiated campaigns to divest from American companies that work with Israel, particularly from American corporations that sell equipment used by the Israeli military in the West Bank and Gaza. The Presbyterian Church (U.S.A.) and the United Methodist Church have been particularly active in this area. More recently, the

Evangelical Lutheran Church of America has taken up this cause. Similarly, there are politically liberal evangelicals who have condemned Israeli policies in the Territories. In July of 2002, Jim Wallis, editor of the liberal journal *Sojourners*, published a letter to President Bush calling on the president "to provide the leadership necessary for peacemaking in the Middle East by vigorously opposing injustice, including the continued unlawful and degrading Israeli settlement movement." Signed by over forty evangelical pastors, the letter pointed out that "the American evangelical community is not a monolithic bloc in full and firm support of present Israeli policy."[72] But as the political trends of the George W. Bush years demonstrated, this was a minority political opinion, and one that did not gain much traction among American evangelicals.

In October 2008, the National Council of Churches of Christ, which includes more than 100,000 churches belonging to thirty-five different church groups and denominations, published a brochure titled "Why We Should Be Concerned about Christian Zionism." The brochure offers reasons why Christian Zionism, "as narrowly defined . . . in beliefs which consider the state of Israel to be divinely ordained and scripturally determined with a central role in ushering in the end of history," causes immediate concern. The first reasons given are that Christian Zionism "is a movement with negative consequences for Middle East peace" and that the movement "fosters fear and hatred of Muslims and non-Western Christians."[73]

Since Vatican II, the American Catholic community, especially its hierarchy, has been generally supportive of Israel. As I point out in Chapter 4, many American Catholics opposed the Vatican's decision to withhold diplomatic recognition from Israel, a reluctance that was not overcome until 1994. (By that time, Israel had been recognized by 144 states.) The Catholic legal scholar Father Robert Drinan, author of *Honor the Promise: America's Commitment to Israel*, was one of the Jewish state's most enthusiastic supporters during his tenure in the House of Representatives in the 1970s. The Vatican opposed his activism on this and other issues. The Drinan case served to highlight the tensions between the Vatican and American Catholics.

$\backsim$

Ambivalence and Enthusiasm

The Jewish Zionist–Christian Zionist relationship, like the Jewish-Christian relationship of which it is a part, has always been fraught with ambivalence. British foreign secretary Lord Balfour, who described himself as "an ardent

Zionist," was not an admirer of Jews in general or of the British Jewish community in particular. As one of his biographers noted, "In common with many Zionists of his time, both Jew and Gentile, he accepted many of the allegations made against Jews by anti-Semites."[74] Other Christian Zionists, including some in the leadership of fundamentalist churches influenced by dispensationalism, had a darker, more conspiratorial view of the Jewish role in history. In the early 1930s the popular American evangelical preacher Arno Gaebelein cited the infamous forgery *The Protocols of the Elders of Zion* as proof of a worldwide Jewish conspiracy poised to control world affairs. This forgery, circulated in 1902 by the Russian intelligence services, claimed to be a secret record of meetings of Jewish leaders. Here Gaebelein clashed with the view of William Blackstone, who had earlier asserted that the *Protocols* were a forgery. Gaebelein's fear of a "Jewish conspiracy" did not stop him from preaching that the aims of the Zionist movement were divinely ordained and directed, as the imminent return of Jesus was dependent on the fulfillment of the biblical prophecy that the Jews return to their land. But Gaebelein felt that while the aim of Zionism was commendable, the Zionist movement, assertively secular, was "displeasing to God." Gaebelein devoted his considerable financial and organizational resources to converting Jews to Christianity. Like William Blackstone, he felt that Orthodox Jews were the best candidates for conversion to Christianity. They would, he was sure, at the time of "Jacob's Tribulation" be witnesses for the Christian truth. Until that time comes, efforts should be made to "bring them to Christ." His conviction that John Nelson Darby's prophecy teachings were true led Gaebelein to leave the Methodist Episcopal Church, which, he asserted, had become too liberal. Gaebelein was one of the seven consulting editors of the *Scofield Reference Bible*, and in this way he influenced fundamentalist perceptions of the relationship between biblical history and current events. At the same time, he was for a time America's most vocal and prominent Christian supporter of Zionist aims.[75] For observers of today's fundamentalist evangelical Christian Zionism, this stark ambivalence toward Jews, an ambivalence still apparent in the writings and sermons of some of today's American fundamentalist preachers, is troubling. Despite the impassioned and highly organized advocacy of fundamentalist Christian Zionism's supporters, many in the American Jewish community are still unsure about the religious and political implications of fundamentalist support for Israel—and many Americans of all religious denominations and secular persuasions want to know more about it.

The six narratives in *Zeal for Zion* relate the histories of the two Zionisms while at the same time reflecting on the complexities of the Christian-Jewish relationship. In each chapter we encounter varying forms of Zionism, and changing forms of Judaism and Christianity. The narratives are presented in chronological order and draw on literary, religious, and historical materials. Chapter 1, on the encounter between Naphtali Herz Imber, the author of *Hatikvah* (which became the Israeli national anthem), and Laurence Oliphant, British novelist, diplomat, and journalist, is set in Ottoman Palestine in the 1880s. Chapter 2, on Theodor Herzl and his friend Rev. William Hechler is set in the European salons, embassies, and diplomatic missions of the late nineteenth and early twentieth centuries. Canon Herbert Danby of Jerusalem's St. George's Cathedral (and later professor of Hebrew at Oxford) is the central figure of Chapter 3. Danby moved to Jerusalem in 1919 and lived in the Holy City until 1936. His professional and personal relationship with Hebrew University scholar and Revisionist Zionist thinker Joseph Klausner exemplifies many of the issues that beset Christians and Jews attempting to work together in British Mandate Palestine.

The remarkable change in the Vatican's attitude toward Zionism and the State of Israel is the focus of Chapter 4. That chapter examines the writings on Zionism of two prominent Catholic thinkers, G. K. Chesterton and Jacques Maritain, and describes the pilgrimages to the Holy Land of two popes, Paul VI in 1964 and John Paul II in 2000. One of the themes that arises in that chapter is the difference between the Vatican's often inimical official stance toward the State of Israel and the positive attitudes of individual Catholics toward the Jewish state. Chapter 5 tells of three modern literary masters, Jorge Luis Borges, Robert Graves, and Vladimir Nabokov, each of whom were deeply interested in the modern history of the Jews and the emergence of the State of Israel. Borges and Graves made pilgrimages to Jerusalem; Nabokov yearned to visit Israel, but it was a journey he was never to make; his plan to visit Jerusalem was cut short by his final illness. Chapter 6, on the Jewish settler movement and American Christian fundamentalists, takes the reader up to the present time. Within the context of both American and Israeli religious history it tells the story of this unexpected relationship between "fundamentalists" of two different religions.

The areas of study that *Zeal for Zion* touch on—Christian-Jewish relations, the history of Zionism, and the clashing narratives of the Arab-Israeli conflict —are fraught with controversy. The emotions about these subjects run high; a book that touches on all three of these topics will no doubt generate strong responses. The public controversy surrounding the publication of Walt and Mearsheimer's *The Israel Lobby* (2007) is a recent example. That book fails to take into account the degree to which American perceptions of the Arab-

Israeli and Israeli-Palestinian conflicts are influenced by the centrality of the Bible's place in American culture. Walt and Mearsheimer refer to an earlier American "biblically inspired fascination with the Holy Land and the role of Judaism in its history." Surprisingly, the authors then proceed to dismiss this central factor: "It is a mistake to see this history of modest and for the most part private engagement as the taproot of America's role in the region since World War II, and especially its extraordinary relationship with Israel today."[76] In contrast, *Zeal for Zion* aims to uncover the deep Jewish and Christian backgrounds of Zionism and place them in historical context.

Zeal for Zion, which focuses on the Jewish and Christian understandings of Zionism and Israel seeks to be nuanced in its portrait of the history of modern Israel. In this sense it is closest in spirit to Mark Tessler's 1994 book, *A History of the Israeli-Palestinian Conflict*. Tessler notes that "many on both sides of the Israeli-Palestinian conflict find it difficult to take the opposing side seriously, not in military or political terms, of course, but as a people with legitimate rights and valid aspirations. On both sides there are those who insist on delegitimizing or even demonizing their adversary, as if the rightness of their cause were justified primarily by the villainy of the opposing party and only secondarily by their own ideals and achievements."[77] Concerning the last century of Holy Land history, Tessler and other observers have noted that there are two conflicting narratives, one Israeli Jewish and the other Palestinian Arab. *Zeal for Zion* adds another dimension to the story: a description and analysis of Christian narratives about the same contested and "much promised" land. As I have pointed out in a review essay in *American Jewish History*,[78] books on Christian Zionism, like much of the large bibliography on Israel, are quite partisan, with supporters of Israel praising Zionism and Israel's critics vilifying it. In *Zeal for Zion*, I aspire to describe and analyze the Christian encounter with Zionism in a nonpartisan, engaging, and illuminating manner.

The Christian Zionists and the Hebrew Poet
Laurence and Alice Oliphant's Encounter with
Naphtali Herz Imber (1882–1888)

In answer to the kind expression contained in your letter, I feel that
although not a Jew myself, as a man I am only doing my simple duty to
my Jewish brethren, in exerting myself to the utmost to help them in this
time of their great trouble. —Laurence Oliphant, 1879[1]

Hatikvah—"Our Hope"

Many modern visitors to Israel have heard *Hatikvah*, the Israeli national anthem, long before they reach the country. Jewish visitors know the song from
youth groups, summer camps, and communal gatherings. American baby
boomers, regardless of religious persuasion, might remember *Hatikvah* from
the 1960 Hollywood film *Exodus*, where the music was blended with great
effect into Ernest Gold's stirring score. The melody, borrowed from a Moldavian folk song and reminiscent of rousing passages in the Czech composer
Smetana's "Moldau," evokes the heady nationalisms of nineteenth-century
Europe. Hebrew poet Naphtali Herz Imber first published the words to *Hatikvah* ("*Tikvoseinu*," "Our Hope") in Jerusalem in 1886, a decade before Theodor
Herzl convened the First Zionist Congress. Soon after Imber published the
poem, Samuel Cohen of Rishon Letzion set the first of the nine stanzas to
music, and the song spread quickly throughout the fledgling Jewish pioneer
communities of Palestine and the Jewish communities of Europe and the
United States. A popular translation of that first stanza reads: "As long as deep
within the heart a Jewish soul beats, / And to the far reaches of the East the
eye yearns for Zion, / Our hope, the hope of two thousand years, is not lost: /
To be a free people in our land, / The Land of Zion, Jerusalem."

   Imber (1856–1909) dedicated *Barkai*, the small volume of Hebrew poetry in which *Hatikvah* was first published, to prominent Christian Zionists Laurence and Alice Oliphant. The Oliphants, members of the English political and social aristocracy, gave a large part of their lives and fortune to the restoration of the Jews. Imber often stated that *Hatikvah* would not have come into being without the Oliphants' help. Late in life Imber acknowledged that hearing *Hatikvah* sung "brings before my eyes the sweet face of Alice, which has always inspired me, and the aristocratic face of Laurence."[2]

An account of the personal relationship between the Oliphants and Imber offers us an opportunity to examine the complex relationships between Christian and Jewish Zionists in the last quarter of the nineteenth century. Between the early seventeenth and late nineteenth centuries a number of English and American Protestants thinkers advocated the return of the Jews to Zion. With few exceptions, this advocacy was linked to millennialist expectations that Jewish return was a necessary step in the unfolding of the Second Coming. Christian advocacy helped pave the way for the birth of Jewish political Zionism. Christians and Jews cooperated in the formation of what became political Zionism in the last years of the nineteenth century. The Oliphant-Imber relationship is a small example of a larger trend. In many ways this unlikely encounter would serve as a model for later Christian-Jewish partnerships in support of Zionism.

The popularity of *Hatikvah* suggests the extended and complicated relationship between Christian and Jewish influences in the development of Zionism. Although it did not become the official Israeli national anthem until 2004, *Hatikvah* had been for decades the official song of the Zionist movement, informally adopted as such at the Fifth Zionist Congress and formally adopted at the eighteenth congress in 1933, along with the white and blue flag displaying the star of David.[3] For years after the declaration of Israeli statehood in 1948, the prospect of declaring *Hatikvah* the national anthem posed two long-standing problems. The "hope of 2000 years," that yearning for Zion that *Hatikvah* valorizes, is the hope of the "Jewish soul." It is not the hope of all citizens of Israel, a modern democratic state, close to 20 percent of whose citizens are Arab. Thus one out of every five Israeli citizens would not find their country's national aspirations expressed in their national anthem. The other major problem for some Israeli Jews is that the anthem is assertively secular and makes no mention of God or Torah. Therefore Israel's *haredim*, its ultra-Orthodox Jews, strongly objected to the song.

Today, the singing of *Hatikvah* opens rallies, meetings, cultural activities, and speeches in the United States by visiting Israeli diplomats and military officers. Initially promoted as the anthem of secular Zionism, it has achieved liturgical status in sectors of American Judaism. Since 2001 some synagogues of the Conservative Movement, with which one-third of American Jews are affiliated (the movement claimed 1.5 million members in 2004), have included the singing of *Hatikvah* in the Sabbath services as an act of solidarity with Israel.

In Imber's lifetime and afterward, it was also sung in some Protestant churches at meetings held in support of the Zionist cause. *Hatikvah* has now entered the liturgies of some evangelical churches, particularly in the southern United States. Christian Zionists who want to demonstrate their unqualified and unflinching loyalty to Israel and its "biblical right to the land" have found in *Hatikvah* a form of identification with both the Christian Right and Jewish national aspirations. In 2006, at the first meeting of Christians United for Israel, a lobbying group founded by fundamentalist pastor John Hagee, *Hatikvah* was sung by hundreds of supporters of this Christian Zionist organization.[4]

Hatikvah also has become well known in what to many would seem unexpected quarters—the repertoire of the Mormon Tabernacle Choir. Along with "Jerusalem of Gold" and other popular Israeli songs, *Hatikvah* is often sung by the choir in its public performances, and it is featured on a popular CD that it recorded in Jerusalem in 2000. The Mormon Church has a unique relationship with Jews and Zionism, a relationship that precedes by a half century the composition of *Hatikvah* and the emergence of political Zionism. In 1841 the founder and prophet of the church, Joseph Smith, sent one of his disciples, Orson Hyde, on a pilgrimage to Jerusalem.[5] Smith instructed Hyde to bless the city and pray for the restoration of the Jews to the Holy Land. In sending Orson Hyde to Jerusalem, Joseph Smith was expressing in a new way a teaching that would soon achieve popularity in Protestant Europe and the United States: Christians had to be active in the restoration of the Jews to their ancestral land. This belief was based on new understandings of the End Time. For Protestants influenced by dispensationalism, the Jewish return to the land that God had promised to them formed an essential part of the drama of the Second Coming. Thus restoration of the Jews was a doctrine of the Mormon Church long before there was a Jewish political movement to create a Jewish state.[6]

Hatikvah was a popular song long before it was harnessed to specific political aims, and the story behind its composition—the story of the Oliphant-Imber relationship—dramatizes the complex interaction of the two components, one Christian, the other Jewish, that would within seventy years of the inception of Jewish colonization in Palestine enable Zionism to develop from a political and cultural movement to the foundational ideology of an independent state. Both the Jewish and Christian religious components were necessary for the cultural and political success of the movement. Until recently there has been considerable resistance to looking at Zionist history in this way. Most major works on Zionism assign Christian Zionism an ancillary, secondary role despite the fact that the British movement for the restoration of the Jews to Palestine was three hundred years old when political Zionism was organized.[7] The standard histories of Zionism represent the movement galvanized by Theodor Herzl's leadership in the 1890s as a secular Jewish adaptation of European nationalist ideas. Religious influence, whether Jewish or Christian, is assigned a secondary, shadow role. Yet forces of secularism and religion, both Christian and Jewish, were constantly in play. In Britain and the United States, Christian Zionism flourished in the first half of the nineteenth century, while Jewish Zionism became a political force only in the last years of that century. A close examination of the relationship between Oliphant and Imber, and of the relationships between other Christian Zionists and their Jewish associates, can illuminate some of the complexities of Zionist history.[8]

Laurence Oliphant (1829–88), well known in the latter half of the nineteenth century as diplomat, adventurer, and author, achieved fame during his lifetime that far eclipsed that of Imber. Yet by the mid-twentieth century, Oliphant was all but forgotten; Imber, however, was famed as the author of the anthem that expressed Jewish national aspirations. On many occasions Imber, who survived both of the Oliphants by twenty years, wrote of his association with the Oliphants, praising them as facilitators of the Zionist dream. In 1906, for example, Imber wrote a memorial to his "two sets of parents," describing the Oliphants, who were decidedly unorthodox Christians, as equally if not more important to him as his biological parents, who were Orthodox Jews. Of the Oliphants he wrote: "Divine Providence propelled me in the course of my wanderings into the care of the late Laurence and Alice Oliphant. They were a second edition of my parents. . . . Credit is due to them that the Zionists have a national anthem."[9] In marked contrast, Laurence Oliphant in his many novels, memoirs, and travel books, never mentions Imber by name, and alludes to him only once or twice in all of his writings. One gets the clear impression that the Oliphants were much more important to the Hebrew poet than he was to them.

We know much more about Oliphant's life than Imber's life. We have Oliphant's own autobiographical volumes, as well as a number of biographical studies, the most recent of which appeared in 1982. Furthermore, both historians of the British Empire and historians of nineteenth-century American

Laurence Oliphant (Emory University Libraries)

"New Religions" find Oliphant of interest. There are, however, far fewer sources for Imber's life. He was neither as fluent a writer as Oliphant nor as assiduous in promoting his own ideas. Yet, while Oliphant slid into relative obscurity,[10] *Hatikvah* granted Imber a type of immortality, a fate he had brazenly predicted for himself.[11]

In Israel, historians of Zionism remember Oliphant as an ardent, if not always effective, supporter of Jewish settlement in Palestine. He worked tirelessly to establish a Jewish colony east of the Jordan. When those plans failed, he supported the *Biluim*, the Russian university student group that in the 1880s pioneered the settlement of colonies in Ottoman Palestine west of the Jordan. That support extended to other groups of pioneers, including those who purchased the land in northern Galilee that became part of the colony of Rosh Pina. Thus the association with Imber is but one of a number of Oliphant's connections to the history of Zionism. In fact, Oliphant's diplomatic activity at the Turkish court would serve as a model for and inspiration to Theodor Herzl, who managed to get an audience with the sultan eighteen years after Oliphant's thwarted attempts. According to Jacob de Haas, Herzl's first biographer, Herzl expressed admiration for Oliphant and his book *Land of Gilead* (1880), which included a plan for an autonomous Jewish colony east of the Jordan River.[12] We shall consider Oliphant's relationship with Naphtali Herz Imber in the context of a wide web of relationships between Christian and Jewish Zionists. Let us look first at Oliphant's story and then return to Imber, who outlived Oliphant by two decades. Imber's story will be followed by an account of the Oliphant's legacy to the Jewish state.

~

Laurence Oliphant

Laurence Oliphant was born in 1829 in what is now South Africa. His mother's father was commander of British forces on the Cape of Good Hope. Laurence's father, Anthony Oliphant, appointed chief justice of Ceylon soon after Laurence's birth, was from a family "ancient and distinguished in Scotland." Maria and Anthony Oliphant were strict evangelicals, deeply influenced by the teachings of Edward Irving, "a Scottish divine of dynamic presence and dictatorial manner," who preached the imminent Second Coming[13] and attracted many followers in Britain and the United States. In addition to loyalty to the ideals of the British Empire, Laurence Oliphant internalized Irving's teachings about the role and place of Israel in the fulfillment of Christian prophecy.[14]

In 1826 Anthony Oliphant had participated in the first Albury Prophecy Conference, which was inspired by Edward Irving and presided over by his wealthy friend Henry Drummond. In Irving's words, conference participants would "deliberate for a full week upon the great prophetic questions which do at present most intimately concern Christendom."[15] The conference, which lasted six days, brought together twenty highly influential British clergymen and laymen of various religious denominations. Most were Tory traditionalists disturbed by liberal tendencies in English public life. For these conservatives, the recent proposal to admit Jews to Parliament was taken as a sign that "our legislature must be no longer regarded a purely Christian institution." While they opposed the admission of Jews to Parliament, these traditionalists favored the establishment of a Jewish colony in the East. Jews were not seen as full members of English political life, but they had an important part to play in the unfolding of divine events. The conference organizers would hold four additional prophecy conferences in the subsequent four years. They also created a journal, *The Morning Watch*.[16] Ultimately, the five Albury Prophecy conferences led to the founding of the English Catholic Apostolic Church. Subsequently, the Prophecy Conference tradition would establish itself in the United States, where a series of highly influential conferences, attended by hundreds of delegates, took place in the 1880s and 1890s. The return of the Jews to their land was a constant theme at these American conferences.

The Albury conferences and their journal, *The Morning Watch*, preached the necessity of the restoration of the Jews to their land. In 1829 the journal published a lecture by the eminent clergyman James Doddridge in which he explained, following biblical prophecy, that the Jews in the End Time would "be gathered from the countries in which they are now scattered, and conducted to their own land, where they shall become a prosperous and honorable, as well as a religious nation." This "recovery and defense of the Jews" would serve as a sign to the world of God's ultimate redemption and "make such impression on the Gentiles as to be a means of bringing in the fullness of them."[17] Here, as in earlier restoration plans, Jews' return to Palestine was linked to their conversion to Christianity. It should be noted that the Albury group's discomfort with the admission of Jews to Parliament did not prevent members from advocating a Jewish Palestine. As with Lord Balfour almost a century later, suspicion of British Jews often went hand in hand with plans to restore the Jews to Palestine.

Edward Irving's millennialist teachings had a deep influence on Anthony Oliphant, who passed these views on to his son Laurence. Although Laurence eventually distanced himself from any formal ties to organized Christianity, he retained his father's proto-Zionist, millennialist views, which would later resurface and lead Laurence to Palestine. This familial tie to millennialist thought makes Oliphant's Zionism all the more complex and difficult to categorize.

Laurence Oliphant spent his childhood in Ceylon. "As soon as he was old enough to understand," writes biographer Anne Taylor, "Laurence was subjected to a daily discipline of self-examination, the results of which had to be submitted to his parents. They cross-questioned him as to the smallest departure from the standard of conduct and thought they imposed. . . . This standard was the strictest possible and required the little boy to renounce the gaieties of the world."[18] As the child of a high-ranking colonial official, Laurence was imbued with a strong sense of loyalty to the British Empire. Throughout his adventurous life he sought to serve the empire, a tendency that would later combine with and shape his religious views, including his support of Zionism, which he was convinced would benefit the British. Rather than attend Cambridge, he convinced his parents that he would learn more from working with his father in Ceylon. He studied law with his father and others before beginning legal work in London. In Victorian London he developed a reputation as a "ladies man," was much sought after by hostesses of the upper crust, and was rumored to be a "sexual adventurer." Family contacts facilitated his ties to the royal family and to the press, and in 1865 he was elected to the House of Commons for a single term. The American writer Henry Adams, who met Oliphant in London in 1861, found him "exceptionally sane and peculiarly suited for country houses, where every man would enjoy his company and every woman adore him."[19]

It would be difficult to exaggerate the extent of Oliphant's overseas travel. Following an early trip to Nepal, he published his first book, *Journey to Katmandu* (1852), at age twenty-three. Next came *The Russian Shores of the Black Sea*, a travelogue of the Russian Empire, which he published right before the outbreak of the Crimean War. British government officials often used Oliphant's penchant for travel and his social graces to support diplomatic contacts, but he never entered the diplomatic service in an official capacity. He served, however, on virtually every continent: in Europe as a war correspondent for the *Times* (London), in Asia as a first secretary of the British embassy in Tokyo, and in the Americas as the personal secretary of Lord Elgin, governor of Canada. He continued to recount his adventures in a series of best-selling books, among them *Episodes in a Life of Adventure*, published in 1887. Oliphant's fluent and engaging prose style made these books eminently readable and very popular. He became well known as an intrepid traveler and explorer.

Early in his journalistic and diplomatic careers Oliphant evinced an interest in the future of Jewish life in Ottoman Palestine, although Palestine would not become the focal point of his life for another two decades. In 1857, while he was working for the British Foreign Office, Oliphant met the philanthropist Sir Moses Montefiore, leader of English Jewry and advocate for the Jewish communities in the Holy Land. Louis Loewe, Montefiore's secretary, noted that Oliphant and Montefiore met in Malta in May: "Mr. Laurence Oliphant, who was now on his way to China, as secretary to Lord Elgin, breakfasted with Montefiore. Mr. Oliphant took a great interest in all matters relating to the Holy Land, and conversed freely with him on certain schemes which might serve to improve the condition of its inhabitants."[20]

In his midthirties, at the height of social and professional success, Oliphant met the American mystic Thomas Lake Harris (1823–1906). Although Oliphant's first allegiance seemed to be to the good life of London society and to the British Empire and its commercial and strategic influence in the Middle East and South Asia, the evangelicalism of his parents was still very much with him. Founder of the Brotherhood of the New Life, one of the stranger new American religions of the mid-nineteenth century, Harris was, according to William James, "America's best-known mystic."[21] English-born and American-bred, Harris demonstrated an early aptitude for public speaking and a tendency to enter mystical states. In his thirties he founded a movement he called Christian Spiritualism. Harris's book *The Marriage of Heaven and Earth, Triumph of Life* was influenced by the teachings of Emanuel Swedenborg. After serving as pastor of the New Jerusalem Church, the Swedenborgian Church of New York, Harris, in search of new converts, brought his message to England, where he was said to be "looking for souls."[22]

Laurence Oliphant first heard Harris lecture in 1859, and for the subsequent seven years, during which he considered himself to be his new teacher's acolyte, Oliphant remained a very active "man of the world." On Harris's instructions, he remained in contact with influential friends. In the mid-1860s, Oliphant was earning a good deal of money from his books and magazine articles. Furthermore, he often traveled and negotiated for England at the request of the foreign secretary. In *Elgin's Mission to China and Japan*, a best seller, he told of an attack on the British legation in Edo (Tokyo), an attack that left him seriously wounded. In 1862 Oliphant also was involved in British diplomatic maneuvering related to the unification of Italy.[23] In 1865 he was elected to a seat in the House of Commons. But by 1867 he had given up his political and journalistic endeavors and settled in the United States. Eight years after first meeting Harris, Oliphant relinquished his stimulating and comfortable life in London and moved with his mother, Maria, and his wife, Alice, to Harris's rural commune in Brocton, New York. The elder Mrs. Oliphant provided much of the funding for the purchase of the land for the commune. On the teacher's orders, Laurence spent two years engaged in grueling physical labor at the Harris commune.

Oliphant decided to join Harris at a moment of spiritual crisis, which was preceded and perhaps precipitated by the death of his father. Laurence, together with his mother, who was predisposed to spiritualism, attended séances and consulted with mediums to "contact" Judge Oliphant. Furthermore, Laurence's term in Parliament had been a disastrous failure and his health was deteriorating, most likely as a result of syphilis. Desperate, he turned to an American "prophet," who promised him "a cure."[24] Perhaps a sojourn on the Brotherhood commune would be of benefit. Harris's commune was one of a number of American communal social experiments of the mid-nineteenth century. The Oneida Community in New York State was perhaps the best known of these communes.

Anne Taylor is quite perceptive about Oliphant's attraction to Harris: "From earliest childhood Laurence had had thrust upon him by his parent's Evangelical teaching a sense of responsibility not only for himself but for all mankind. The grace with which he bore this appalling burden was part of his charm, but the strain it imposed must have been almost intolerable. Now here was Harris, exhorting him to 'live the life' and ready to tell him exactly how to do it."[25] Within a decade, Oliphant would move from being an obedient follower of his American spiritual teacher to an independent leader and teacher of his own movement in a communal setting in Palestine.

Laurence Oliphant indicated his disillusionment with the worlds of diplomacy, journalism, and publishing at the end of his *Episodes in a Life of Adventure; or, Moss from a Rolling Stone* (1887). The book takes the reader up to 1864, when Laurence Oliphant was thirty-five years old. Replete with detailed reports of battles, diplomatic wrangling, secret negotiations, and far-flung travels, *Episodes in a Life of Adventure* reminds us that in the first half of the nineteenth century, travel was still dangerous and exciting. In the concluding chapter, "The Moral of It All," Oliphant declares: "Most people are, I suppose, more or less conscious of leading a sort of double life—an outside one and an inside one. The more I raced about the world, and took as active a part as I could in its dramatic performances, the more profoundly did the conviction force itself upon me, that if it was indeed a stage, and all the men and women only players, there must be real life somewhere."[26] Sick of this "false" life, Oliphant and his family moved to upstate New York in search of that "real life," as they did again two decades later when they sought "real life" as pioneers in Ottoman Palestine.

Oliphant's ideas might strike today's reader as belonging more to the late twentieth century than the late nineteenth century. His disillusionment with fame and his invocation of "inside" and "outside" lives reminds us of Jung's analysis of the modern condition. Laurence Oliphant concluded that the state of human affairs was increasingly precarious: "The world, with its bloody wars, its political intrigues, its social evils, its religious cant, its financial frauds,

Alice Oliphant (Emory University Libraries)

and its glaring anomalies, assumed in my eyes more and more the aspect of a gigantic lunatic asylum."[27] In a world gone insane, Oliphant sought a spiritual anchor. First he joined a new American communal experiment. Then, when he became disillusioned with its leader, he turned to Christian Zionism, a movement he would help shape.

Oliphant's mystical ideas, challenged and refined during his years with Harris, would later influence his understandings of Judaism and Zionism. Harris's teachings were a mixture of Swedenborgian mysticism and late-nineteenth-century American Spiritualism. Swedenborg spoke of "angelic revelation" as the basis for a new "spiritual science." Harris would go into trances—he dubbed himself a "trance lecturer"—and in that altered state he would compose and recite long mystical poems. Strangest of Harris's principles was the notion of "heavenly counterparts." Harris taught that a person's choice of an "earthly spouse" was most often an error. As a true prophet, Harris could identify a devotee's heavenly counterpart and bring the "ideal" couple together. Whether Harris meant for the new couple to consummate their relationship "on the physical plane" was unclear. What Harris made explicit was that the newly identified "ideal couple" should engage in "breathing exercises" together with other members of the commune. An arcane mystical terminology surrounded his description of these exercises; what really went on at the group exercises would later be the subject of a late-nineteenth-century American scandal.[28] Harris dubbed these breathing exercises *sympneumata*; toward the end of his life Oliphant would write a book with this title.

Soon after he met Harris, Oliphant became engaged to Alice Le Strange, a very beautiful and wealthy English aristocrat. Harris did not approve of the marriage; Alice's family was similarly disapproving. Eventually, Harris gave his approval, as did Alice's family. To her family's surprise and chagrin, Alice followed Laurence to the United States and Harris's Brotherhood of the New Life commune. According to Rosamond Dale Owen, Laurence Oliphant's second wife, under Harris's influence Laurence and Alice were married for twelve years without consummating their marriage—because Prophet Harris told them that they were not compatible souls. While Harris's detractors claimed that he was advocating "free love"—or as "free" as he, the teacher, would allow,[29] others claimed that the prophet and his followers were held to a vow of celibacy. This confusion about communal practice, and the polarized descriptions of either total celibacy or "free love," was typical of mid-nineteenth-century discourse about new religious sects. A similarly confused discourse emerged in the late-nineteenth-century polemic about the American colony in Jerusalem. Selah Merrill, the U.S. consul in Jerusalem, accused the colonists of conducting orgies; other critics of the colony claimed that all of the colonists were celibate and that marriage was banned.

On the basis of his thoroughly modern reading of the world's ills, in *Episodes in a Life of Adventure* Laurence Oliphant reconsiders the public and adventurous life so vividly described in his book: "Looking back upon the period described in the foregoing pages, it appeared to me distinctly a most insane period. I therefore decided upon retiring from public life and the confused turmoil of a mad world, into a seclusion where, under the most favorable conditions I could find I could prosecute my researches into the more hidden laws which govern human action and control events."[30] In Victorian fashion, he makes no explicit mention of his sexual life, but a history of promiscuity and venereal disease (a possibility suggested by some of Oliphant's biographers) would fit with his expression of retreat from the "insane" world. Perhaps he felt that a discipline imposed by a religious system would help him control his sexual appetites. Communal living—first in America, then in Palestine—and Swedenborg's and Harris's ideas about sexuality would stay with Oliphant and were later transmuted into a belief in the "bi-sexuality of God" and his human creations. These ideas would later manifest themselves in the commune that the Oliphants tried to establish in Haifa. The idea of the commune, according to Oliphant biographer Philip Henderson, was not "connected with Jewish colonization so much as with the founding of their own community on Harrisite lines—for curiously enough, though they had become disenchanted with Harris, they still founded their lives on the main tenets of his teaching."[31]

In "retiring from public life" Laurence Oliphant did not stay a hermit for long. Thomas Lake Harris recognized quickly that Oliphant's talents lay in the public sphere and that it was detrimental to the Brotherhood to keep Laurence out of public life. After his two year "initiation" period at the guru's commune in upstate New York, Laurence Oliphant returned to England in 1869, and to public life, at Harris's suggestion. He remained, according to his friends in England, as personable and engaged as ever, although his new religious ideas struck his conversation partners as odd at best. On a number of occasions Oliphant had audiences with Queen Victoria. Her journal entries reveal that she was always impressed by his knowledge of foreign affairs but troubled by what she heard of his spiritual searches. The queen wrote, "He has very peculiar religious views."[32]

Alice Oliphant did not escape Harris's grasp as easily as her husband had. As his movement became riddled with dissension and beset with financial difficulties, Harris became more dictatorial and unreasonable. In order to separate Alice from Laurence, Harris sent her to a satellite commune that his followers had established in California, a commune from which Alice later fled. After a period in which she supported herself as a schoolteacher, Laurence was able to rescue her and bring her back to England.

For thirteen years, beginning in 1865, the Oliphants were linked to Harris and his Brotherhood. The final break came in 1878, a year before the Oliphants began working tirelessly for Jewish settlement. Harris frowned on Laurence's developing philo-Judaism. Harris's negative obsession with Jews and Judaism[33] as well as his attraction to the "enlightened religions of the East" relied heavily on the influence of Swedenborg.[34] Swedenborg's deep hostility toward Jews and Judaism manifested itself not only in the form of traditional stereotypes ("The Jews are among the nations the most avaricious, for they are in the mere love of money without regard to its use.") but also as a rejection of the role of the Jews in End Time scenarios ("It would be easier to convert stones to faith in the Lord than the Jews. How mistaken they are who think that the church will ever pass to them.").[35] The Oliphants reacted violently against these prejudices and became advocates of Jewish political and national rights.

In 1878 Oliphant expressed support for Zionism; a year later he was in Istanbul petitioning the Ottoman court to permit Russian Jews to settle in Palestine. In discussions with European Jewish leaders, Oliphant advocated Jewish emigration to Palestine, not to the United States, the preferred destination of many of Eastern Europe's destitute Jews. In that same year, Oliphant toured Ottoman Palestine, seeking information on areas that might be appropriate for Jewish agricultural settlement initiatives. From Damascus Oliphant wrote to Lord Salisbury, the British foreign secretary, and described a large area east of the Jordan River that might be suitable as the site of a Jewish colony under British auspices.[36] A year later, Oliphant published his book *Land of Gilead*, which presented this settlement proposal in great detail.

Disillusioned with Harris, the Oliphants departed to seek spiritual fulfillment in a biblical setting. They would replicate some of Harris's communal ideas in their homes in Haifa and the neighboring Druze village of Dalyat al Carmel. Perhaps the Palestine effort was a substitute for the failed American communal effort. We have seen this model in the story of Clorinda Minor, who moved to Palestine in 1849 after serving as Adventist Prophetess during the Great Disappointment of 1844. When America failed as the land of promise, those influenced by new forms of biblically referenced prophecy attempted to realize their vision in the biblical Promised Land.

After leaving Harris's commune and circle of influence, Laurence and Alice Oliphant dedicated themselves completely to Jewish settlement in Palestine. As the Oliphants had given considerable sums of money and property to Harris, Laurence traveled to the United States in 1881 in an attempt to retrieve some of the funds. He reached a settlement with Harris's small group of followers and used the money to move to Haifa. This total commitment to Zionism extended to the end of their lives in the late 1880s. The Oliphants' Zionist advocacy would take a number of forms, including diplomacy, fund-raising, political organizing, and cooperation with Jewish individuals and groups. More importantly, they took direct action to bring about Jewish restoration. They moved to Palestine and from their base in Haifa worked tirelessly for the welfare of the Old and New Yishuv. Just as they were in the process of moving to Palestine, the Oliphants met the Hebrew poet Naphtali Herz Imber in Istanbul.

~

Naphtali Herz Imber

N. H. Imber's humble origins are a stark contrast to those of Laurence Oliphant. Imber was born in 1856 in Bukovina, then part of the Austro-Hungarian Empire. The impoverished Jewish population in this region of the Carpathian Mountains lived in an uneasy truce with the equally impoverished Christian population. Naphtali Herz was one of six children. Gifted with a prodigious memory, he was acclaimed an *"iluy,"* a prodigy of rabbinic learning, as a youngster. Naphtali Herz's brother Shmaryahu writes that Naphtali Herz, at the age of eight, was discoursing on Talmudic matters with the mental agility of a fifteen year old and that "he soon became known throughout Bukovina as 'the *iluy* of the *illuyim'* —the genius of the geniuses."[37]

Imber wrote many brief sketches of his own life, but factual accuracy was not his strength. His brother Shmaryahu is a more reliable source of information about the poet's childhood and youth. Shmaryahu Imber sketches a family portrait of piety, poverty, and dedication to rabbinic learning. Naphtali Herz was closer to his warm and nurturing mother than to his distant father, who did not appreciate the child's talents or understand his shifting moods. "From childhood," wrote his brother, "Naphtali Herz would lie in bed until noon, and even then it wasn't easy to get him out of bed. We had to drag him to the living room."[38]

From the age of ten, Naphtali Herz composed poems in Hebrew that celebrated Austro-Hungarian national events. In his Hebrew poem "Austria," for which he was awarded a medal and a cash prize, he expressed the general Jewish enthusiasm for the Austro-Hungarian emperor Franz Josef. Emperor Franz Josef had granted civil rights to the Jews of the empire in the 1860s. Jewish leaders praised the emperor's long benevolent rule, and included his name in the synagogue prayer for the government that had become institutionalized in European Jewish communities. The emperor's cash prize enabled Imber to travel from his native town to the cultural capitals of the Austro-Hungarian Empire, and it set up a model for the rest of Imber's life. He would no longer write poems about Austria, since his European nationalist sentiments gave way to advocacy of Zionism, but he would continue to depend on wealthy and prominent patrons for his livelihood. Like the medieval troubadours on whom he modeled himself, Imber sought patrons in each of the many cities and countries in which he resided.

With this initial recognition of his literary talents, Imber began writing poems for official and unofficial occasions within both the Jewish community and the wider Austro-Hungarian society. In his late teens he cultivated the company of Jewish intellectuals, first in Brody and then in Lemberg/Lvov, the cultural capital of Galicia. On his extended journey from his hometown to Brody and to Lemberg, Imber cut off his *payyes* (sidelocks), the sign of male adherence to ultra-Orthodox practice, and adopted conventional European clothing. He also gave up halacha, formal rabbinic law and practice. On this journey he was introduced to the educational reformer Abraham Krochmal and to Joshua Heschel Schorr, editor of *Hechalutz*, a Haskalah journal in which Imber published some early poems.[39]

The next step up on the European Jewish cultural and publishing ladder for aspiring poets and intellectuals was Vienna. Imber arrived there in 1876. He was twenty years old. Continually on the move, restless and curious, Imber did not stay long in the imperial city. He was seeking "poetic experience" as he set out on a six-year journey that would lead him to Constantinople by 1882. Unlike Oliphant, Imber left no detailed account of his youthful travels and adventures. At times he supported himself by tutoring the children of wealthy Maskilim who wanted their offspring to be familiar with European languages and literature as well as with the literature of the emerging Hebrew revival, a revival that began in Eastern Europe and Russia and only later spread to Palestine with the first settlers of Hovevei Zion (Lovers of Zion). On reaching a European city with a Jewish literary or cultural institution, Imber would visit that institution. He sought funds, preferably through a wealthy patron, and a place to publish his work. He moved south through Europe, following the Danube through Hungary, Serbia, and Romania. When he could find neither work as a tutor nor publishing outlets for his poems, Imber took to the regional markets as a peddler. One literary historian has dubbed Imber "the first bohemian." He had a weakness for alcohol and later delighted in announcing to friends that he wrote *Hatikvah* when drunk, "for only when I drink myself into a stupor can I create."[40]

In a 1904 conversation with the American Yiddish writer Abraham Reisen, a down-and-out Imber asserted presciently that because of *Hatikvah*, his name would be remembered forever.[41] In his twenties, when his first book of poems, which included *Hatikvah*, was published, he was dubbed the "Hebrew National Poet," a prototype later fulfilled in the life of Hayyim Nahman Bialik.[42] Yet many popular accounts and some serious histories of Zionism dismiss Imber's literary career, denigrating his work and downplaying his role as national poet. His Zionist contemporaries remembered his personal failings, despite the success of *Hatikvah*. Imber's bohemian ways and his raucous, disruptive presence embarrassed many of the more conventional Zionist leaders. This was especially true in the United States. Louis Lipsky, who first encountered Imber at a 1901 Zionist meeting, wrote: "He was certainly not an attractive character. He had the head of an Indian, his face was bronzed, his hair was long and his clothes always in tatters. He was indescribably dirty and always exuded the aroma of stale whisky." Not content to damn Imber for his drinking and lack of proper grooming, Lipsky went on to attack both Imber's poetry and his politics: "He was not really much of a poet. . . . *Hatikvah* was made the text of a song which struck a responsive chord by reason of its sentiment and melody. He had no philosophy nor was he really a lover of Zion. In fact, he was not interested in Palestine over much. He mocked the seriousness of the Zionists, their romantic ideas, their tendency to mourn over the past."[43]

Many things about Imber bothered Lipsky, the "organization man" of early American Zionism. To say that Imber was not a "lover of Zion" strikes one as inaccurate at best, vicious at worst. What irked Lipsky and other organizational Zionists was that Imber, who lived and wrote in Palestine from 1882 to 1887—a period in which he celebrated and joined the struggles of the *halutzim*, the "pioneers" of the first aliyah, chose not to remain in Palestine. Rather, he preferred to live in the United States. The American Zionist leadership, bound by the myths and tasks of Zionism to encourage Jews to immigrate to Palestine, or at the very least to support financially those Jews who chose to immigrate to Palestine, could not countenance Imber's behavior and choices. In a prescient way, Imber was the first "Israeli" in the United States. Today, the many Israeli residents in the United States present a similar challenge to American Zionist ideology and leadership.[44] As Israeli historian Tom Segev has noted, "No one knows just how many Israelis have settled in America since Israel's founding, but the number almost certainly exceeds the number of Jews who have moved to Israel from America. There is no more stinging affront to the Zionist ego than people's decision to leave Israel and live abroad."[45]

A 1902 postcard featuring the lyrics to Hatikvah *(Beit Hatefutsot)*

Recently, literary scholars have challenged the tendency of the Israeli literary establishment to minimize Imber's importance in the history of modern Hebrew poetry. One of the reasons for the negative evaluation of Imber's poetry and prose was that it was not collected until decades after his death in 1909. Imber's "Complete Poems" was not published until 1950. In his introduction to that volume, titled *Gypsy and Bohemian*, critic Dov Sadan noted that the lack of a complete volume of Imber's works made an honest critical evaluation of its value impossible. "Most of those who have written about him hadn't fulfilled the basic requirement: read the work. They based their critiques on a crumb here and a crumb there."[46] Sadan pointed out that Imber's tenuous claim to the position of "national poet" or "poet of the Hebrew revival" was undermined by his departure from Palestine in 1887 and by his erratic behavior and eccentric pronouncements. Louis Lipsky's damning dismissal of Imber's poetry and personality resonated with Israeli historians and Hebrew literary critics. They, too, unjustly minimized Imber's accomplishments.

Imber claimed at one point to have written what was to become his most famous poem early in his European journeys. As his brother Shmaryahu writes, "In 1878, in the house of Baron Moshe Waldberg, he wrote *Hatikvah* . . . that is what my brother told me. In the beginning, only a chosen few knew the poem. A few years later, when the Jewish colonies began and the Lovers of Zion movement spread, *Hatikvah* became famous in virtually every Jewish community. The poem became the national anthem."[47] Yet, in Imber's book *Barkai*, which he dedicated to the Oliphants, the first printed copy of *Tikvoseinu* bears the subscript "Jerusalem, 1884."[48] Did Imber write the poem in Romania or Palestine? If, as he later said to Abraham Reisen, he was indeed drunk when he wrote the poem, perhaps Imber himself was not sure of the place or date of its composition. The question of the date of the poem's composition is significant because Imber stated on many occasions that he wrote *Hatikvah* specifically in honor of the Oliphants. Perhaps he penned the poem in the late 1870s in Romania but revised and printed it—with the aid of and in honor of the Oliphants—in the mid-1880s, when he was living in Palestine.

~

The Oliphants and Imber

N. H. Imber tells the story of his first meeting with the Oliphants in *Leaves from My Palestine and Other Diaries*: "My acquaintance with Laurence Oliphant began badly. For I was at this period such a zealous nationalist that I was angry to hear that a Christian like Mr. Oliphant was mixing himself up with a Jewish national movement. What business had a Christian to interfere?, I thought. And so I determined to pay the said Christian a visit and give him a piece of my mind."[49]

In the dramatic conversation that ensued, Laurence Oliphant—when challenged by Imber about his right to speak on Jewish matters—presented the Hebrew poet with a German newspaper article in which Oliphant had stated publicly that "he and his wife had definitely abandoned Christianity twenty-five years ago." After expressing sympathy for Jewish suffering, Oliphant asked Imber about his religious beliefs. Imber presented himself as a Kabbalist, and spoke of the *Shekhina* (the divine presence) and the dual nature of God—male and female. As Imber himself explained, "During my explanation Mr. and Mrs. Oliphant exchanged glances of surprise and pleasure, and when I had done they cried out how wonderful it was that they should meet me, for they too believed in this dual nature of God. They said that God must have sent me to them."[50]

This encounter captures the complexity of Jewish responses to Christian Zionists: attraction, interest, confrontation, doubt, and hostility—all adding up to a cautious ambivalence. In Imber's case it led to devotion and admiration mixed with lingering suspicion. Imber and his Jewish contemporaries could make their peace with "Christian Zionists" who were not "Christian" in the evangelical, missionizing sense. To the extent that this support of the Jewish cause was not grounded in millennialism or evangelism, causes that both religious and secular Jews considered a direct threat, it was welcome. The Oliphants assured Imber that they had "left Christianity" a quarter century ago. Unlike most Christian restorationists who preceded them, starting with Thomas Brightman and Henry Finch in the seventeenth century, the Oliphants did not speak of the return of the Jews as part of an End Time scenario. Two and a half centuries after Finch, the Oliphants never directly endorsed a literalist reading of prophecy. Unlike most Christian advocates of Jewish restoration they saw no theological imperative at work in the contemporary unfolding of Jewish fate. At times Laurence even mocked End Time beliefs.[51] Although the Oliphants' Zionist work had religious underpinnings, it was not predicated on End Time beliefs or on the eventual conversion of the Jews.[52] But, as we shall see, the Oliphants' Zionism was not totally secular, either.

In his memoirs Shmaryahu Imber provides a different account of his brother's first meeting with the Oliphants:

After the Russian-Turkish War Imber came to Istanbul and there became a peddler. By accident he met in 1882 Sir Laurence Oliphant, one of the Righteous Gentiles and an enthusiastic Lover of Zion. Oliphant sought, as was well known, to direct Russian Jewish emigration to the Land of Israel, though most of it was going to America. Sir Laurence and his wife invited Imber, who met them in a public garden, to travel with them. They would take care of all his expenses. He thanked them but said that he never accepted charity. This response pleased the couple and they suggested to him that he become their secretary for Jewish affairs and travel with them to the Land of Israel. . . . He accepted with great joy and wrote to us of his great joy. The family also received a letter in German from Mrs. Oliphant. In it she told our mother to no longer worry about her son, for she and her husband love him as if he were their son.[53]

In Shmaryahu's account the first Oliphant-Imber meeting is accidental and it is the Oliphants who take the initiative and offer a job to Imber. There is no mention of mystical teachings that the Jewish and Gentile seekers find they have in common. Shmaryahu elevates "Sir Laurence" to knighthood, a status he did not achieve but with which he was honored in Jewish journalistic accounts of his exploits on behalf of Jewish refugees and colonists. Shmaryahu presents Alice Oliphant as a maternal figure who writes to Imber's mother, woman to woman, to assure her of her son's welfare. Imber's own account of his first meeting with Alice was more dramatic and eroticized. She is there when he first meets Laurence, but she does not speak: "A servant led me into a small sitting room. As I entered, my eye fell first on Mrs. Oliphant, and as it did so I felt myself thrilled by the same inexplicable fascination that her sweetness exercised over everybody with whom she came in contact." After his Zionist and mystical conversation with Laurence, Imber recalled, "[I] kiss[ed] my host and hostess in Oriental fashion. Hence forwards I was the attached and devoted slave and friend of the noble-hearted Mrs. Oliphant, I thought of her night and day."[54]

Laurence and Alice Oliphant met Naphtali Herz Imber just as the Oliphants' own hopes for an autonomous Jewish colony in Gilead had collapsed. This was a critical moment in Laurence Oliphant's Zionist career. Diplomatic maneuvering had failed. Subsequent to that failure, Laurence and Alice forged contacts with Jewish individuals and institutions. Now they were in need of a "Hebrew secretary," who could facilitate their contacts with Jews. They hoped that Imber's knowledge of Hebrew, Yiddish, German, and Romanian would enable them to correspond with Jews throughout Europe and Palestine.

Imber was also in dire need at this time, a need of a more immediate and essential kind. Reduced to peddling in the markets of Istanbul, his hopes of visiting Palestine were fading quickly. For the previous six years he had traveled through southern Europe, writing poems, observing, visiting, and "schnorring" (begging, cajoling) from Jewish communities large and small. In the Oliphants he found financial, emotional, and spiritual support. They would take him to Eretz Israel, give him regular, meaningful employment, and perhaps most importantly act as surrogate parents.

Imber settled with the Oliphants in Haifa and served as their secretary and general amanuensis, but he did not stay long. After a few months, the Oliphants sent him to "tour the land" and visit the settlements of the New Yishuv. Imber journeyed to the colony of Rosh Pina, near Safed, and met the *halutzim* who had settled there. Oliphant had met with representatives of these Romanian Jewish colonists during his 1879 sojourn in Istanbul and later had given the colonists some of the land for the colony. Imber then went to Petah Tikvah, and found that the *halutzim* had set his poems *Mishmar hayarden* and *Tikvoseinu* to popular folk tunes. He was inspired by the settlers and the land to write more Hebrew poetry. Imber soon returned to the Oliphants and as their secretary recorded the visits of many famous British visitors to the Oliphant compound in Haifa, including General Charles "Chinese" Gordon, who was killed the following year in Khartoum. Imber noted that the Oliphants had established links with the German Templer colony of Haifa and with the Druze village of Dalyat al Carmel, where they built a summer home. The Oliphants became patrons of the Druze villagers; they sought to aid the villagers as they aided the *halutzim*. In both Haifa and Dalyat Imber found opportunities to socialize and drink with the locals. Their association with the German colonists had amusing consequences. On Christmas Day, a German colonist brought the Oliphants a festive boar's head as a gift. Imber writes that out of politeness he was prepared to taste the dish. But as soon as their German neighbor left the Oliphant residence, Alice threw the offending dish in the garbage, saying, "My Herzl won't taste a pig's head." Imber also befriended the Jewish pioneers of Zichron Yaakov. "Imber was always attracted to places and occasions where the food and drink were free, and for this reason he formed a fast friendship with the men of the German Colony in Haifa."[55]

⌒

The Oliphants in Palestine

The record of the Oliphants' Zionist activities is clear, but the reasons for their commitment to Zionism are difficult to pin down. As Israeli historian Yosef Nedava wrote, "Oliphant was a declared 'Lover of Zion'. But it is hard to define precisely the motivations that brought him to the Zionist camp and to support for Jewish settlement efforts."[56] To some extent, Zionism was a replacement for the Oliphants' commitment to Thomas Lake Harris's Brotherhood of the New Life. With Laurence and Alice Oliphant, however, political motivations seem more important than theological ones. Some scholars have suggested that the Oliphants' proto-Zionism did have Christian religious roots but that they deliberately obscured those roots so as not to alienate members of the British ruling class, who saw these beliefs as quaint at best and "lunatic" at worst. Laurence also was aware that Jewish Zionist leaders with whom he wished to collaborate would be put off by an appeal to Christian millennialist expectations. As he wrote to a Zionist leader, "So far as my own efforts are concerned, they are based upon considerations which have no connection whatever with any popular religious theory upon the subject."[57] Oliphant had a pragmatic and nationalistic understanding of Zionism, an understanding that foreshadowed the emerging views of Jewish Zionists. From Laurence Oliphant's actions during the twenty years before he embraced "Zionism," it was clear that he was concerned about the situation of persecuted Jews of Russia and Romania. Like his Jewish Zionist counterparts, he saw Zionism as the solution to persistent anti-Semitism.

Jewish Zionist leaders for the most part were enthusiastic in their support of the Oliphants' efforts in Palestine. Zionist leader Moses Lilienblum said, "I hope that Laurence Oliphant will be the Messiah of Israel."[58] Lilienblum was invoking the biblical description of Cyrus, king of Persia, as Messiah. In the Hebrew Bible, the only messianic figure identified as an actual person is Cyrus, the monarch who allowed and enabled the return of the Jews from their exile in Babylon to their home in Zion.[59]

Several years before moving to Palestine Oliphant had petitioned the British government to consider a plan for Palestine that would satisfy both British imperial needs and Jewish nationalist aspirations. In his 1879 letter to Lord Salisbury, Oliphant detailed a plan to lease a large area of eastern Palestine from the Ottoman Empire. European Christian and Jewish supporters would finance the twenty-five-year lease of the land. Laurence noted that the Palestine Exploration Fund had pledged 40,000 pounds sterling to the effort, which he called the "Gilead Plan." Gilead was the territory east of the Jordan River that, according to the Book of Numbers, chapter 32, Moses had granted to the Israelite tribes of Reuben and Gad and half of the tribe of Menassah.[60] That the Palestine Exploration Fund of Great Britain agreed to provide some financial support to the project indicated emerging links between Christian "biblical researchers" and Christian advocates of Jewish return to the Holy Land. Oliphant, however, chose not to involve Jewish philanthropists or intellectuals in the early phase of the Gilead Plan. The proposed colony, which would fall under British auspices, would be based on diversity in agriculture and on exploitation of the mineral wealth of the Dead Sea. The British foreign secretary, acting on Oliphant's proposal, consulted with Prime Minister Benjamin Disraeli, who was enthusiastic about the project.

When Eliezer Ben-Yehuda, then living in Jerusalem, read of the Gilead Plan, he endorsed it enthusiastically, as did other Zionists. The *London Jewish Chronicle* assured its readers that Laurence Oliphant was not motivated by missionary reasons. The *Chronicle* writer expressed the hope that "Oliphant would serve as God's representative," a precursor of the Messiah. "Heaven may lead a man of great intelligence, but of little faith, to become the precursor of the Messiah."[61] The description of Oliphant as being "of little faith" would have mollified Jews wary of millennialist Christian enthusiasm for a Jewish national home. Eliezer Ben-Yehuda, fiercely secular and a vocal opponent of rabbinic authority, was none the less outspoken in his opposition to Christian missionary efforts. Initially he cleared the Oliphants of any suspicion of missionary intentions, but within a few years of praising Oliphant's Gilead Plan he condemned Oliphant's protégé Imber as a tool of Christian missionaries in Jerusalem. What evidence Ben-Yehuda had of Imber's apostasy we do not know; but he seemed sure of this assertion. When it became clear that the Turks would not approve Oliphant's Gilead Plan, a disillusioned Ben-Yehuda wrote a fiery newspaper article in which he mocked the plan and asked if there was not enough room west of the Jordan for Jewish settlement.[62]

As we can see from his correspondence with Lord Salisbury, there were British diplomatic aspects to Oliphant's proto-Zionism. As he had spent decades serving the interests of the British Empire, only setting aside these efforts to join Thomas Lake Harris's Brotherhood, it would only make sense for him to combine his Zionist sentiments with his pro-empire orientation. One of Oliphant's pet projects was the Palestine Railroad. The railroad would enable the implementation of his larger Gilead Plan, linking by rail the proposed Jewish colony east of the Jordan with the port of Haifa on the Mediterranean. He met with the Duke of Sutherland, who had shares in other Middle Eastern railroad endeavors, and tried to convince him to support the plan.[63]

Thus from 1878 onward Oliphant was engaged in activities he thought would benefit both the British Empire and Zionist aspirations. Oliphant argued that the Gilead Plan with its creation of an autonomous Jewish territory in the area east of the Jordan River in what is now the Kingdom of Jordan, would strengthen the Ottoman Empire and British influence in it. Under Benjamin Disraeli's leadership the British government had developed a policy of support for the Ottoman Empire against what both the Turks and the British saw as a Russian threat. Russia's search for a warm-water port led it to seek an outlet at the Bosphorus, and it was thought to have designs on Palestine. The large number of Russian Orthodox pilgrims to Jerusalem and the consequent Russian presence in Jerusalem convinced Britain of Russia's intention to gain influence in this and other parts of the Ottoman Empire. Britain feared that waning Ottoman power in Palestine would give Russia a foothold in the Eastern Mediterranean. The Ottomans had to be supported, and establishing Jewish settlement was one way to do it. Disraeli's own Jewish heritage may have made him sympathetic to Oliphant's plans, though there is no direct evidence of this.

Oliphant supported the Ottomans as a bulwark against Russian intentions, but British interests were only one factor in his considerations. His pro-Zionist activities may have been catalyzed by his wish to serve the empire, but he soon developed a real sympathy for the welfare and safety of Jews of Europe. Oliphant argued that the Turks should welcome a Jewish presence in Palestine—here he played on Turkish ideas of Jewish financial power—and claimed that Russian Jewish emigrants would be especially loyal to the Turks, as Russia was a common enemy. On this basis, Oliphant had high expectations for the outcome of his negotiations with the Ottoman court in 1879.[64]

Arriving in Istanbul, he managed to establish contact with lower-level Turkish officials through whom he hoped to gain an audience with the Ottoman sultan. The Ottoman government, however, put off by British naval maneuvers in the Bosphorus, did not want to see a British-influenced Jewish colony in Palestine, and so rejected Oliphant's Gilead Plan. In 1880 Oliphant, undeterred, decided to move from diplomacy to public advocacy. He sought the support of Jewish Zionists. He now turned to Jewish activists and philanthropists for support for his plans to assist Jewish refugees and colonists.

Oliphant decided that the case for Zionism was strongest when presented as the most effective response to the problem of European anti-Semitism. In the introduction to *Land of Gilead* (1880), he articulated what would later become the central Zionist claim, that settlement in Palestine was the only possible solution to the Jewish situation in Europe: "The Jews themselves have borne repeated testimony to the fact that as far as they are concerned, Christian fanaticism in Eastern Europe is far more bitter than Moslem; indeed the position of the Jews in Turkey is relatively favored."[65] For Jews, life in Palestine under Turkish rule would be an improvement over the conditions in Europe. Oliphant further rehearsed many of the classic Zionist formulations: "The Arabs have very little claim for our sympathy . . . they have laid waste this country."[66] He compared "the luxuriant exuberance of Gilead" with "the hard rock of Judea."[67] For Oliphant, man and nature had shaped the country's harsh features; the returning Jews could redeem the land.

Within two years of Oliphant's sojourn in Istanbul, the Russian pogroms of 1881–82 broke out. In London there were mass demonstrations in favor of Jewish rights. The British government, with broad public support, established the Mansion House Fund to support the victims of the pogroms and called upon Laurence Oliphant to administer it. Oliphant wrote of his journey to Russia:

> I was the emissary of the Mansion House committee, for the purpose of distributing relief to some fifteen thousand distressed refugee Jews, who had taken refuge there in a starving condition. . . . So intensely wrought up were the expectations of the much-suffering race who form the largest proportion of the population of this part of Europe, that at every station they were assembled in crowds with petitions to be transported to Palestine, the conviction haven taken possession of their minds that the time appointed for their return to the land of their ancestors had arrived, and that I was to be their Moses on that occasion.[68]

Through these efforts, Oliphant became a hero to many Eastern European Jews. Lest we think that Oliphant's comment about "being their Moses" was mere self-aggrandizement, we have a confirming observation by early-twentieth-century historian of Zionism N. M. Gelber: "It shouldn't surprise us that Eastern European Jews spun great stories about Oliphant's activities, as if he was their deliverer from misery. In cities and small towns in Russia, Romania, and Galicia, you could find in the houses of poor Jews a picture of Oliphant. It would be hung right next to the pictures of the great philanthropists Moses Montefiore and Baron Hirsch."[69] On his trip to Russia, Oliphant was accompanied by Reverend William Hechler, an associate of Theodor Herzl. As we shall see in the following chapter, Reverend Hechler was to play a pivotal role in establishing political Zionism's international diplomatic credentials.

Oliphant traveled to Lemberg/Lvov, and there he met with Zionist intellectual Peretz Smolenskin to discuss emigration plans for Russian Jews. Oliphant was in favor of emigration to Palestine, not the United States; with this idea the Zionists concurred. In a letter to Smolenskin, Laurence Oliphant noted that he favored settlement in the Land of Israel "though most of the Jewish philanthropists of Europe oppose this idea." In a letter to American

Jewish scholar Ephraim Deinard, Smolenskin stated that he had total trust in Oliphant and his wife, for "they have only the welfare of Israel in their hearts."[70] As a pragmatic Zionist, Peretz Smolenskin was more concerned about the feasibility of Oliphant's land acquisition plans than about the purity of his religious or political motives.

At the Lemberg/Lvov Conference of 1882, Oliphant also gained the endorsement of Rabbi Samuel Mohiliver.[71] Rabbi Mohiliver was a central Rabbinic figure in the early development of religious Zionism. From the 1870s until his death in 1898 Mohiliver worked tirelessly to bridge the ever-growing gap between secular and religious concepts of Zionism. "He served as an example for various movements and organizations that sought to merge traditional Jewry and the Zionist movement."[72] Rabbi Mohiliver assured his coreligionists that Laurence Oliphant did not have missionary intentions: "Our brethren should not suspect that his intention is to strengthen the Christian religion and divert our people from their faith. . . . He told me that twenty-five years ago he left all of the established Christian churches, and that he and his wife wish only for the fulfillment of the words of the prophets that Israel will be restored to its land, *and that they should do this in a way that enables them to keep every detail of the Jewish religion.*"[73]

Oliphant influenced emergent Zionism in a number of ways. He derided the *Halukah*, the charity system by which Old Yishuv Jews received money from their coreligionists in the West.[74] The *Halukah*, for Oliphant, was a hindrance to the development of Jewish independence. In his account of a sojourn in Safed in 1883, Oliphant described the Jewish section of the town

> One seems transported into the ghetto of some Romanian or Russian town, with a few Eastern disagreeables added. . . . The majority of the Jews here are supported by a charitable fund called the *Halukah*, which is subscribed to by pious Jews all over the world as a sacred duty. . . . The practical result of this system is to maintain in idleness and mendicancy a set of useless bigots, who combine superstitious observance with immoral practice, and who, as a rule, are opposed to every project which has for its object the real progress of the Jewish nation. Hence they regard with alarm the establishment of agricultural colonies, or the inauguration of an era of any kind of labour by Jews in Palestine.[75]

Oliphant's heated polemic against the orthodoxy of the Old Yishuv could have been written by one of many Jewish champions of political Zionism and its heroes, the *halutzim*, or pioneers. The pioneers were the New Jews—Jews able to work the land, in contrast to the Jews of the Old Yishuv, who spent their days in study while supported by charitable contributions from the Diaspora. These traditional Jews would naturally oppose the agricultural initiatives of their modernizing coreligionists. All the more reason, said Oliphant, to support those agricultural initiatives.

But unlike many Zionist thinkers, Laurence Oliphant did not want the *halutzim* to jettison Jewish ritual observances. Zionists had to be observant Jews. In this he differed from the Zionist secularism of many of his Jewish colleagues. For Oliphant and other Christian Zionists the return to Zion was inextricably linked to their notion of the Jewish people as a people of religion and religious observance. Yes, the social and economic lives of Jews had to be modernized, but not so modernized as to undo their religious underpinnings. This conflict between a Christian Zionist view of the Jewish return as a religious phenomenon and a secular Jewish view of Zionism as a modern nationalist movement persists until today. The current alliance between the religious Zionist settler movement and American Christian fundamentalists is predicated on the resolution of this conflict.

Laurence Oliphant's admiration for the pioneering agriculturalist Jews of Palestine was not untouched by vestiges of Christian anti-Jewish sentiment. In *Haifa*, he tells of his visit to Bukeia (Peki'in), a village that some Zionists claimed had an uninterrupted settlement of Jews from Second Temple times. Oliphant's reaction to Bukeia is startling. He described the various religious and ethnic groups of the village: "Then there were the Jews—the only group of Jews existing in the world whose ancestors have clung to the soil ever since that Teacher's tragic death, and whose fathers may have shared in the general hostility to him at the time—representing still the faith which was the repository of the highest moral teaching prior to Christianity, prior to Mohammedanism."[76]

Despite these references to Jewish hostility to Jesus, Laurence Oliphant remained firmly supportive of Jewish colonization: "There are three prejudices which have operated against the colonization of Palestine by Jews, and which are all absolutely unsound, and these are, first, that the Jew cannot become an agriculturalist; secondly, that the country is barren; and thirdly, that it is unsafe. The real obstacle in the way to Palestine colonization does not lie in any of these directions, but in the fact that the government is most determinedly opposed to it."[77] Contrast Oliphant's statements with those of Selah Merrill, U.S. consul in Jerusalem during Oliphant's sojourn there. In 1891 Merrill wrote to his superiors at the U.S. State Department that "the Jews are not ready for Palestine and Palestine is not ready for the Jews." Merrill, an ordained Congregationalist minister who served as consul during a period of twenty years, did all he could to obstruct Jewish emigration to Palestine. Oliphant did all he could to fight Merrill's intransigence and encourage Jewish agricultural settlement.

Another overtly Zionist activity that Oliphant helped pioneer was the linking of specific sites in Palestine with their Jewish past. The modern originator and systematizer of the link between biblical narrative and Holy Land geography was the American explorer Edward Robinson, who visited Palestine in 1836 and 1852. A few decades later, in the 1880s, Oliphant extended Robinson's methods to northern Galilee and the Golan. In his travels through that northern mountain range Oliphant examined many ancient ruins. In his archaeological reports to the Palestine Exploration Society Oliphant highlighted the remains of ancient Jewish villages and synagogues in Galilee and Golan.[78]

Trouble in Paradise

After eight months together, Imber and the Oliphants began to quarrel. Their communal idyll had lasted from November 1882 to July 1883. Imber began to drink heavily, and his restlessness reasserted itself. What exactly happened between the Oliphants and Imber? No easy answers are forthcoming from the many letters and memoirs left by the principals. In Shmaryahu Imber's biography of his brother we read that "the reason for their quarrel never became known." I would suggest that sex "reared its ugly head" among these Victorian visionaries. Imber, throughout his writings, repeatedly and a little too insistently refers to Alice's "purity" and "nobility," saying that she was "devoid of sensuousness." Yet, if the accounts of Alice Oliphant's "breathing exercises" are true—accounts first published in the 1920s, long after her death—perhaps Alice attempted to seduce Naphtali Herz, and he, still a yeshiva student at heart, rejected her. In the early 1880s, she was a beautiful woman in her mid-thirties in a supposedly platonic marriage. Was Imber trying to protect her reputation? He wrote, "Her goodness is indescribable. She was pure and passionless as an angel. Nor were her intellectual gifts below her moral endowments."[79] Perhaps Imber was in love with Alice and could not bear to stay within the household any longer.

The question of Alice's alleged promiscuity would haunt Oliphant and his followers. Laurence was quite explicit that his relationship with Alice had not been "burdened" by sexual relations. The Oliphants' English detractors, however, argued that Alice, outside of her marriage to Laurence, was not so chaste. According to Hannah Whitall Smith,

> Very remarkable things are reported to have gone on in that community, and finally it had to be closed at the instance of the Vigilance Association of London, which threatened a complete exposure if it continued. It seems that Mrs. Oliphant, in helping the Arabs towards what she and her husband called 'Sympneumata', or the union of the spiritual counterpart with the earthly one, was so forgetful of self that, in the real Lily Queen manner, she would accomplish this by getting into bed with these Arabs, no matter how degraded or dirty they were, and the contact of her body brought about, as she supposed, the coming of the counterpart. It was a great trial to her to do this, and she felt that she was performing a most holy mission.[80]

Later, during his years in the United States, Imber often wrote about the Oliphants and their commitment to Zionism, never mentioning his falling out with them. For example, in articles for the *Reform Advocate*, Imber speaks glowingly of the Oliphants: "It was in the year 1882 . . . the year when thousands of brethren fled from drunken Russian mobs, seeking refuge and safety in the metropolitan of the grand old Turk. . . . I sailed with the noble family of the late Laurence Oliphant, who, both he and his noble wife Alice, have done so much to gladden the hearts of these sufferers, and cheer the fallen spirit."[81]

From the relative security and prosperity of the Oliphant household in Haifa Imber moved to Jerusalem. Without the support of the Oliphants, he was quickly reduced to poverty. The poet lived in a cramped room outside the walls of the Old City. A visitor described it as "dingy and narrow" and said that Imber had covered the walls with his poems and notes. He began to drink heavily and was known for pestering the city's Hebrew publishers and lit- terateurs. After a few months, Imber fell ill with kidney trouble, which was no doubt related to his drinking habits. At this point, despite their falling out, the Oliphants stepped in and offered to help, sending Imber to the Jewish colony of Rishon Letzion for rest and recuperation. Imber rested, and his health improved. He then went to Beirut to train as a watchmaker—again at the Oliphants' expense. Imber briefly ran a watch store in Haifa, but he and Oliphant clashed over Laurence's insistence that Imber keep the watch store closed on the Sabbath, as demanded by rabbinic law, something Imber would not do on his own.[82] Here we encounter a paradox that weaves itself throughout the history of the Christian encounter with Zionism. Christian enthusiasts for Jewish return expected Jews to observe rabbinic law. When they didn't, their Christian friends were often bewildered and disappointed. After abandoning the watch store, Imber left Palestine, never to return to its shores. He had been in the "land of our hopes"—*Eretz Tikvoseinu*—for four years and four months.[83]

Throughout his four years in Palestine Imber continued to write both poetry and prose. He published many articles in the emergent Hebrew press and engaged in heated polemics with Eliezer Ben-Yehuda, journalist and "reviver of the Hebrew language." Ben-Yehuda had initially supported the Oliphants' Gilead Plan and approved of their Zionist efforts, but he later accused Imber of being a tool of Protestant missionaries in Jerusalem, an accusation that would follow Imber during his later years in England and the United States.

For Imber, leaving the Oliphants meant leaving Palestine. So strong was his attachment to the couple, and so powerfully were they linked to his own vision of Jewish settlement, that he could not stay in Palestine and be out of contact with them. Imber set out on a long journey to Rome, Paris, and Bombay.[84] These travels are undocumented; we know about them only through Imber's writings, and there are reasons to question whether he actually reached all of the places that he claimed to have visited. Whether or not he went to all of these places, he wrote of them quite evocatively, if not always accurately. He published many articles in Hebrew and Anglo-American Jewish newspapers, in which he told of his visits to far-flung Jewish communities.

Imber would remain assertively Jewish, but he was a Jewish nationalist without a ritual practice and without a nation-state. He had left the world of Orthodox Jewish observance as a teenager; as an adult he had left the nation-state in formation. Yet he continued to assert a Jewish identity. When he was told that his brother Mordechai had changed his first name to "Marcus," Imber wrote to Shmaryahu: "I pass through countries and states and I encounter officials and rulers—and I have never changed my name. In front of all I am proud of my Jewish name Naphtali Herz. And is the name 'Marcus' prettier than 'Mordechai?' "[85] Imber, as a wandering cosmopolitan, a poet, and a Jew, was defining his identity in a new way: he was a secular Jew. In his essays he mocked the rabbis and their rule of law. In his journalistic writings, many of which appeared in American Jewish publications, Imber mocked the piety of the Chasidim and what he saw as the hypocrisy of their rebbes. He did not attend synagogue services, nor did he pay his respects to the synagogue leaders of the many cities he visited. He was a "Lover of Zion" and claimant to the mantle of the "Poet of Zion," but he mocked the Jewish Zionist leadership. Imber was a thoroughly modern figure, and his Jewish secularism confused both Jews and Christians in Palestine and the United States.[86]

During his four years in Palestine, Laurence and Alice Oliphant had given Imber a home and a job. While he was with the Oliphants, Imber stayed away from alcohol, composed poetry, and wrote for the Hebrew press in Palestine and Europe. After he left them, Imber's support structures crumbled. At the end of the 1880s, when he returned to Europe, Imber resumed his travels to European cities and, as he had done a decade earlier, visited Jewish cultural and literary institutions—literary clubs, newspapers, magazines, and publishing houses for Yiddish and Hebrew literature. Jewish literary memoirists of the period recall Imber's sudden appearances. Many note that he was often drunk, and in that state he would launch into a spirited rendition of *Hatikvah*. This was Imber's second "wandering life." First there were his six years in southern Europe, culminating in his fateful meeting with the Oliphants in Istanbul. Then he spent a little over four years in Palestine. His poems inspired the young Jewish pioneers. Imber, in turn, was inspired by their bravery and determination. But he did not want to be a permanent member of the new Jewish social experiment in Palestine. Although he was disillusioned with the reality of Jewish Palestine, the idea of a renewed Jewish commonwealth still held a powerful hold over him. In his post-Palestine period, Imber continued to write poems that praised the *halutzim*, the pioneers. He was in fact one of the first Hebrew writers to use the term *"Halutz"* to describe the Jewish pioneers in Palestine. Previously the term had been reserved for the Maskilim of Eastern Europe, those intellectual, literary pioneers who were forging a new secular Jewish culture.[87]

Where Imber wandered was never as important to him as the people, like the Oliphants, that he encountered. In 1890 Imber met the popular English journalist and literary figure Israel Zangwill. During the two years he spent in London, Imber and Zangwill became fast friends. In private, Zangwill was somewhat skeptical of Imber's literary talents. Imber's brother Shmaryahu, however, records that Imber and Zangwill quickly understood each other, "even though their personalities were so different—and they loved each other."[88]

Zangwill and Imber exchanged language lessons. Imber taught Zangwill Hebrew, and Zangwill taught Imber English. Zangwill, after translating Imber's *Hatikvah* into English, set himself to translating another of Imber's most popular poems, "The Watch on the Jordan."

Like the crash of the thunder
Which splitteth asunder
The flame of the cloud,
On our ears ever falling
A voice is heard calling
From Zion aloud:
Let your spirits' desires
For the land of your sires,
Eternally burn.
From the foe to deliver,
Our own holy river,
To Jordan return.
Where the soft flowing stream
Murmurs low as in dream,
There set we our watch.[89]

Like *Hatikvah*, this poem had been set to rousing music and was sung at Zionist meetings throughout the Jewish world, most notably at the first Zionist congresses.

When Imber began to write articles in fluent and fluid English, Zangwill saw to it that they were published in the London *Jewish Standard*, an Orthodox Jewish newspaper. Soon Imber became the editor of that journal, but his assertive and flamboyant secularism clashed with the leadership of the Orthodox community that the paper represented. His tenure as editor was short lived.

Imber's friendship with Zangwill also proved short lived. In articles he wrote for *Pall Mall Magazine*, Zangwill featured some of London's more colorful Jewish characters, a thinly disguised Imber among them. He refined these magazine pieces in his book *Children of the Ghetto*, which became a British and then a transatlantic bestseller. In the book, Imber is immortalized in the character of Melchitsedek Pinchas, Hebrew poet and socialist revolutionary: "He is a great wit with an inflated sense of his importance as a poet. The poet was a slim, dark little man, with long, matted black hair. His face was hatchet-shaped and not unlike an Aztec's. The eyes were informed by an eager brilliance. He had a heap of little paper-covered books in one hand and an extinct cigar in the other."[90]

Zangwill, in his less than flattering representation, has Pinchas sparring with the local rabbi over rumors that he had sought support from the Christian missionaries of the London Jews Society. "Why accuse me?" Pinchas asks.

"Because I lived there for a week, hunting out their customs and their ways of ensnaring the souls of our brethren, so that I might write about them some-day?"[91] Pinchas denies any connection to the missionaries, arguing that if he indeed benefited from their largesse, it was only in order to observe their missionary tactics.

In another scene, Zangwill has Pinchas give a rousing speech at a Jewish workers strike. Despite the misgivings of the more religiously observant workers, the union meeting is held on a Friday night. Pinchas tells the assembled workers, "Our great teacher, Moses, was the first socialist. The legislation of the Old Testament—the land laws, the jubilee regulations, the tender care of the poor, the subordination of the rights of property to the interests of the working man—all this is pure socialism!" The speech galvanizes the mostly Orthodox crowd, but then Pinchas unthinkingly lights a cigar. As it is the Sabbath eve, the Orthodox contingent among the workers is outraged, and they turn on Pinchas with a fury, denouncing him as a hypocrite.[92]

Zangwill's satirical portrait of Melchitsedek Pinchas in *Children of the Ghetto* infuriated Imber, and within a few months of the book's publication, he set sail for the United States. Just as he left the Oliphants and Palestine under a cloud, Imber left London a comic figure, disgraced and parodied in a very popular novel. In the United States, Imber would meet much the same sad fate.

~

The Oliphants after Imber's Departure

While Imber was traveling in Europe, the Oliphants remained in Haifa. They cultivated relationships with varied supporters of Zionist enterprises and established homes in both Haifa and the neighboring Druze village of Dalyat al Carmel. In 1886, Alice Oliphant, forty years old, contracted malarial fever on an excursion to Tiberias. Malaria was the scourge of Western colonists in nineteenth-century Palestine. It had claimed the lives of dozens of the settlers of the American Adams Colony at Jaffa, 165 of whom had traveled from Maine and New Hampshire to Jaffa in 1866. After only four years in Palestine, Alice Oliphant died of the dreaded disease. She was buried in view of her beloved Mt. Carmel in the cemetery of the German Templer colony.

Laurence fell ill at the same time. He recovered from malaria but was sunk in depression at the loss of his wife: "For a time after Alice's death it seemed impossible to Laurence that he should go on living."[93] But soon after her death he felt her spirit: "She seems sensationally to invade my frame," Laurence wrote, "thrilling my nerves when the sad fit is coming on and shaking me out of it, flooding my brain occasionally with her thoughts so that I can feel her thinking in me, inspiring me."[94] In a letter to his friend Ernest Bruckner, written soon after Alice's death, Laurence noted, "A marriage between two people, thinking more of how they can help their fellow creatures, than of how then can secure their own carnal gratification, will be infinitely blessed to them, as my own was—no natural marriage could procure the joys that Alice and I knew,—*now far more intensely than when she was alive.*"[95]

To the surprise of his friends and of the British public who followed the exploits of celebrities much as they do today, Oliphant married again soon after Alice's death. Rosamond Dale Owen was the granddaughter of the famous American social reformer Robert Dale Owen, and she had grown up in her grandfather's utopian community in New Harmony, Indiana. As a young woman, she lived in Europe with her father, who served in a number of diplomatic posts. There she was active in the suffrage movement. It was in Indiana that Oliphant sought her out, having heard of her spiritualist powers from his English friend and disciple James Murray Templeton. Upon reading a letter from Rosamond, Oliphant was smitten, and he told Templeton he would travel to the United States to meet the author of the letter. When they met, Laurence Oliphant told her, "We must combine our forces." He then asked her to return to Palestine with him. Ten days later, they sailed from New York.[96]

Laurence and Rosamond married in England in 1888. They organized a group of fifteen associates and planned to take them to Oliphant's homes in Haifa and Dalyat al Carmel. Almost immediately afterward, en route to Palestine, Laurence fell ill with a recurrence of malarial fever. Four months later, at the age of fifty-seven, he died. Laurence Oliphant was buried in Twickenham Cemetery in London after a small private funeral ceremony.

Reports soon spread in the British press that Oliphant's illness and demise were the result of a curse placed on him by his still-living former guru, the American "prophet" Thomas Lake Harris. Harris was said to have exulted at Oliphant's death. According to one of Harris's devotees, the prophet spoke of "how he killed Oliphant. He kept repeating, 'When Laurence Oliphant died, I was at the death; I watched him die and heard him talk. I did it.'"[97] Harris never forgave the younger man for his "betrayal" of the Brotherhood of the New Life and its commune. Alice and Laurence's efforts on behalf of the Jews particularly enraged Harris, who had developed an intense anti-Semitic worldview in the 1880s. In a satire on Palestine colonization plans, Harris had ridiculed the idea that the Jewish people could be redeemed by labor and

restored to their land, arguing that "the day of the Jew is over." The Oliphants'
break with Harris "turned his stomach against the whole Jewish proprium
and led him to seek refuge from the Near East in the Far East."[98] Harris
represented the beginning of a trend that would later dominate twentieth-
century Western spiritual seeking, a rejection of the "Judaeo-Christian" past
and a turn to the "enlightened religions of the East."

Imber was in London in 1888 when he learned that Oliphant had died.
"The news of the death of my friend and patron, Mr. Oliphant, to whom
I dedicated my volume of poems *Barkai*, has been a great shock to me,"
he wrote.

> . . . He called himself a rolling stone. I too have been a rolling stone.
> And if rolling stones gather no moss, they at least knock up against one
> another; and that is how I have had the privilege of knowing him. His
> admiration for the Jewish religion, and his love for the Jewish nation
> were very intense. His journey to Palestine was only undertaken in
> connection with the colonizing movement in the Holy Land. He
> believed that peace could not come into the world until the words of
> the Jewish prophets had been fulfilled, and the children of Israel should
> be restored to their own land.[99]

Imber attended Oliphant's funeral[100] and later wrote an obituary notice for
him in the December 1888 issue of the Hebrew-language journal *Hahavatzelet*:
"Mr. Oliphant, the great English traveller and writer, the true Lover of Zion, is
no longer with us, for he has been taken from the land of the living. . . . His
love for the people Israel and its land, a love that had no hidden agenda, a love
not dependent on any other cause, this I will relate here. . . . Many said that he
aided the missionaries . . . in saying this they spread lies about him."[101]

~

Imber in the United States

Imber spent the last seventeen years of his life (1892–1909) in the United
States, where he was known as "the king of the Jewish Bohemians." An impoverished and chronic alcoholic, he nevertheless found a patron in the eminent jurist Mayer Sulzberger, who supported him until the end of his life.
Although some believe that Imber sunk into alcoholism and despair during these years, the written and published record suggests otherwise. Imber
wrote many articles for the Anglo-Jewish press. His wide-ranging pieces appeared in New York's *Hebrew Standard*, in Boston's *Jewish Chronicle*, and in

Chicago's *Reform Advocate*. He collected Jewish legends in two anthologies: *Treasure of Ancient Jerusalem* (1898) and *Treasure of Two Worlds* (1910).[102] Imber was constantly in motion, traveling from city to city, living a hand-to-mouth existence, and he must have dashed his articles off quickly. They are not deep, but they are lively and informative and have an enduring appeal, although, alas, the "information" is often inaccurate. The essays and Hebrew poems that Imber produced during his final two decades are of uneven quality, but they do represent a sustained body of literary work.

Imber, in search of new adventures and a steady income, also began presenting himself as a Kabbalist, offering classes in Jewish mysticism. In New York, his efforts met with great resistance as the city's rabbis denounced him. He then tried his luck in Boston, where he launched the journal *Uriel*, a magazine of "Cabbalistic Science," which went out of business in the summer of 1895 after only two issues.[103] In his essays on comparative mysticism he denounced Madame Blavatsky, the Russian mystic whom late-nineteenth-century Americans found so fascinating, and the other leaders of the theosophical movement. It is not clear whether Imber knew that Laurence Oliphant had also denounced Blavatsky.

Imber, as restless in the New World as he had been in the Old, was determined to travel throughout the United States. Although he was no longer young—he was forty years old when he left Boston in 1896—he set out for the West. In Chicago in 1900 he met and married an American Christian woman, Amanda Katie Davidson. Shmaryahu Imber described her as a beautiful, educated woman who loved Imber so deeply that she "sacrificed her Protestant faith to him," that is, she converted to Judaism in order to marry Imber. Both Shmaryahu and Naphtali Herz claimed that Davidson was a physician; others, including Israel Zangwill, who called her "an American Christian crank," were skeptical of these claims.[104] Sadly, the marriage lasted no longer than a year. Imber began to drink heavily; it seems that he hid his alcoholism from his new wife. Imber left Amanda in Denver and continued his journey west. What survived of their marriage was a cycle of poems dedicated to Amanda Davidson: "La Shulamith." The erotic imagery of the poems is remarkably explicit for Hebrew poetry of the period. One critic, writing of the book in the mid-1950s, said it "verges on pornography."[105]

With the end of his marriage to Amanda Katie Davidson, Imber's financial and personal situation deteriorated. He returned to New York City and took up residence in a small room on the Lower East Side. Those who met him found him dejected and dispirited, and his daily intake of alcohol increased. He stopped writing poems and articles, until a Jewish tragedy jolted him out of his downward spiral and forced him to set pen to paper. He was at his best when he was fired up, angry on behalf of his persecuted coreligionists.

What galvanized Imber was the Kishinev pogrom of 1903. Twenty years earlier, Imber had heard of the 1882 pogroms while in Palestine with the Oliphants. These signaled the beginning of a dire period of government-sponsored persecution of Russia's Jews. Oliphant, it will be recalled, headed the Mansion House Fund, which disbursed funds to Jewish victims of pogroms. In the twenty years since 1882, hundred of thousands of Jews had emigrated to the United States and a few thousand had emigrated to Palestine. World opinion influenced the Czarist government to suppress anti-Jewish riots, but in 1903, violence against Jews erupted again, this time in the Moldavian town of Kishinev.

The Kishinev pogrom of 1903 galvanized public opinion in the West—among both Christians and Jews. As the news of the pogrom spread throughout Europe and the Americas, the systematic persecution of Russian Jews that had been going on since the pogroms of the 1880s could no longer be ignored. This pogrom entered Jewish literary and political history, through Hayyim Nahman Bialik's "On the Slaughter," a brilliant poetic response to the attacks. While Bialik railed both against the attackers and against the inaction of the Jews of Kishinev, Imber, in a series of poems, written in both Hebrew and English, reserved his anger for the drunken mobs and the Czarist government. He called God's fury down on them—and called for vengeance both human and divine. In "To Ivan the Terrible: A Prophecy," Imber situates Russian anti-Semitism in the history of the millennial antipathy to Jews and Judaism. And he invites God's vengeance on the Russians:

TO: IVAN THE TERRIBLE

A PROPHECY

I will invite a nation from a land so far,
Foreign to thee is his tongue,
His legions all fierce and brave,
Will come upon thee as stormy waves,
To avenge for my people the wrong.

I called my warriors in battle array,
Pride of my legions inspired by wrath.
Thy fortress will be crashed,
Thy stronghold will be smashed,
They will march on the victorious path.

I the Lord before them will go,
Will lead to victory all my braves,
Japan and China's hordes
Will cast upon thee their swords,
And set free all thy slaves.

Art thou better than Ancient Rome?
Who wronged my people in the past.
Where are the Romans? Where the Edomites?
Who wronged Israel in spite.
With them thy lot will be cast.

Not in secret, Ivan, to thee I speak,
In wilderness from people afar,
Israel will tell in song,
To every nation and tongue.
Of my revenge in the land of the Czar.

This poem was published in the *New York Jewish World* in June 1903.[106] In February of the following year, the Russo-Japanese War broke out. It ended with Russia's defeat at the hands of the Japanese army. Many American Jews felt that Russia had deserved the defeat at the hands of the Japanese. Imber was lauded as a prophet of the Russian defeat.

Imber reprinted the poem in his collection *Barkai Hashelishi*. The volume was dedicated to Emperor Mitsuhito of Japan: "Your Majesty—the horrors of Kishinev which took place a year before the outbreak of the present war, has inspired me to prophesy the punishment of the Russians in the victory of your Majesty's arms."[107] The first *Barkai* volume has been dedicated to the Oliphants. Imber sought and found patrons for his nationalist poetry—as he had when he was only ten years old and the Austro-Hungarian Crown awarded him a cash prize for a nationalist poem. The third *Barkai* collection was dedicated to a Japanese nobleman.

In addition to being the inspiration for a major character in Zangwill's *Children of the Ghetto*, Imber also appears in an important account of the Jewish immigrant culture of New York, Hutchins Hapgood's *The Spirit of the Ghetto* (1902). Interviewed at a Lower East Side café, Imber claimed, "I've now perfected Zionism, so I'm free to pass to mysticism, on which I'm deeply at work. It is difficult to persuade Americans to become mystics; their philosophy is what I call Barnumism." Thus Imber passed into literary history through two landmark books of others: *The Spirit of the Ghetto* and *Children of the Ghetto*.

Imber spent his last few years living in a small Lower East Side tenement room. His dependence on alcohol deepened and his sources of income shrunk. Admitted to the hospital in September 1909, he was released two weeks later. After making the rounds of his favorite bars, Imber collapsed and was brought back to the hospital. He died soon afterward—on 8 October 1909. He was fifty-three years old. The *New York Times* covered Imber's illness and death in an article that identified him as the author of *Hatikvah*. His funeral attracted close to ten thousand mourners. Such was the power of *Hatikvah* and the Zionist ideals that it represented. Though forgotten in the last few years of his life, he was remembered for *Hatikvah* as soon as he passed away. There was competition among the mourners as to who should deliver the final honors. An argument ensued between Jewish organizations as to where he should be buried and which group would have the honor of interring the composer of "the national anthem."[108] Imber's funeral was one of the largest Jewish assemblies the Lower East Side had ever seen. In a very rare show of unity, leaders of the various factions of the Jewish community participated. The socialist parties participated as did the religious leaders. Imber was eulogized by three rabbis. Rabbi Joseph Scheff spoke in Yiddish, Rabbi Buechner spoke in German, and Rabbi Judah Magnes of Temple Emanuel delivered his eulogy in English.[109] Ironically, no one delivered a Hebrew-language eulogy, which would have been most appropriate at the funeral of a Hebrew poet.

Israel and the Oliphants

The deaths of Alice and Laurence did not end the Oliphant connection to the cause of Jewish restoration. Laurence had asserted that he felt Alice's "presence" in the months after her death. Similarly, Rosamond Dale Owen, after Laurence's death, claimed to be in contact with both Laurence and Alice. In the brief four-month period that he was married to Rosamond, Laurence conveyed to her many of his mystical and political ideas, among them his commitment to Zionism. For Oliphant, Jewish restoration was among his mystical ideas. He was the most pragmatic of Zionists, focusing on land acquisition and diplomatic maneuvering, not on the promotion of religious ideas—and not on the conversion of the Jews as a prerequisite or outcome of their return. But his devotion to the idea of Jewish restoration had a religious quality. This set of ideas and expectations played out in his widow Rosamond's life in a very strange way.

After Laurence's death, rather than return to the United States and the town her grandfather founded at New Harmony, Indiana, Rosamond decided to carry on Laurence and Alice's work in Palestine. I emphasize her connection to *both* her late husband and his first wife, for that is how Rosamond understood Laurence's legacy. Two weeks after Laurence's death, Rosamond reported that she had received his message from beyond the grave: "Death is delicious." She then knew that "to all eternity Laurence, Alice's Laurence, would be my deeply loved friend. . . . The widest chasm which death can cleave has no power to sunder soul from soul." For Rosamond, Laurence, even in death, remained "Alice's Laurence."[110] Rosamond would dedicate the rest of her long and active life to the legacies of both Oliphants.

Gathering around her a group of fifteen British associates of the Oliphants, Rosamond Dale Owen made plans to return to Haifa. Her adventures there—which she chronicled in *My Perilous Life in Palestine*—extended the Oliphant–Holy Land connection into the first decades of the twentieth century. Soon after Laurence Oliphant's death, Rosamond married James Murray Templeton, Laurence Oliphant's most devoted disciple. But that marriage, too, was to end in tragedy. Templeton, always melancholic, committed suicide within two years of their marriage—jumping off a boat returning from Beirut to Haifa.[111] Until the end of her long life—she died in 1934—Rosamond called herself "Mrs. Templeton; the former Mrs. Laurence Oliphant." In her actions and writings she explicitly championed two seemingly unrelated causes, causes she dubbed the "two great world problems"—the need for a Jewish home in Palestine and the need for "sexual purity in spiritual marriage." This was one of a number of nineteenth-century ideas that called for celibate marriage. Thus, through Mrs. Templeton, Laurence Oliphant's spiritual teaching, a synthesis cobbled out of the ideas of Thomas Lake Harris and other nineteenth-century spiritualists, were explicitly joined to the search for a Jewish homeland. As mentioned earlier, this connection was implicit in Laurence and Alice's settlement efforts. Alice and Laurence Oliphant expressed this synthesis when they set up their commune in Haifa in 1882; Mrs. Templeton would carry out these ideas in a radically different way.

Perhaps we can see both of Mrs. Templeton's issues, "sexual purity" and Zionism, as elements of the search for "restoration," redemption, and purity. Celibacy, within marriage and without, can be related to Christian doctrine rather than to Jewish ideas. There is no celibacy in the Jewish traditions, and the attitude toward sexuality is significantly more liberal than in classical Christian thought.[112] We see a similar conjunction of ideas at work in American Protestant reform movements of the nineteenth century. Along with diet, exercise, and new forms of worship, sexual behavior was a malleable variable in many new churches and religious communities. As to the Oliphants' communal experiment in Haifa, Rosamond defended them against attacks on their reputation, in particular against claims made by the English National Vigilance Association that Alice was sexually promiscuous, a "profligate."[113] Yet again we find this nineteenth-century trope: dissidents and nonconformists are either celibate or promiscuous, or somehow both at the same time. Either option is viewed as an extreme, a threat to the social order.

Rosamond Dale Owen died at the age of ninety-two in 1937. She spent most of her last years in Haifa. Over the years, her ideas on Jewish restoration changed. In her last decades she called for a renewal of Christian missions to the Jews. This view is in sharp contrast to the ideas of Laurence and Alice, who were quite explicit about not engaging in a mission to the Jews. But Rosamond saw things differently: "The Jews are a great people, and they can do a great good for the world. They can save it, but first they must be converted to Christianity by accepting their own teachings in the Old Testament."[114] These ideas reflect one powerful strain of fundamentalist Christian Zionism, a strain that considered the conversion of the Jews a prerequisite to their return to the Holy Land. But there are many variations on this conversion theme. Rosamond saw the conversion of the Jews as the way to bring peace to Palestine: "They, the Jews, are coming into his Land; may God grant that they may enter also into His Kingdom, so that welcomed and beloved they may bring at last peace to Palestine." Anticipating late-twentieth-century "Messianic Jewish" ideas, Rosamond expected Jews to become Christian yet remain distinctively Jewish: "May it not be true then, that Israel may arise, remaining forever Israel, and yet blessing backward Palestine as it never yet has been blessed, because it is a Christian Israel, proudly great and yet most meekly humble, losing none of its great ancient Prophets, while furnishing Prophets yet greater?"[115]

~

Armageddon

Laurence Oliphant had acquired quite a bit of land during his years in Palestine; some of it he hoped would be earmarked for the Palestine Railway he had vigorously campaigned for. He had mapped out and surveyed a rail route from Haifa to Damascus and purchased land in Haifa that could serve as a railway terminal. As his heir, Rosamond kept track of and extended these holdings; among them were many sites associated with biblical history.[116]

In the early years of the twentieth century, Rosamond made a startling acquisition: "When the Turkish government put Armageddon, in the Plain of Esdraelon, up for sale at auction, I was guided to seek to hold in my own name this celebrated spot."[117]

Armageddon (the New Testament Greek form of *Har Meggido*, the mountain of Megiddo) is the spot associated in Christian thought with the great battle of the End of Days. This idea is based on Revelation 16:13–16, which speaks of the "kings of the whole world" gathered by demonic spirits "to assemble them for battle on the great Day of God the Almighty." The apocalyptic imagination has embellished this already vivid narrative with details of the chaos and destruction that will follow this battle. Eventually, though, the forces of evil will be destroyed. Armageddon will not have been the last battle, though. It will be followed by one last confrontation between good and evil.[118]

Rosamond utilized the term "Armageddon" in another, quite striking, way. "But the real Battle of Armageddon . . . so I was led to perceive more clearly," wrote Rosamond, "is a moral battle, and the context plainly indicates that it is a sex battle, for when victory is one, Babylon, the Mother of Harlots, falls. I have been made the owner of Armageddon, then, because of the task given me in the beginning of my mission. I was told to undertake the most difficult work in the world, to cleanse, so far as my feeble strength permitted it, sex-filth; and the harassing ownership of Armageddon is the outward sign of my inner, my hidden responsibility; a responsibility borne quite alone, in the end."[119] The title page of *My Perilous Life* describes Rosamond Dale Owen as "Mrs. Oliphant, the owner of Armageddon."

Here is a convergence of themes found throughout accounts of nineteenth-century Christian travelers who sought spiritual enlightenment in the sacred landscape of the Holy Land. Their hope was that the sacred sites would redeem and give meaning to their lives. In nineteenth-century Victorian "moral crusades" to free spiritual aspirants of "the sex-filth," the future battlefield of cosmic purification, the battlefield of Armageddon, was a metaphor for achieving a state of purity. For Armageddon was not only the site of the *future* great battle, it was also the place where many great battles of the past had been fought. The New Testament Book of Revelation, in situating the great battle of the End Time at Armageddon, was echoing and evoking Old Testament stories of the great battles at Megiddo in the Valley of Jezreel. For some nineteenth-century Christians, Armageddon was a metaphor for the battle against "the temptations of the flesh."

In Second Kings, and again in Chronicles, we read of the death of Josiah, king of Judah, in the seventh century B.C., at Megiddo (Armageddon), where he was defeated in battle by the pharaoh of Egypt. Josiah had been a reformer; he cleansed the Temple of pagan idols and cult objects. The righteous king's death in battle signaled the end of Davidic rule over the people of Israel. The messianic hopes of Israel focused on the restoration of David's kingship. The followers of Jesus appealed to this hope when they presented Jesus's genealogy (in Matthew 1) as directly descended from David, king of Israel.

Thus the choice of Megiddo as the site of the great battle between good and evil, a battle whose conclusion would hasten the redemption and usher in the reign of the returned Messiah. Mrs. Templeton's choice of the actual and metaphoric "Armageddons" resonates with the use of this term in American political life of the period, particularly in the rhetoric used by President Teddy Roosevelt in 1912: "We stand at Armageddon, and we battle for the Lord."[120] Eighty years later another American president, Ronald Reagan, would employ Armageddon references in his remarks on America's Cold War with the "Evil Empire," the Soviet Union.

A visitor to Haifa today finds the Oliphants memorialized at two sites. In the German colony neighborhood of Haifa (on and near Ben Gurion Avenue) stands the former home of Laurence and Alice Oliphant—at 16 Ben Gurion Avenue. In the Druze village of Dalyat al Carmel (twelve miles from Haifa) the former "country home" of the Oliphants has been renovated and preserved by the government. Known as Beit Oliphant (the House of Oliphant) it serves as both a Druze cultural center and a memorial to the fallen Druze soldiers of the Israeli army.[121]

Two of Laurence Oliphant's books have appeared in Hebrew. Zionist luminary Nahum Sokolow translated *Land of Gilead* soon after its English publication, and it was widely read in its Hebrew version. The Hebrew edition included Oliphant's Hebrew-language map of Palestine with many of the biblical sites identified. This identification of modern sites with biblical sites presaged British Mandate–period Jewish identification of places of the Bible. These links helped shape and solidify a strong sense of Jewish identification with specific sites in the Land of Israel. Also rendered into Hebrew was Oliphant's *Haifa; or, Life in Modern Palestine* (1887), translated in the 1970s with an introduction by Rehavam Ze'evi, the high-ranking Israeli general and head of the nationalist Moledet Party. Ze'evi, a military hero and ultra-nationalist was assassinated in 2001 while serving as a member of the Israeli cabinet during the second intifada.[122]

Oliphant was eulogized in Jewish publications in Russia, Poland, and the United States. At his death he was heralded as a champion of Jewish rights.

Jewish journals had earlier written favorably about Oliphant's efforts. Upon the 1880 publication of *The Land of Gilead* the London *Jewish Chronicle* printed an enthusiastic review. The reviewer pointed out that the book's plan for Jewish settlement "should not be taken as a utopian fantasy, for *such a plan, advanced by a non-Jew, will be of benefit to Jews.*"[123] Looking back at the entwined histories of Jewish and Christian Zionisms one could apply this observation to three centuries of non-Jewish plans for the restoration of the Jews to their land. These settlement plans, advanced most often by Christians, were drafts of blueprints for the Jewish state-in-the-making, one that came into being in 1948.

⌒∙

Imber, "Baal *Hatikvah*," Revisited

The death of Laurence Oliphant's second wife, Rosamond Dale Owen, in 1937, ended the Oliphant connection to the Holy Land. The Oliphants' protégé, Naphtali Hertz Imber, had died a quarter of century earlier in New York City. With the 1948 declaration of Israeli statehood and the informal adoption of *Hatikvah* as the "national anthem," Imber's reputation was restored. His claim to immortality through *Hatikvah* had in a sense come true. And if he was to be fully restored to the pantheon of Zionist visionaries, it only made sense that his bodily remains would be brought to Israel.

With the declaration of the State of Israel, the new government sought the reburial in Israel of famous Zionists who had been interred in exile. Foremost among these leaders was Theodor Herzl, whose remains were removed from a Jewish cemetery in Vienna and reburied in a public ceremony in Jerusalem in 1949. Later, other Zionist politicians and intellectuals were brought to an Israeli reburial, and in 1953 Imber was similarly honored. In 2007 Herzl's children and grandson were brought to burial in Israel.

Hatikvah, and to a lesser extent its author, Imber, have acquired great cultural prestige over the last half century since Israel's establishment. In the late nineteenth century, *Hatikvah* spread as a popular folk song. It was sung at the first Zionist congresses in the early twentieth century, and from 1934 onward it was the official song of the Zionist movement. With the establishment of the State of Israel, *Hatikvah* achieved canonical, and one might say, liturgical status. Because of objections to its ideological content (it overlooks the presence of Israel's Arabs and mentions neither God nor Torah), it didn't become the official Israeli anthem until the beginning of the twenty-first century, when the Knesset declared *Hatikvah* the national anthem in 2004.

Christian Zionists of various denominations use *Hatikvah* to celebrate Israeli holidays and to mark political events. Jews and Christians join in *Hatikvah* at the annual American Israel Public Affairs Committee (AIPAC) conference, and in 2006, it was sung at the founding meeting of John Hagee's Christian advocacy group Christians United for Israel (CUFI).

Laurence Oliphant and his books proposing Jewish resettlement of Palestine were profoundly influential in nineteenth- and early-twentieth-century European Jewish cultural circles. Oliphant's detailed plan for an autonomous Jewish colony on Ottoman lands east of the Jordan River fired the imaginations of many early Jewish Zionist visionaries. For Oliphant's *East of the Jordan*, unlike many other English tracts advocating the return of the Jews to their land, provided a detailed plan of settlement, a plan supported by Hebrew-language maps, budget figures, and plans for self-rule, economic self-sufficiency, and self-defense. Oliphant endeavored to create settlement blueprints attractive to the Ottoman authorities, the British government (which he imagined would exert considerable influence in the proposed colony), and potential settlers from among Eastern European Jews.

Most significantly, Oliphant's *East of the Jordan* fired the imagination of Theodor Herzl, whose own Zionist settlement plans, outlined both in his tract *The Jewish State* and in his novel *Altneuland*, were directly influenced by Oliphant's book, published fifteen years before *The Jewish State*. Oliphant was one of a number of Christian Zionist visionaries who inspired Herzl to action and whose ideas Herzl put to eminently practical use. The next chapter will tell of Herzl's association with another Christian supporter of Jewish restoration, Reverend William Hechler, an enigmatic and charismatic Anglican clergyman who faithfully served the Zionist cause for half a century.

2

Theodor Herzl and His
Christian Associates (1883–1904)

"We are here to lay the foundation stone of the house which is to shelter the Jewish nation." — Theodor Herzl, First Zionist Congress, 1897[1]

Hebrew poet N. H. Imber, in his more boastful drunken moods, often claimed that he was the "original Zionist." But in reality, Imber, Oliphant, and other Jews and Christians of the late nineteenth century were only some among many "dreamers of Zion." A glimpse at the standard histories of Zionism reveals accounts of scores of such dreamers. Though the term "Zionist" was first used in 1892, plans to restore the Jews to Palestine were evolving over the preceding decades. Jews, of course, were at the forefront of these late-nineteenth-century movements; however, Christians often played significant roles in them. Earlier in the nineteenth century and in the two preceding centuries, "Zionist" proposals and intermittent settlement attempts came from Christian supporters of the restoration of the Jews to their land. Christian hopes for that restoration were tied, in almost all cases, to aspirations that Jews would convert, in the process of their return to Zion, to Christianity.

As a result of the Russian pogroms of 1881, some Russian Jewish intellectuals turned toward a Palestine-centered territorial solution for the amelioration of the precarious situation of the Jews of Russia. Loosely organized societies of "Lovers of Zion" sprung up in many American and European cities. They collected donations for Zionist pioneers in Ottoman Palestine and published newspapers, books, pamphlets, and broadsides promoting Jewish settlement there. From the 1880s onward, small groups of European Jewish *halutzim* (pioneers) established agricultural settlements in Palestine. A growing base of European Jewish financial support encouraged and sustained their efforts.

In the mid-1890s Theodor Herzl articulated the aspirations of these Zionists and gave them political direction. Herzl's decision to convene the First

Zionist Congress in 1897 galvanized and organized a diverse and hitherto disorganized array of advocates for a Jewish national home. At that congress and those that followed the forces of both unity and division within the movement were quite apparent. There was unity on the need to establish a Jewish homeland or state; there was disagreement about how to achieve this goal. First and foremost, where should this Jewish state be situated? Palestine was the obvious but not the only choice. Other places, such as Uganda, were considered and eventually rejected. The issue of religion loomed large: Was Zionism to be a secular or religious movement? Was the envisioned state to be organized on socialist or capitalist lines? What was the movement's relationship with the Ottomans who ruled Palestine, and with the Arabs who lived there? Herzl sought a consensus among the delegates on these and other pressing questions.

In terms of literary production and political activism, Theodor Herzl and Naphtali Imber's mentor Laurence Oliphant had much in common. Both Oliphant and Herzl were successful journalists who saw Zionism as a solution to the "Jewish Question." Both understood that the struggle for a Jewish Palestine had to be carried out on the diplomatic level. Oliphant, a sort of untenured British diplomat who never formally joined the British Foreign Office, traveled widely in support of Jewish causes, and in 1879 spent months in Istanbul attempting to get the sultan's approval for a Jewish colony east of the Jordan. Caught in the intricacies of Ottoman imperial intrigues, he eventually despaired of obtaining the sultan's approval. Twenty-four years later, Herzl went to Istanbul with similar hopes. As we shall see, Herzl, too, failed to negotiate the torturous bureaucracy of the Turkish court.

N. H. Imber, who first met Oliphant in Istanbul, never met Herzl. At the time of the First Zionist Congress, Imber, who had lived in Palestine from 1882 to 1886, was living in the United States, where he would remain until his death in 1909. Imber's song *Hatikvah* was sung at the Basel Congress—and at every subsequent Zionist congress, as well as at countless Zionist assemblies around the world. In 1901 Imber wrote to Herzl, requesting that *Hatikvah* be recognized as the official Zionist anthem and that Imber be acknowledged as its creator. Herzl, engaged in what he no doubt felt were far more important issues, never answered Imber's letter.

There is one further link between Imber, author of *Hatikvah*, and Herzl, "founder of the Jewish State." Both legendary Zionist figures were reburied in Israel. In 1949 Herzl's remains were removed from Vienna and reinterred in a national ceremony on a mountain in Jerusalem renamed in his honor. Four years later, in 1953, Imber's remains were removed from a New York City cemetery to a grave in Jerusalem. These were two of a series of reburials carried out by the government of Israel in keeping with the biblical and Jewish idea that the ideal place of burial for a Jew is in the Holy Land. The biblical model was Genesis 47 and 50, where we read of Jacob's request to Joseph, "Bury me not, I pray thee, in Egypt," and Joseph's request to his brothers that they "bring his bones" to Canaan from Egypt. When Moses leads the Israelites out of Egypt he takes Joseph's bones with him. Moses' successor, Joshua, later buries them in Canaan. These texts provided the model for the ancient Jewish custom of burying the dead in the Land of Israel, a tradition that emphasized and strengthened the ties between the Jews of the Diaspora and the Land of Israel. In his will, Herzl had requested that when possible, he and his family be buried in the Land of Israel. As recently as 2007, Herzl's request was again in the news, as we shall recount at the end of this chapter.

⌇

The First Zionist Congress

On Sunday, 29 August 1897, the First Zionist Congress opened in the Stadt Casino, a concert hall in Basel, Switzerland. Close to 200 Jewish delegates from all over the world were in attendance. Of these 200 delegates, 69 represented Jewish organizations. The others were individuals in leadership roles in Jewish communities worldwide. Twenty countries were represented. More than sixty delegates came from Russia; the next largest delegations came from Austria and Germany. Also in attendance were a few Christian guests and many Jewish and Christian observers. Among the Christian guests were Jean Henri Dunant, the founder of the International Red Cross, and Rev. William Hechler of Vienna and London.

The congress was first scheduled for Munich, Germany, but "the Jewish Community of Munich protested openly and officially against the holding of the Congress in that city."[2] The German Federation of Rabbis, a Liberal rabbinical association, issued a statement to the leading Berlin newspapers describing the planned congress as a "nonsensical distortion of the meaning of Judaism and of the ideas of the confessors of the Jewish faith."[3] This description was in keeping with early Reform Jewish responses to Zionism. Reform Judaism envisioned a Judaism shorn of its nationalistic aspects. Prayers that called for the renewal of Temple sacrifice were eliminated from the Reform prayer book. Also in opposition to the congress were most Orthodox rabbis, both within Germany and without. The German Rabbinical Council condemned a congress "which contravenes the messianic promise and the obligation to serve one's fatherland."[4] The promise contravened was the promise of divine intervention to end the Exile under the leadership of an actual Messiah. Prior to that divine intervention, Diaspora Jewry was expected to endure the vicissitudes of Exile. Another fear expressed by the rabbis was that loyalty to a Jewish state would undercut loyalty to the European states in which Jews reside. Some of these states had granted Jews civil rights in the nineteenth century. At the close of that century, argued these rabbis and their supporters, why endanger Jewish civil status by embarking on a nationalist adventure?

Herzl found ways, in print and speech, to counter both Orthodox and Reform rabbinic hostility, and he was able to garner the support of a small group of European rabbis, most dramatically the support of Orthodox Rabbi Cohn of Basel. Initially, Rabbi Cohn opposed holding the conference in Basel. The passion and enthusiasm of delegates from all over the world won him over in the end, and he became an enthusiastic supporter.[5] The assembled delegates accepted the Basel Program, formulated by Herzl, Max Nordau, and other close associates of Herzl. They defined the movement's objective: "Zionism seeks to obtain for the Jewish people a publicly recognized, legally secured homeland in Palestine."[6] At the congress, Herzl masterfully kept the contending Jewish factions in line. He prevented the political, religious, and social divisions among the delegates from destroying the movement. The central question, which would emerge most powerfully at the Sixth Zionist Congress in 1903, was the question of whether another territory would be acceptable as a temporary alternative to Palestine. At that meeting Herzl brought forth the suggestion that British territory in Uganda be considered as a place for an initial Jewish state. The ensuing controversy threatened to tear the young movement apart. Though Palestine, "the Land of Israel," was the traditional object of Jewish hope, Herzl argued that any territory, on any continent, would suffice now as a homeland for Jews. Yes, Palestine would be ideal, but if it were not attainable, a territory in South America or Africa would provide a temporary solution to the Jewish situation. Other major issues that beset the young movement were questions of religious observance and political orientation, divisions that would later bedevil the State of Israel. At the tumultuous closing session of the first congress, all divisions seemed to have been overcome. The cheering crowd broke out into song. They sang two songs by Naphtali Herz Imber, *Hatikvah* and *Mishmar Hayarden*.

In March of 1896, a year and a half before the Basel Congress, Herzl had confided to his diary that the infighting between Jewish socialists and their opponents was threatening the movement: "We haven't got the country, and they already want to tear it apart."[7] An additional source of tension was the

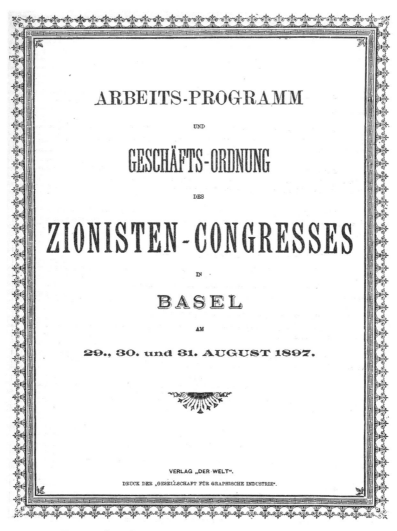

ARBEITS-PROGRAMM

UND

GESCHÄFTS-ORDNUNG

DES

ZIONISTEN-CONGRESSES

IN

BASEL

AM

29., 30. und 31. AUGUST 1897.

VERLAG „DER WELT".
DRUCK DER „GESELLSCHAFT FÜR GRAPHISCHE INDUSTRIE".

Program from the First Zionist Congress (author's collection)

question of religion and secularism. Was the envisioned Jewish state to be a religious or secular entity? In correspondence and conversation Herzl sought the support of many rabbis. In the year preceding the congress, Herzl carried on a dialogue with Rabbi Moritz Güdemann, chief rabbi of Vienna. A moderate Orthodox leader who was a vocal opponent of Reform Judaism, Güdemann wavered on giving his unqualified approval to Herzl's movement. Perhaps the rabbi was shaken by his visit to the Herzl household. As one of Herzl's biographers noted, "Güdemann arrived at Herzl's home just as he was lighting the Christmas tree. Herzl did not think it necessary to offer an apology, noting privately that 'for all I care Güdemann could call it a Hanukah tree.' "[8]

Master strategist that he was, Herzl kept an eye out for potential Christian allies of influence and included them in what he was sure was a historic moment, the First Zionist Congress. Herzl had made a point of inviting Christian friends of the emerging movement to the congress. Among these guests was the Reverend William Hechler, chaplain of the British embassy in Vienna. Herzl understood something that many of his less assimilated Jewish associates did not—that the diplomatic success of the Zionist movement was dependent on the help of Christians sympathetic to Zionism.

Herzl and Hechler had met six months before the congress, and in those six months, from March to August of 1896, Hechler rendered great service to Herzl's political aspirations. As Israeli historian Isaiah Friedman put it, "In Herzl's quizzical eyes, Hechler appeared a 'naïve visionary,' but it is undeniable that it was he who raised Herzl's cause to the diplomatic plane by introducing him to the Grand Duke of Baden."[9]

The diplomatic activity that Hechler set in motion led to a series of important meetings: Herzl's encounter with the Grand Duke of Baden, an audience with Kaiser Wilhelm and members of the kaiser's diplomatic service, and eventually an audience with the Turkish sultan. These meetings fit into Herzl's developing diplomatic strategy. "His strategy was multilateral, though evolving in response to opportunities rather than by design. His basic principle was that the 'Jewish Question' was an international one and should therefore be tackled within the framework of international law."[10] Herzl acknowledged in his opening and closing remarks the presence of Hechler and other Christian friends of Zionism at the congress. The opening address was brilliantly constructed. It started with this declarative sentence: "We are here to lay the foundation stone of the house which is to shelter the Jewish nation."[11]

Christians sympathetic to Zionism were drawn to Herzl and his cause, as were, of course, many Jews. Local Zionist organizations in Russia and elsewhere had been organizing since the 1880s, and they had been supporting Zionist settlement activity in Palestine. Jews had founded and supported these organizations; Christian enthusiasts, Laurence Oliphant foremost among them, had aided Jewish efforts. In 1881, soon after the outbreak of Russian pogroms, Oliphant, on behalf of the London Mansion House Fund, traveled to Russia and Romania to visit and support the victims of the pogroms. It was his responsibility to distribute equitably charity funds to Jews harmed or displaced by the pogroms. Traveling with Laurence Oliphant was Rev. William Hechler of London. Like Oliphant, he, too, was an ardent philo-Semite. Fifteen years after accompanying Oliphant on his journey of mercy to Russia and Romania, Hechler would meet Theodor Herzl in Vienna. The meeting would have considerable significance for the success of the Zionist movement.

At the forefront of European and American Jewish concerns in the 1880s was the growing threat that European anti-Semitism posed to the Jewish communities of Central and Eastern Europe. Fifteen years before the First Zionist Congress, politicians and church leaders in Austria and Germany organized the first anti-Semitic congress in Dresden. By 1882 organized opposition to "undue Jewish influence" was expressed in the formation of European political parties for whom anti-Semitism was the unifying factor. In France and Austria local Catholic authorities, engaged in a battle against "Jewish" liberalism and secularism, supported these parties. Theirs was an unembarrassed and assertive anti-Semitism, and the newspapers affiliated with these parties competed in their vilification of Jews and Judaism. One paper, *La Croix*, advertised itself as "the most anti-Jewish newspaper in France."[12] In Italy, the *Civilta Cattolica* served a parallel function.

During the years of the Dreyfus Affair (1894–99) Herzl would become acutely aware of the currents of anti-Semitism engulfing France. As one of Herzl's biographers put it: "The problem, as Herzl saw it, was as simple as the solution. The rise of even more brutal anti-Semitism in Western as well as Eastern Europe proved the failure of the emancipation; therefore, the only possibility for Jews to live in peace and dignity is to have a country of their own."[13]

Jewish groups ardently embraced Christians sympathetic to Zionism. When Herzl organized a world Zionist movement, and convened its first congress in 1897, Jewish and Christian activists already committed to the cause flocked to him. They viewed him as a prophetic, messianic figure, a Jewish king. Jews and Christians shared this impression, for each group was heir to a messianic tradition that envisioned redemption by a leader who would return a biblical people to their promised land. For many Jews of his time, Herzl seemed a messianic figure. For some Christians, Herzl's plan presaged the events of the End Time.

⁓

Herzl's Political Zionism

What Herzl brought to Zionism was a political program that created a semblance of Jewish unity in the face of mounting anti-Semitic sentiment and activity. If those responding to his call were people of influence, Herzl and his aides capitalized on their connections. Herzl was very adept at finding the most talented person for the task at hand, whether it was educational, financial, or diplomatic. In Herzl's opinion, diplomatic contacts were essential to the success of the cause. In the late nineteenth century very few Jews were in the position to introduce and promote the Zionist agenda to European and Turkish nobility and officialdom. For the most part, those wealthy Jews who might have had such influence were reluctant to support the Zionist cause. For high-level political contacts, Herzl was dependent on non-Jewish supporters. Herzl understood that the Jewish colonies in Palestine, then under Ottoman control, could not move to the next stage of growth and development, and could not form the basis of a state-in-the-making, without the Zionist movement's gaining some diplomatic recognition from both the European powers and the Ottomans.

Herzl's great success in embodying and galvanizing the disparate strands of the movement joined together two competing tendencies within emergent Zionist groups. The "practical" Zionists, organized under the aegis of the Lovers of Zion, were focused on Jewish emigration to Palestine, raising money, and creating a spiritual center in the Land of Israel. In contrast, the "political" Zionists focused on diplomacy and appeals to powerful Jewish and Christian figures of influence. Herzl was identified with the latter, diplomatic, orientation, but at the early Zionist congresses he was able to appeal to both groups and draw them together. After Herzl's death, Chaim Weizmann articulated this new amalgamation as "synthetic Zionism," synthesizing practical settlement of the Land of Israel with international political activity.[14]

Herzl is most often portrayed as the child of assimilated urban parents, and his awakening to Zionism is portrayed as a response to the Dreyfus trial, which he covered as a journalist. The case for Herzl's "conversion" to Zionism as the result of the Dreyfus trial is often overstated. Herzl was exposed to Zionist ideas as a child; his grandfather was a devotee of Rabbi Zvi Hirsch Kalischer (1795–1874), an early precursor of religious Zionism. Also missing in this description of Herzl's family as assimilated is an understanding of the non-Jewish context in which many members of the European Jewish communities lived. Whether a given family or community was traditional or assimilated, it was always living in relationship to the non-Jewish world around it. The description of Herzl as assimilated overlooks the part that Christian thought and Christian activists played in the implementation of what would become political Zionism. Especially relevant here is the influence of nineteenth-century European nationalism, particularly German and Italian nationalisms, in the development of Zionist thought. German and Italian nationalisms were the conscious models of many Zionist thinkers; if those nationalist struggles had succeeded, so could Zionism. Christian articulation of proto-Zionist ideas, most significant among them George Eliot's *Daniel Deronda* (1876), had a profound impact on Jewish readers. Both Eliezer Ben-Yehuda, reviver of the Hebrew language, and David Ben-Gurion, political architect of the Israeli state, wrote of the galvanizing effect that *Daniel Deronda* had on each of them when they read the book in their youth.

Herzl's narrative of his ancestors, a narrative that he admitted was shrouded in legend, both highlighted and reinforced Jewish-Christian difference. Herzl told his earliest biographers that his paternal great-grandfather, Lobel Herzl, "was a Spanish Jew who was forced in Spain to accept Christianity. To escape the Inquisition he emigrated, and as a Marrano, re-Judaised in Constantinople." Jacob de Haas has noted that "this tradition was related to the author by Herzl at almost their first meeting in London in 1896."[15] Alex Bein, another confidant and early biographer of Herzl, relates an even more elaborate and mythic version of this origin tale. In this retelling Herzl's distant ancestors were two Spanish Jewish brothers who were forced by the Inquisition to convert to Christianity and join a monastic order. Their intellectual and organizational talents were such that they rose to leadership levels in the order, although secretly they observed Jewish ritual whenever possible. Years later the head of their order sent the brothers overseas on a secret mission for the church. Taking the opportunity to flee, they made their way to Constantinople "and renounced the religion which had been forced upon them."[16] Herzl's self-image and the image he promoted were in the heroic mode. He was descended, he claimed, from kings and heroes and he would emulate them. Note his oft-quoted diary entry of late 1897, a declaration that has a regal tone: "Were I to depict the Basel Congress in a word—which I shall refrain from uttering publicly—it is: In Basel I founded the Jewish State. If I said this aloud today, the answer would be universal laughter. Perhaps in five years, in any case in fifty years, everyone will recognize this. In truth a state exists by the people's will to be a state."[17]

For Herzl and his early Zionist colleagues, the establishment of a Jewish state was the only way to solve the Jewish question. The Jews were stateless and unprotected; others decided their fate. The most powerful impulses in the development of Zionism were those that sought Jewish independence and self-sufficiency. The question of self-definition was foremost. Were French Jews, for example, "Frenchmen of the Mosaic persuasion?" Or were they members of a "Jewish nation" who resided in France? Should Jews remain Jewish? In the nineteenth century many European Jews, particularly in West-

Theodor Herzl, 1896 (Nachum T. Gidal Archive, Steinheim Institute)

ern Europe, were attracted to Christianity. Conversion, many felt, would erase Jewish separateness and solve the problem of anti-Semitism. Herzl himself once proposed—though only half seriously—that mass baptism was the best solution to the Jewish dilemma: "The idea of a general baptism is half jest and half earnest. I am permitted to say it, I who would not baptize. But what about my son Hans . . . when he grows up I hope he will be too proud to renounce his faith, even though he has as little from it as I."[18] As we shall see, Herzl's predictions about his son, unlike his predictions about a Jewish state, were far off the mark. Herzl's son Hans, after his father's death, converted to Christianity, first to a Baptist denomination and then to the Catholic Church.[19] Late in his short life Hans would return to Judaism and join a liberal congregation in London. Soon afterward, however, he committed suicide at age forty.

<hr />

Anti-Semitism and Zionism

As a cosmopolitan European journalist Herzl was familiar with European anti-Semitic politics and with both Catholic and Lutheran doctrines hostile to the Jews. He was also well aware of the Catholic Church's antagonism to a Jewish return to Zion. In 1893 Herzl wrote of his fantasy of meeting the pope and saying to him, "Help us against anti-Semitism and I in return will lead a great movement among the Jews for voluntary and honorable conversion to Christianity."[20] Eleven years later, in 1904, Herzl actually had an audience with Pope Pius X, who declared, "If you come to Palestine and settle your people there, we want to have Churches and priests ready to baptize all of you."[21]

Herzl's life and career, especially his last decade (1894–1904), were shaped in part by Christian culture, or rather, by a variety of Christian cultures. Contrary to the narrative of early Zionist historians, Jewish political separatism was achieved after, not before, the success of Zionism. For Zionist ideologues, separation from the political rule of Christendom—and from Islamdom—was the objective of political Zionism. Zionism enabled Jewish separatism. According to the Zionist narrative of the past, once that separation had been achieved, Jewish efforts brought the State of Israel into being. The actual process of building support for a Jewish state, however, a process in which Jews and some Christians participated, was much more complicated. It involved Jews and Christians of different affiliations and denominations, and they were moved to further the cause for a wide variety of reasons.

Herzl's establishment of political Zionism and his convening of the First

Zionist Congress can now be viewed in a different light, one that incorporates non-Jews in the narrative. Zionism was not a solely Jewish idea that developed in isolation. Rather, it was a Jewish implementation of an idea that had been developing in Christian circles for more than 300 years. In short, Jewish Zionism would not have succeeded without the help of Christian Zionism. The movement for the restoration of the Jews to their ancestral land started with Christian thinkers and activists—and they kept the idea alive for centuries until it could be implemented. Some early Zionist historians recognized this; most, did not.[22]

Herzl, European journalist, essayist, and dramatist, was the product of the Christian schools, universities, and newspaper offices in which he was educated and shaped. His family, fully acculturated members of Prague's mercantile bourgeoisie, gave him a rudimentary Jewish education, preparing him for his Bar Mitzvah in Prague's Liberal synagogue. Herr and Frau Jacob Herzl invited their guests to Theodor's "confirmation"—as it had become the custom to call Bar Mitzvah in Reform circles—on 3 May 1873. Despite the superficiality of Herzl's Jewish education, from a young age he assimilated a sense of exalted destiny. From his father's side of the family, he heard stories of exotic ancestors who fled Christianity and returned to Judaism. His mother told him that both sides of her family were descended from the Hebrew kings.[23]

Herzl began his career as a journalist and playwright, and when he found his cause in Zionism, he chose the form of the novel to promote his ideas. His play *The New Ghetto*, although on a Jewish theme, was decidedly non-nationalist. The following year Herzl wrote *The Jewish State*, his argument for political Zionism.

The title of Herzl's tract, *Der Judenstaat*, is more precisely translated as "The Jew's State." The English translators chose the phrase "The Jewish State." "Medinat Hayehudim," the Hebrew translation of the book's title, preserves the meaning of the German original. Herzl envisioned a European-style, German-speaking country. It would be Jewish in the sense that its inhabitants were Jews. Though preferring Palestine, Herzl was willing to consider other places, such as Uganda or Argentina. As a western colony within the Ottoman Empire—a Jewish Palestine would not be other than ethnically Jewish. It would not be a theocracy. In contrast, Jewish religious Zionists had long before Herzl envisioned a state whose character would be "Jewish" both religiously and culturally. With the 1897 publication of *Der Judenstaat*, each faction saw in the book what it wished. The tension between the two views expressed in the translations of the title of Herzl's book has informed and influenced the course of Zionist history. Is Israel to be a state where Jews safely reside? Or is it a state whose very character is "Jewish," a term notoriously difficult to define? Herzl's nontheocratic vision was further expanded in his 1902 novel *Altneuland*. Herzl accommodated his more religiously minded Jewish and Christian followers; but he did not give up his western secular vision. When he first heard himself hailed as "Messiah" and "King of Israel" he recognized the irony of a "secular Messiah." Similarly, his reaction to Rev. Hechler's messianism was dismissive and acerbic.

When Herzl wanted to imagine the future Jewish state, he wrote his utopian novel *Altneuland* ("Old-New Land"). This novel was in the European and American traditions of espousing and promoting political ideas through the novelistic medium. *Daniel Deronda* and *Uncle Tom's Cabin* are prime examples. Though the Dreyfus Affair may not have been the direct catalyst of Herzl's Zionist awakening, he was deeply disturbed by the manifestations of anti-Semitism generated by the affair, in which Colonel Dreyfus, a French officer, was wrongly accused of betraying state secrets to Germany. As a newspaper correspondent in Paris, Herzl witnessed anti-Jewish riots and read the canards of the anti-Semitic press. In an 1895 conversation with French author Alphonse Daudet, Daudet confessed to Herzl that he was an anti-Semite. The French man of letters added that he identified with the French political parties that called for the elimination of "Jewish influence" in public life. Herzl wrote: "I explained to him my own standpoint and once again grew ardent. . . . When I told him that I wanted to write a book for and about the Jews, he asked: 'A novel?' 'No,' I ventured, 'preferably a man's book.' " (Novels were deemed women's books.) To which Daudet replied: "A novel reaches farther. Remember *Uncle Tom's Cabin*?"[24] A year after his conversation with Daudet, Herzl wrote his short book *The Jewish State*. Two years later he published his Zionist novel, *Old-New Land*.

In the society Herzl depicted in *Old-New Land*, which is set in the future, in 1923, religion had no place in the public life of the recently established Jewish state. Religious observance would be a completely private affair; members of all religions, not only Jews, would be insured of freedom to observe their own rituals. The Arabs of Palestine would welcome Jewish immigration, as it would bring the scientific advances of the West to the Ottoman realm. That Herzl's utopian vision was unrealistic was apparent to many critics of the time, but that did not diminish the appeal and power of Herzl's book. Ideas that would coalesce in political Zionism were developing in Herzl's mind over a dozen or more years. This contradicts a standard trope in Herzl biographies, that Herzl was thoroughly assimilated to the German culture of fin de siècle

Vienna and as an intellectual and journalist had little interest in Jewish matters. In this often repeated version of events, it was only the Dreyfus Affair of
the mid-1890s that brought him "back to Judaism" and to the espousal of
territorial nationalism. To be sure, there is some truth to this view. He was
"completely absorbed by German literary culture,"[25] and when he left Budapest for Vienna, in 1884, he had decided to become a writer, a German writer.
From 1880 onward he wrote—and published—plays, novels, and essays in
German.[26]

Thus the idea that the Dreyfus trial was the catalyst for Herzl's Zionism
is not completely off the mark. But the full flowering of his Zionist ideas
emerged from very deep Jewish soil. For fifteen years preceding the trial while
engaged in writing plays and journalistic pieces, he had read in the growing
body of anti-Semitic literature, much of it published in the popular press, and
within him the internal process of imagining a different future for the Jews of
Europe began. In a 7 June 1895, diary entry Herzl traced the development of
his ideas: "It took me at least thirteen years to reach the simple conclusion I
have now reached. Only now can I see that many times I came close to these
conclusions."[27] Herzl's long intellectual journey led him back to the Lovers of
Zion ideology he was exposed to as a child. His grandfather's devotion to
Rabbi Kalischer's fusion of religion and Zionism was a seed that sprouted in
Herzl's adulthood after a long dormancy.

Central to the development of Herzl's thought was his reaction to Edouard
Drumont's *La France Juive* (1885)—"One of the great book-selling successes of
the nineteenth century. . . . It provided the foundation for a definite, rounded-
out system of anti-Semitism."[28] Drumont's anti-Semitism was linked to his
support of reactionary politics. In one of the ironies of history, the early
Zionists and the organized anti-Semitic parties were in agreement about one
thing: that the Jews were "strangers" in European culture.

A month before the First Zionist Congress, Herzl was asked by his associate Reuben Brainin how he became a Zionist. Herzl answered: "You ask
me how did I become a Zionist? God knows! It seems that the Zionist idea
was growing in me without my knowing it."[29] Herzl said that before reading Drumont's anti-Semitic book he encountered another troubling volume,
During's *The Jewish Question*, published in Germany in 1882. During spoke of
the "racial inferiority" of Jews and called for their exclusion from Austrian and
German society. When many of Herzl's fellow students in Vienna praised the
book, Herzl began to distance himself from Austrian nationalist groups and to
think more deeply about Jewish matters. During's book was followed three
years later by Drumont's *La France Juive*. Organized political anti-Semitism

now had intellectual credentials. To these Herzl felt he had to respond.[30] As historian Steven Beller has observed: "There is a very long catalogue of incidents which conspired to provoke Herzl to study this (Jewish) question, both in Paris and in Vienna. It is not true that the Dreyfus Affair was the major cause of Herzl's conversion, as legend would have it."[31]

A parallel to the "Dreyfus awakening" hypothesis is the myth of Herzl's ignorance of Hebrew and his opposition to it as a spoken language. According to Israeli scholar Shlomo Haramati, Herzl learned some Hebrew as a child, although we have no indication as to how much of the biblical text he prepared for his confirmation ceremony.[32] Though at first Herzl doubted that Hebrew could be a national language, he changed his mind on this issue as the result of his encounters with Eastern European Jewish intellectuals. Later he joined them in envisioning the rebirth of spoken Hebrew in a Jewish state.

Thus proto-Zionist ideas had been developing in Herzl's mind for some two decades before he organized the Zionist congress. It was during this same period, the last decades of the nineteenth century, that some highly influential British and American Christians were renewing their call for the restoration of the Jews to their land. Once he realized this, Herzl was determined to capitalize on the synergy between the two Zionisms, Christian and Jewish.

Herzl Meets Hechler

In the fifteen years before the First Zionist Congress, Zionist ideas were latent and nascent in Herzl's mind; during that same period, they were uppermost in the mind of his Christian contemporary, the Reverend William Hechler of London and Vienna. In 1883 Hechler wrote a broadside on "the Restoration of the Jews According to the Prophets" and distributed it on the streets of London. Replete with biblical quotations from the Old and New Testaments, Hechler's broadside states that "the duty of every Christian is to pray earnestly and to long for the restoration of God's chosen race, and to love the Jews; for they are still beloved for their father's sake. . . . With reference to the conversion of the Jews, a) some passages speak of their conversion before restoration b) other passages, however, state that their conversion will follow after their restoration. From these passages we conclude, that some will return, believing in Jesus, their Messiah; whilst others will see their error only at the sight of the Messiah." Rev. Hechler signed the broadside, a "Lover of God's Ancient People."[33]

Since writing this broadside, Hechler had been promoting restorationist ideas. When Herzl embarked on his Zionist endeavors, Hechler was ready and able to assist him in his campaign to influence European rulers to consider Zionist plans. In September of 1898 the Grand Duke of Baden, uncle of Kaiser Wilhelm of Germany, received a letter from Hechler, then serving as Anglican chaplain to the British embassy in Vienna. Hechler was a German-speaking Anglican priest who was active in fostering close ties between Anglicans and German Lutherans. The British and German royal families were close cousins, and the Anglican and German Lutheran Churches had grown closer during the mid-nineteenth century. Sixty years earlier, in 1840, the Anglican and German Churches had established a joint bishopric in Jerusalem and built Christ Church in Jerusalem's Old City. Situated in the "Protestant compound" near Jaffa Gate, the church is still in use today. The establishment of this church, whose first bishop was Michael Solomon Alexander, a converted rabbi, had inspired Hechler to work for further Anglo-German cooperation and for greater emphasis in the churches on attempts to convert Jews to Christianity.

Reverend Hechler, as a guest of Theodor Herzl, attended the first Zionist congresses. In his letter to the duke, Hechler noted that the congress "proved again how literally the Jews are fulfilling God's prophecies, and they do not know it. . . . It is wonderful how these Jews are unconsciously fulfilling the Scriptures concerning the events, which the prophets tell us are to lead up to the Lord's Second Coming, and they are doing this just as unconsciously as their forefathers fulfilled God's prophecies, when Christ came the first time and lived in Jerusalem."[34] That Jews were unaware that they were fulfilling Christian messianic expectations became in the late twentieth century one of the central tenets of Evangelical Christian Zionism. Despite Jewish "ignorance" of their place in the unfolding events of the End Time, Christians were enjoined to assist Jews in Zionist endeavors.

Hechler noted that "every detail of this most remarkable movement is of interest to us Bible students and especially to us clergy, who stand as watchmen on the spiritual walls of Zion and are allowed to see God's hand still overruling all, even the wrath of man, fulfilling His own Word, and that not always as we expected, but as He wills it."[35] Hechler's concern for Jewish welfare, although it sprang from eschatological hopes, extended beyond Zionist activities. Any Christian persecution of Jews greatly disturbed him. Hechler "was the first English clergyman to go to Russia and help the persecuted Jews on the spot: he visited at that time Odessa, Mohilev, Kishinev and Balta."[36] He joined Laurence Oliphant on this mission, an episode that further connects the Jewish and Christian proto-Zionism of N. H. Imber and Laurence Oliphant with the political Zionism of Herzl and Hechler.

William Hechler, 1899 (Central Zionist Archives)

Herzl and Hechler first met in a way that made a deep impression on both men. Both were very imposing, handsome, and biblical-looking men. They sported long beards and looked "Messiah-like." In David Ben-Gurion's memoir, *Recollections*, he recalls his first impression of Herzl: "He was a finely featured man whose impressive black beard flowed wide down to his chest. One glimpse of him and I was ready to follow him then and there to the land of my ancestors."[37] Israel Zangwill, British journalist and friend of N. H. Imber, said of Herzl's appearance: "A majestic Oriental figure not so tall as it appears when he draws himself up and stands dominating the assembly with eyes that brood and glow—you would say one of the Assyrian Kings, whose sculptured heads adorn our museums, the very profile of Tiglath Pileser."[38]

While the London-based Zangwill saw Herzl through the lens of the British Museum collection of Assyrian art, East European Jewish delegates to the Basel Congress saw him as a *Hebrew* king. In the words of journalist Ben Ammi: "Before us rose a marvelous and exalted figure, kingly in bearing and stature, with deep eyes in which could be read quiet majesty and unuttered sorrow. It is no longer the elegant Dr. Herzl of Vienna; it is a royal scion of the House of David, risen from the dead, clothed in legend and fantasy and beauty."[39] Herzl seemed biblical and regal to his East European Jewish admirers; Hechler looked biblical to Herzl. He had a long flowing beard and a flowing mane of long hair. Each of them was well aware of the effect their biblical countenances had on their listeners. As historian of Zionism Michael Berkowitz has noted: "One might say that [Herzl's] was the specific countenance of the movement. Herzl's looks were professed to be serious, proud, intelligent, noble, attractive, unique, and at the same time—recognizably Jewish. He was ultimately respectable and manly."[40]

The first meeting of the Viennese journalist and the English clergyman was quite dramatic. On 14 March 1896, Rev. Hechler appeared unannounced at Herzl's apartment in Vienna. Herzl noted in his meticulously kept diary that he saw before him "a sympathetic and sensitive man with a long grey prophetic beard." Hechler told Herzl that the publication of Herzl's *The Jewish State* a few months earlier was a "prophetic event."[41] But as his diaries reveal, Herzl was suspicious at first of what he saw as Hechler's naïveté and religious enthusiasm. "He waxed eloquent about my solution—one he had foretold two years ago." Religious zeal, whether Jewish or Christian, did not appeal to the worldly Viennese journalist. "Hechler declares my movement to be a biblical one," Herzl wrote, "even though I go about it rationally."[42] But when he understood that Hechler was associated with the British embassy and that he had previously served as a tutor to the Grand Duke of Baden, Herzl saw the opportunities and possibilities at hand. For it was at this point, in early 1896, that Herzl, despairing of substantial assistance from Europe's Jewish philanthropists, had decided to turn to Christian interlocutors who could intercede for him with European rulers and diplomats.

Hechler called himself a "student of biblical prophecy." Citing the biblical prophecies of the Book of Daniel, he calculated that the Second Coming would begin in the years 1897–98. The enigmatic prophecies of Daniel 8 and 9, with their mysterious allusions and numbers, had long fed the imaginations of students of prophecy in various Christian and Jewish traditions. Sir Isaac Newton, the great seventeenth-century mathematician, devoted a good part of the last twenty years of his life to the decipherment of Daniel's prophecies. Using the mysterious numbers, Newton attempted to calculate the precise date of Christ's return and predicted, within an End Time context, the return of the Jews to their land. In the final days, wrote the great mathematician, we will see "the ruin of the wicked nations, the end of weeping and of all troubles, the return of the Jews from captivity and their setting up a flourishing and everlasting kingdom."[43] For Hechler, moved by biblical prophecy, the only possible place for a Jewish state was in the biblical Holy Land. Herzl, in contrast, was willing to consider the possibility of places other than Palestine. When the "Uganda Controversy" erupted at the 1903 Zionist congress, Hechler was firmly against the suggestion that the Zionist movement consider a British proposal to establish a colony in what is now part of Kenya.

William Hechler's interest in Jews and Judaism was kindled in his childhood. Hechler's father, Dietrich Hechler, had been an Anglican missionary to the Jews and in that capacity learned Hebrew. Dietrich Hechler's first missionary assignment was in India from 1844 to 1849. William was born in Benares in 1845. Dietrich's wife, Catherine, died within a few years of their moving to India; soon afterward, father and son returned to England. The elder Hechler then threw himself into missions to the Jews: "His passion for the Jewish people, which he much regretted not being a child of, pushed him to work for the London Society for Promoting Christianity Among the Jews."[44] Commonly known as the London Jews Society, this group, in addition to their efforts throughout the British Empire to convert Jews to Anglican Christianity, was one of the first English missionary groups to call for the restoration of the Jews to their land. Thus, like Laurence Oliphant before him, William Hechler was brought up in a "proto-Zionist" Christian home. But unlike Oliphant, who renounced any intentions to "bring Jews to Christianity," Hechler retained his belief that it was a Christian's duty to show Jews "the Christian truth." To the end of his long life Hechler saw the realization of Zionist aspirations as a step toward the conversion of the Jews.

Hechler's personal and religious ambitions were joined to his prophetic understanding of the unfolding of history. "He was ready. His highest ambition in life was to become Bishop of Jerusalem in time to welcome the Savior at the gate."[45] The joint German-British Jerusalem bishopric had been established in 1840, a few years before Hechler's birth. The first appointee to the office of bishop in Jerusalem was Michael Solomon Alexander, a converted rabbi. The joint Lutheran-Anglican Church experiment lasted for forty years; it was dissolved in the early 1880s because of worsening German-British relations. Hechler wrote a book-length history of the Jerusalem bishopric and aspired to become the bishop and lead the Jerusalem Church.

Only a few days after their meeting in Herzl's apartment, Herzl visited Hechler's house.[46] The house was filled with Bibles, books of biblical commentaries, maps of the Holy Land—and a few small-scale models of the Temple of Jerusalem. Hechler was anticipating and studying the rebuilding of the Temple of Jerusalem in the context of a Christian End Time scenario. We learn from his diaries and correspondence that Herzl was repelled by this eschatological frame of mind, but he saw that Hechler might be of great assistance to his secular Zionist vision. For the British clergyman, convinced that Herzl was a modern Jewish prophet, offered to introduce him to the Grand Duke of Baden and through the duke to Kaiser Wilhelm. The entry from Herzl's diaries that records his first impressions of Hechler's residence and library is worth quoting in full:

March 16, [1896]

Yesterday (Sunday) afternoon I visited the Rev. Hechler. Next to Colonel Goldsmid, he is the most extraordinary character I have encountered in the movement. He lives on the fourth floor. His windows overlook the Schillerplatz. While mounting the stairs I heard the sound of an organ. The room in which I entered was lined with books on every side, floor to ceiling.

Bibles, all of them.

A window of the brightly lit room was open, letting in the cool spring air, and Mr. Hechler showed me his biblical treasures. He spread out before me his comparative history-tables, and finally a map of Palestine. It was a huge military-staff map in four sheets which, when laid out, covered the entire floor.

"We have prepared the ground for you!" he said triumphantly. He showed me where, according to his calculations, our new Temple must be built: in Bethel! For that is the center of the country. He also showed me models of the ancient temple: "We have prepared the ground for you."

We were interrupted by the visit of two English ladies, to whom he likewise displayed his Bibles, mementoes, maps, etc.

After this tedious interruption he sang and played for me on the organ a Zionist song of his own composition. From the woman who teaches me English I had heard that Hechler was a hypocrite. I rather take him to be a naive enthusiast, with a streak of the collector's mania. Still, there is something fetching in his naive enthusiasm; I particularly felt it when he sang to me his little song.

Next we came to the heart of the business. I said to him: "I must put myself into direct and publicly-known relations with a responsible or non-responsible ruler—that is, with a minister-of-state or a prince. Then the Jews will believe in me and follow me. The most suitable personage would be the German Kaiser. But I must have help if I am to carry out the task. Hitherto I have had nothing but obstacles to combat, and they are eating away my strength."

Hechler declared on the spot that he was ready to go to Berlin and speak with the Court Preacher [Dryander], as well as with Prince Günther and Prince Heinrich. Would I be willing to cover the travel expenses?

Of course I assented at once. It will come to several hundred florins—a considerable sacrifice in my circumstances. But I am willing to risk it on the prospect of speaking with the Kaiser.

At the same time I am by no means blind to the possibility that Hechler, whom I really do not know, is only an impecunious clergyman with a taste for travel, and that he will come back with the word: it was impossible to reach the Kaiser.

Moreover, if he is actually admitted to their presence, I have no idea of how these princely families regard him. In truth, here is a serious riddle lying athwart my path. My experience tells me that persons in exalted station do not reason more broadly or see more clearly than the rest of us. It is therefore quite as likely that the German princes are accustomed to laugh at the old tutor for his collecting-mania as they are prepared to share his artless enthusiasm. The question now is: when he comes to Berlin will they pat him ironically on the shoulder and say, "Hechler, old man, don't let that Jew stuff your head with nonsense"? Or will he stir them? In any case I will take the precaution to impress upon him that he must not say he "came at my behest."

He is an incredible figure when looked at with the quizzical eyes of a Viennese Jewish journalist. But I have to imagine that people altogether different from us see him quite differently. With the mental reservation, then, that I shall not have been his dupe if he merely desires to take a journey at my expense, I am sending him on to Berlin. I seem, though, to detect from certain clues that he is a sincere believer in the prophets. For instance, he said I have only one scruple: namely, that we must do nothing toward the fulfillment of the prophecy. But this scruple is laid, for you began your work without me and would accomplish it without me.

If, however, he only feigned the signs which aroused my faith in him, the presumption grows that he [is] a fine instrument for my purposes.

He considers our departure for Jerusalem to be close at hand, and showed me the coat-pocket in which he will stow his big Palestine map when we shall be riding together around the Holy Land. That was yesterday his most naive and convincing touch.[47]

On 17 March 1896, the day after his first visit to Hechler's apartment, Herzl, who in his aspiration to create a new Jewish political movement had been driving himself to the point of exhaustion, went to see his doctor. As his diary entry from that date relates: "Dr. Beck, the old family doctor of my parents, has examined me and diagnosed a weakness of the heart, caused by powerful excitement. He fails to understand why I concern myself with the Jewish cause, and among the Jews he frequents no one else can understand it."[48] This was a telling remark. For Herzl was well aware that for the most part the assimilated Jews of Vienna had little understanding of or sympathy for Zionism. Many, in fact, were hostile to the movement.

〜

Herzl Meets the Duke of Baden

True to his promise, Hechler arranged a meeting in Karlsruhe between Herzl and the Duke of Baden, uncle of Kaiser Wilhelm. The meeting was set for late April of 1896, only five weeks after Hechler had arrived unannounced at Herzl's flat in Vienna. From that point in 1896, Herzl was with Hechler at many political and diplomatic high points of the next eight years—all that remained of Herzl's short life. Hechler accompanied Herzl to each of the first five congresses; he was with him on his 1898 journey to Palestine, where Herzl met Kaiser Wilhelm; and he was one of the few people at Herzl's deathbed in 1904.

It was through Hechler that Herzl made his first contacts with European heads of state. Herzl had grown weary of courting the great Jewish philanthropists of Europe, including Rothschild and Baron Hirsch, and had decided to turn to potential Gentile supporters of the Zionist cause. He articulated this shift to Hechler at their meeting at Hechler's Vienna apartment.

Herzl recorded the arrangements for the meeting with the Grand Duke in his diary entry for 16 April 1896: "For today, the plan (for the Jewish state) has possibly taken a historically memorable step towards its realization. Reverend Hechler, who traveled to Karlsruhe to win over the Grand Duke and through him the Kaiser, has telegraphed that I should be prepared to come to Karlsruhe."[49]

On 23 April, after he and Hechler had been ushered into the duke's salon, Herzl took the opportunity to present the case for political Zionism. It was an intense two and a half hour conversation. Writing in his diary later that day Herzl noted that the duke "took my project for building a state with the utmost earnestness. His chief misgiving was that if he supported the cause, people might accuse him of anti-Semitism. I explained to him that only those Jews will go who wish to. The Jews of Baden, for example, who are perfectly content under his beneficent reign will not want to go; and they are right."[50]

During the conversation it became clear to Herzl that Hechler's earlier communications with the duke focused on the prophetic implications of the Zionist movement. Wishing to avoid these End Time questions, Herzl focused on the diplomatic and economic benefits to Germany if it were to sponsor a Jewish colony in Palestine. Summing up his long diary entry on this meeting, Herzl said of the duke, "Now that I reconsider it all, it seems to me that I have won him over."[51] Here, too, the Herzl-Hechler dialogue presages the subsequent century of Jewish Zionist–Christian Zionist relations. Christians focused on the Jewish role in the End Time; Jews focused on establishing and maintaining the Jewish state.

Herzl also recorded his thoughts about Hechler, who had delivered on his promises, although they had seemed at the time quite unrealistic: "Hechler is at all events a curious and complicated character. He is given to pedantry, undue humility, and much pious rolling of the eyes; but, on the other hand, he counsels me superbly, and with unmistakably genuine good-will. He is at once shrewd and mystical, cunning and naive. So far, with respect to myself, he has backed me up in quite a wonderful way. His advice and precepts have been consummate; and unless it turns out later that in one way or another he is a double-dealer, I would wish the Jews to show him a full measure of gratitude."[52] Returning by train from the meeting with the Duke of Baden, Herzl and Hechler spent the journey to Vienna evaluating their conversation with the German nobleman. Hechler, convinced of the success of the conversation, pulled out his large map of Palestine and "began teaching Herzl the geography of Palestine."[53] For this was a topic about which Hechler, a lifelong student of biblical geography, knew much more than Herzl. Hechler had been studying biblical geography for fifteen years; Herzl had never taken an interest in the topic.

Historian Franz Kobler wrote of the meeting between the Viennese Jewish journalist and the Anglican clergyman: "When in 1896 the Restorationist William H. Hechler stood in Vienna face to face with Theodor Herzl their encounter signified that the British movement for the Restoration of the Jews and Jewish Zionism had reached their predestined crossroads."[54] In the sixteen months between the audience with the Duke of Baden and the First Zionist Congress, Hechler was often at Herzl's side.

In his diary entry of 6 October 1896, Herzl confided: "Of all the people drawn across my path through the 'movement', the Rev. Hechler is the most genuine and enthusiastic. But I believe he wants to convert me. Often for no apparent reason, he sends me a postcard telling me that he couldn't sleep the previous night because Jerusalem came into his mind."[55] Here Herzl's experience provides us with a template for future Jewish Zionist–Christian Zionist relations. Both parties have a shared vision of Jewish return, but they are divided by religious sensibilities and expectations. Some prominent Christian Zionists, Hechler first and foremost among them, never jettisoned their conversionist agenda. As we shall see, Hechler persisted in his zeal to "bring Jews to Christ" long after Herzl's death.

Two month's after recording his suspicions about Hechler's motives, Herzl made another rare entry about his health: "I feel that I am growing exhausted. Oftener than ever I believe that my movement is at an end. While I am still absolutely convinced of its feasibility, I cannot overcome the initial difficulties."[56] A few days after New Year's Day, 1897, Herzl again referred to Hechler's obsession with the End Time: "Here we are in the year 1897—one of the 'critical' years of my friend Hechler."[57] This is a reference to Hechler's "prophetic" calculations, in which 1897 was the year in which the process of Redemption would advance.

Herzl, persistent and adamant, busy with thousands of details and scores of assistants, kept up the pressure on Hechler to arrange a meeting with the kaiser. From Herzl's diary, 21 May 1898: "Hechler is going to attend the Church conference in Berlin. I again exhorted him to try to induce the Kaiser to receive me. . . . He appreciated the great weight I attach to this audience and begged me to go to the English church tomorrow, which is Sunday, and pray with him. . . . At this I began to speak about how things were growing in our garden where we happened to be sitting."[58] As we have seen a number of times and as we shall see again, the conversionist agenda of a number of Christian Zionists, and of Hechler in particular, was hard to repress. For the most part, Jewish Zionists tended to ignore this agenda.

The Kaiser and Herzl Meet

Through Hechler's efforts, Herzl had met the Duke of Baden and influenced him to raise the Zionist issue with his nephew, Kaiser Wilhelm II. Hechler's letters to the duke make constant reference to biblical prophecy and the place of the Jewish people in that prophecy. The Anglican priest asked the German duke to intercede with the kaiser and persuade him to meet with Herzl. But Hechler also asked that the duke speak to other members of European royalty about the Zionist cause:

> If I could I should go quite quietly to every European sovereign and plead for God's ancient people begging that the Land of Promise might be given back to the Jews, to whom God gave it for everlasting possession some four thousand years ago. . . . If I could only persuade every one to read Dr. Herzl's "Judenstaat" and see how wonderfully it agrees with the Bible prophecies, and he wrote it without knowing it himself. The Jews must return to Palestine according to the Bible and therefore I am helping in this movement as a Christian and a believer in the Truth of the Bible, for God wills it![59]

The duke knew that his nephew the German emperor was interested in the state of the Ottoman Empire and the situation in Palestine. He understood that the emperor's interest was purely political, not theological. In his letter to the emperor, the duke mentioned political advantages that might accrue to Germany if it were to support Zionism. He suggested that with German intervention in the Middle East, "the German Emperor will soon be the Protector of all the Protestants and Jews in the East."[60] Middle Eastern Catholics were then under the protection of the Vatican and of France. Protestants, and in the duke's imagination, Jews, would benefit from Germany's protection and representation. In addition to the Duke of Baden's plea to Kaiser Wilhelm, Count Philip Eulenberg, a good friend of the kaiser, also intervened. Eulenberg knew of Herzl's journalistic work and was very impressed with his Zionist project.

Despite the political focus of his letter to the kaiser, the duke could not help but join it to religious issues and quote Hechler's claim that the Ark of the Covenant was about to be discovered on Mount Nebo in Palestine. Hechler, inspired by a series of Near Eastern archaeological discoveries at the end of the nineteenth century, hoped for what would be the greatest discovery of all, the discovery of the "Lost Ark." The duke, intrigued by Hechler's enthusiasm and high expectations, wrote:

> The two tablets of stone were in the ark and the discovery would bring great glory to the German court. I propose telling the German Ambassador to Vienna all about Mount Nebo and try to persuade him to have that whole district of East Jordan, near the Dead Sea, given to the Emperor of Germany by the Sultan, so that, when the Ark of the Covenant is found, his Majesty will possess it with the two tables of stone with the Ten Commandments written by God on Mount Sinai, and probably the original manuscript of the Five Books of Moses, written by Moses, which were hid in the Ark and which will prove how foolishly so called Higher Criticism tries to make out that Moses could not have written this and that."[61]

Here the duke, no doubt influenced by Hechler, is responding to the Documentary Hypothesis, the theory of biblical scholars in Germany and England that the Hebrew Bible was composed of four distinct documents, each from a different historical period. According to this theory, these documents were later redacted into the text we now refer to as the Hebrew Bible/Old Testament. In Hechler's thinking and in the duke's retelling, the discovery of the actual tablets of the law and the five books of Moses would signal the death-knell of that hypothesis. This discovery would serve to bolster the authority of the Bible and the church.

Kaiser Wilhelm's response to his uncle is worth quoting in full, as it reveals the kaiser's thinking about Jews and about Middle Eastern affairs. He indicates that he had already been asked to meet with Zionists in Palestine and intercede with the Turkish sultan on their behalf. The letter also reveals some of the kaiser's crude misconceptions concerning Jews and Judaism.

The German Emperor, William II, to his uncle the Grand Duke Frederick of Baden. September 29, 1898. (Original in German)

Rominten Hunting Lodge   September 29, 1898
My Dearest Uncle:

A momentary pause in the amorous concerts of my deer gives me a chance to write a few lines to you. You were kind enough to send me late this summer a rather voluminous and very interesting sheaf of documents whose contents concerned the Zionists and their movement. I have examined the material and have gone over it together with Count Eulenburg in Vienna. The result of my investigations is the following: First of all, I must give you my most sincere thanks for kindly providing the impetus and direction in this matter with which I had hitherto been acquainted only superficially from newspapers and pamphlets, an activity that had chiefly been carried on by the notorious and well-know Baron Hirsch. The basic idea had always interested me—in fact, I have been in sympathy with it. Studying what you kindly sent me has convinced me that we are dealing with a question of the most far-reaching significance. Therefore I have cautiously established contact with the promoters of this idea. I have been able to notice that the emigration to the land of Palestine of those Jews who are ready for it is being prepared extremely well and is even financially sound in every respect. Therefore I have replied to an inquiry from the Zionists as to whether I wished to receive a delegation of them in audience that I would be glad to receive a deputation in Jerusalem on the occasion of our presence there. I am convinced that the settlement of the Holy Land by the financially strong and diligent people of Israel will soon bring undreamt-of prosperity and blessing to the land, something that may with further expansion grow into a significant resuscitation and development of Asia Minor. But that in turn means millions into Turkish money-bags— including those of the great lords, the effendis—and consequently a gradual *curing* of the so-called "Sick Man," which would quite imperceptibly avert the troublesome "Eastern question" at least from the Mediterranean and gradually solve it. Then the Turks will get well again, i.e., they will get money in a natural way, *without mooching* it. Then the Turks won't be sick any more; they will build their roads and railroads themselves, without foreign companies, and it won't be so easy to partition Turkey then. *Q.e.d.!* Besides, the energy, creative power, and productivity of the tribe of Shem would be directed to worthier goals than the exploitation of Christians, and many a Semite who incites the opposition and adheres to the Social Democrats will move off to the East where there is more rewarding work and the end is not, as in the above case, the penitentiary. Now, I realize that nine-tenths of all Germans will be horrified and shun me if they find out at some later date that I am in sympathy with the Zionists and might even place them under my protection if they call upon me to do so. I should like to state the following: that the Jews killed our Savior the Good Lord knows better than we do, and He has punished them accordingly. But neither the anti-Semites nor I nor anybody else has been instructed or authorized by Him to ill-treat these people in our own way *in majorem Dei gloriam* [for the greater glory of God]. I believe here one may also say: "He that is without sin among you, let him first cast a stone." To this one could also add the words "Love your enemies." And from the point of view of secular *real-politik*, we must not disregard the fact that, considering the tremendous power represented by international Jewish capital in all its dangerousness, it would surely be a tremendous achievement for Germany if the Hebrew world looked up to our country with gratitude. Everywhere the hydra of the crudest, most hideous anti-Semitism is raising its horrible head, and full of anxiety the Jews, ready to leave the lands where they are in danger, are looking for a protector. All right, then, those who return to the Holy Land shall enjoy protection and security, and I shall intercede with the Sultan in their behalf, for Scripture says: "Make to yourselves friends of the mammon of unrighteousness" and "Be ye wise as serpents, and harmless as doves."

> With all my heart,
> Your loving nephew
> Wilhelm.[62]

Note the classic anti-Semitic stereotypes in the kaiser's letter. If they were to move to Palestine, the Tribe of Shem, instead of continuing to exploit Christians, "would be directed to worthier goals." Jews attracted to socialism, a threat to German imperial rule, will "move off to the East." The kaiser then moves to the theme of the Jews as killers of Jesus. Here he provides an interesting twist. God has punished the Jews for their alleged deicide; it is not the job of the German government to punish them. Despite this negative view of Jews, the kaiser sees anti-Semitism, a destabilizing social force, as a dangerous and "horrible" phenomenon.[63]

More than two years had passed since Hechler had initiated the process that, together with the diplomatic intervention of Count Eulenberg, would culminate in a meeting between Herzl and the kaiser. That meeting would take place in the Ottoman Empire, not in Germany. Learning that the kaiser was to pay a state visit to Istanbul and then proceed to Palestine, Herzl traveled to the Ottoman capital in the fall of 1898. Through the intervention of the duke, Herzl was able to get a one-hour audience with the kaiser while he was in Istanbul.[64] The audience was held at the sultan's Yildiz Palace. The kaiser openly expressed his anti-Jewish sentiments, which were mixed with admiration for Jewish power. Herzl bristled at the kaiser's remark that Jewish moneylenders in Germany should "take their capital and settle in the (Palestine) colonies. That he (the Kaiser) should identify the Jews with a few moneylenders irritated me; my displeasure restored my self-possession and I launched into a brief attack on anti-Semitism which, I said, was stabbing the rest of us to the heart. We had been deeply hurt."[65]

Herzl and the kaiser moved beyond that moment of contention; according to Herzl, the conversation from there on was a very affirming and positive one. Most importantly for Herzl, the kaiser said he would bring the proposal for a German-sponsored Jewish colony in Palestine to the sultan when the German imperial delegation met with him.

Hechler's advice and connections had paved the way for these conversations with Kaiser Wilhem, and as the result of his conversation with Herzl, the kaiser brought the Zionist idea to the Turkish court. But there the proposal interminably stalled. The court's opposition to Zionism was by 1898 fully developed. Laurence Oliphant, nineteen years earlier, had met with an earlier form of Ottoman opposition to Jewish settlement. The kaiser's short flirtation with the idea of a German protectorate for the Jews of Palestine ended in the Yildiz Palace.[66] Kaiser Wilhelm's attitude toward Jews and Zionism may be glimpsed in his comments in a letter to his mother—written on the return journey from Palestine to Germany: "What a dismal arid heap of stones the latter country [Palestine] is. The want of shade and water is appalling. Jerusalem is very much spoilt by the large quite modern suburbs, which are mostly formed by the numerous Jewish colonies newly erected by Rothschild. 60,000 of these people were there, greasy and squalid, cringing and abject, doing nothing but making themselves obnoxious equally to Christian and Mussulman by trying to fleece these neighbours from every farthing they manage to earn. Shylocks by the score!"[67]

Herzl traveled to Palestine at the same time as the kaiser and had a brief audience with him in Jerusalem. It is immortalized in a photograph often displayed in histories of the State of Israel. Herzl had a second audience with the kaiser at the agricultural school Mikveh Israel soon afterward, but neither his Istanbul visit nor his Jerusalem audiences with the kaiser yielded direct political benefit. While Herzl's meeting with the kaiser led to no further German support, his visit to Palestine did have an electrifying effect on the Jews in Palestine, both the new settlers and the old Orthodox community. In those old and new communities Herzl had both critics and supporters; all, it seems, were thrilled by his visit and its implications for the Jewish situation in Palestine. Like Laurence Oliphant almost twenty years earlier, Herzl, working through the kaiser, was unable to move the Turkish court to ease restrictions on Jewish settlement activity. The Ottoman sultan would not countenance large-scale Jewish settlement in Palestine and therefore saw no reason to meet with Herzl. Herzl, although aware of the sultan's opposition, was nevertheless determined to meet with him. To arrange an audience with the Ottoman sultan, Herzl turned to another Christian Zionist, Arminius Vambery of the University of Budapest.

⌒

A. Vambery (1823–1913): "The Human Tower of Babel"

As we can see from the story of William Hechler, Herzl's Christian associates, who helped him forge the diplomatic alliances essential to the success of the Zionist cause, were a romantic, varied, and eccentric lot. We have read of the Rev. Hechler's close relationship with Herzl and followed that Anglican clergyman's wanderings and adventures as he enabled Herzl's contacts with the Duke of Baden and Kaiser Wilhelm of Germany. Hechler was at Herzl's side when he died, as he had been at the founder's side at the first Zionist congresses and during the pilgrimage to Palestine in 1898. He was among the most dedicated of Christian Zionists.

Just as Herzl made use of Reverend Hechler's contacts to meet the kaiser, he made use of other non-Jewish interlocutors to reach the Turkish sultan. He had tried to get the kaiser himself to arrange for an audience with the sultan, but this attempt failed. Herzl had hoped that the close ties between Germany and Turkey, ties diplomatic, economic, and cultural, would bring the Ottoman court to a reconsideration of Zionist aspirations. At the same time, other paths to Istanbul's Yildiz Palace were pursued. For entré to the Turkish court, Herzl sought the assistance of another Christian associate, Hungarian Orientalist Arminius Vambery.

Vambery, however, was Christian only in a limited sense. For he had been born into a Jewish family and later converted first to Islam and then to Christianity. Born in 1832 into a Hungarian Orthodox Jewish family, Vambery became a Muslim in his youth and a Protestant Christian in middle age. As one historian wrote of Vambery, "He was of Jewish origin, but he changed religions with the same speed and facility as he acquired languages."[68] In his voluminous writings, Vambery assures his readers that he never truly "went native," that he remained at heart "a Westerner," and that his religious conversions were insincere. I refer to him as Christian because it was as a member of Hungarian Christian society that Vambery was able to aid the Zionist cause.

It was Vambery's linguistic ability that led him to careers in both Muslim and Christian societies. Chaim Herman Wamberger, later known as Arminius Vambery, used his great memory and ear for language to lift himself out of poverty and cultural isolation. He studied Arabic, Persian, and Turkish in his youth and made his way to Constantinople in his twenties. There, Vambery found a tutoring job in the Ottoman court, eventually becoming the tutor of Princess Fatima, sister of future sultan Abdul-Hamid. Years later, Vambery would use his connection to the sultan's family as a way of exerting influence in the Turkish royal court. During his long sojourn in Turkey and travels in Central Asia he converted to Islam. At times he posed as a Sunni Muslim; in Shia areas he presented himself as Shia. Vambery denied the sincerity of this and other subsequent conversions. Working his way up the ladder of Ottoman bureaucracy from tutor to secretary, Vambery served as secretary to the foreign minister, Mehmet Fuad Pasha. From then on he was known as "Vambery Pasha."[69]

Writing of his early years in Istanbul (1857–63) Vambery tells us of his studies with Ahmed Effendi, a mullah from Baghdad. He praises Ahmed's "astonishing, almost supernatural memory; he was a thorough Arabic and Persian scholar and knew a whole list of classics by heart." Vambery credits this teacher with enabling his own "transformation from a European into an Asiatic." But lest we think that this transformation was genuine and sincere, Vambery assures us that "the more I studied the civilization of Islam and the views of the nations professing it, the higher rose, in my estimation, the value of Western civilization."[70]

The reader of his first autobiography, *Arminius Vambery: His Life and Adventures, Written by Himself* (London, 1884), is given no hint that the author is of Jewish origin. We read of his lameness from birth, the death of his father and the grinding poverty in which his mother struggled to raise him and his siblings, and later of his escape from poverty through a remarkable facility with languages. This talent, allied to a powerful memory, enabled him to tutor the children of the wealthy when he himself was little older than his students. A love of literature and the ability to read the classics in many languages led him to an infatuation with the peoples and places of Asia: "No scenes had such a charm for me as those acting in the land of the rising sun, Asia—which then seemed to be so very far away. . . . How could it be otherwise with one who, in his youth had read *The Arabian Nights*, and who, as in my case, was by birth and education half an Asiatic himself?"[71] This is Vambery's only reference in the book to his Jewish background and upbringing—that he was by birth "half an Asiatic."

Twenty years later, Vambery offered a very different presentation of himself in his expanded autobiographical memoir, *The Story of My Struggles* (1904), a book written after his efforts on behalf of the Zionist cause. In the first book he had hidden his Jewish background. To insure the widest possible circulation, Vambery wrote both autobiographies in English, although the rest of his considerable literary and scholarly publications were in Hungarian, German, and French.

From his second autobiography we learn that Vambery's mother was from Moravia, from a well-to-do Jewish family; his father was from Pressburg in Hungary, from a poor Jewish family. Chaim was born near Bratislava in Slovakia. His father was a devoted Talmudist who had no aptitude or inclination for business and the support of his growing family. In time-honored European Jewish tradition, his wife took the family finances in hand and the husband retreated to his study. When the elder Wamberger died in the cholera epidemic of the late 1820s, his widow remarried, had three more children, and soon found herself again in charge of her growing family's business affairs. Her second husband was equally incompetent; more embarrassing, he was not even a scholar.

Vambery's explanation of his intellectual development strikes a comparative note: he was successful in his studies of Muslim cultures because of his childhood immersion in Jewish texts and practices. He makes the point that for Orthodox Jews, study is a form of devotion, as it is for Muslims.[72] This was a startling suggestion for English and American audiences of the time and part of Vambery's "pro-Islam" political stance. In late-nineteenth- and early-twentieth-century European discourse hostile to Islam, Vambery was an advocate of positive engagement with Muslims, especially with the Turks.

Other talents that emerged in Vambery's youth were mimicry and imitation. "From my earliest youth," Vambery commented, "I had learned to imitate the outward expression of various kinds of people; this I had accustomed myself to wear alternately the mask of Jew, Christian, Sunnite, and Shiite, although any form of positive religion was objectionable to me."[73]

Vambery's mother was determined that her son's obvious intellectual gifts have practical application. Her late husband's Talmudic erudition had put no bread on the table. Vambery wrote of his mother, "Devout and God-fearing though she was, she seems to have come to the conclusion that the study of Torah and Talmud may be all very well to open the gates of Paradise, but that they are of little use to help one on in the world."[74] Influenced by his mother, he was determined to use his scholarly talents to earn money and gain status. Vambery's various religious conversions, from Judaism to Islam and from Islam to Christianity, were part of his struggle for status. He used his expertise in exotic cultures to gain a foothold in elite Hungarian society.

Vambery's *The Story of My Struggle* is studded with comparisons of Jewish and Islamic ritual observances and orthodoxies—and their effect on young children: "Such a religion necessarily exercises a profound influence upon the youthful mind, it absorbs him entirely, it captivates his senses and his thoughts."[75]

Between the ages of ten and twelve, Vambery was "farmed out" as a tutor to local middle-class Jewish families. At age thirteen, he returned home to celebrate his Bar Mitzvah. "Strange to say," he recalled, "the whole ceremony made little impression on me."[76] A few days after the ceremony in the synagogue, he left home again to enroll in the Latin Catholic School near Pressburg. During his school years and afterward, he supported himself by tutoring the children of the Hungarian middle and upper classes.

At the Latin Catholic School, which was run by the Piarist Order of St. George, Vambery suffered the same uncomfortable fate as the other non-Catholic students. "Catholic ecclesiastical discipline was kept up in many respects," he wrote. "Lutherans, Calvinists and Jews were obliged to recite the Our Father and the Hail Mary. . . . In fact, there was a sort of silent pressure exercised on the scholars in the hope of their embracing the Catholic religion."[77]

In his second year of study, Vambery's new professor received him with "the not very flattering remark 'well Moshele (the name given to the Jews in general), why do you study? Would it not be better for you to become a Kosher butcher?'" "Unfortunately," Vambery recalled, "this was the prevailing tone among the priests who were entrusted with school teaching . . . and from his earliest childhood the Jewish boy of that period received the saddest impressions of the position he was to fill in the future."[78] Young indigent Vambery, determined to succeed in school yet still remain faithful to his principles, ignored the pressures on him to embrace the Catholic faith—or in fact, any faith. "The vast difference I found between principle and action in my Catholic teachers," he wrote, "had nearly upset all my beliefs." But rather than jettison all religious affiliation, Vambery sought a middle path: "Of a complete want of religious feeling or of conversion to another faith there could be no question." But he was determined to remain aloof from doctrinal issues: "In the midst of the hard struggle for life I had neither time nor inclination to soar to the higher regions of metaphysical contemplation."[79] Later in life his resolve on the issue of conversion would weaken.

For the third and fourth years of his high school education he moved to a school run by Benedictine monks and there had the freedom to educate himself. He claims that when he arrived at the school his mastery of languages was superior to that of his teachers: "The fact that when I began my studies I knew four languages—Hungarian, German, Slav, and Hebrew—was the reason I turned my attention to the acquirement of other languages."[80]

Vambery spent six years as a private tutor after finishing school. He used that time to master new foreign languages. He was a true autodidact. Decades later, when he was appointed a professor, he expected his students to teach themselves. He was only there to make sure they taught themselves adequately.

As a young man, Vambery began by tutoring Jewish students; eventually he moved up the social ladder to tutor Christian students. In Turkey he earned a living by teaching the sons and daughters of the Muslim elite. Tutoring and the entrée to the homes of the elite that this profession provided were his techniques for pulling himself out of dire poverty. He kept moving up the social and intellectual ladders and soon deemed himself an "aristocrat of the mind." That Vambery managed to do this in mid-nineteenth-century Turkey and Central Asia is all the more remarkable. Vambery praised the power of foreign-language mastery: "Truly speech, the spoken word, is a mighty instrument! By it mountains are leveled and hearts hard as rocks are softened. Differences of faith and nationality vanish before it; and as I had the good fortune to experience all this at the very outset of my adventurous career in Asia, many dark outlines of the far-off future were smoothed away."[81]

Despite this grand rhetoric, we might wonder whether Vambery actually achieved the linguistic mastery he claimed. His students at the University of Budapest expressed skepticism about his claims to language mastery. Today, many scholars concur. His travel accounts are filled with generalities and clichés, and his knowledge of nineteenth-century Muslim Asia seems superficial.

~

Vambery in Turkey

Vambery's passion for Asiatic cultures led him to the study of Turkish. He claimed that within a year his reading skills enabled him to enjoy Turkish poetry. Vambery then took up the study of classical Arabic. He was in his twenties and resolved to travel to Constantinople. With the help of a grant from the Hungarian writer Baron Joseph Eotvos, he made his way to Turkey.[82]

In Istanbul Vambery became a tutor to palace aristocrats, including Princess Fatima. Through these teaching jobs he moved easily among the upper crust of Ottoman society. Note how radically different Hebrew poet Naphtali Imber's experience of Istanbul was. Imber, with no formal education, no mastery of languages, and no letters of introduction, was reduced to penury and supported himself by peddling during his Istanbul sojourn of the early 1880s. Laurence and Alice Oliphant would rescue him from poverty by bringing him to Palestine.

In 1857, twenty-five years before Imber and the Oliphants met in the Ottoman capitol, Vambery converted to Islam ("became a Turk") in the Imperial City. He then spent six years in Constantinople, where he deepened his knowledge of Islam and Turkish language and culture and broadened his knowledge of other Middle Eastern and Central Asian cultures. In 1858 he published the first Turkish-German dictionary. Later he published his *Etymological Dictionary of the Turkish Language*. Late in life he was proud that he had entered into and distinguished himself in the world of scholarship without the benefit of a formal university education: "The fact that I, self-taught, with no scholastic education—a man who was no grammarian, and who had but very vague notions about philology in general should dare to venture on a philological work, and that, moreover, in German; that I should dare to lay this before the severe forum of expert philology—this, indeed, was almost too bold a stroke, well nigh on a par with my journey into Central Asia. Fortunately at that time I was still ignorant of the *furor teutonicus*, and the spiteful nature of philologists."[83]

Vambery's study of Turkish led him to "discover" the linguistic kingship between the Magyar (Hungarian) language and Turkish.[84] This discovery in his twenties made him a Hungarian national hero. By uncovering Magyar national origins, he aided the Hungarian struggle for cultural autonomy within the Austro-Hungarian Empire.[85] Jacob Landau has suggested that Vambery's childhood poverty and years of wandering in Asia sensitized him to the plight of the downtrodden and especially to the plight of religious and ethnic minorities: "A scholar and traveler, essentially a self-made man, Vambery characteristically inclined to defend such groups, while condemning bigotry and hatred of sects." Landau sees Vambery's advocacy for Zionism in the context of "his persistent campaigns on behalf of the oppressed."[86]

As we have seen, the Reverend William Hechler stayed within one tradition, the Anglican Church, and maintained links with German Lutherans and

Jewish Zionists. He was later able to influence some Anglican bishops to support the Balfour Declaration of 1917. Vambery, in contrast, could stay within no synagogue, mosque, or church for long. Hechler had stood by Herzl in all circumstances and asked for little in return. Vambery, with a much stronger ego and greater financial needs, proved something of an opportunist. Despite his claim to wealth, he often asked Herzl for money to facilitate his contacts within the Ottoman court. Vambery's many religious conversions seem to have been more out of expediency than honest belief. This contrast resulted in friction between Hechler and Vambery. When they met, each of these eccentrics bristled with contempt for the other. It was only Herzl and the Zionist cause that brought them together.

Vambery Returns to Hungary

When, after twenty years of wandering, Vambery was finally awarded an academic post—the chair for Oriental languages at the University of Budapest, he still faced prejudice and opposition. He described this appointment in his autobiography:

> The fact that this Hungarian, who had been so much feted abroad, was of obscure origin, without family relations, and moreover of Jewish extraction, spoiled the interest for many, and they forcibly suppressed any feelings of appreciation they may have had. The Catholic Church, that hotbed of blind prejudice, was the first in attack. It upbraided me for figuring as a Protestant and not as a Catholic, as if I, the freethinker, took any interest in sectarian matters. I was the first non-Catholic professor appointed according to Imperial Cabinet orders to occupy a chair at the philosophical faculty of Budapest University.[87]

Thus Vambery was appointed to a lectureship at the University of Budapest and tolerated as a Protestant scholar of Jewish origin in the Catholic culture of the Austro-Hungarian Empire. Vambery's brilliant student Ignaz Goldziher would wait thirty years for a university appointment at the same institution. But at least he could do so as a Jew.[88] Vambery did so as a member of the Protestant minority in predominantly Catholic Hungary.

Why did Herzl think that Vambery, a Hungarian university professor, had entrée to the Ottoman court of Abdul Hamid, a court so riddled with intrigue and corruption that few Europeans could forge any effective relationship with it? Yes, in his youth Vambery had been a tutor at the Ottoman court, and

Princess Fatima the sister of the future sultan had been one of his pupils. But that had been in 1858, more than forty years earlier; it was in 1900 that Herzl sought Vambery's help. How did Herzl expect Vambery to bridge a gap of four decades? How was Vambery able to do just that and arrange a royal audience for Herzl?

The answer seems to lie in Vambery's link to the British Foreign Office. Foreign Office documents released in 2005 reveal that Vambery was a paid agent of the office for decades. Throughout the nineteenth century, the British government took a lively interest in Turkish affairs, and Vambery had been recruited as an agent. Abdul Hamid ascended to the throne in 1876; in the Russian-Turkish War of 1878 the British supported the Turks. Since that time, British-Turkish ties had strengthened. The sultan, knowing of Vambery's ties to the British Foreign Office and of his eminence as a scholar of Turkish and Islamic culture, invited his old acquaintance to Constantinople. From 1888 onward, with the opening of the Budapest-Constantinople railroad line, Vambery made annual visits to Turkey, eventually becoming a paid adviser to the sultan, while still working as a British agent.[89] The sultan and Vambery could converse in Turkish; in fact, Vambery claimed that his Turkish was a bit more literary than the sultan's. Abdul Hamid considered Vambery a reliable advocate for Turkey in Britain. But Vambery could not always agree with Turkish policies, particularly on the Turkish mistreatment of the Armenians.[90]

In the post-9/11 Western attempts to unravel the history of Western interactions with Islam, Vambery's name and work have often been invoked. He was a European scholar who claimed to be profoundly knowledgeable about the Muslim East. In his travels he assumed a multitude of identities and disguises. He displayed what we now identify as "Orientalist" tendencies, and was loyal to England and to the aims of the British Foreign Office. What is more, he was an Orientalist whose career reinforced all of the contemporary stereotypes and condemnations of that profession. In contrast, the career of his student Ignaz Goldziher, who would far surpass his teacher as a focused and scholarly expert on Islam, refutes the "Orientalist" charge. Goldziher, deeply sympathetic to Islamic culture, emerged as an anti-imperialist.[91] For those critics who track links between Zionism and Orientalism, Vambery's career is a strong case in point.

It was to Professor Vambery, Hungarian scholar and British agent, that Herzl turned in 1900 to influence the Turkish sultan to support—or at least not hinder—the Zionist cause. The Duke of Baden and Kaiser Wilhelm had failed in their efforts to gain an audience for Herzl at the Turkish court.

Herzl's 1898 visits to Istanbul and Jerusalem had led to meetings with the German kaiser, but not with the Turkish sultan. Herzl hoped that salvation of sorts would come from Arminius Vambery. Herzl met Vambery in June 1900, four years after his first meeting with Hechler.[92] William Hechler knew of Vambery but did not approve of him. Hechler was a believer; Vambery was not. Hechler knew that Vambery had donned and shed faiths like sets of clothes. Herzl first tried contacting Vambery through Hechler, but Vambery, not "a man of faith" despite his string of conversions, did not take to Hechler. Vambery, for his part, dismissed Hechler as "an unctuous crackpot."[93] The dislike between the two men was mutual and powerful. It was a tribute to Herzl's political and social skills that he could cultivate friendships with these radically different individuals.

Herzl Meets Vambery

In June of 1900 Herzl wrote of Vambery:

> I have met one of the most interesting men in this lame, seventy-year-old Hungarian Jew who doesn't know whether he is more Turk than Englishman, writes in German, speaks twelve languages with equal perfection, and has professed five religions, serving two of them as a priest. With this intimate knowledge of so many religions he was naturally bound to end up an atheist. He told me one thousand and one tales of the Orient, about his intimacy with the sultan, and so on. He immediately trusted me completely and, after swearing me to secrecy, told me that he was a secret agent for both Turkey and England. His professorship in Hungary . . . was now merely a cover. He showed me a mass of secret documents, which however I could only admire rather than read, since they were in Turkish, including writings in the Sultan's own hand . . . "I don't want any money, he began. I am a rich man. I cannot eat golden beefsteaks. I have a quarter of a million, and I can't use even half the interest I earn. If I help you, it will be for the sake of the cause." . . . I told him: Vámbéry bácsi [Uncle Vámbéry]—may I call you as Nordau does?—Ask the Sultan to receive me: (1) because I could be of service to him in the press, (2) because the mere fact of my appearance would raise his credit. I would like it best if you could be my interpreter, I told him, but he fears the hardships of summer travel. My time was up.

It remained uncertain if he would do anything, and most particularly, if he would immediately write to the sultan about my audience. But he embraced and kissed me when we parted.[94]

Herzl sensed correctly that Zionism would appeal to the eccentric Hungarian professor. When the two Hungarian intellectuals first met, Herzl was forty years old, Vambery close to seventy.[95] They spoke in Hungarian. Herzl called the older man "uncle." Thus Vambery became Herzl's associate late in life, but in a sense his whole life was pointing the way to reengagement with Jewish life through Zionism. Vambery is an example of how allegiance to political Zionism served as a solution to the problem of Jewish identity in Christian Europe. For Vambery, who had lived as a Christian for decades, Zionism was a way to identify with a Jewish cause without returning to Jewish religious practice or to ethnic identification with fellow Jews. Therefore, when Herzl, denied an audience with Abdul Hamid in 1899, turned to Vambery in 1900 for help, Vambery was willing to be a go-between, although he feared Abdul Hamid's well-known paranoid tendencies.

Herzl, aware of Vambery's self-concept as a sophisticated man of the greater European Christian world, knew how to appeal to Vambery's yearning to be identified with diplomatic efforts on behalf of Zionism but without a commitment to the religion or peoplehood of the Jews. He wrote to Vambery soon after their initial meeting.

June 17, 1900
Dear Uncle Vámbéry:
    There is a good Hungarian word: *zsidóember* [Jewish man]. You are one, and so am I. That is why we understood one another so fast and so completely—perhaps more even at the human than at the Jewish level, although the latter is certainly strong enough in both of us. Help me, no, help us. Write to the Sultan, ask him to send for me . . . the details we can discuss after the congress, when I have you along as the interpreter. The audience as such is all I want before the congress. *Takhles* [essentials] later. I don't want *khokhmes* [to get smart] with you. You would render our cause an enormous service if you could get me the audience now. I well understand what you wish to achieve with your autobiography: a royal tomb. Crown your pyramid with the chapter: "How I helped prepare the homecoming of my people, the Jews." Your whole strange life will appear as though it had been leading toward this goal.[96]

Herzl was using Vambery, but he remained skeptical of him. In his diary Herzl wrote of Vambery's tendency to embellish the accounts of his adventures.[97]

Herzl had first heard of Vambery through Max Nordau. Nordau (1849–1923) had met Vambery twenty-five years earlier, in 1875, and the two popular authors became fast friends. Of their first meeting Nordau wrote: "He was the Eastern fairy-tale teller who carried his blissful, world-forgetting listeners up to the seventh heaven. . . . He was Scherazade translated into the masculine and endowed with a precious touch of humor."[98]

Max Nordau, son of an Orthodox rabbi, became a medical doctor, a psychiatrist, and a very popular European author. His 1892 book *Degeneracy*, a treatise on madness and genius in art and philosophy, was an international best seller. Nordau was for a time Herzl's physician. In 1895 Nordau "converted" to Zionism and eventually became a central figure in the Zionist movement. Within the movement he remained a staunch secularist hostile to traditional religion. He brought word of Vambery's association with Sultan Abdul Hamid to Herzl's attention, and suggested that through Vambery a meeting between the sultan and Herzl might be arranged.

Herzl, Nordau, and Vambery, all estranged from their Jewish religious roots, were now joined together in the Zionist cause. As Herzl said of Nordau: "I never realized how much we belong together. That has nothing to do with religion—but we are of the same race. . . . Moreover, we both agreed that it was only anti-Semitism that has made Jews of us."[99] In the stories of Jewish "converts" to Zionism this is a persistent, constant theme: anti-Semitism as the disease and Zionism as the cure. Dr. Nordau, as a physician, was particularly fond of this metaphor. For these acculturated European Jewish intellectuals, religion and culture had little to do with their self-understanding. "Race" was their common bond. Dr. Nordau's hostility to religion in general and rabbinic Judaism in particular would become a bitter point of contention in relations between the secular Zionist founders and the Orthodox rabbis whose support they sought. Nordau's antipathy to organized religion is evidenced in the following selection from one of his essays:

> As a literary monument the Bible is of much later origin than the
> Vedas; as a work of literary value it is surpassed by everything written
> in the last 2000 years by authors even of second rank; and to compare
> it seriously with the productions of Homer, Sophocles, Dante,
> Shakespeare or Goethe would require a fanaticized mind that had
> entirely lost its power of judgment. Its conception of the universe is

childish and its morality revolting, as revealed in the malicious vengeance attributed to God in the Old Testament. . . . And yet men, cultivated and capable of forming a just estimate, pretend to reverence this ancient work, they refuse to allow it to be discussed and criticized like any other production of the human intellect . . . and they pretend to be edified and inspired when they read it.[100]

In Herzl's terms Vambery succeeded in advocating for Zionism at the Turkish court, but only in a limited way. In May 1901 Herzl did get an audience with Sultan Abdul Hamid, but the audience did not result in any direct benefit for the Zionist cause. Vambery's agreement with the Ottoman court was that the sultan would receive Herzl as a prominent European journalist, but not as the Zionist leader. A few months before the Herzl–Abdul Hamid meeting the Turks had placed greater restrictions on Jewish immigration to Palestine. Surprisingly, Herzl was encouraged by this move; he saw it as a sign that the Turks were negotiating for a higher price. They obviously wanted their European loans restructured or forgiven, something that Herzl hoped that wealthy Jewish supporters of the movement could arrange. Writing to Vambery, Herzl said that Turkish intransigence was a positive development: "The whore wants to raise the price by telling us she can't be bought. Am I right?"[101] Herzl's meeting with the sultan lasted for two hours. From Herzl's standpoint, little was accomplished. After the sultan voiced his opinion on various European newspapers, Herzl's among them, Herzl brought up the question of Jewish settlement in Palestine. The sultan, through his interpreter, made clear that Jews were welcome anywhere in the Ottoman Empire *but* Palestine. The Arabs of Palestine were fearful of Jewish immigration; the presence of more Jews would make Ottoman rule in Palestine all the more difficult. Perhaps, the sultan suggested, Europe's Jewish financiers could aid the Ottoman state, a country historically responsive to Jewish needs, starting with the aftermath of the expulsion of the Jews from Spain and their settlement in Ottoman lands. Disappointed at the negative outcome of this long-awaited audience with the sultan, Herzl sank into depression, despairing of ever getting the Turks to agree to a Jewish state in their domains.[102]

~

Herzl's Pragmatism and Jewish Theology

Herzl enlisted both Hechler and Vambery in his appeals to and negotiations with influential non-Jewish figures, including diplomats, statesmen, and military men. The key to understanding Herzl's plans for a Jewish state was that he was an optimist about the conduct of human affairs, at both the individual and the state level. He believed in the power of logical argument and appeals to self-interest to persuade individuals and statesmen. In Herzl's opinion, establishing a Jewish state, preferably in Palestine, would solve the precarious situation of the Jews in Europe. Jews from all over the world, especially the persecuted, would move there. The Arabs of Palestine, happy to benefit from the large-scale Jewish immigration, would welcome the Jews. His optimism extended to his belief in his ability to influence Christians as well. In his opinion, anti-Semitism, widespread in Christendom, was a permanent fixture of European culture. It could not be extirpated, but it could be alleviated by the establishment of a national state for Jews. In Herzl's view, Christians, whether they were philo-Semites or not, could help build European sentiment for support of Zionism. Zionism was something even anti-Semites could support. If they wanted Jews to leave Europe, they should support the establishment of a Jewish state in Palestine.

In short, Herzl used every means possible to advance the Zionist cause. A year before the First Zionist Congress, he wrote in his diary: "Great things don't need a solid foundation. . . . The earth floats in the air. Thus I may perhaps be able to found and consolidate the Jewish state without any firm support. The secret lies in motion."[103]

Exhausted by his constant endeavors on behalf of the movement, and especially by the controversy over the Uganda proposal at the Sixth Zionist Congress, Herzl died in 1904 at age forty-four. His will of March 1903 stated: "I ask for a funeral of the most modest kind, with neither speeches nor flowers. I wish to be buried in a metal coffin in a grave beside my father until the Jewish people raise my bones to Palestine, to which my father's coffin will also be conveyed." This part of the will is often quoted in the standard accounts of Herzl and Zionism. Often overlooked is the following request: "My sister Paulina, who died in the epidemic of 1878, will also be buried beside me. The remains of my family, my mother and my children, should they die before my coffin is raised to Palestine, will also lie beside me. My wife—only if she so wishes."[104] As we shall see, this request would prove difficult for Herzl's successors to fulfill.

Vambery died in 1913, nine years after Herzl. William Hechler would survive both Vambery and Herzl by many years, passing away in 1931. At Herzl's death in 1904 there was an outpouring of grief, but not in all quarters of the Jewish world. Generally, Eastern European rabbinical leaders were indifferent to his passing. An exception was Rabbi Abraham Isaac Kook. Rabbi Kook had immigrated to Palestine only a few weeks before Herzl's death and wrote a remarkable eulogy for him.[105]

In his eulogy, Kook adopted the rabbinic idea of the Messiah son of Joseph as a way of harmonizing two conflicting views of the return to Zion, the avowedly secular view and the outspokenly religious view. In the rabbinic tradition, the Messiah son of Joseph is the pragmatic military leader who prepares the way for the more spiritual son of David. Kook said of Herzl, "We consider him the harbinger of the Messiah son of Joseph, in terms of his role of achieving the great aim of national rebirth in the general, material sense."[106] Herzl was thus understood as a secular facilitator of the developing redemptive process. The culmination of that process would be the appearance of the Messiah son of David. To prepare for the coming of the Messiah son of David, religious Zionists would have to infuse the movement with spiritual meaning and content. The body of Zionism needed a soul. As Rabbi Kook said, "This soul cannot be injected into the Zionist movement as long as the forehead of the latter bears the Mark of Cain, the declaration that 'Zionism has nothing to do with religion.' "[107]

Rabbi Kook's statement of 1913 was a direct reference to Max Nordau's articulation of secular Zionism's estrangement from religion, an articulation that Herzl and Nordau embodied. For inherent in Herzl's thought was a secular messianism based on romantic nationalism. The Jewish people *as a nation* would be redeemed by their own efforts, not by the intervention of God in history. In this secular view, the messianic idea, as prophesied in the Hebrew prophets, promises and predicts a redemption understood as a gradually unfolding process achieved through human effort. Before their exile, the Jews were a people in their land; their redemption would return them to that same "national" status. As Arthur Hertzberg said of Herzl, "Messianism is the essence of his stance, because it proclaimed the historical inevitability of a Jewish State in a world of peaceful nations."[108]

As Herzl and his secular associates saw it, Jews would never be at home in the emerging nation-states of Europe. In *The Jewish State* Herzl claimed that the question of Jewish citizenship was a "national question, and to solve it we must first of all establish it as an international political problem to be discussed and settled by the civilized nations of the world in council."[109] The outcome of that council should be support for the Zionist program. Organized religion was of interest to these early Zionist leaders only in so far as it could lend support to the political idea.

Though much is now made of the fact that a Jewish state was declared within a half century of the First Zionist Congress, the process by which the

State of Israel came into being was the reverse of Herzl's plan. For Herzl, an international political solution to the Jewish question would precede Jewish immigration to Palestine. In actuality, immigration came first, followed by nation building. There were 600,000 Jews and 1.2 million Arabs in Palestine when the State of Israel was established in 1948. The Jews of Europe, the great potential reservoir of Jewish immigrants to Palestine, were trapped in Europe from the late 1930s onward. After the Nazi conquests, they were doomed. It was only in the aftermath of World War II, in 1948, that the State of Israel was established.

For early political Zionists, the messianic component of their ideology was a metaphor, though a potent one. In religious Zionism as articulated by Rabbi Kook and his followers, the European idea of nationalism was conflated with the biblical and rabbinic idea of actual messianic deliverance and national restoration.[110] Redemption was not a metaphor, but an imminent actual event. Oddly, for followers of religious Zionism, Herzl, although avowedly secular, was seen as a messianic figure. In Rabbi Kook's religious messianism, Herzl was the beginning of this process, the Messiah son of Joseph. He would be followed by the Messiah son of David.

Highly offensive to Rabbi Kook and other religious Zionists was Max Nordau's 1897 statement of the secular nature of Zionism. According to Nordau, "Zionism has nothing to do with religion; and if a desire has been kindled in Jewish hearts to establish a new commonwealth in Zion, it is not the Torah or the Mishnah that inspire them, but hard times."[111] Rabbi Kook attacked this statement with great vigor. For Rabbi Kook, allegiance to the teachings of the Torah and the Jewish return to the land were inseparable. For the secular settlers to whom he would soon minister as chief rabbi of Jaffa, Zionism was a rebellion against, and replacement for, the rule of Torah. This made Rabbi Kook's aspiration to be their rabbi all the more quixotic. Kook was willing neither to condemn Zionism as a heresy, nor to fully embrace it as a form of secular nationalism. With great skill he was able to occupy, for a while, a middle position. Rabbi Kook's understanding of Zionism as a spiritual enterprise would live on long after his death in 1935. His legacy would be adapted and expanded by his son, Rabbi Zvi Yehuda Kook, who forged a political movement out of his father's religious ideas. From the mid-1970s onward, this movement, Gush Emunim ("The bloc of the faithful"), would transform the State of Israel by advocating and enabling the expansion of Jewish settlement into the territories conquered by Israel in the 1967 war. In Chapter 6, we will return to the political consequences of the ideas of the Rabbis Kook, father and son.

⟞⟍

Legacies: Hechler, Vambery, Herzl

Vambery and Hechler were two of Herzl's closest Christian associates. Both made significant contributions to early Zionist diplomacy. Both survived Herzl. Vambery lived until 1913; Hechler until 1931. As far as the record shows, these two Christian Zionists, hostile to each from their first meeting, never communicated after Herzl's death. Early historians of Zionism acknowledged their contributions to Zionism, but in the past half century these contributions have been largely forgotten. Of the two, Hechler remained in touch with the Zionist movement after Herzl's death in 1904. Vambery, however, moved away from Zionism and focused on his professorship in Budapest and on his intelligence-gathering activities for the British Foreign Office. From 1904 until his death in 1931, Hechler attended all of the Zionist congresses. Before the seventh congress, held in London in 1905, Martin Buber and other young Zionist activists hosted a dinner in Rev. Hechler's honor. When Hechler left the chaplaincy of the British embassy in Vienna in 1911, he retired to London, where he remained active in the Zionist movement, whose center was now in that city. Hechler lived out his life in genteel poverty, supported at times by financial contributions from British Zionists. While he remained a committed Zionist, Hechler did not give up his hopes of converting Jews to Christianity. The Orientalist A. S. Yahuda, who knew Hechler well, recalled in his memoirs that to the end of his days Hechler was an enthusiastic though most often discreet missionary to Jews:

> (Hechler's) sympathy for the Jews was not the sole factor in his
> adherence to the Zionist idea. There was another motive which drove
> him with great force toward Zionism; and this was the missionary idea
> that when the Jews would be relieved of their sufferings in many
> countries and given full liberty to settle in the Holy Land, they would
> come nearer to the Kingdom of Heaven, and eventually come upon the
> road which would bring them to Jesus Christ. Although he never spoke
> about his missionary aims to the Jews, he very frankly expressed his
> tendencies to Christians, more especially to clergymen and high
> personages when soliciting their support for Zionism.[112]

Along with all Zionists, Jewish and Christian, Hechler rejoiced when the British government issued the Balfour Declaration, and he was heartened by the League of Nations' acceptance of the British Mandate in Palestine. But as a believer in biblical prophecy, Hechler was disturbed that these two declarations were not framed in scriptural and religious terms. Rather, they were couched in the language of international diplomacy. A similar reaction to the Balfour Declaration was forthcoming from the elder Rabbi Kook. He, too, felt that the declaration was a religious event, and should be marked and appreciated as such. The irony here is in the now well-documented understanding that Lord Balfour, the British foreign secretary, was himself deeply religious and that his thinking on the projected post–World War I fate of Palestine was influenced by his expectations of the fulfillment of biblical prophecy. What disappointed Balfour, Hechler, and Kook was that the secular Jewish settlers of British Mandate Palestine did not see divine Providence at work in international affairs. As Hechler said to A. S. Yahuda in the 1920s:

> Instead of seeing the hand of God in the return of the Jews to the Holy Land and the initiation of a new religious movement, which would bring the Jewish people to the right path, what is happening in Palestine now? There is not a trace of religious life; the young people who are flocking to Palestine foster all kinds of subversive ideas—socialism, atheism and even Bolshevism. It was not for such a Palestine that I was working. I, as well as many of my friends who supported me, entertained the hope that the return of the Jews to Palestine would inspire them with the conviction that it was the Will of God to bring them back to the Holy Land, and this would mean a return to a true religious life and that the Jewish people would realize that, though many prophecies have yet to be fulfilled, some of them have already gone into fulfillment.[113]

Pauline, Hans, Trude

While Herzl's political legacy was of enormous significance, his personal legacy, the fate of his children, proved tragic. The Jewish-Christian relationship, a major theme in Herzl's sense of self and narrative of origins, intruded in its most troubling forms in the lives of his three children: "Although Herzl's political child, Zionism, managed to survive incredible difficulties to become the Jewish Homeland to which he dedicated his life . . . his physical children did not, struck down by relentless fate like protagonists in a Greek tragedy."[114]

The children lost their mother, Julia, in 1907, three years after Herzl's demise. Each of them suffered greatly from the loss of their parents. Pauline, Herzl's eldest child, had a very unhappy adolescence. Her short-lived mar-

Theodor Herzl and his children, 1899 (Central Zionist Archives)

riage ended in an early divorce. Pauline became addicted to drugs in her twenties, and within a few years she died from an overdose. Her brother and sister were devastated by her death. Hans, in particular, was burdened by terrible feelings of guilt for not being able to save his sister from the ravages of addiction.

The middle child, Hans, suffered the strangest fate. Defying Jewish custom, his parents decided not to circumcise him in infancy. His mother objected to the procedure; his father did not insist on it. News of this defiance of Jewish law angered many in the Zionist movement. When Hans was fifteen, two years after his parents' deaths, his wards in the Zionist leadership pressured him to undergo circumcision. Afterward, Hans was schooled in England, where he was attracted to various Christian doctrines. After a few years in England, despairing of finding a spiritual home within a Jewish environment, Hans converted to Christianity. Dissatisfied in the Baptist denomination into which he was first received, Hans turned to the Roman Catholic Church. He soon left the church and returned briefly to British liberal Judaism, before committing suicide in 1930. He was forty years old.

Theodor and Julia Herzl's youngest child, Trude, was ravaged by mental illness. She was married briefly to textile manufacturer Richard Neumann. Their only child, Stephen Theodor, was brought up in England. Trude was institutionalized for many years. During World War II she was taken from her mental hospital to the Nazi camp at Terezienstadt, where she died. Thus two of the Herzl children took their own lives while the third fell victim to the forces of anti-Jewish hatred that Herzl had predicted and feared.

When in 1949 the Israeli government arranged for the removal of Herzl's remains from Vienna and their reburial in Jerusalem, it also moved the remains of his parents from Budapest and reburied them in the national shrine on Mt. Herzl, the mountain named for Herzl. But the bodies of Herzl's children Pauline and Hans were left in their graves in the cemetery at Bordeaux.

In 2004, Israel marked the 100th anniversary of Herzl's death and the government passed a law setting a date for a annual commemoration of the founder's legacy. Renewed attention to Herzl's legacy brought the fate of his children to public attention. Some secular members of the Knesset, now aware of the unfulfilled request in Herzl's will, proposed the "repatriation" of Pauline's and Hans's remains. Members of the religious parties objected, as Hans had converted to Christianity and Pauline had been addicted to drugs.

In a long-debated move, the Israeli government in 2007 had the remains of Pauline and Hans reburied in Jerusalem on Mt. Herzl. To enable their burial in a Jewish cemetery, the Sephardic chief rabbi Shlomo Amar declared that Hans's conversion to Christianity was the result of mental illness, and not the result of a rational decision. The ashes of their mother, who was cremated in 1907, have been lost, and the ashes of their sister, Trude, murdered by the Nazis, were, of course, lost among the myriad dead of World War II. Most controversial in Israel was the decision to rebury Hans Herzl. Both his apostasy and his suicide could have constituted grounds for exclusion from a Jewish cemetery.

Herzl's own narrative of origins, which emphasized the story of his ancestors' forced baptisms and their eventual return to Judaism, was thus subverted by his children's stories, particularly by the story of his son, Hans. As Hans himself realized, Herzl's children were fated to be neither Jewish nor Christian. The Jewish state Theodor Herzl envisioned came into being forty-four years after his death. The family he and his wife established came to an end with the death of their only grandson, Trude's son Stephen Theodor Norman, in Washington, D.C., in 1946. Not long after he found out that most of his family had died during the war, Stephen Theodor Norman committed suicide. In 2007 the Israeli government arranged the transfer of his remains for reburial in the Herzl plot on Jerusalem's Mt. Herzl.

Herzl, when he first met Hechler, had been surprised by his "biblical" orientation. Today, Christian Zionists continue to espouse a biblical view of the Jewish return to Palestine. Jewish Zionism, unlike Christian Zionism, followed a secular path, although within that path there were religious ideas, such as messianism, percolating beneath the surface. All of these elements played a part in the stories of Theodor and Julia Herzl and their children, as well as in the stories of William Hechler and Arminius Vambery. Our next chapter, on Canon Herbert Danby of Jerusalem, tells of one Christian intellectual's attempt to integrate the various and conflicting Zionisms, Jewish and Christian, religious and secular.

The Reverend Herbert Danby
Scholar of Rabbinics, Zionist, Christian Missionary (1889–1953)

If the Jew did, in truth, become the deepest hater of Christianity,
it was most certainly the Christian who had the largest share
in making him so. —Herbert Danby[1]

～

Jerusalem, 1919

The Balfour Declaration of 1917 presented a challenge to the hierarchy and laity of the Anglican Church. Some Anglicans were supportive of Jewish aspirations for "the establishment in Palestine of a national home for the Jewish people"; others were troubled by them. Some of the leading Anglican bishops supported the Balfour Declaration. It is thought that Rev. William Hechler had some influence on them. But the Anglican bishop in Jerusalem, the Right Reverend Rennie Miles MacInnes, charged with revitalizing Anglican life in the Holy City, opposed Zionism. His sympathies lay with the Arabs of Palestine, and more particularly with the Christians among them.

For the Zionist movement, the Balfour Declaration and General Allenby's entry into Jerusalem, later in the same year, were momentous occasions. These events revitalized the worldwide Zionist movement and allowed the renewed growth of the Yishuv. British victory affirmed the view articulated in 1914 by Zionist leader Chaim Weizmann that the future of Zionism was entwined with the fortunes of the British Empire. Both the empire and Jewish nationalism would benefit from the relationship. According to Weizmann, "England[,] which would be instrumental in the redemption of Israel[,] would derive an enormous benefit from it."[2] Religious Zionists, foremost among them Rabbi Abraham Isaac Kook, saw the Balfour Declaration and the British victory as signs of divine favor, the beginning of the redemptive process.

Similarly, Theodor Herzl's associate Rev. William Hechler, a Christian religious Zionist, as almost all Christian Zionists were and are, understood these events as divinely ordained, and the facilitators of the events as divinely inspired. Bishop MacInnes had a decidedly different view.

During the first years of the British occupation of Palestine, Bishop MacInnes often expressed his opposition to Zionism. This opposition was noted in the Jewish newspapers of Palestine and was the cause of considerable tension between the Zionist rank and file and the clergy and laity of the Anglican Church. In 1919, faced with the complexities of intercommunal relations in the Holy City, MacInnes sought to employ an Anglican cleric who was familiar with the Jewish tradition and who could serve as a much-needed interlocutor with the city's various Jewish communities. That cleric would join the community at St. George's Cathedral, the Anglican seat in Jerusalem.

MacInnes's meeting with Chaim Weizmann in December 1919 made clear the bishop's dire need of a consultant on Jewish matters. The meeting was an uneasy one. Bishop MacInnes was disturbed by Jewish protests against the Anglican schools in Palestine, which some Jews saw as "mission schools." The city's Jewish communities, both religious and secular, boycotted Anglican institutions. In keeping with precedents dating back to 1830s encounters between the Old Yishuv and Protestant missionaries, some of Jerusalem's rabbis threatened the families of Jewish children at the schools, and the Jewish patients in the Anglican hospital, with *herem*—excommunication. In 1919 Jewish newspapers in Palestine embarked on a press campaign against the mission schools. In his response to the bishop, Weizmann explained the Jewish communities' opposition in the context of the legacy of Christian persecution of Jews, of which missionizing was understood to be a form. Bishop MacInnes was confused and disturbed by this reaction.[3]

After consulting with colleagues in England, Bishop MacInnes found a candidate who seemed ideal for the job. The young man, Herbert Danby, quickly accepted the position of church librarian and consultant to the bishop and arrived in Jerusalem in 1919. He was thirty years old and had served in the Anglican ministry for the previous six years, having been ordained an Anglican priest while at Oxford. As a historian of St. George's Cathedral noted, "Bishop MacInnes planned to have a consultant in matters relating to Jews and Judaism. . . . Reverend Danby accepted to work under the Bishop."[4] It is to Bishop MacInnes's credit that he hired and retained a clergyman whose views were so different from his.

Danby would soon become a supporter of Zionism; MacInnes's opposition to the movement would only grow more forceful and strident. In a 1921 letter to clergy and laity of the Anglican Church, MacInnes wrote, "At a time when Palestine is so unhappily disturbed by the unjust and intolerable demands of the Zionists, it is good to see the missionary schools contributing something of great worth to the Holy Land in the leveling and uniting influence they bring to bear on all these young and opening minds."[5]

Herbert Danby's attitude toward Zionism was diametrically opposed to that of Bishop MacInnes. In Danby's case, the relationship between Christian Hebraism, philo-Semitism, and support of Zionism was unusually direct. Danby's intellectual interest in Jewish texts began when he was as an undergraduate at Keble College, Oxford, where he excelled in the study of Hebrew. At Oxford, Hebrew was an esteemed topic of study, though few undergraduates undertook the study of the language. The Regius Professorship of Hebrew, established by order of Henry VIII, was among the oldest and most prestigious of the university's professorships, though its prestige had considerably diminished by the beginning of the twentieth century. Danby studied Hebrew comparatively, in the context of other Semitic languages, and was awarded both the Houghton Syriac Prize and the Junior Septuagint Prize. While a student he took an interest in the revival of the Hebrew language and began reading contemporary Hebrew literature. From philology he moved to textual study; in 1914 he was awarded an M.A. for translations of sections of Mishnah Berachot into English. Unlike some of his English Hebraist predecessors whose scholarly endeavors were joined to hostility toward Jews and Judaism, Danby's study of Hebrew and Judaica led him to a sympathetic attitude toward the object of his study. Danby was well aware that in previous centuries Christian scholars at Oxford and Cambridge had studied rabbinic texts for polemical anti-Jewish purposes. Reasons for Christian interest in Hebrew varied, of course, but often it was the result of a wish to engage in polemics with Jewish scholars or to use the texts in missionary efforts. Hence the Christian Hebraists concentrated on biblical Hebrew and avoided the study of rabbinic Hebrew. In the late 1920s Danby wrote, "Of living Gentile Hebraists . . . perhaps a dozen or more have ventured the uncomfortable passage from the comparatively easy and well-charted biblical language and literature to the superficially repellent and turbid post-biblical depths. . . . Nevertheless is it very evident that, among non-Jews, rabbinic studies lack today both the appeal and the prestige which was theirs from the sixteenth to the eighteenth century."[6] From the beginning of his career, Danby endeavored to restore the prestige of rabbinic studies. After earning his M.A., Danby continued to work on the translation and explication of rabbinic texts. Four years after he settled in Jerusalem, Oxford awarded him a Doctor of Divinity degree on the strength of his translation of Mishnah Sanhedrin.

Danby, who had spent the First World War years as a church librarian and priest in England, was the ideal candidate for the job of consultant on Jewish affairs. He had excelled in the study of Semitics at Oxford, where he was awarded series of academic prizes, culminating in a first in Oriental languages. He was deeply interested in Christian-Jewish relations and had embarked on an independent study of rabbinic texts. Jerusalem, "the city of three faiths" now under British rule, seemed an ideal place for him. He was to live and flourish there for seventeen years. By the time he left the Holy City and returned to Oxford, he had had a positive effect on Jewish-Christian relations in England and Palestine—and he would continue and expand upon that interfaith work when he returned to Oxford in the mid-1930s. In 1936 Danby was appointed Regius Professor of Hebrew at Oxford, and there he achieved great eminence as an internationally recognized expert on the Hebrew language and rabbinic texts.

For many twentieth-century scholars of Judaica, Danby served as an invaluable and reliable guide to scholarly developments in what we would now call Jewish Studies. In 1933 Oxford University Press published Danby's translation of the complete Mishnah, a translation that is still in use today. In a series of scholarly works, reviews, and articles published before and after that translation, Danby apprised readers of the landmark Jewish scholarship projects of the period. He introduced, explained, and contextualized these new works for his Christian colleagues, thus establishing those Jewish scholars' academic reputations.

Since its publication in 1933, Danby's Mishnah translation has achieved near canonical status, and one would be hard-pressed to find in the translation evidence that the translator was anything but a rabbinic Jewish scholar. To this day, many Jewish readers of the Mishnah translation are surprised to learn that Danby was an Anglican priest. Danby's motivations and personal religious views are even more surprising. Despite his immersion in the world of rabbinic texts, his commitment to the Church of England never wavered, and his interest in Judaism remained, naturally, subservient to that commitment. This chapter examines Danby's view of Judaism in the context of his commitment to the church, exploring his support of political Zionism in the context of both his religious and intellectual projects.[7]

St. George's Cathedral, the Anglican church in Jerusalem, was established in 1892. Throughout the church's history most of its hierarchy was anti-

Zionist. This anti-Zionism drew on a tradition of Anglican missionary views of Jews and Judaism, a view especially strong at St. George's Cathedral Church. In an 1893 clergy meeting at the residence of Bishop George Blyth, the assembled heard a report on the "Difficulties of Mission-work in Palestine." Most of the report concerned the difficulties inherent in attempts to convert Jerusalem's Eastern Christians and the city's Muslims. A brief paragraph on Jerusalem's Jews is a veritable litany of anti-Judaism: "In preaching the Gospel to the Jews there must be special difficulties caused by their upholding the Talmud, misunderstanding the nature of sin, deeming things of other people as lawful to them, being accustomed from fear to deceit, lying and slyness, and by their belief that they are Abraham's children and heirs of Israel's blessing and the first born son of God, etc., which subject I shall not enter upon, but leave to someone of you who know by experience a great deal more than I do."[8] Against this anti-Judaic, and specifically anti-Talmudic statement, Danby's interest in rabbinics and his willingness to engage Jewish scholars of Judaica are all the more compelling.

Subsequent to the 1948 Arab-Israeli war the cathedral was in Jordanian Jerusalem. During Jordanian rule, and then under Israeli rule after the 1967 war, St. George's became a center of Palestinian nationalism and opposition to Israeli rule. The great irony here is that it was in this church that Danby developed his strong identification with the Zionist cause. By the end of the twentieth century, St. George's was a center of Palestinian nationalism. The church hierarchy, including the bishop of Jerusalem, was now Palestinian Arab. In 2002, Mordechai Vanunu, freed after eighteen years in an Israel jail on charges of disclosing Israel's nuclear secrets, took up residence in the cathedral's guesthouse, further exacerbating relations between church officials and the Israeli authorities.

A half century before St. George's was built, another Anglican church was consecrated in Jerusalem. Built within the city walls—unlike St. George's, which was built outside of the city walls a kilometer east of the Damascus Gate—Christ Church, established in 1842, was the home of the Anglo-Prussian bishopric, a rare example of Anglican-Lutheran cooperation. St. George's Cathedral and Christ Church are thus a study in contrasts. St. George's was High Church; Christ Church was Low Church. Long before the establishment of Israel, they differed widely about Zionism. Christ Church was the home of the Hebrew Christian Mission founded by the London Jews Society. Its first bishop was Michael Solomon Alexander, an English rabbi who converted to the Church of England in the 1840s. To this day, 150 years after its founding, Christ Church maintains its missionary function and is assertively Zionist. It hosts a weekly prayer service in Hebrew, a tradition it initiated in the mid-nineteenth century. St. George's Cathedral, in contrast, is assertively anti-Zionist, and directs its evangelizing efforts toward Jerusalem's Christian Arab population. It has little to no contact with Jerusalem's Jewish communities.

During the British Mandate (1920–48), the clergy of these two Anglican churches gave radically different advice to the British and international committees that came to Jerusalem to investigate the competing claims of Palestine's Arabs and Jews. Bishop Rennie MacInnes often spoke against Zionism, which must have troubled Danby. In contrast, in 1930, Christ Church called for the establishment of a Jewish state: "We can take comfort in the knowledge that the return of the Jews to the Holy Land is assured as in the purposes of Almighty God for the World."[9] The British Peel Commission of 1936 heard testimony from MacInnes's successor, Bishop Graham-Brown, who issued a statement negating any biblical connection with the Jews in modern Palestine: "As to any 'Biblical' claim for the establishment of a Jewish state, the claim was based on a false premise." And in 1945 Graham-Brown's successor, Bishop W. H. Stewart of St. George's, told the Anglo-American Commission on Palestine:

> There is an uncommon tendency today both in England and in America, to base large Zionist claims on the Old Testament history and prophecies, and thereby to win support from many Christians whose respect for the Bible is perhaps greater than their understanding of it. . . . The Christian doctrine of the New Testament is that the new spiritual Israel of the Christian Church, with its descent by the spiritual birth of baptism, is the sole heir to the promises themselves also spiritualized, which had been fortified by the Old Israel after the flesh, with its descent by human generations.[10]

In this formulation, support for Zionism is directly at odds with Christian doctrine.

⌀

At Work in Jerusalem

Danby arrived in Jerusalem at a remarkable historical moment. The British had taken the city from the Ottoman Turks in 1917. Before the mandate government was established in 1920, the British administration of Jerusalem was under the authority of Ronald Storrs, the military governor. Storrs had a powerful political and cultural interest in smoothing relations between Muslims, Christians, and Jews, and it was under his auspices that the Palestine Oriental Society was formed in March of 1920. Herbert Danby was appointed secretary of the group and editor of its scholarly publication, *The Journal of the Palestine Oriental Society* (*JPOS*).[11] The society's purpose was "the cultivation and publication of researches on the Ancient East." But the journal's mandate was much wider than the study of "the Ancient East." It soon was to publish articles on modern Middle Eastern cultural developments, among them the study of local Palestinian folklore and the revival of the Hebrew language. Among the contributors were Christian, Muslim, and Jewish scholars. Most of the articles appeared in English. Some were published in French or German.

The editorship of the *JPOS*, which Danby retained until he left Palestine in 1936, was but one of many editorial and reporting assignments that he assumed during his sojourn in Palestine. He also wrote for the *Times* (London).[12] His many articles were favorable to the Zionist cause. For several years in the early 1930s, Danby would share editorial responsibilities for the *JPOS* with the American archaeologist William Foxwell Albright. Albright, of Johns Hopkins University, would later be acknowledged as "the Dean of Near Eastern Archaeologists." In 1946 he was among the founders of the American Christian Palestine Committee, a group that advocated for the establishment of a Jewish state in Palestine.

Controversy broke out in 1922 when the *JPOS* under Danby's leadership published an article written in Hebrew. On the occasion of Eliezer Ben-Yehuda's death, the journal published a tribute to "the reviver of the Hebrew language" by his colleague David Yellin. The article appeared in Hebrew with a facing English translation, prepared, it seems, by Danby.[13] The publication of this and other articles on Hebrew and Jewish subjects, and the presence of Jewish scholars on the editorial board, led to accusations that the editor favored Jews and Jewish subjects and neglected Christian and Muslim subjects and authors. In a later article in the *JPOS*, William Foxwell Albright addressed this issue obliquely. He praised Danby for his "faithful and competent editorship" and acknowledged the society's debt to his "general popularity in all circles." Albright concluded: "I shall naturally not speak of my own modest services, which consisted mostly in assisting Danby and in helping to pacify certain groups which were bent on dragging the Society into politics. . . . We have succeeded in avoiding the pitfalls of politics, and our Society is known to all who are really *au courant* with its activities, as strictly neutral."[14]

The "pitfalls of politics" is a reference to the growing Arab-Jewish tension in 1930s Palestine. When, in June of 1920, Sir Herbert Samuel was appointed the first British High Commissioner for Palestine, Zionists within Palestine and without were thrilled by the British government's decision to appoint an English Jew to that office. The Arab leadership understood Samuel's appointment in much the same way, and saw it as a move against Arab interests. Jerusalem's Muslim leadership complained that the appointment of Herbert Samuel signaled a British turn toward the Zionists. The growing tension between Christians, Muslim, and Jews made Danby's work all the more difficult.

While at St. George's Danby also founded *Bible Lands*, a scholarly journal aimed at a wide readership. It reported on biblical textual research and archaeological excavation, often supplementing articles with photographs. Danby wrote many of the articles. Through his contacts in England and the United States he made sure that the journal had a wide readership. Protestant clergy and laymen throughout the English-speaking world read *Bible Lands* until it ceased publication in the late 1950s.

∽

Danby on Judaism

Danby's intensive and comprehensive study of rabbinic texts led him to surprising conclusions about the nature of Judaism, conclusions that were at odds with the then-dominant Anglican understandings of the Jewish faith. In a 1937 review of the first volumes of Salo Baron's *A Social and Religious History of the Jews*, Danby, praising Baron's presentation of Judaism, criticized the tendency of many Christian scholars to view Judaism through a "Bible-centered" lens. Judaism, Danby pointed out to his Christian readers, had a life and literature that were referenced to the biblical text but extended far beyond the confines of that text.[15] If they were to understand Judaism as a living tradition, Christian scholars had to move beyond the Hebrew Bible and study rabbinic texts. Danby had been promoting this point of view among Christian scholars since the early 1920s. For those unable to read rabbinic texts in the Hebrew and Aramaic originals, Danby's fluid translations would open up that world to them. His essays and lectures on Jewish subjects challenged earlier conceptions of Judaism and did much to counter anti-Semitic tendencies in the English-speaking world. The long-term effect of Danby's translations and essays was quite remarkable. Because of his work, Christians now had access to accurately translated Jewish texts, and these translations were often accompanied by essays sympathetic to the rabbinic tradition and to contemporary Jewish causes, foremost among them Zionism.

Danby warned his readers, "If we identify Judaism with formalism, legalism and stereotyped practices, we see it in the wrong perspective; Judaism is not only pure mind applied to ancient revelation; there certainly does exist much of this legalism and formalism, and sometimes excessive emphasis placed on the intellect as opposed to the feelings . . . (but) such was not the essence of Judaism as a living faith; still less was it the dominant note in the bulk of the Jewish people." He warned his readers that "Judaism is wrongly envisaged if it is looked upon solely as a process of restricting its content to code and rule and law; on the contrary, the truer view is to see it in repeated revolt against such limitations."[16] Danby argued for the continuing intellectual validity of Judaism explicitly in his essays and implicitly in his masterly translations.

~

Danby and Joseph Klausner's *Jesus of Nazareth*

During his seventeen years in Jerusalem, Danby cultivated the friendship of Jewish scholars, many of whom had arrived in Jerusalem to teach at the Hebrew University of Jerusalem, established in 1925. Among the most fruitful of these associations was his friendship with Professor Joseph Klausner. Klausner and Danby had arrived in Palestine in the same year, 1919. Klausner and his wife arrived from Odessa, Danby from Oxford. Klausner's academic specialty was the Late Second Temple Period, and in the years before he left Russia he was engaged in a study of Jesus in the context of Second Temple Judaism. He did this within a scholarly tradition established in the late nineteenth century, a scholarly tradition in which Jewish researchers focused their study of Christianity on its earliest period. This approach required a further set of enquiries about the historical context of Jesus's time: "In order to clarify the relationship of early Christianity to the Judaism of its time, researchers had to perform additional work. They had to delineate the nature of Judaism in the Land of Israel at the end of the Second Temple Period."[17]

Klausner, a powerful cultural force in Jewish Palestine, was a prolific historian and literary scholar. Ideologically, he was a supporter of Vladimir Jabotinsky, the founder of Revisionist Zionism. This placed him on the political right of the Zionist spectrum. Revisionists advocated a militant approach to the establishment of a Jewish state and defined that state's future borders in the widest possible way; theirs was a maximalist stance that envisioned a Jewish state on both sides of the Jordon River. Culturally, Klausner was an ecumenist who called for Jewish reevaluation of Jesus and early Christianity. As editor of the Hebrew journal *HaShiloah*, the journal founded by Ahad Ha'am,

Joseph Klausner, 1903 (Massadah Publishers)

Klausner wielded great influence and authority in the Hebrew-speaking liter-ary world. Klausner opened up the journal to a very diverse set of writers and subjects—Christianity among them.

When the Hebrew University opened in 1925 Klausner hoped to be ap-pointed Professor of Second Temple History in the history department. The political and cultural orientation of the university's founders and faculty was liberal and socialist. The university's first president was Dr. Judah Magnes, a Reform rabbi from New York. As Klausner's political orientation was rightist/ Revisionist he was denied the position he sought and was appointed Professor of Modern Hebrew Literature, a field in which Klausner also excelled. He taught and wrote on Hebrew literature for eighteen years, from 1925 to 1944, when a fund was created that gave Klausner an additional appointment in Jewish history, his chosen field of endeavor. Of the opponents of his appointment as a historian Klausner wrote that they were "the enemies of my true and complete Zionism . . . which was the complete opposite of the half-Zionism of the socialists."[18]

In 1921 Klausner published his epochal Hebrew-language work *Jesus of Nazareth*. In this work he placed Jesus's life and teachings within the context of Late Second Temple times and the development of rabbinic Judaism. Klausner's ideal reader was the "new Jew" of Palestine who, he anticipated, would be free of anti-Christian feelings resulting from centuries of Christian persecution. This fresh portrayal of Christianity and Jesus would, Klausner hoped, speak to the educated readership of the Yishuv.[19] Klausner also hoped, naively, that its message would appeal to Jews in the English-speaking world.

Underlying Klausner's publication of his reconsideration of Christianity was a startling assumption: Jews living in an independent Jewish state would be able to free themselves of their fear of, and aversion to, the central figure of the Christian faith. Klausner felt that this reevaluation, by bringing Christians to a more sympathetic view of Judaism, would both strengthen the Jewish claim to Palestine and free Jews of their fear of Christianity.

In reevaluating and valorizing Jesus in a Jewish context, Klausner was breaking with his mentor Ahad Ha'am (Asher Ginzberg). In a long article in his Hebrew-language journal *HaShiloah*, Ginzberg had argued against Claude Montefiore and other Jewish scholars who wrote sympathetically of Jesus.[20] Danby, a regular reader of *HaShiloah*, wrote that Ahad Ha'am "insisted that while Christianity was all very well for Christians, Jews could have nothing to do with it short of denying the most fundamental characteristics of Judaism."[21] In contrast, Klausner, Ahad Ha'am's successor as editor, opened up *HaShiloah* to discussions of Christianity.

According to Danby, his own early conversations with Klausner influenced the final shape of Klausner's Jesus book. As Klausner knew little spoken English and Danby had no Russian or German, the conversations were carried on in Hebrew. This was a remarkable moment, as these two men, a Russian Jew and an English Christian, would later help shape the content and structure of modern Hebrew usage. Klausner was among the founders of the Hebrew Language Academy, the group first proposed by Eliezer Ben-Yehuda. Danby, working with Hebrew University professor M. Z. Segal, produced one of the first modern Hebrew dictionaries. Herbert Danby took on the considerable task of translating Klausner's 350-page book on Jesus into English.

Klausner wrote that he and Danby "went over each and every line of the translation and Dr. Danby praised my knowledge of literary English, though I never learned to speak English and we conducted our conversations in Hebrew."[22] The project held different meanings for writer and translator. Klausner called for a Jewish reevaluation of Christianity; Danby sought a Christian reevaluation of Judaism. Klausner and Danby, both ardent Zionists, supported the modernization of Hebrew and its adoption as the language of everyday speech by the Jews of Palestine. Klausner, in an introductory note to the English translation, expressed the hope that the appearance of his book on Jesus would convince English and American Jews of the significance of modern Hebrew. Considering the heightened sensitivity of American Jewish individuals and organizations to books about Jesus, which they linked to Christian missionary tracts, it is remarkable that Klausner could get it so wrong. A Hebrew book about Jesus was the last thing American Jewish leaders wanted. It reminded them of missionary activity. And perhaps, under Klauser's influence, Danby, too, got it wrong, as he, too, expected a wide Jewish readership for Klausner's book. He overestimated Klausner's influence among American Jews, and he underestimated the negative reaction to a new Jewish evaluation of Jesus.

Danby, it seems, had an inflated view of Klausner's prestige, and of the potential of Klausner's book to change Jewish attitudes toward Jesus. Danby dubbed Klausner "a writer with a most responsible position in the world of Jewish thought, even a leading figure in the concentrated, intensified atmosphere of the very centre of that world of Jewish thought in Palestine—such a man had thought it worth the trouble, and even his duty as a Hebrew of the Hebrews, to write in Hebrew for the benefit of his fellow-Hebrews, a weighty learned treatise. . . . That treatise is a most unexpected by-product of the rise of the Jewish nationalist instinct and the revival of Hebrew culture."[23]

But as reviews of *Jesus of Nazareth* began to appear in both English- and Hebrew-language journals, Danby became aware that Jewish opposition to Klausner's project and thesis was often enraged and virulent. At issue here were two radically different modern Jewish responses to Christianity. To some extent these responses were shaped by the circumstances of the Jewish communities from which they emerged. In general, American Jewish readers were more hostile than their European coreligionists to Klausner's book and Danby's translations. By the 1920s, American Jews were responding forcefully to the renewed missionary efforts directed toward them by Christian groups. This reaction had been forming since the mid-nineteenth century. With the large influx of Eastern European Jews arriving in the United States after

1881, Christian missionary efforts grew considerably. The organized Jewish response, as in the mid-nineteenth century, was to form organizations that would counter missionaries, to publish Jewish newspapers in response to missionary activity, and to strengthen self-help organizations, foremost among them B'nai Brith.

Klausner's book on Jesus, in Danby's translation, was the direct inspiration for Rabbi Stephen Wise's famous "Jesus Speech" on Christmas Day 1925. This speech generated considerable controversy, with many Jews denouncing Wise's call for a reevaluation of Jesus's Jewishness and many liberal Protestants hailing his speech. Among Wise's most quoted observations in this lecture was that "Jesus was a Jew, Hebrew of Hebrews. Whatever I believe with respect to the imputed miracle of his birth, his mother, Mary, was a Jewish woman. He was reared and taught as a Jew. He worshipped in the synagogue." Rabbi Wise, a leading figure in the Reform movement, had spoken before about Jesus the Jew. Nine years earlier, in 1916, he told a large audience of Jews and Christians, "The Jew recognizes, marvels at the radiance, the benignity of the personality of Jesus, the Nazarene Jew, but we do not class that personality by the side of God. God is One—unique, not humanly inimitable, but humanly attainable."[24] His 1925 speech, made when he was one of the most prominent and popular Jewish orators in New York and one of the leaders of American Zionism, caused a veritable firestorm in more religiously traditional circles, particularly among the Orthodox. But opposition also came from Wise's Reform rabbinical colleagues. Rabbi Samuel Schulman of New York's Temple Beth-El deemed Wise's call for a Jewish reevaluation of Jesus "indelicate and undignified and shows a lack of moral and spiritual virility."[25]

Mizrahi, the religious Zionist organization, demanded that Wise resign from the Zionist leadership. Concerned that the evolving "Jesus scandal" would hurt the Zionist movement's fund-raising efforts, Rabbi Wise offered his resignation. As Wise's biographer Carl Voss described it: "Nathan Straus (the founder of Macy's) turned the tide. He expressed his faith in Stephen Wise and gave six hundred and fifty thousand dollars as an additional gift to the United Palestine Appeal. . . . After a long discussion, the executive committee of the U.P.A. voted overwhelmingly for Wise and informed him of their decision that his resignation would be declined."[26] Thus support of Zionism, which was slowly but surely becoming the unifying force among contending American Jewish factions, won out over concerns for ideological purity or unity on theological questions.

The secular elites of the Yishuv in Palestine were in a radically different cultural and political situation than American Jews. Engaged in creating an autonomous Jewish society, a society whose "other" was Muslim, not Christian, the "new Jews" of Palestine no longer had to fear Christian doctrine and teachings, or so Klausner hoped. For the most part they were as disinterested in Christianity as they were in Jewish religious doctrine. All religious teachings seemed to them outmoded. To secular members of the Yishuv, Christian missions did not seem a direct threat, though many secularists viewed Christian missionary efforts as an attack on Jewish identity. By the 1920s, Protestant missionary activities in Palestine were directed primarily toward Eastern Christians and Catholics; most missionaries had decided to no longer target Jews.

This situation left open a space and an opportunity for Jewish investigations of Christian origins, particularly in the figure of Jesus. The roots of this endeavor were in the work of Abraham Geiger and other European Jewish scholars of the mid-nineteenth century. Klausner's Hebrew-language study of Jesus was the first of a series of Hebrew-language books by Jewish scholars who reexamined Jesus in a Jewish context. In the 1950s, novelist Abraham Kabak published *On the Narrow Path*, a Hebrew novel that sets Jesus's story squarely within the rabbinic tradition. Then in the early 1960s, Hebrew University professor David Flusser published his landmark Hebrew-language study of Jesus.[27] This interest in Jesus was limited to the Jews of Mandate Palestine and, later, the State of Israel. Jews living in the United States and Europe, at least those who were affiliated with Jewish cultural or religious organizations, demonstrated little to no interest in new understandings of Jesus's Jewish background. In American Jewry, a writer demonstrating such interest was suspected of apostasy. In the mid-twentieth century, the case of novelist Sholem Asch was a prime example.[28]

The harshness of responses to Jewish interest in Jesus was reflected in American Jewish publications both scholarly and popular. In the 19 November 1926 issue of the American Hebrew-language journal *Hadoar*, the Hebrew critic Gershon Schoffman condemned Danby's translation of Klausner's book —and along with it the tendency of Hebrew writers to use Christological terms and Christian themes in their writings: "It seems that some of our young writers take great pleasure in using the words 'crucifixion', 'golgotha', and other terms of this sort—words that they seem to find elevating. 'Jesus' especially makes them want to set pen to paper. . . . How they love that name. . . . It would be best if that name never came to our minds again."[29]

The most sustained and lengthy attack on Klausner and Danby's *Jesus* appeared in the American scholar Ephraim Deinard's *Herev LaHashem Uleyisrael*, of 1924. The book's subtitle is "Against the book *Jesus of Nazareth* by Dr. Joseph Klausner, in which he strives to bring us under the canopy of the new Shekhinah, as he is so inspired by the spirit of the son of Miriam." In his autobiography, Klausner, writing thirty years after the publication of his Jesus book, was still smarting from Deinard's attacks: "Deinard, that crazy/dirty old man who only knew how to attack and curse, printed three filthy books attacking my *Jesus of Nazareth*. In these books he accused me of accepting money from Christian missionaries. The truth was that those very missionaries in Jerusalem cursed my book, calling it 'full of lies and a blasphemy against our Lord Jesus Christ.' "[30]

In an essay published in 1930, Danby translated and quoted Deinard's blistering attacks on both the author and the translator. It seems that Danby derived an odd satisfaction from Deinard's pronouncement on his translation of Klausner's book: "From heaven above to hell below," Deinard said, "nowhere can you show me a single Christian scholar in the whole world capable of understanding the Hebrew language of your book. . . . Not even twenty priests, let alone one, could translate a book written in Talmudic Hebrew or in the Modern Hebrew literary style, difficult enough for a learned Jew to understand, still more for a Christian who learns his Hebrew from the Bible."[31] Danby was the obvious target of this slur. He was an Anglican priest who did understand rabbinic Hebrew, and this rankled Deinard. Danby took pleasure in being the priest who could translate rabbinic and modern Hebrew texts, and who could also read and respond to his Hebrew critics in modern Hebrew.

Danby's translation of Klausner's *Jesus* was an attempt to bridge the Christian-Jewish divide by altering Jewish perceptions of Christianity. But was it more than that? Was it an attempt to bring Jews closer to Christianity? Deinard and other conservative Jewish critics claimed that Klausner and Danby were serving the interests of Christian missionaries. Klausner stated that he wanted to change Jewish perceptions of Jesus. Danby stated that he wanted to change Christian perceptions of Judaism. He made this clear within three years of moving to Jerusalem. But this does not preclude other motives, such as attempts to bring Jews to Christianity.

In a remarkable series of lectures delivered at St. George's Cathedral in January of 1922, Danby addressed Christian misperceptions of Judaism and sought to correct them. The lectures were titled "Mind Versus Emotion in Judaism" and "Hasidism: Present Day Jewish Mysticism." In these lectures Danby established three main points. First, the conventional Christian view of Judaism as "a religion of unrelieved legalism" (in the words of the German historian Emil Schurer) was mistaken. Danby pointed out that "for many Christians, legalism has become both the definition and also the condemnation of Judaism."[32] His second point followed directly: "Spirit" as well as "mind" animated Jewish thought. Finally, Hasidism exemplified the current dynamism of Jewish thought and life.[33] Danby arrived at this conclusion after a period of intensive study of Hasidic texts—and, it seems, limited study of Hasidim in Jerusalem.

Danby's second lecture opened with a startling confession: "First of all I have to make the confession that until some two and a half years ago I had never heard of this movement of Hasidism."[34] It was his move to Jerusalem that brought him into contact with the city's insular communities of Hasidim. Danby's residence at St. George's Cathedral was only a few minutes walk from Meah Shearim, the ultra-Orthodox stronghold. Unlike most of his Jewish and Christian colleagues, he sought to understand both the ideas and practices of these Hasidic communities. This was in sharp contrast to the attitude toward ultra-Orthodox Jews displayed by Bishop MacInnes, Danby's superior. In *The Living Church* of 26 November 1929, MacInnes wrote:

> The first objective of the Anglican Church in Palestine was the Jew, and the Jewish problem was never more insistent than it is today. There are large numbers in Jerusalem itself of the old Orthodox Jews. You can see them in the streets on a Sabbath, a New Year, or a Feast of Tabernacles . . . Shylocks in purple velvet coats, fur cap, long ringlet, and praying shawl—a devout pathetic people, still wailing every Friday at the ruined wall of the Temple Area, still hoping and seeking for Him to whom Christendom, for very lack of His spirit in dealing with them, has failed to open their eyes.[35]

In contrast to the hostile reviews in the Anglo-Jewish and Hebrew press, Christian scholarly reception of Danby's translation of Klausner's *Jesus* was quite positive. In a review in the prestigious *Journal of Religion*, Professor E. F. Scott of Union Theological Seminary wrote: "We are reminded by this book that a Jewish state has not only come into being, but has begun to make its own contribution to the world's culture. The book was written in Hebrew— once more a living language—and was published three years ago in Jerusalem. . . . Klausner writes for Jews, and his own sympathies are those of a fervidly patriotic view. . . . Though he cannot adopt the Christian estimate of Jesus, his tone is one of generous appreciation. . . . That such a book should be the first fruits of a new Zionist culture may be taken as a happy augury."[36]

We would be mistaken to read Danby on Judaism as completely irenic, understanding, and conciliatory. Perusing Danby's translations and explications of the Mishnah, Maimonides, and modern Jewish literature, one might think that Danby had accepted Judaism's own understandings of its historical role. On the face of it Danby seemed to view Jewish legalism as viable and intellectually vibrant for Jews and students of Judaism, whether these scholars be Jewish or Christian. But what was his view of the church's responsibility toward the Jewish people?

A very different view of Danby's translation of Klausner's *Jesus*, and a very different understanding of Danby's greater project, emerge from a reading of the transcript of Danby's remarks at the 1935 "Budapest and Warsaw Conference on the presentation of the Christian Message to the Jews," a conference convened by American and European missionaries to the Jews:

> The consequence of the Klausner translation: whether it was a
> good thing or a bad thing? There was never a word of doubt but
> that the translation (the original would have remained in comparative
> obscurity but for the English version) has done good[,] that it gives the
> missionary a long-wanted "jumping-off place" and especially, an insight
> into the strength or weakness of the present educated Jewish opinion,
> and some knowledge of the point of Jewish sympathy or of Jewish
> antipathies as to the subject in general. The most subtle and accurate
> comment (by Dr Zwemer) was that the book was another and strong
> factor which made for the ploughing up of the soil of the Jewish
> mentality, hitherto trampled down hard by mutual prejudices and
> ignorances; and that now that the soil was well and thoroughly
> ploughed and broken up was the time to sew and irrigate. The soil was
> fruitful; it only remained to seen what seed would be sown—whether
> Christian influences or non-Christian.[37]

This "Report submitted by Dr. Danby to the Bishop," which I found in typescript in the archives of Jerusalem's St. George's Cathedral, tells us that in the mid-1930s, Danby's loyalty to a conversionist agenda was unwavering. He saw no possibility that a Jewish religious ideal would influence the young generation of Zionists. Either they would adopt a political ideology, whether of the Right or of the Left, or they would see the light of the Christian message. Now that "the soil of the Jewish mentality" had been ploughed up by Klausner's book, Christians could plant the seeds of belief in Jesus. Danby's hope was that the seed would sprout and Jews would accept Christianity. Secular Jewish rejection of rabbinic law encouraged Danby's expectation that Christianity would prove a viable religious alternative to traditional Judaism.

We can assume that Danby kept this report from coming to the attention of his friend Joseph Klausner. Klausner was sure of the purity of Danby's intentions. In a tribute written after Danby's death in 1953, Klausner recalled: "When Danby offered to translate *Jesus of Nazareth* it was only natural that I would think his intentions were Christian. . . . But in Danby's act of translation there was no missionary intent. As a man of science Danby wanted Christians to have a clear and correct idea what a nationalist Jewish scholar conversant with the ancient Hebrew literature has to say of the origins of Jesus and his teachings."[38]

Danby, resident in Palestine from 1919 to 1936, during which time he immersed himself in the emerging culture of the Yishuv, was acutely aware of tensions between the Orthodox and secular Jewish sectors and of secular Jewish antipathy to the Talmud: "The super-Jews of Eretz-Yisrael may toss it aside as a potsherd fit only for Jews to scratch themselves with." It was this antipathy that convinced him that the members of the New Yishuv would continue to reject rabbinic Judaism and search elsewhere for a religious ideology to sustain them. It was his hope, and the hope of Christian missionaries generally, that Jews would choose Christianity over a secular version of Jewish identity.

❧

Danby on Jewish Attitudes toward Christianity

In a series of lectures titled *The Jew and Christianity: Some Phases, Ancient and Modern, of the Jewish Attitude Towards Christianity* (1927), first delivered at London's Sion College under the auspices of the Society for the Promotion of Christian Knowledge, Danby devoted the concluding lecture to Jewish reactions to Klausner's book. As he noted, "By some Jews the book has been looked upon as a startling and dangerous monstrosity; by others as a welcome novelty."[39] Contextualizing interest in the book among the secular elites of the Yishuv, Danby compared that interest to the "extraordinary excitement and interest . . . shown by the Jews in Palestine in the (1926) performance of a Hebrew play called Ha-Dibbuk."[40] Just as the folklore of the Hasidim was appealing as the subject of artistic treatment, so might the story of Jesus be told in Jewish context. At this point, Danby cautioned his audience that they would be wrong to read this new interest in Jesus as a Jewish interest in Christian dogmas and institutions: "The Jew is as much repelled by these as ever he was; to him they are symbols of bitterness, cruelty, savage, senseless and fanatical persecution and wholesale murder. No, it is not a sign of Jewish approach to Christianity; but it is an attempt to rescue from the hands of Christendom a figure whom the Jews can claim to be, historically and humanly, their own."[41]

Here Danby returns to the central theme of these five London lectures and to one of the recurring themes in his life's work, that Christians, by their "unChristian" behavior, have made Christianity an anathema to Jews, and that the persistence of Judaism offers Christians "a systematic, consistent, independent, external criterion of the various forms of Christianity at various stages of its history. . . . The results of this search are, on the whole, far from flattering to us Christians."[42] Thus for Danby, as for James Parkes in the 1950s, and for the Catholic writers Robert Drinan in the 1970s and James Carroll in the 1990s, Christian mistreatment of Jews is a betrayal of Christian ideals. European Jewish history offered these Christian critics a yardstick with which to measure Christian aspirations and find them wanting. Their philo-Semitism constituted a critique of the established churches, and in a sense a critique of the church was the primary focus of their writing and research.

~

Danby and H. N. Bialik

Danby's fascination with the Hebrew language and rabbinic texts expressed itself in his friendship with the "Hebrew national poet" Hayyim Nahman Bialik. Bialik, a towering figure in the revival of Hebrew literary culture, immigrated to Palestine in 1923. Bialik and a group of fellow litterateurs in Odessa, Berlin, and Warsaw had shaped the canon and diction of modern Hebrew poetry and prose. In the early 1920s, in the years immediately after the Russian Revolution, Bialik and a group of his colleagues were living in the Crimean port of Odessa. The intervention of Maxim Gorky enabled Bialik and four other Hebrew writers to leave Soviet Russia and immigrate to Palestine. There he was welcomed in the Yishuv as a great hero. In Palestine Bialik focused on teaching, lecturing, collecting, and editing Jewish texts for a new Hebrew-speaking audience. His early poems had made him famous, but he would write few major poems in Palestine, with the exception of some poems for children.

In Europe, Bialik and Joseph Klausner moved in the same literary and social circles. As editor of the influential Hebrew journal *HaShiloah*, Klausner published a great deal of Bialik's poetry. In response to the Kishinev pogrom of 1903 Bialik wrote his great poem "On the Slaughter." Klausner decided to publish the rousing, revolutionary poem in *HaShiloah*, despite fears that the

Russian government censor would not permit it.[43] When Klausner and Bialik both were living in British Mandate Palestine, political differences bedeviled their friendship. Klausner was a cultural figure on the political right; Bialik an icon of the political left.

In his translation of Klausner's *A History of Hebrew Literature, 1785–1930*, Danby emphasized and elaborated upon Klausner's praise of Bialik's work. Klausner's study was originally written and published in Russian, then expanded and translated by the author into Hebrew—and then translated from the Hebrew into English by Danby. Danby had been reading Bialik's prose and poetry long before the "national poet" moved to Palestine in 1923, and Danby was thrilled to meet and befriend the great writer. Danby brought Klausner's work to English-speaking readers; later, he did the same for Bialik's prose work.[44]

Both Bialik and Danby toiled in the twin realms of the rabbinic tradition, the legal and the narrative, the halachic and the aggadic. Danby's 1933 translation of the complete text of the Mishnah was his great contribution to Western study of halacha, Jewish law. His 1938 translation of Bialik's *And It Came to Pass* was his parallel contribution to the study of Aggadah.[45]

Danby was familiar with Bialik's influential essay "On Halachah and Aggadah." His close friendship with Bialik committed him to a series of English translations of Bialik's books. In 1938, four years after Bialik's death, Danby produced a vivid English translation of Bialik's *"Vayehi Hayom"—And it Came to Pass: Legends and Stories About King David and King Solomon*. This anthology was first published in Hebrew soon after Bialik's death in 1934. It consisted of thirty-five stories of these two kings of ancient Israel. Bialik had published these tales in literary journals during the last seven years of his life.[46]

And It Came to Pass is a kind of younger sibling to Bialik's grand project, *The Book of Legends*, an anthology compiled with the help of Y. H. Ravnitzky.[47] In both of these projects Bialik's technique was to mold the Talmudic legends into accessible and entertaining folktales that would appeal to both adults and children. To the ancient legends Bialik added material from later elaborations and retellings, including retellings of his own construction. Both books were readily accepted by the emergent Hebrew readership of the Yishuv. Part of Bialik's contribution was the translation of Talmudic legends from Aramaic into modern Hebrew. For young secular Palestinian Jews of the 1930s and 1940s Aramaic was a dead language; therefore, the vast compendium of lore and law in the Talmud was for them a closed book. The translation of this Aramaic material into modern Hebrew opened a new world of the imagination to readers young and old. As critic Mordechai ben Yehezkel noted: "It seems to me that no other book in its generation appeared in so many copies as this volume. The light of Torah and life suffuse it; and even though the translation from Aramaic to Hebrew causes some changes in the legends, this is something that only those with a classical Talmudic education will notice. . . . The influence of this book is so great, in both the moral and literary spheres, that it is hard to estimate its overall value."[48]

The Book of Legends enriched the vocabulary of modern Hebrew and provided a rich source of motifs for Hebrew poets, novelists, and short story writers. Bialik had written of the importance of the Jewish bookshelf, a literary canon in which secular Jews could find both enrichment and entertainment. *And It Came to Pass* and its elder sibling *The Book of Legends* were to become central texts of that new Jewish bookshelf. From the mid-1930s to the mid-1970s the book was read by generations of Israelis and copies could be found in many Israeli Jewish homes.

A year after the publication of his English translation of *And It Came to Pass*, Danby produced another translation of a work by Bialik—his *Knights of Onions and Garlic*. This is a delightful Hebrew poem that reflects Yiddish culture and humor. Danby's short introductory note describes the poem as "an elaboration of an anecdote current among the Jews of Eastern Europe." Published by New York's Hebrew Publishing Company, the volume is beautifully illustrated by Emanuel Romano. In both its Hebrew original and English translation *Knights of Onions and Garlic* delighted generations of readers. It was a folkloric piece of "wisdom literature" on the perils of greed and ambition.[49]

After devoting time to translating Bialik's renditions of Jewish legends, Danby returned to his first scholarly love, the translation of rabbinic legal texts. He was mindful that legends were but "handmaidens of the law" and delighted in citing Maimonides' injunction to memorize and analyze the rules of ritual purity: "If the greatest sages of the Mishnah found difficulties, how much more so must we? Do you not see how Rabbi Eleazar ben Azariah says to Rabbi Akiva, 'Akiva, why are you trifling with Aggadah. Let it be, and turn to (more serious problems like) leprosy signs and corpse uncleanness.' "[50]

Danby's most useful and widely used contribution to the study of Jewish texts was his Mishnah translation. This translation quickly became a standard text in the English-speaking world, and it remains in print seventy years after its publication. When, in 1988, Yale University Press published a new translation of the Mishnah, its editor, Jacob Neusner, made it clear that "publishing this fresh translation of the Mishnah constitutes no criticism of the great and pioneering translation by Herbert Danby. His translation has one fundamental flaw. . . . He does not make the effort to translate the Hebrew into English words following the syntax of Mishnaic Hebrew . . . that is what the present translation, into American English, provides."[51] While Neusner's translation takes us closer to the syntactical structure of the Hebrew of the Mishnah, Danby's translation renders that text more immediately accessible, and for that reason it remains the translation of record.

~

Danby as Regius Professor of Hebrew at Oxford

In 1936, after seventeen years in Jerusalem, Herbert Danby left St. George's and returned to Oxford University, where he was appointed Regius Professor of Hebrew and canon of Christ Church. While at Oxford Danby continued to make contributions to the development of modern Hebrew. Working with Professor M. Z. Segal of the Hebrew University, Danby produced a series of Hebrew-English and English-Hebrew dictionaries that had a significant effect on the development of modern Hebrew usage.[52] Danby taught his students at Oxford classical and modern Hebrew. In a course titled "From Kohelet to Klausner," Danby provided a year-long survey of Hebrew from its beginnings to its flowering as a written and spoken language in British Mandate Palestine.

Danby's return to the university in which he had been educated was the occasion for extended reflection on his career. In *Bible Lands*, the quarterly review that Danby founded in the 1920s, the new editors bid him farewell and provided a note on the church's understanding of why Bishop MacInnes had invited Danby to Jerusalem in 1919:

> The Bishop felt that the British Mandate for Palestine with promise of a National Home for the Jews would mean that the Church must rethink its way of approach to the Jews. He sought a man who could not only present Christianity to the Jews, but also one who from his knowledge and understanding of Jewish aspirations, could explain the Jewish mind to Christians. He found this man in Dr. Danby. . . . While Dr. Danby's work with and for the Jews had a first claim upon his time, his advice was constantly sought and used on all matters connected with the Christian schools in the Bishopric.[53]

This *Bible Lands* article glosses over the sharp contrast between Danby's positive view of Zionism and the Anglican Church's emerging negative view of it. By the end of the 1930s the dichotomy had sharpened. The various Palestine partition plans that were bandied about in the late 1930s were greeted by the Anglican Church with dismay: "In 1938 the Church of England's Council for Foreign Relations condemned the proposed partition of Palestine into Arab and Jewish states as against Christian interests, deplored political Zionism, and recommended that Britain retain Palestine indefinitely and put an end to Jewish immigration. Canon Danby was the only member of the Council to dissociate himself completely from the document."[54]

After he left Jerusalem for Oxford, Danby became more explicit about his interfaith work with Christians and Jews in Palestine. In a 1941 survey of the history of the Anglican Church in Jerusalem he presented his understanding of Zionism and of the young Jews who had come "to *live* in Palestine and there create a system of life, which while distinctively Jewish should rid itself of the deformities which had made Jews hateful to themselves and to others." In this survey Danby makes clear that his, and the church's, ultimate goal was to "bring the Jewish people into closer sympathy with the Christian faith. . . . May it be in our power to bring them still closer—into allegiance to the one Saviour."[55] We saw this conversionist agenda made explicit earlier in Danby's report to the bishop at the Budapest and Warsaw Conferences of 1935.

A less charitable view of the secular Jews of Palestine may be found in the memoirs of a colleague of Danby's at St. George's, Rev. C. H. Gill. Gill, like Danby, highlighted the differences between "Jews who had come to Palestine to die and those who had come there to live." Unlike Danby, he found the "new Jews" even more objectionable than the "old": "These new Jewish immigrants were of a type widely different from that of their Jewish predecessors. They were highly cultured, yet a very large proportion of them were without any effective religious faith."[56] The distinction between "old" and "new" Jews was a constant theme in Christian reflections on the Jews of British Mandate Palestine. In 1935, the Rev. G. L. B. Sloan, Anglican missionary in Tiberias, wrote of the *halutzim* of the neighboring kibbutzim: "These are not the old, stooping, decrepit type, relics of the Ghetto, with whom one so often comes in contact in Eastern Europe. They are fresh in their veins. With right they call themselves Halutzim—Pioneers."[57]

Advocacy of Christian missions to the Jews of Palestine did not mean a lessening of Danby's protective attitude toward Jews in general. In 1937, Danby, responding to an anti-Semitic tract by Nazi ideologue Alfred Rosenberg, penned a spirited defense of the Jewish tradition and the Jewish people. "Danby severely criticized Rosenberg, the Nazi scholar and the head of the German Foreign Affairs Section, who had just published his book *The Immorality of the Talmud*. Danby said that the book was full of malice, malignity and misquotations."[58] An anti-Nazi group in London, Friends of Europe, published selections of Rosenberg's *Unmoral im Talmud* as part of their pro-

gram "to provide accurate information about Nazi Germany for use . . .
wherever the English tongue is known." Danby's foreword and notes to that
translation present Rosenberg's attack on the Talmud within the context of
German historical anti-Semitism: "Utilization of selected extracts from ancient Jewish writings to bring discredit and ridicule on the Jews of more than a
thousand years later . . . is a practice with a long history in Germany."[59]

Danby was acutely aware that his own lineage of Christian Hebraism had
a legacy of anti-Semitic endeavors. He connected Rosenberg's twentieth-
century anti-Semitic tract to the seventeenth-century anti-Jewish anthologies
of Wagenseil and Eisenmenger: "Herr Rosenberg's pamphlet is but a puny
imitation of Eisenmenger's colossal volume; yet the spirit is the same, and it as
true to type as it is, like Eisenmenger, loose in its canons of accuracy."[60]
Descrying the "malice and malignity" with which Rosenberg selects and
presents quotations from the Talmud that put Jews and Judaism in a bad light,
Danby directs his readers to a familiar source: "It would be merely tiresome to
deal with each quotation in turn. . . . Much is made in Rosenberg's Chapter
Five of the alleged scurrilous references to Jesus in the Talmud. The reader
can find these objectively treated in Klausner's *Jesus of Nazareth*."[61]

∽

Danby after World War II

The aftermath of the murder of European Jewry during the Second World
War had a profound effect on Christian relationships to Jews and Judaism.
Danby led this shift in attitudes. Before the war, he had warned against anti-
Semitism. He had condemned Nazi policies and ideology, as we saw in his
polemic against Alfred Rosenberg. At the same time, he promoted missions to
the Jews. After the war, he gave up his conversionist ideas, or at least he never
spoke of them publicly.

In England, Danby developed a close friendship with the eminent Ortho-
dox Jewish scholar Rabbi Isadore Epstein. Another Jewish scholar with whom
Danby had both a personal and scholarly relationship was the American
Talmudist Saul Leiberman of the Jewish Theological Seminary. Working with
Leiberman, Danby translated sections of Maimonides' Laws of Purity for the
Yale Judaica series.[62]

At Oxford, Danby served in a prestigious professorship that had been
established by Henry VIII. Among his illustrious predecessors was Hebraist
Edward Pusey. Like Danby, these Oxford dons had been Anglican clergymen,
and their scholarly projects and conversations were conducted with other

Christian Hebraist colleagues. Rarely did Jewish Hebraism and Christian Hebraism meet. Danby, in contrast, brought the two disciplines, and their practitioners, together. He was the first holder of the Regius Professorship in Hebrew who was in direct scholarly conversation with Jewish scholars of Judaica.

At the time of his death in 1953, Herbert Danby was engaged in an ambitious and taxing project, the translation of Maimonides' *Code of Cleanliness*, a manual on the laws of purity and impurity. This translation was undertaken for the Yale Judaica series. Danby completed the translation part of the project —over 600 pages of English text in its final version. He did not live to complete an analytical introduction to this section of Maimonides' *Code*. Some of Danby's observations were summed up in editor Julian Obermann's foreword. Obermann wrote of Danby's work on the Maimonides translation, "Our esteem for his vast learning and scholarship became inseparable from our appreciation of his great wisdom and his glowing humanity."[63]

Danby, a philo-Semitic Christian Hebraist, was aware that criticism of the Talmud was also a theme in modern Jewish discourse. "Liberal Jews may rise superior to the Talmud," he wrote. But he emphasized that a Christian would benefit from studying it, "to scrutinize his specifically Jewish historical and religious origins." Such scrutiny, added Danby, might preserve Christians "from many vagaries"—including the heresy of Marcion, which rejects the Hebrew Bible, and the anti-Semitic trends of the 1930s.[64] For, "if the Jew did, in truth, become the deepest hater of Christianity, it was most certainly the Christian who had the largest share in making him so."[65]

It would be productive to compare Danby's work and life to those of another pro-Zionist Anglican clergyman, James Parkes (1896–1981). Parkes, Danby's slightly younger contemporary, attended Oxford University's Hertford College. It was at Oxford that Parkes first encountered British Jews and learned of the anti-Semitism they often encountered. During his last year at Oxford, he joined the staff of the Student Christian Movement (SCM). He later served as an SCM representative to European student organizations and learned of the worsening situation of Jewish students at European universities.[66] Though he was an excellent Greek and Latin student, Parkes did not embark on the study of Hebrew. This was a striking decision, as he was soon to make advocacy for Jewish rights and the call for Christian-Jewish understanding his life's work.

Danby, in contrast, had embarked on the study of biblical and post-biblical Hebrew while an undergraduate and made his language skills the key to his grand scholarly project, the complete and accurate translations of rabbinic classics. Danby worked within institutions: the Anglican Church and Oxford University. Parkes attempted to establish his own institutions for Jewish-Christian understanding and did not work directly for church institutions or serve a regular parish. Most often Parkes's work was supported by Jewish organizations that sought to advance Jewish-Christian dialogue.

Parkes sought reconciliation between Judaism and Christianity. Long before World War II, he objected to Christian missions to the Jews. Parkes, not knowing Hebrew, relied on translations, Danby's among them. Parkes's many books on Jewish history, Jewish-Christian relations, and the Land of Israel were informed by these translations. These books called for Christian support of Jews and Zionism. In *Judaism and Christianity* (1948), *The Story of Jerusalem* (1949), *A History of the Jewish People* (1962), and *Whose Land? A History of the Peoples of Palestine* (1970), he made the case for the Jewish state.

In a 1970 event that would have gladdened the heart of Herbert Danby, James Parkes was invited to preach at Jerusalem's St. George's Cathedral, an institution well-known for its anti-Israeli stance. In his sermon he called on Christians to reevaluate Judaism. He said that he considered it "the greatest tragedy of the first two millennia of Christian history that the apostolic age convinced itself that it had replaced Judaism."[67]

Unlike James Parkes, an outsider who was invited back on occasion to preach, Danby, in contrast, stayed within the institutions of the church. His life's work was in the translation and explication of rabbinic texts, and his support of Jews and Zionism was implicit within his work. Danby's decision as an Oxford student to study biblical and rabbinic Hebrews was pivotal in his life. But that decision did not subvert his commitment to the welfare of the Anglican Church and the furtherment of its missionary aims. Though Klausner and other Jewish associates of Danby overlooked, or were not aware of, his commitment to the conversion of the Jews, they were correct in assessing his enthusiasm for Zionism and the revival of the Hebrew language. In his eulogy of Danby, Klausner wrote that "even among the English, who produced George Eliot and Lord Balfour, there weren't many like him. . . . His pure memory will live among his people and his land, as it will live in our people and land—as a great person and an exemplary English Christian."[68]

Over the period that Herbert Danby and his fellow Anglican clergyman James Parkes were challenging anti-Zionism and anti-Semitism within their churches, the Catholic Church was undergoing its own very gradual transformation on these issues. It is that remarkable story that will concern us in the next chapter.

4

Rome and Jerusalem
Two Catholic Thinkers on Zionism and
Two Papal Visits to Jerusalem, 1964 and 2000

*In Catholic doctrine, adopted in the main also by the Protestant Episcopal
Churches, the survival of the Jewish people was held necessary merely to
bear visible witness to the truth of the biblical narratives and of the
Prophecies foretelling its downfall, humiliation, punishment.*[1]

In 1904, a few months before his death at the age of forty-four, Theodor Herzl
met with the Vatican secretary of state, Cardinal Merry del Val. Herzl asked
for Vatican diplomatic support to further the international recognition of the
Zionist cause. In response, the cardinal said: "I do not quite see how we can
take any initiative in this matter. As long as the Jews deny the divinity of
Christ, we certainly cannot make a declaration in their favor. Not that we have
any ill will toward them. On the contrary, the church has always protected
them. To us they are the indispensable witnesses to the phenomenon of God's
term on earth. But they deny the divine nature of Christ. How then can we,
without abandoning our own highest principles, agree to their being given
possession of the Holy Land again?"[2] This well-known statement by the
Vatican secretary of state did not indicate implacable hostility toward Jews.
Cardinal Merry del Val's declaration that the church has always protected the
Jews has a degree of historical validity that was given credence by his actions a
few years after his meeting with Herzl. With the revival of European blood
libels at the beginning of the twentieth century, del Val labeled the libels "an
incredible myth." He told Catholics that between the thirteenth and eighteenth centuries the popes had rejected again and again the veracity of claims
that Jews killed Christian children and used their blood in religious rituals,
particularly those of Passover. The cardinal reminded church congregants
that in the thirteenth century Pope Innocent IV had forbidden Catholics "to
accuse any Jew of using human blood in their rites, since it is clear in the Old

Testament that it is forbidden to them to consume any blood, let alone the blood of humans."[3]

A vivid illustration of papal protection of Jews occurred in the French city of Avignon in the fourteenth century. The papacy had moved its seat to Avignon in the first decades of that century and soon created an independent enclave in which the church had spiritual and temporal rule. Within that enclave the Jews of the city escaped the persecution that was the fate of many of their coreligionists in other parts of Western Europe. In 1913, Merry del Val, in keeping with this tradition, condemned strongly the prosecution of Mendel Beilis, a Jew of Kiev accused of ritual murder. Powerful members of the Russian Orthodox clergy had promoted these accusations, but the Roman cardinal spoke out against them.

Christians in each denomination developed varied understandings of the sanctity of the Holy Land. The land of Christian origins had always been an object of veneration and a place of pilgrimage for Christians because of its association with Jesus. What then should Christians make of Jewish claims to the Holy Land? On the question of a Jewish return to Palestine, the religious and political issues were radically different for Catholics and Protestants. Generally, Catholics, until Vatican II, upheld the teaching that the Jews were guilty of "deicide," and that the punishment for their crime was eternal exile. In keeping with that view, "Zionism must therefore be regarded as an arrogant presumption, in opposition to the will of God, who has punished His people, condemning them to exile and wandering."[4] For a growing number of Protestants in the past two centuries, Jews were spoken of as a people who retained a degree of chosenness; their claims to their ancestral land might still be considered. Of course, Protestant denominations differed among themselves in their understandings of the possibility of Jewish return and on interpretations of the Holy Land's role in their Christian doctrine.

Modern Jewish claims to, and eventual possession of, the Holy Land thus presented a formidable challenge to centuries-old Christian ideas. This was especially true for Catholics. How these challenges were met is the subject of this chapter. Changes in Catholic attitudes toward Zionism are here examined in the light of Catholic theology and papal diplomacy. A shift in attitude took place over the course of the twentieth century and culminated in Vatican diplomatic recognition of Israel in 1993 and Pope John Paul II's pilgrimage to Jerusalem in 2000.

Following the 1948 establishment of the State of Israel and its inclusion in the United Nations—both acts that the Vatican opposed—there was a series of low-level diplomatic conversations between Israeli officials and Vatican officials. High-ranking Catholic clergymen also made many visits to Israel. The church was concerned about both its real estate holdings and its flock in the Holy Land. Contacts between Israel and the Vatican waxed and waned over the subsequent forty-five years; it was not until 1993 that the Vatican granted Israel diplomatic recognition. The gradual steps that led to that recognition forms the structure of this account.

⌁

Popes and Theologians on Zionism and Israel

As of 2008, two popes have visited the State of Israel, Paul VI in 1964 and John Paul II in 2000. This chapter tells the stories of these two very different visits against the background of the dramatic ideological and political changes that led to these pilgrimages. The differences between these two papal visits highlight the dramatic change in Israel-Vatican and Jewish-Catholic relations during the second half of the twentieth century. This change, from mutual suspicion and rejection to an awkward embrace, came about gradually, with an acceleration of the process following World War II. The papal visits of 1964 and 2000 were important signifiers of the process of accommodation. During Paul VI's 1964 visit there was limited Vatican-Israeli interaction. John Paul II's visit to Jerusalem in 2000 was dramatically different. Although the visit seemed sudden, it was in fact the result of a long, drawn-out process. Both papal visits are best understood in the context of changes in both Middle Eastern political alliances and changes in Catholic-Jewish relations.[5]

This dramatic change in Catholic-Jewish and Vatican-Israel relations was influenced by two leading Catholic intellectuals, G. K. Chesterton (1874–1936) and Jacques Maritain (1882–1973). Both took stands on Catholic-Jewish relations and the question of Zionism, Chesterton in the 1920s and 1930s, Maritain from the 1930s through the 1960s. Chesterton, the twentieth century's most prominent Anglican convert to Roman Catholicism, visited Jerusalem in 1919. His account of this visit, *The New Jerusalem*, was widely read and commented upon in Britain and the United States. Considering Chesterton's often expressed unease with and hostility toward Jews and Judaism, his enthusiastic appraisal of Zionism was all the more surprising.

Maritain, like Chesterton, was a convert to the Roman Catholic Church. He was brought up in a secularized Protestant family and joined the Catholic Church as a young man. As the author of many philosophical works and a scholar of St. Thomas Aquinas's works, Maritain wielded considerable influence. By the 1950s and 1960s Maritain's influence extended to the Vatican and the papacy. His teachings were decisive in changing both official and unofficial Catholic views of the Jews. Maritain not only helped formulate the Vatican II response to the Nazi murder of two-thirds of Europe's Jews but also influenced the Vatican's reformulation of attitudes toward the State of Israel.

During their long and prolific careers both Chesterton and Maritain were accused of anti-Semitism. Endorsement of the Zionist cause enabled them to counter these charges and "repent" for earlier statements that might be read as inimical to Jews and Judaism. Both Chesterton and Maritain exerted considerable influence on Catholic intellectuals in the United States, particularly on the issue of Zionism. Chesterton, who lived in England, visited and wrote about the United States in the 1920s and recorded his impressions in his book *What I Saw in America*. His influence in the United States has grown in the post–World War II period. Maritain, who was born in France, lived in the United States for long periods between 1940 and 1960, part of that time as a professor at Princeton University.[6] He made a dual contribution to Catholic intellectual life, first in the more narrowly focused area of the history of ideas, particularly Aquinas studies, and then in the more general liberalization of Catholic attitudes toward other religions, a change reflected in the innovations of Vatican II.

Of these two literary and theological masters, Maritain's influence on Vatican policies toward Jews and Zionism was more direct. Chesterton exerted his influence through the popularity of his many books, *Orthodoxy* foremost among them, and through his wide readership among the Anglican and Catholic laity and clergy. Two popes, Paul VI and John Paul II, called Maritain their teacher. Marcel Dubois, a Dominican monk who moved to Israel in 1964 and spent the rest of his life there, most clearly demonstrated the influence of Maritain's pro-Zionist thought. Deeply engaged in Israeli cultural and religious life, Dubois taught in the Hebrew University philosophy department, of which he was chairman for many years. Along with his friend Father Bruno Hussar, Dubois lived at Jerusalem's Isaiah House. Father Hussar established Isaiah House in West Jerusalem in 1962 as a Catholic research center dedicated to Catholic-Jewish understanding. It also served as a community resource for Jerusalem's then small community of Hebrew-speaking Catholics.

After the 1967 war, these two Dominican friars helped found Neve Shalom/ Wahat al-Salam (Oasis of Peace), a multi-ethnic community in Israel. There Muslim, Christian, and Jewish families live in a small village on the outskirts of Jerusalem. The community serves as a living example of the possibility of peaceful interfaith relations within Israel. That the Dominican order would be a positive force in interfaith relations was a surprising development. For the

Dominicans, in the order's earliest years, had been one of the most vigorous opponents of Judaism.[7]

The Dominicans, founded in the thirteenth century by St. Dominic de Guzman, was charged with pursuing heretics, particularly those charged with the Albegensian heresy, and bringing them back to the church. Soon, the order directed its efforts toward the Jews. Along with the friars of the Franciscan order, Dominicans preached to captive Jewish audiences in synagogues. According to historian Jeremy Cohen, these friars "subjected Jews to offensive harangues, participation in debates whose outcomes had been predetermined, and the violence of the mob. The intent of the friars was obvious: to eliminate the Jewish presence in Christendom—both by inducing the Jews to convert and by destroying all remnants of Judaism even after no Jews remained."[8]

The Franciscan order, founded in the same period as the Dominicans, was given a related responsibility. They were to be the custodians of the sacred places in the Holy Land. St. Francis founded the order's trusteeship, the Custodia Terrae Sanctae (Catholic Custodian of the Holy Lands), on his visit to the Crusader Kingdom of Jerusalem. From the time of its founding in 1217, the Custodia has maintained a presence in Jerusalem, where it has often come into conflict with other Christian groups vying for real estate, power, and influence in the city. After 1948, and especially after 1967, the Custodia was in constant contact with the Israeli authorities. At times, there was considerable friction between the Franciscans and the Israeli authorities.

The twentieth-century Dominicans Dubois and Hussar, both of whom were influenced by the ideas of Jacques Maritain, transformed the Dominican order's attitudes toward Jews and the State of Israel, and facilitated the great change in the Catholic Church's understanding of the State of Israel. In the mid-1960s Father Hussar participated in the drafting of *Nostra Aetate* at Vatican II. To understand the full impact of Chesterton and Maritain on Catholic responses to Zionism, let us look at the church's stand on this issue before the writings of these two intellectuals facilitated a radical change in official church policy towards Jews, Judaism, and the State of Israel.

~

Early Political Zionism and the Vatican

The antagonistic response that the Vatican hierarchy gave Herzl in 1904 was not the first indication of Catholic displeasure with Zionism. Seven years earlier, the Vatican press had greeted Theodor Herzl's announcement of the First

Zionist Congress with scorn. The newspaper *Civiltà Cattolica* condemned Zionism in theological terms:

> 1[,]827 years have passed since the prediction of Jesus of Nazareth was fulfilled, namely that is that Jerusalem would be destroyed . . . that the Jews would be led away to be slaves among all the nations, and that they would remain in the dispersion till the end of the world. . . . According to the Sacred Scriptures, the Jewish people must always live dispersed and wandering among the other nations, so that they may render witness to Christ not only by the Scriptures . . . but by their very existence. As for a rebuilt Jerusalem, which would become the center of a reconstituted state of Israel, we must add that this is contrary to the prediction of Christ Himself.[9]

This article clearly stated the theological grounds for the Vatican's opposition to Zionism. *Civiltà Cattolica* was a Jesuit newspaper known for its anti-Semitic tendencies. Founded in 1850, "it came to be regarded as the unofficial voice of the pope himself."[10] Informed readers understood what it had to say about Zionism as the official Vatican response to Herzl's request for Vatican support for a Jewish state.

The histories of the Catholic and the Protestant churches are riddled with anti-Jewish statements and actions. But on the question of Zionism there is a significant difference between official Protestant and Catholic views. In contrast to the diversity of Protestant responses to Zionism, some of which were positive and some negative, the official Catholic response was clearly negative. The Vatican opposed Zionism in both its political and cultural manifestations. The prospect of a Jewish state in the Christian Holy Land, a land hallowed for Christians by its association with the life of Jesus, was threatening to the Vatican. Zionism, and later the State of Israel, presented the church with a problem. Renewed Jewish sovereignty in Palestine, and the possibility of Jewish cultural and religious renaissance in the reclaimed land, challenged the Catholic Church's view of Judaism as a superseded religion and its view of Jews as a people condemned to permanent exile.

With the advent of Zionism, the church's uneasy relationship with the Jewish people, marked by frequent persecution and humiliation of Jews in Catholic lands, was intensified by the addition of a Jewish territorial claim, a claim that the church hierarchy mocked. In the words of mid-twentieth historian Jules Isaac, the essence of Christian anti-Judaism was "the teaching of contempt," a teaching inculcated by the Catholic Church. Throughout the

Second Christian millennium this contempt was a dominant aspect of Christian attitudes and actions toward Jews. The Dominican and Franciscan orders were founded, in part, to convert Jews and heretics to the true church. What, then, were Catholics to make of plans to establish a state for and by a people that the church had held in contempt since its establishment by St. Peter? Since the Jews had rejected Jesus, they had lost their chosenness; the church had replaced the Jews in God's favor and thus had become Verus Israel, the true Israel. The old or "carnal" Israel no longer had a claim to what the Catholic Church deemed the Christian Holy Land. Why, then, should the church support Zionism, a political movement that aimed to end the exile to which the Jews had been justly condemned?

A few weeks after the 1897 condemnation of Zionism in *Civiltà Cattolica*, Herzl met with the papal nuncio in Vienna. For Herzl, the results of the meeting were discouraging. He recorded the following in his diary: "Result of the conversation: I believe Rome will be against us, because she does not consider the solution of the Jewish question in a Jewish state, and perhaps even fears it."[11]

Although he was pessimistic about Catholic support for Zionism, Herzl remained optimistic about Anglican and Protestant support. He had been in close contact with Protestant clergymen since the preparations for the First Zionist Congress of 1897. Anglican clergyman Rev. William Hechler, who had articulated support for the restoration of the Jews as early as 1883, helped Herzl obtain an audience with the Duke of Baden and his nephew Kaiser Wilhelm. Other Protestant clergymen and laymen, including a number of Americans, were associated with the seemingly contradictory nineteenth-century combination of Protestant missions to the Jews and support for a Jewish home in Palestine. In the late nineteenth century, Christians assisting in the restoration of the Jews to their land were for the most part Protestants of the various denominations; Catholic and Eastern Orthodox Christians tended to be hostile to Zionist aims.

~

Christian Holy Sites and the Ottomans

When approaching Vatican officials, Herzl was well aware of the church's political and theological opposition to Zionism, and he had no illusions about countering it or changing it. Rather, he hoped to convince the church that Jewish rule in the Holy Land would be better for Vatican interests than the past

400 years of Ottoman Turkish rule had been. Since the schism between the Eastern and Western churches in the eleventh century, control over Christian sacred sites in Palestine had been continuously contested. From the thirteenth century onward, the Custodia Terrae Sanctae, administered by the Franciscan order, controlled the Catholic holy sites in Jerusalem. From the Vatican perspective, the Ottoman authorities had for centuries favored the competing claims of the Greek Orthodox Church. There was thus great tension between the Greek Orthodox Church, which owned many of the Christian holy sites in Palestine, and the Roman Catholic Church. Under these conditions, Anglican and Protestant missionaries and churches had little chance of establishing a presence in Palestine. This situation changed when Mehmet Alis's conquest of Palestine in 1831 opened Palestine to Western influence.

After 1840, with British help, Palestine returned to Ottoman control; Protestant officials and missionaries then were able to gain considerable influence. Many Protestant missionaries—British, American, and others—were living in Palestine, a situation that threatened Catholic authority. The Vatican, alarmed by the formation of the joint Prussian-British Jerusalem bishopric and the growing presence of Protestant missionaries, strengthened its presence in the Holy Land. Despite its unhappiness with Ottoman control of the Holy Land, the Vatican preferred that situation to the possibility of either Protestant or Jewish control.

As Protestant denominations were formulating their attitudes and policies toward the holy places in Palestine, some Anglican intellectuals found these new policies disturbing and unsettling. The Anglican-Lutheran alliance of the 1840s, an alliance formed to establish the Jerusalem bishopric at Christ Church in Jerusalem, helped drive John Henry Newman into the arms of the Catholic Church. At Oxford, he had emphasized the spiritual ties between England and Rome. Newman had begun his spiritual pilgrimage to the Roman Church much earlier, but the Anglo-Lutheran alliance alienated him ever further from the leadership of the Anglican Church. In Newman's eyes, the alliance between Anglicans and German Lutherans threatened the integrity of the Church of England. According to Newman: "The Jerusalem Bishopric was the ultimate condemnation of the old theory of the *Via Media*—if its establishment did nothing else, at least it demolished the sacredness of diocesan rights. If England could be in Palestine, Rome might be in England."[12] As Frank M. Turner, Cardinal Newman's most recent biographer, has noted, "From its inception, the Jerusalem bishopric provoked a negative reaction in Newman, recognized by almost all of his friends as disproportional, extreme, and vehement. . . . Newman further complained to his sister Jemima that by cooperating with the Prussians in appointing a bishop for Jerusalem, the Church of England was 'forming a special league which she has never done before with the foreign Protestants.' "[13]

The German kaiser's reason for supporting the Protestant bishopric had less to do with the sanctity of Jerusalem and the conversion of the Jews than it had to do with achieving Protestant unity within Germany. In sharp contrast to the motives of the kaiser, both British diplomatic authorities and Anglican ecclesiastical authorities linked the joint bishopric to support for restoration of the Jews to their land and their eventual conversion to Protestant Christianity. For this reason the first bishop chosen for this new church—Christ Church—was Michael Solomon Alexander, an English rabbi who had apostatized in the late 1830s and then actively sought the conversion of the Jews of Jerusalem to Anglican Christianity. Herzl's associate Rev. William Hechler was drawn to support the Jerusalem bishopric seat in Christ Church and record its history. As a young man, Hechler had aspired to lead that church some day. The worship services in Christ Church, which was built near the Jaffa Gate, were conducted in Hebrew for the small but growing group of Jewish converts to the Anglican Church. In the 1880s there were perhaps fifty converted Jews who were regular members of Christ Church. By 1900 their number had grown to close to a hundred. Shunned by Jerusalem's diverse Jewish communities, these Jewish converts soon constituted yet another religious minority in Jerusalem.

At Herzl's 1897 meeting with the papal nuncio, the vexed question of the Christian holy sites came immediately to the fore. If a Jewish state were established, who would control the Christian shrines? Aware that, aside from its theological resistance to the notion of a Jewish state, the church was deeply concerned not only about its role in Jerusalem as protector of Catholic sites but also about competition with non-Catholic churches, Herzl immediately explained to the nuncio that the Zionist plan aimed to make parts of Jerusalem "extraterritorial." To which the nuncio replied, "You propose, then, to exclude Jerusalem, Bethlehem and Nazareth, and set up the capital, I take it, more to the north?" To this comment Herzl gave a vaguely affirmative reply, which seemed to mollify the nuncio.[14] If the Zionists did not claim the Christian holy places, thought Herzl, perhaps the Vatican might consider Zionist aspirations more positively. But Herzl's vague assertion did not satisfy Vatican officials, who wanted firm assurances that Christian holy places would not be under direct control of Jewish authorities.

Disappointed that the Vatican, Germany, and France had all failed to support Zionism, Herzl and the other leaders of the official Zionist movement chose to seek support in England. Chaim Weizmann and other leading Zionist thinkers suggested that the future of the Yishuv and of the Zionist movement generally, should be linked to British power and influence. In the nineteenth century some clerics in the Anglican Church and many of the dissenting churches had supported Zionist plans. Some British cabinet members had expressed support for the restoration of the Jews to their Land. Therefore, in the first years of the twentieth century, the Zionist movement greatly strengthened its presence in London, where it was supported by many but not all English Jews and many influential Christians—both Anglicans and Dissenters. Within a few decades this move would have far-reaching consequences. With its strong English presence, the Zionist movement was situated to influence English public opinion during and after the First World War. A parallel and analogous development was the decision by David Ben-Gurion and his associates in the mid-1940s to shift the center of the Zionist movement to the United States. With war raging in Europe and Britain standing alone against the Nazis, it made sense to reestablish and revitalize the Zionist organization in the United States.

Seven years after his 1897 meeting with the papal nuncio in Vienna, a meeting at which control of the Christian holy places dominated the conversation, Herzl obtained an audience with Pope Pius X. This audience, held three days after his discouraging meeting with Cardinal Merry del Val, was equally disappointing. Pius X told Herzl: "We won't be able to stop the Jews from going to Jerusalem, but we could never favor it. . . . The Jews have not recognized our Lord, and so we cannot recognize the Jewish people. . . . The Jewish faith was the foundation of our own, but it has been superseded by the teachings of Christ, and we cannot admit that it enjoys any validity." When Herzl asked about the church's attitude toward Jerusalem, the pope replied: "I know it is not pleasant to see the Turks in possession of our holy places. We simply have to put up with that. But to support the Jews in the acquisition of the holy places, that we cannot do."[15] Herzl's hope that the Vatican would prefer Jewish rule in Jerusalem to Turkish rule were dashed. As distasteful as it was for the Catholic Church in Jerusalem to be subject to the local dictates of the Muslim authorities, it was less objectionable than reversing the church's age-old power relationship with the Jews, a relationship in which Judaism was understood as vanquished and Jews in Catholic lands were subject to the dictates of the church.

⌒

G. K. Chesterton on Jews and the Zionist Movement

Early in the twentieth century, Zionist leaders recognized that some Catholic intellectuals were sympathetic to Zionist aspirations despite the official position of the Vatican. In 1922, Chaim Weizmann wrote that he did not believe that "the Vatican policy in this matter necessarily corresponds to the views of the Roman Catholic world at large. . . . On the other hand, so far as the Curia was concerned, there is no doubt that we have to contend with an implacable hostility."[16] To what extent did the views of the Catholic laity differ from the official positions of the church hierarchy? One dissenter from the then dominant Catholic view of Zionism was G. K. Chesterton (1874–1936), who was among the most influential writers of his time. Today his literary legacy and influence is still very much alive. Many of his books are still in print, and they continue to influence religious thinkers and the general public.

Chesterton's books were read widely in the United States. As historian Patrick Allitt has noted: "Among the English Catholics whose work was widely read in America in the late nineteenth and early twentieth century, nearly all were converts. . . . Chesterton was widely recognized in his day and since as a master of English prose, and he gave to this convert generation much of its distinctive voice and mood."[17] Throughout the twentieth century and into the twenty-first, Chesterton's ideas and attitudes have influenced many Americans of all religious traditions.

Chesterton's many works, especially his early books, are sprinkled with derogatory comments about Jews. His accounts of early-twentieth-century financial scandals in Britain and on the Continent are riddled with accusations that Jewish financiers were behind each of the scandals. Chesterton's antipathy to Jews was inspired and fostered by his friendship with the British Catholic critic and essayist Hilaire Belloc. Together, they opposed Britain's entanglement in the Boer War. Chesterton "came to share Belloc's view that a Jewish oligarchy, only partially assimilated to British life, was corrupting the government and Parliament."[18] That Jewish oligarchy, Chesterton and Belloc claimed, had maneuvered Britain into the war. Later, both Belloc and Chesterton smarted under the accusations that they were anti-Semites. Eventually, both would support Zionism, though with differing degrees of enthusiasm. Belloc was a reluctant supporter; Chesterton an enthusiastic one.

Today, Britain's G. K. Chesterton Institute is overly sensitive to charges that Chesterton was an anti-Semite. On its website the institute directors note that

G. K. Chesterton (Sheed and Ward)

the author "certainly made anti-Jewish remarks. . . . These need to be understood in their social and historical context, not in order to whitewash Chesterton, but to see how they do not invalidate his entire intellectual or spiritual legacy."[19]

British sensitivity to Chesterton's anti-Jewish remarks emerged only after World War II. In a February 1945 essay titled "Anti-Semitism in Britain," George Orwell noted that "Chesterton's endless tirades against Jews, which he thrust into stories and essays upon the flimsiest pretexts, never got him into trouble—indeed Chesterton was one of the most generally respected figures in English literary life. Anyone who wrote in that strain *now* would bring down a storm of abuse upon himself, or more probably would find it impossible to get his writings published."[20] Chesterton's anti-Jewish tirades included allegations that Jews were in control of international finance and that they were a threat to English Christian values. For Chesterton, a Jew could never change; he would always remain a foreigner to British culture. And as resident foreigners, wealthy Jews were attempting to control Britain. "The Jews," he wrote, "already exercise colossal cosmopolitan financial power."[21] In Chesterton's view, the "Jewish Problem" stemmed from the fact that Jews were essentially different from the peoples among whom they lived. That difference should always be made apparent and openly marked; therefore, Jews should not be allowed to assimilate. This marking would enable non-Jews to distance themselves from any "Jewish taint": "Let a Jew be Archbishop of Canterbury, if our national religion has attained to that receptive breadth that would render such a transition unobjectionable and even unconscious . . . let him preach in St. Paul's Cathedral, but let him sit there dressed as an Arab."[22]

In contrast to these condemnations of Jews, Chesterton's *The New Jerusalem*, an account of his 1919 tour of Palestine, concluded with a spirited defense of Zionism. That Chesterton made anti-Semitic remarks within the very same book should not surprise us. He admired the "new Jew" of Palestine and hoped that British Jews would move to Palestine and transform themselves into the Middle Easterners they really were. It was the "old Jews" of Europe that he disdained. Chesterton's account of his Christmas 1919 voyage to Jerusalem described a transformative spiritual pilgrimage. *The New Jerusalem*, published in 1920, proved a very popular book in both England and the United States. Some of Chesterton's remarks on the Holy Land now seem prescient, or perhaps indicative of a mind-set that was later to become dominant. Visiting the Temple Mount/Haram al-Sharif, Chesterton felt "the burden of Palestine: there is no place for the Temple of Solomon but on the ruins of the Mosque of Omar. There is no place for the nation of the Jews but in the country of the Arabs. . . . I felt almost a momentary impulse to flee from the place, like one who has received an omen. For two voices had met in my ears; and within the same narrow space and in the same dark hour, electric and yet eclipsed with cloud, I heard Islam crying from the turret and Israel wailing at the wall."[23] Chesterton's remark was not meant to equate the two religious claims to the city but, rather, to highlight their incompatibility. For him, neither Muslims nor Jews, but Christians, held the true claim to Jerusalem's spiritual legacy.

Chesterton was a journalist and polemicist, not a systematic thinker. He wrote more than 100 books, so perhaps it is unreasonable to expect his views to be consistent throughout his work. On one level, *The New Jerusalem* is an extended meditation on the history of the monotheistic religions, a meditation composed on the eve of Chesterton's conversion from Anglicanism to Catholicism. On a more superficial level, the book is a travel narrative. Primarily, the book calls for a return to medieval Christian ideals. Contrasted to these ideals is the culture of Islam. Throughout the book, Chesterton condemns Islam, which he dubs "the way of the desert." For Chesterton, complexity and contradiction marked the history of Christianity; Islam "takes everything literally, and does not know how to play with anything." Muslims, Chesterton claims, "suffer from a lack of vitality that comes from complexity, and of complexity that comes from comparison." He dubs Islam "This great religion of simplicity."[24] But despite his aversion to Islam, Chesterton is susceptible to the charms of Islamic cities, especially Cairo, which he visits on the way to Jerusalem.

Chesterton claims that Jews, caught between the idea of chosenness and the harsh reality of exile, can be redeemed only by a return to their homeland. His condemnation of the old "ghetto Jew" and his praise of the "new Jew" of the Zionist pioneers endeared Chesterton to Chaim Weizmann and other Zionist spokesmen. For both Chesterton and political Zionists valorized the emergence of the "new Jew" and the decline of the "old Jew." Freed from the burdens of exile, Jews would no longer exhibit the traits that made them objectionable to Christians. Thus through Zionism the "Jewish question" would be solved to the satisfaction of both Christians and Jews. Muslims, of course, were never brought into consideration in this European-oriented equation.

Chesterton found support for his critique of Jews in the Zionist analysis of Jewish life in exile. Zionists, he noted, offer "a diagnosis and a remedy." The diagnosis is that "any abnormal qualities in the Jews are due to the abnormal position of the Jews . . . for exile is the worst kind of bondage."[25] The remedy, for Zionists as for Chesterton, is a return to the land and physical labor. For Chesterton, this return to the land might not bring Jews to Jesus, but it would "cure" them of their attachment to urban landscapes, scholarly pursuits, and financial chicanery. Two years after Chesterton published *The New Jerusalem*, his friend Hilaire Belloc published *The Jews*. A strange work, the book purports to condemn anti-Semitism but at the same time indulges in it. Belloc writes that "the anti-Semitic movement is essentially a reaction against the abnormal growth in Jewish power, and the new strength of anti-Semitism is largely due to the Jews themselves."[26] As to whether Zionism could provide a solution to the Jewish issue, Belloc, unlike Chesterton, was somewhat skeptical. He did not believe the Jews were capable of fighting for and protecting their own state. Fifteen years later, however, in a 1937 introduction to a third edition of *The Jews*, Belloc was somewhat more sympathetic toward Zionist aspirations, but he remained doubtful that Jews would be accepted in the Arab Middle East.

A remarkable aspect of Chesterton's advocacy for the Zionist cause was that in the early 1920s, the years in which he published *The New Jerusalem* and wrote pro-Zionist articles, the Vatican was engaged in a vigorous diplomatic campaign to stop the League of Nations from assigning to Britain the Palestine mandate, a mandate that the Vatican feared would enable the emergence of a Jewish state. In a May 1922 letter to the League of Nations, Cardinal Pietro Gasparri, the Vatican secretary of state, wrote, "The Holy See is not opposed to the Jews in Palestine having civil rights equal to those possessed by other nationals and creeds, but it cannot agree to the Jews being given a privileged and preponderant position in Palestine vis-à-vis other confessions."[27] In contrast, Chesterton, who had recently converted to Catholicism, advocated giving Jews a privileged position in Palestine. The Zionist movement welcomed his support warmly.

When *The New Jerusalem* was published, some American Jewish leaders, familiar with Chesterton's earlier diatribes against Jews and alarmed by echoes of this hostility in his new book, condemned the book's "Jew baiting." Chesterton's support of Zionism was often mentioned or applauded as a way of countering these charges of anti-Semitism. Ultimately, this argument seems to have won out. Prominent Jewish spokesmen declared Chesterton "a friend."

In a January 1921 sermon at New York City's Temple Beth El, Rabbi Samuel Schulman delivered a sermon titled "Chesterton's *The New Jerusalem* and his Jew Baiting." Rabbi Schulman, a vocal anti-Zionist within the Reform movement, felt compelled "to take note of a book which has great literary merit, and therefore, is guilty of proportionate moral delinquency." In an interview with the *New York Times*, Rabbi Schulman said: "I am not a Zionist, and one of the reasons why I am not a Zionist is that I have always felt that Zionism would coax from every hole an anti-Semitic serpent. I will not do Mr. Chesterton the favor of becoming a Zionist."[28] Despite Rabbi Schulman's condemnation, Chesterton's reputation among Jewish readers soared. The Zionist argument prevailed. Ultimately, Chesterton was exonerated in the eyes of the American Jewish community.

Chesterton's support of Zionism in the 1920s and his condemnation of Hitler in the 1930s earned him the gratitude of some Jewish leaders. Soon after Chesterton's death in 1936, Rabbi Stephen Wise, then among the country's leading Zionists, wrote, "Indeed I was a warm admirer of Gilbert Chesterton. . . . Apart from his delightful art and his genius in many directions, he was, as you know, a great religionist. When Hitlerism came, he was one of the first to speak out with all the directness and frankness of a great unabashed spirit. Blessing to his memory."[29] As we saw in the previous chapter, Rabbi

Wise's 1925 lecture on Jesus, which was widely condemned by American Jewish leaders, was also a target of Rabbi Schulman's ire. Attacks on Rabbi Wise, chairman of the United Palestine Appeal, threatened the fund-raising capabilities of the American Zionist movement. As in the case of Chesterton, Zionist pragmatism won out over Christian-Jewish theological difference.

Michael Coren, one of Chesterton's most astute biographers, notes that to say that Chesterton and Belloc were not anti-Semites *because* they supported Zionism "is a fatuous and ludicrously badly informed explanation." Rather, says Coren, they should be seen as among a group of "chauvinistic intellectuals of the 1920s who spent a lot of time and ink on the possibility of 'resettlement' and for a brief period felt confident that a Jew-free Europe could be achieved."[30] For Chesterton and Belloc, Jews, fundamentally "other" in Christian Europe, should have a land of their own. J. Pearce, another Chesterton biographer, notes that, "The main reason for the eventual reconciliation between Chesterton and the Jews was, ironically and paradoxically, the anti-Semitism of Hitler. The Jews forgave Chesterton his earlier indiscretions because 'he was the first to speak out when the real testing time came,' and Chesterton softened his attitude to Jews because he was horrified to see the hardening of attitudes in Germany and its results."[31]

Chesterton's work exerted great influence on the Anglican and Catholic laity. Many in the clergy praised his work, particularly his book on Thomas Aquinas. Maritain, Chesterton's younger contemporary, who survived the English writer by thirty-seven years, had greater influence on the Catholic hierarchy. Both writers wrote books on the continuing relevance of the works of Thomas Aquinas. In this they were both part of the neo-Thomist revival in early-twentieth-century Catholicism. In Chesterton's immensely popular *St. Thomas Aquinas*, published in 1933, the older writer approvingly cites the young Maritain's early work on Aquinas, the "Angelic Doctor."

Chesterton died at seventy in 1936; a few years earlier he had condemned Nazi persecution of the Jews and distanced himself from Hilaire Belloc's vitriolic anti-Jewish statements. Perhaps the most perceptive assessment of Chesterton's relationship with Jews is from Anthony Read and David Fisher's *Kristallnacht: The Nazi Night of Terror*: "Belloc, like his friend Chesterton, like so many of the English Middle class, was prejudiced against Jews. He did not like them. . . . [Chesterton] nevertheless, was not anti-Semitic, certainly not in the Nazi sense, and the idea of employing physical brutality against a single Jew would have appalled him. He was an honourable man, uneasily aware that there was something going on in Germany of which, in conscience, he could not approve."[32]

Chesterton, who was considered by many in the English-speaking world a leading spokesman for Catholicism, condemned Nazi persecution of the Jews in a way that the official spokesmen of the Catholic Church could or would not. In the 1920s and 1930s, the Vatican concluded a series of agreements with Italian and German Fascists, creating the perception among some observers that the church supported the anti-Semitism endemic in Fascist regimes. While many in the church protected and saved Jews from Nazi persecution, the Vatican did not or could not issue an unequivocal condemnation of Nazi racial policy. And, as we have seen, the Vatican was clearly opposed to Zionism. Chesterton advocated for a Jewish state in Palestine during the same period when the Vatican was doing all it could to prevent that state from coming into being.

~

Jacques Maritain, the Shoah, and Israel

Jacques Maritain helped shape Catholic attitudes toward the Jewish people and the State of Israel. From 1944 to 1947 he served as French ambassador to the Vatican and in that capacity worked to improve Vatican-Jewish relations. His great standing as a scholar of Catholic thought and doctrine—including his early work on Aquinas—brought him into close contact with members of the Vatican hierarchy. At Vatican II Paul VI called Maritain "my teacher." On the establishment of Israel in 1948, Maritain wrote about the new state and its place among the nations: "Israel is the Jesus among the nations, and the Jewish diaspora within Europe is one long Via Dolorosa."[33] This concern for and interest in Jews occupied the philosopher throughout his intellectual life. From before his conversion to Catholicism in 1906 to shortly before his death in 1973, Maritain wrote often about Catholicism's relationship to the Jewish people.

Maritain married Raissa Oumansoff, a Russian Jewish woman, in 1904. She was one year his junior. Soon after they met, they had promised each other that they would commit suicide if they could not live a meaningful religious life. Jacques was from a secularized French Protestant family. Raissa's parents were from a secular Jewish family; her grandparents were Hasidic Jews. Did Maritain's marriage to Raissa sensitize him to Jewish concerns? It seems so. Both students at the Sorbonne, they were married in a civil ceremony. Each had cut their ties to the religious traditions of their families. Together they embarked on a spiritual journey that led to their baptism into the Catholic Church two years after their marriage. The young couple then found a spiri-

Jacques Maritain (The Jacques Maritain Center)

tual home in the Catholic Church. In their writings the Maritains often make reference to their early life outside of the church and of the solace they found within it.

The strongest early influence on young Jacques and Raissa were the teachings of French philosopher Henri Bergson. Raissa's close reading of Aquinas's *Summa Theologica*, to which she introduced her husband, led Jacques to write his first monograph, *Bergsonian Philosophy and Thomism*, in 1914. Their study of Aquinas's teachings, which would be their intellectual focus and anchor for the rest of their lives, allowed the couple to "reconcile their artistic interests with their religious activities . . . intellectually, as Christians, they could thereby be devotees of the latest poetry, the latest music, and the latest literature."[34]

Among the artists they admired and befriended in the artistically vibrant Paris of the first decade of the twentieth century was novelist Léon Bloy. Jacques Maritain dubbed Bloy a "critic of bourgeois values, a writer of great originality . . . prophet of authentic Christianity."[35] Bloy's novels mocked the French bourgeoisie and joyfully anticipated the violent end of a complacent social order. In Léon Bloy's life and work the Maritains found absolute religious conviction linked to artistic integrity, a combination so appealing that it led them to join the Catholic Church. Bloy lived in great poverty, and the Maritains, "disgusted with their education, their social class, and modern life, were fascinated with the absolute conviction with which Bloy . . . prophesied the end of the world."[36] Though Bloy's main ire was directed at "the self-satisfied niceties of a supposedly Christian society," he often expressed disdain for Jews and Judaism. "Strictly speaking," wrote Bloy, "I know that the Jews can be called our 'brothers.' But to love them as such is a proposition revolting to nature."[37]

What makes Maritain's later advocacy for Jews and Israel so remarkable is that early in his career he supported the ideology of Léon Bloy and other conservative French Catholic thinkers of the 1920s. In a 1921 essay influenced by Bloy's work, Maritain wrote that Jews "fatally play a subversive role in the world." He called for the Jewish renunciation of Zionism. Like Bloy, Maritain saw the "good Jew" as a convert to Catholicism. The context here is the French Catholic Right's fear of Jews as agents of liberalism and subversion, a fear that the young Maritain was caught up in.

At the end of the 1920s Maritain disassociated himself from Léon Bloy and his colleagues in Action Française, the French Catholic reactionary movement. The Vatican had condemned the Rightist group. From then on Maritain allied himself with political liberals; religiously he remained a devout Catholic. During the Spanish Civil War he spoke out in defense of the Republican cause, although many other French Catholic intellectuals supported Franco. During World War II Maritain attacked Catholic leaders and thinkers who allied themselves with Fascism.[38] In the postwar period, his ideas were considered too liberal for mainstream Catholic institutions in Europe and the United States. During his sojourn in the United States, Notre Dame University, wary of Maritain's liberalism, declined to invite him to teach. Princeton, with its Protestant roots, was more receptive to his political and religious views.

To today's Jewish reader, much of what Maritain wrote in his early years about Jews and Judaism remains deeply disturbing. Like Chesterton, his early view was that Jews' "contrary" nature was immutable. The Jewish refusal to accept Jesus was a stumbling block to any Christian embrace of the Jewish people. In the 1930s, Maritain changed his attitude toward Jews and Judaism. In response to Rightist French criticism of Jews, Maritain wrote: "Israel is a priestly people. I have met arrogant Jews; I have also encountered high-minded Jews of generous heart, men who were born poor and died poorer still, whose happiness was in giving, not acquiring."[39] With the rise of Nazism in Germany, Maritain joined other French intellectuals in a call to distance the church from political anti-Semitism. In 1935, responding to the Nuremberg Laws, Oscar de Ferenzy, one of Maritain's close colleagues argued: "I defend Israel because Jesus was the descendant of David. I defend Israel because I am a Christian; as a Christian, I have the duty to come to its aid."[40]

In his 1939 book *A Christian Looks at the Jewish Question*, Maritain condemned the Nazi persecutions: "If the world hates the Jews, it is because the world clearly senses that they will always be outsiders in a supernatural sense, it is because the world detests their passion for the absolute and the unbearable stimulus which it inflicts. It is the vocation of Israel which the world execrates. To be hated by the world is their glory, as it is also the glory of Christians who live by faith."[41] Despite his harsh critique of Christian persecution of Jews, Maritain was insistent on maintaining the Vatican's century-old distinction between anti-Semitism and anti-Judaism. In a postwar letter to Sir Robert Mayer dated 9 November 1954, Maritain wrote: "Christianity is not, and cannot be, anti-Semitic . . . but any kind whatever of *Christian civilization* is neither the church, nor Christianity. Medieval anti-Semitism . . . was totally different from racist anti-Semitism."[42] A full exposition of the defense of the church against charges that Christian doctrine was the source and cause of the Nazi murders may be found in Father Edward Flannery's *The Anguish of the Jews: Twenty-three Centuries of Anti-Semitism*. Referring to Jules Isaac's critique of Christian anti-Semitism, Flannery claimed that Isaac "exaggerated the historical bond between Christian anti-Semitism and the Hitlerian model. How much more historically plausible it is to see Hitlerian racist anti-Semitism as the creature of modern laicism, the modern revolt against God, rather than a fruit of Christian teaching. . . . It is possible, nonetheless[,] to agree that anti-Semitic forces in Christian tradition exerted a secondary or tertiary influence on the emergence of racist anti-Semitism."[43]

Critics of this distinction argue that the historical record demonstrates the continuity of classical medieval anti-Semitism with nineteenth- and twentieth-century racialist anti-Semitism. According to historian David Kertzer, the Catholic Church, by denying this connection, tried to exonerate itself from complicity in the Nazi persecution and murder of Europe's Jews.[44]

The rise of fascism, the Nazi rape of Europe, and the murder of Europe's Jews in World War II changed Maritain's actions and to some extent his theology. He became a lifelong supporter of politically liberal causes—including the United Nations—and an advocate for the establishment and support of a Jewish state. Among Maritain's Jewish interlocutors was Maurice Samuel, author of *The Great Hatred*, a 1940 study of anti-Semitism in European Christian history. Maritain was taken with Samuel's reading of Nazi ideology as "anti-Christian." He quotes approvingly from Samuel's analysis of Nazi anti-Semitism as a thinly disguised hatred of Christianity: "We shall never understand the maniacal, world-wide seizure of anti-Semitism unless we transpose the terms. It is of Christ that the Nazi-Fascists are afraid. . . . Therefore, they must, I repeat, make their assault on those who were responsible for the birth of the spread of Christianity. They must spit on the Jews as 'Christ-killers' because they long to spit on the Jews as Christ-givers."[45]

Maritain spoke out against anti-Semitism before the outbreak of World War II and he continued to condemn it both during and after the war. He would become a pivotal figure in the Catholic Church's postwar reassessment of its relationship with the Jews, a relationship unalterably transformed by the murder of two-third's of Europe's Jews during the Second World War. Still, it was not until the early 1960s that Maritain's teachings on Israel began to reach and influence the corridors of Vatican power. During and immediately after the war, the Vatican remained adamantly opposed to the creation of a Jewish state, a position that popes, cardinals, and papal nuncios had expressed from the time of the First Zionist Congress of 1897. In a 1943 letter to Myron Taylor, U.S. representative to the Vatican, Amleto G. Cicognani, the apostolic delegate to the United States, reiterated Vatican opposition to plans to create a Jewish state in Palestine:

> Catholics the world over are piously devoted to this country
> [Palestine], hallowed as it was by the presence of the Redeemer and
> esteemed as it is as the cradle of Christianity. If the greater part of
> Palestine is given to the Jewish People, this would be a severe blow to
> the religious attachment of Catholics to this land. To have the Jewish
> People in the majority is to interfere with the peaceful exercise of these
> rights in the Holy Land already vested in Catholics.

It is true that at one time Palestine was inhabited by the Hebrew race, but there is no axiom in history to substantiate the necessity of a people returning to a country they left nineteen centuries before.

If a "Hebrew Home" is desired, it would not be too difficult to find a more fitting territory than Palestine. With an increase in the Jewish population there, grave new international problems would arise. Catholics the world over would be aroused.[46]

Cicognani is here responding to various American and British proposals to create Jewish and Arab states in Palestine.

Although its hostility to Zionism remained implacable, the Vatican did respond indirectly to Nazi racial policies. Vatican attitudes toward the rise of Nazism were expressed in two documents of the 1930s. A year after the Nazi seizure of power, in February 1934, Pope Pius XI declared, "We are living in historically tragic times . . . when racial pride has been exalted to the point of being a pride of thoughts, doctrines, and practice, which is neither Christian nor human."[47] Thus, the church condemned Nazi racism, but the primary object of that racism, the Jewish people, was not identified. The papal encyclical *Mit brennender Sorge* of 1937 condemned all who "take race or state . . . and makes them divine through an idolatrous cult that overturns and falsifies the order of things created and ordained by God. The experiences of recent years bring the responsibilities completely to light: they reveal the intrigues which from the beginning were aimed solely at a war of extermination."[48]

These statements strike the modern reader as vague and unfocused. Direct and explicit condemnation by the Vatican of German anti-Jewish violence in the 1930s was not to be found. While Pius XI spoke out against anti-Semitism in private conversations, he seemed reluctant to issue these pronouncements publicly. In September 1938 he told a group of Belgian pilgrims to Rome, "Through Christ and in Christ, we are spiritual descendants of Abraham. No! It is not possible for Christians to participate in anti-Semitism. . . . We are spiritually Semites."[49]

Following the death of Pius XI in February of 1939, Cardinal Eugenio Pacelli became Pope Pius XII, reigning until October of 1958. It is Pius XII around whom controversy still rages, especially since the publication of Rolf Hochhuth's 1963 drama *The Deputy*. Hochhuth's play accuses the Vatican of indifference to the fate of the Jews—and to some degree of complicity in their murder. The pontificate of Pius XII thus became the focus of fierce debate about the Catholic Church, the Jews, and the Second World War. Catholic writer James Carroll has acknowledged the influence of Hochhuth's play and the role it played in igniting controversy about Pius XII's actions during the war. As Carroll said, "The play *The Deputy* broke over us seminarians in that period (the 1960s) like a crushing tidal wave. For it called into question the ground of our faith in the church, in its essential sinlessness. . . . We Catholics prized the image of the church as Hitler's mortal enemy. And to have the illusion of the church's heroism questioned, if not ripped away, was traumatic."[50]

Immediately after World War II, Maritain tried to influence Pope Pius XII to confront and transform church policies toward the Jewish people. As French historian P. Cheneaux has noted, "After the horrible fate that struck the people of Israel, Maritain hoped that the church, through the voice of the pope, would make itself heard and condemn anti-Semitism solemnly."[51] Maritain worked through Cardinal Montini, the Vatican secretary of state who would be elected Pope Paul VI in 1963, to influence Pius XII, but to no avail. The full impact of Maritain's teachings on Jews and Israel would begin to be felt only in the last years of the pontificate of John XXIII.

In the first two decades after the close of World War Two, many Jewish scholars wrote approvingly of Pius XII's actions during the war. In the past two decades, however, attitudes have shifted and some Jewish spokesmen have held Pius XII fully complicit in the Nazi attempt to exterminate the Jews of Europe. In 1999 Rabbi Marvin Hier of the Wiesenthal Center in Los Angeles labeled Pius XII "the pope of the Holocaust."[52] Among the supporting evidence for Rabbi Hier's accusation is the fact that Cardinal Pacelli, serving as Vatican secretary of state for Pius XI, negotiated the Reichskonkordat, the Vatican-Nazi agreement of 1933. Once he became pope in 1939, Pius XII seemed to some critics "Hitler's silent partner." In this analysis of events, Communism was the force that Pius XII most feared, and he was willing to let the Nazis fight against it, weaken it, and, he hoped, triumph over it. Most damning of charges against the wartime pope is that he did not prevent or condemn the Nazi roundup and murder of 1,200 Roman Jews in October of 1943. They were sent to Auschwitz from a roundup point visible from the pope's windows.

In contrast to this wholesale condemnation of the wartime pope, Rabbi David Dalin, in his edited volume *The Pius War: Responses to the Critics of Pius XII*, offers a more balanced view of Pius XII's wartime actions. Dalin reminds his readers of the positive view of Pius XII expressed by Jewish writers in the immediate postwar period. In a scathing review essay titled "Pius XII and the Jews," Dalin singles out John Cornwell's *Hitler's Pope* as "a vicious attack" on the papacy. Dalin brings considerable evidence to support his contention that "Pius XII was not Hitler's pope, but the closest Jews have come to having a papal supporter—and at the moment when it mattered most."[53] The controversy surrounding Pius XII's actions during the war has heated up recently, and it shows no signs of cooling down.

It was Pope John XXIII, Pius XII's successor, who initiated the process that led to a radical change in the church's relationship with Jews, Judaism, and Zionism. This process was part of the larger liberalizing project of the Second Vatican Council and its focus on redefining and improving the church's relationship with other religious traditions, both Christian and non-Christian. The deliberations about Catholic–non-Catholic relations in general, and Catholic-Jewish relations in particular, were influenced directly by Maritain's teachings. John XXIII directly acknowledged Maritain's influence, as did John XXIII's successor, Paul VI, who was Maritain's friend and student.

Maritain was "embraced by Pope Paul VI at the time of Vatican II and honored as a major source and inspiration of the Council's teachings."[54] In the years before the council issued *Nostra Aetate* (In Our Time) the Vatican's teaching on relations with other faiths, Maritain met often with the church hierarchy. His access rested on his eminence as a Catholic philosopher and his diplomatic service as French ambassador to the Holy See from 1944 to 1947. Maritain's influence was affirmed by Paul VI's gesture at the closing ceremony of the council—in which he chose Maritain to deliver the Vatican's message to the world's intellectuals. Maritain wished to show support for Israel by visiting the country. According to Rabbi Leon Klenicki, Maritain intended to visit Israel on a pilgrimage in the 1960s but was unable to travel because of ill health.

The ideology of secular Judaism, especially as espoused by Ben-Gurion and other Israeli leaders, disturbed Maritain, as it did many Catholic and Protestant supporters of Zionism. As Paul Merkley has noted, "Christian Zionists would have preferred, other things being equal, to find believing Jews at the helm of the new state. But this was not to be . . . the leading figures in the new government itself were all secularists."[55] Jewish secularism had long bothered Vatican officials. In 1921 Cardinal Gasparri conveyed Vatican concern to Zionist leader Chaim Weizmann: "The Zionists are not religious and are even antireligious, and therefore Zionism cannot be regarded as the fulfillment of prophecy. Zionism has no connection with the promised return of the Jews to the Holy Land."[56]

Maritain lived in the United States from 1940 to 1952. In the 1940s he was a member of the American Christian Council on Palestine, which was later renamed the American Christian Palestine Committee. The committee's public statements were unambiguously pro-Zionist. Esther Feldblum noted a discrepancy in tone when Maritain wrote in a Catholic publication: "Maritain ambiguously stated: 'it appears that the solution of the Hebrew state in Palestine, inevitably, will be the next solution attempted by the angel of an ever-sorrowful and frustrated history.' "[57]

During Vatican II, Maritain influenced the deliberations on Catholic-Jewish relations. These deliberations produced a series of drafts of what would become *Nostra Aetate*, which the church issued a few months after John XXIII's death. It is worth looking at a communiqué describing the draft of *Nostra Aetate* before examining the full text of the document:

Communiqué of the Secretariat for Promoting Christian Unity, regarding the Chapter on the Jews, issued November 8, 1963.

This morning there was distributed to the Fathers of the Second Vatican Council a draft on "The Attitude of Catholics towards Non-Christians, particularly towards the Jews." This draft was prepared over a period of two years by the Secretariat for Promoting Christian Unity, of which His Eminence Augustine Cardinal Bea is President. It is to form the fourth chapter of the schema on Ecumenism, the first three chapters of which had already been submitted to the bishops.

The document is entirely religious in its content and spiritual in its purpose. It is out of an ever-growing appreciation of the church's sacred heritage that the Council pays attention to the Jews, not as a race or a nation but as the Chosen People of the Old Testament. The clear and unequivocal language of the text gives the Secretariat confidence that no other motive will be read into it than that of the all-embracing love of the late Pope John who himself had wished that the theme be prepared for the Council Fathers.

The draft deals first with the deep bond that ties the church to the Chosen People of the Old Testament. According to God's merciful design, the church has its roots in the covenant made by God with Abraham and his descendants. This plan of salvation for all mankind finds its culmination in the coming of Jesus Christ, Son of David and descendant of Abraham according to the flesh. Through Him the divine call first given to the Chosen People of old is extended through His church to the entire world.

A second point the draft makes is that the responsibility for Christ's death falls upon sinful mankind. It was to atone for the sins of every man that the Son of God willingly offered Himself on the Cross. The part the Jewish leaders of Christ's day played in bringing about the crucifixion does not exclude the guilt of all mankind. But the personal guilt of these leaders cannot be charged to the whole Jewish people either of His time or today. It is therefore unjust to call this people "deicide" or to consider it "cursed" by God. St. Paul, in his letter to the Romans, assures us that God has not rejected the people whom He has chosen.

The document presented goes on to affirm that the church can never forget that it was from Abraham's stock that Christ, His Blessed Mother and the Apostles were born.

In keeping with its objectives, the Council document does not propose to deal with the various causes of anti-Semitism. However, it does indicate that the sacred events of the Bible and, in particular, its account of the crucifixion, cannot give rise to disdain or hatred or persecution of the Jews. Preachers and catechists, the text states, are admonished never to present a contrary position; furthermore, they are urged to promote mutual understanding and esteem.

It is clear, therefore, that both the contents and purposes of the document are purely religious. It cannot be called pro-Zionist or anti-Zionist since it considers these as political questions and entirely outside of its religious scope. In fact, any use of the text to support partisan discussions or particular political claims or to attack the political claims of others would be completely unjustified and contrary to every intention of those who have composed it and presented it to the Council.[58]

This description of what would be issued two years later as *Nostra Aetate* was circulated among the council participants, and it reached some Jewish leaders. At least four other drafts were considered. Some traditionalists among the council's participants wanted *Nostra Aetate*'s declaration on the Jews to include a statement affirming that the church's ultimate goal was to convert the Jews to Christianity. One draft did have such a statement: "The church expects in unshakable faith and with ardent desire the union of the Jewish people with the church." Rabbi Abraham Joshua Heschel, on reading this draft, wrote a statement addressed to the Vatican Council. Heschel deemed the clause calling for the eventual conversion of the Jews

not only ineffective, but also profoundly injurious. . . . Since this present draft document calls for "reciprocal understanding and appreciation, to be attained by theological and fraternal discussion," between Jews and Catholics, it must be stated that *spiritual fratricide* is hardly a means for the attainment of "fraternal discussion" or "reciprocal understanding." A message that regards the Jew as a candidate for conversion and proclaims that the destiny of Judaism is to disappear will be abhorred by the Jews all over the world and is bound to foster reciprocal distrust as well as bitterness and resentment.[59]

Heschel asked to meet with the pope. Because of scheduling problems, the audience was arranged for the day before Yom Kippur, the Day of Atonement. Heschel spent thirty-five minutes with Paul VI. As Heschel later recalled: "The schema on the Jews is the first statement of the church in history, the first Christian document dealing with Judaism, which is devoid of any expression of hope for conversion. And, let me remind you, that there were two versions."[60] Here Heschel implies that he convinced the pope to amend the document. According to religion scholar Susannah Heschel, "My father's objection was unequivocal: the phrase had to be eliminated. . . . My father met with Pope Paul VI to make his objection clear, and he said many times that he was told after their meeting that the pope took his pen and crossed out the sentence."[61]

In the final draft, read aloud by Paul VI on 28 October 1965, Section IV on the Jews read as follows:

As the sacred synod searches into the mystery of the church, it remembers the bond that spiritually ties the people of the New Covenant to Abraham's stock.

Thus the Church of Christ acknowledges that, according to God's saving design, the beginnings of her faith and her election are found already among the Patriarchs, Moses and the prophets. She professes that all who believe in Christ, Abraham's sons according to faith, are included in the same Patriarch's call, and likewise that the salvation of the church is mysteriously foreshadowed by the chosen people's exodus from the land of bondage. The church, therefore, cannot forget that she received the revelation of the Old Testament through the people with whom God in His inexpressible mercy concluded the Ancient Covenant. Nor can she forget that she draws sustenance from the root of that well-cultivated olive tree onto which have been grafted the wild shoots, the Gentiles. Indeed, the Church believes that by His cross Christ, Our Peace, reconciled Jews and Gentiles, making both one in Himself.

The church keeps ever in mind the words of the Apostle about his kinsmen: "theirs is the sonship and the glory and the covenants and the law and the worship and the promises; theirs are the fathers and from them is the Christ according to the flesh" (Rom. 9:4–5), the Son of the Virgin Mary. She also recalls that the Apostles, the church's main-stay and pillars, as well as most of the early disciples who proclaimed Christ's Gospel to the world, sprang from the Jewish people.

As Holy Scripture testifies, Jerusalem did not recognize the time of her visitation, nor did the Jews in large number, accept the Gospel; indeed not a few opposed its spreading. Nevertheless, God holds the Jews most dear for the sake of their Fathers; He does not repent of the gifts He makes or of the calls He issues, such is the witness of the Apostle. In company with the Prophets and the same Apostle, the church awaits that day, known to God alone, on which all peoples will address the Lord in a single voice and "serve him shoulder to shoulder" (Soph. 3:9).

Since the spiritual patrimony common to Christians and Jews is thus so great, this sacred synod wants to foster and recommend that mutual understanding and respect which is the fruit, above all, of biblical and theological studies as well as of fraternal dialogues.

True, the Jewish authorities and those who followed their lead pressed for the death of Christ; still, what happened in His passion cannot be charged against all the Jews, without distinction, then alive, nor against the Jews of today. Although the church is the new people of God, the Jews should not be presented as rejected or accursed by God, as if this followed from the Holy Scriptures. All should see to it, then, that in catechetical work or in the preaching of the word of God they do not teach anything that does not conform to the truth of the Gospel and the spirit of Christ.

Furthermore, in her rejection of every persecution against any man, the church, mindful of the patrimony she shares with the Jews and moved not by political reasons but by the Gospel's spiritual love, decries hatred, persecutions, displays of anti-Semitism, directed against Jews at any time and by anyone.

Besides, as the church has always held and holds now, Christ underwent His passion and death freely, because of the sins of men and out of infinite love, in order that all may reach salvation. It is, therefore, the burden of the church's preaching to proclaim the cross of Christ as the sign of God's all-embracing love and as the fountain from which every grace flows.[62]

The framers of *Nostra Aetate* were careful to dissociate their call for a new relationship with the Jewish people from the question of Zionism. The Catholic Church's relationship with the State of Israel would have to wait another thirty years for resolution.

The process initiated by John XXIII in the early 1960s, a process by which the church dramatically changed its attitude toward Jews and Judaism, was continued by his successor, Paul VI. In the period from 1960 to 2000 Jewish identification with the State of Israel solidified to the point of total identification. Thus Jews identified themselves with Israel, and Catholics, in turn, identified Jews with Israel. A remarkable sign of growing Catholic grappling with Jewish sensibilities was the 1965 publication of Father Edward Flannery's *The Anguish of the Jews: Twenty-three Centuries of Anti-Semitism*. The first book on anti-Semitism written by a Catholic priest, it clearly shows the influence of Jacques Maritain's ideas. In a chapter titled "The Roots of Anti-Semitism," Flannery cites Maritain's work directly: "Jacques Maritain has justly warned against a certain 'blasphemous impersonation of Divine Providence,' whereby the woes of the Jews are accepted or encouraged as willed by God. . . . However, it is not to the divine plan but to the study of human perversity that we must look first for explanations of these manifestations of inhumanity."[63] As noted earlier, Flannery condemns the church's role in anti-Semitism while at the same time emphasizing the difference between the history of Christian anti-Semitism and the implementation of Nazi racial policies.

Moving from scholarship to activism, Father Flannery decided to work on Catholic-Jewish relations at the organizational level. He was appointed the first director of Catholic-Jewish relations at the National Conference of Catholic Bishops. Flannery and other followers of Maritain's approach to Catholic-Jewish relations achieved great success in the United States. Among the figures who moved the reconciliation process forward were Thomas Merton, Sister Rose Thering, Msgr. John Oesterreicher, Rabbi Marc Tennenbaum, Rabbi Abraham Joshua Heschel, and Cardinal John O'Connor. When the Vatican at last recognized the State of Israel in 1993, the move was understood by many as a marker of reconciliation between Catholics and Jews, both of whom now identified Jews with the State of Israel.

Over the nine decades between Herzl's 1904 audience with Pius X and Vatican recognition of Israel in 1993 there had been a number of meetings between Zionist leaders and the popes. From the Zionist viewpoint, few of the meetings before the mid-1960s had any positive consequences. This view is perhaps shortsighted. In retrospect, we can say that Vatican-Zionist and Catholic-Jewish conciliation moved forward through many small steps, with, of course, many setbacks. In the years between 1904 and 1993, 1964 and 2000 were the key dates in this process of accommodation.

~

Paul VI's 1964 Visit to the Holy Land

When the Vatican announced in December 1963, five months after he had been elected, that Pope Paul VI would visit the Holy Land—Jordan and Israel—the visit was framed in terms of an attempted reconciliation between the Catholic Church and Eastern Orthodoxy. What struck observers as most remarkable about the pope's pilgrimage was that he was the first pope in 150 years to travel outside of Italy. There was no mention at the time of an improvement in Vatican-Israeli or Catholic-Jewish relations. Jerusalem, then under Jordanian rule, was chosen for its symbolic value as the sacred site of Christian origins, and as an intermediate site: it was neither Istanbul nor Rome, the seats of Orthodox and Catholic authority. The pope and the Orthodox patriarch, Athenagoros, could meet as equals in Jerusalem. This pilgrimage was presented by the Vatican as "the first visit to the Holy Land by a pope since the days of St. Peter."[64]

Paul VI was careful to emphasize the purely religious nature of his trip. It was to be a pilgrimage, not a political meeting. This was meant to distance the Vatican from any involvement in the Arab-Israeli conflict. Such involvement would be perceived in Arab and Muslim states as de facto recognition of the State of Israel and it was feared that such recognition would adversely affect the situation of Catholics in the Arab world.

According to Xavier Rynne, Vatican correspondent for *The New Yorker*, the pope explained his pilgrimage in this way:

> We are so convinced that, for the final, happy conclusion of this Council, prayers and good works are necessary that, after careful deliberation and much prayer, we have decided to become a pilgrim ourselves to the land of Jesus our Lord. In fact, if God assists us, we wish to go to Palestine in January to honor personally, in the holy places where Christ was born, lived, died and ascended to heaven after His Resurrection, the first mysteries of our faith, the Incarnation and the redemption. We shall see that blessed land whence Peter set forth and where not one of his successors has returned. Most humbly and

briefly we shall return there as an expression of prayer, penance and renovation to offer to Christ His church, to summon to this one holy church our separated brethren, to implore divine mercy on behalf of peace among men, that peace which shows in these days how weak and tottering it is, to beseech Christ our Lord for the salvation of the entire human race.

Rynne wrote of the papal visit, "The pope's historic announcement that he intended to make a trip to the Holy Land was probably one of the best-kept secrets of recent years. . . . To the majority of hearers and the vast world outside, the news came as a breath-taking disclosure of incalculable significance. Nobody was prepared for it."[65] Vatican spokesmen, echoing the pope's statement, made sure to emphasize that this pilgrimage was "a purely religious act, absolutely extraneous to any kind of political or temporal considerations."[66]

On many occasions before the pope's 1964 visit to Jordan and Israel, the Vatican had made clear its sympathy for the plight of the Palestinian refugees. In 1949 the Vatican established the Pontifical Mission for Palestine. There were approximately 20,000 Catholics among those Palestinians displaced within Israel and among those who fled to the neighboring Arab states. The Israeli government was, of course, displeased by the Vatican's support of the Palestinian cause, but it understood that it had to maintain a working relationship with the Vatican, even if it was not about to grant Israel diplomatic recognition.

That a pope's visit to the Holy Land might presage or indicate reconciliation or rapprochement with Jews and Judaism was, in the mid-1960s, not considered. Paul VI's pilgrimage antedated the final publication of the church's 1965 *Nostra Aetate* document on the Jews. The reconciliation attempted in this pilgrimage was between Catholics and Eastern Orthodox Christians. Jews were not mentioned. The Jews of Israel were considered only insofar as the Jewish state controlled part of the Holy Land, the land sacred to Catholics because of its association with the life of Jesus.

Most of Paul VI's 1964 pilgrimage was in Jordan, at the sites associated with the life of Jesus. Prior to the 1967 war the Old City of Jerusalem was in Jordanian hands and its government was the guardian of Christian holy sites. In order to visit Nazareth, the pope had to cross over into Israel, where he spent eleven hours. Much of that time was spent in ceremonies at the Catholic shrines of the city and in conversation with the Orthodox patriarch. The entire trip lasted three days, two of which were spent in Jordan, the third in Israel. Gifts were exchanged, and an Israeli Pilgrims' Medallion was struck and presented to the pope. The Israeli postal service issued a special first day cover in honor of the papal visit. Even if the Vatican avoided actual diplomatic recognition of Israel, the government saw that it could gain legitimacy by commemorating the pope's visit. "Paul VI's pilgrimage," writes Michael Signer, "was entirely focused on affirming the principles articulated in the early sessions of Vatican II that concentrated exclusively on internal Christian concerns. The most important mission for Paul VI was healing the schism between the Eastern and Western churches. Israel as a Jewish state was only marginally a consideration."[67]

From the Israeli government's standpoint, the results of Paul VI's one-day pilgrimage to Christian holy sites in Israel were mixed. Though no diplomatic recognition of Israel was implied (in fact, any hint of it was denied), the logistics of the pilgrimage necessitated diplomatic contacts between Jerusalem and the Holy See. Both sides were wary about these contacts; every detail seemed fraught with great significance. In the 1960s, Israel's leadership was composed of former European Jews, many from Catholic and Russian Orthodox countries where anti-Semitism was endemic. Suspicion of the church hierarchy was difficult for these leaders to overcome. The Catholic Church's leadership was for many of the Israeli leadership still the symbol of European Christian anti-Semitism.[68]

Some pundits pointed out that the pope avoided using the name of the State of Israel during his speeches on the pilgrimage and that he limited his contacts to meetings with Israeli elected officials and shunned meetings with Israeli religious leaders. Paul VI met with the Israeli prime minister and the president, Zalman Shazar, but would not agree to a meeting with Israel's chief rabbis.[69] According to some Israeli journalists, the chief rabbi had himself objected to meeting with the pope, so the aversion to an official Catholic-Jewish encounter seemed to be mutual.[70] Golda Meir, then Israel's foreign minister, met with Paul VI during his day in Jerusalem. Meir's impressions of the meetings between Paul VI and the Israeli leadership were quite negative: "It had not been the happiest of meetings. The pope had made it clear that his visit in no way constituted full recognition by the Vatican of the state of Israel; he had made Jordan, rather than Israel, his headquarters for three days, and the parting message he had sent us from his plane was carefully addressed to Tel Aviv, not Jerusalem."[71] As Rabbi David Rosen noted some forty years later, the 1964 papal visit "had left a bitter taste that had not been forgotten in Israel."[72]

⌒

In Between the Two Papal Visits

Many observers would understand the next papal journey to Jerusalem—that of John Paul II in 2000—as an act of reconciliation between Catholics and Jews. But there were other interfaith and ecumenical aspects to it as well, for John Paul II was committed to reconciliation with the Orthodox churches, the project that had impelled Paul VI to visit Jerusalem in 1964. That the ceremonies and meetings designed to help John Paul II move the Catholic-Orthodox process along were destined for trouble became clear during the pope's visit to the Sinai in February 2000, a month before the Jerusalem pilgrimage. At St. Catherine's monastery at the foot of Mt. Sinai, the pope and his entourage celebrated a mass. The Greek Orthodox monks of St. Catherine's refused to join the pope in prayer. Their tradition, they told Vatican officials, did not permit them to pray with Roman Catholics.

The 2000 papal visit to Israel signaled the implementation of the 1993 Vatican-Israel accords. In the thirty-six years between Paul VI's pilgrimage and that of John Paul II, the Vatican had changed its approach to the State of Israel, a change from nonrecognition to the implementation of full diplomatic relations. Jacques Maritain's understanding of Zionism had fully exerted its influence in the church. This radical change in Vatican-Israel relations was mutual; both parties made remarkable adjustments. From 1948 to 1993 the Vatican had been reluctant to establish full diplomatic relations with Israel. In the first nineteen years of Israel statehood, from 1948 to 1967, there was little improvement in Israel-Vatican relations. As historian Uri Bialer noted, "Two decades of tortuous political ties between Israel and the Vatican had brought Israel almost nothing but frustration."[73] Similarly, the Israeli government, which was led by officials born and raised in Polish Catholic and Russian Orthodox towns and cities, had an aversion to dealing with Catholic hierarchy. Less than twenty years after the end of World War II, fears of European anti-Semitism were still alive among Israelis. It was only in the aftermath of the 1991 Madrid Peace Conference in which Israeli and Palestinian leaders met that the Vatican initiated the process that culminated in the Fundamental Agreement of 1993.

In between the two papal visits of 1964 and 2000 there were a number of landmark changes in Vatican-Israel and Catholic-Jewish relations. Some were geopolitical. Israel's victory in the 1967 war led to its annexation of East Jerusalem. The Christian holy places, previously controlled by Jordan, were now under Israeli control. The Vatican could not long ignore this radical change. Soon after the 1967 war, the Vatican sent an emissary to Israel to negotiate the status of Catholic property in the territories now occupied by Israel.

Between 1963, when the text of *Nostra Aetate* was first drafted, and 1993, when the Vatican granted Israel full diplomatic recognition, the papacy signaled its intent to change the church's relationship to the Jewish people in a number of large and small ways. Pope John XXIII wrote in 1963: "We are conscious today that many, many centuries of blindness have cloaked our eyes so that we can no longer see the beauty of thy chosen people nor recognize in their faces the features of our privileged brethren. We realize that the Mark of Cain stands upon our foreheads. Across the centuries our brother Abel has lain in the blood which we drew, or shed tears we caused by forgetting thy love. Forgive us the curse we falsely attached to their name as Jews. Forgive us for crucifying them a second time in their flesh. For we know not what we did."[74]

This dramatic statement, and others like it, reflected Maritain's influence. John Paul II, also influenced by Maritain, later expanded on this teaching by explicitly linking the Nazi murders to the need for a Jewish state. In 1980 the pope noted that Jews, having undergone "tragic experiences connected with the extermination of so many sons and daughters, were driven by the desire for security to set up the state of Israel."[75] In 1985 the Vatican issued "Notes on the Correct Way to Present Jews and Judaism in Preaching and Catechesis on the Roman Catholic Church." Not only did this decree condemn the charge of "deicide" imputed to the Jews as a people, but it redefined the church's understanding of its relationship to Judaism: "Because of the unique relations that exist between Christianity and Judaism—linked together at the very level of their identity—relations founded on the design of God of the Covenant, the Jews and Judaism should not occupy an occasional and marginal place in Catechesis: their presence there is essential and should be organically integrated."[76] These were powerful words; acts that backed them up would soon follow.

Until Pope John Paul II's millennium pilgrimage to the Holy Land, the most dramatic act signaling a shift in the Catholic Church's relationship with the Jewish people was the pope's visit to Rome's Great Synagogue in April of 1986. On this visit, the pope spoke of the Jewish people as "the beloved elder brothers of the church." At the ceremonies, the chief rabbi of Rome, Rabbi Toaff, asked the pope to establish diplomatic relations between the Vatican and the State of Israel. The pope did not reply to this request.[77] In his speech to Jews and Christians assembled in the Rome synagogue, the pope noted the full implications of Vatican II's reassessment of the church's relation with the

Jewish people: "Once again, speaking through me, the church deplores, in the words of 'Nostra Aetate,' the hatreds, the persecutions, and all the manifestations of anti-Semitism directed against the Jews at any time by whomever."[78]

The relationship between earlier persecution of Jews and the murderous onslaught of the Nazi fury was most clearly articulated by the preacher of the papal household in a survey of that pope's legacy: "As John Paul II once observed, all of this made Christians of our century less vigilant when the Nazi fury was unleashed against the Jews. It eased the way, albeit indirectly, for the coming of the Shoah, the Holocaust."[79]

Other signals of Catholic-Jewish and Vatican-Israel reconciliation were not as loud; but they were, nevertheless, clear. An important player in this slow and gradual reconciliation was Father Marcel Dubois. Since 1964 Dubois had lived in Jerusalem, where he taught in the Hebrew University philosophy department, of which he was chairman for many years. Dubois, in a theological statement unique in the Catholic discourse of his time, spoke of the establishment of Israel as "an event which must be read in the perspective of the history of the design of God."[80] While working for Catholic-Jewish reconciliation, Dubois also championed Arab-Jewish understanding as a path to Israeli-Palestinian peace. For Dubois, as for Jacques Maritain, the improvement of both Catholic-Jewish relations and Arab-Jewish relations were closely related to human rights issues. For both thinkers, Jewish rights were safest only in the general context of universal human rights. In 1982 Dubois told an interviewer for the Israeli newspaper *Ha'aretz*, "I feel close to the (ultra-Orthodox) people of Meah Shearim because of the similarity of our absolute faith in God and in prayer. But if it was up to them, I would have to pack my bags and leave this place. On the other hand, the Kibbutzim invite me to lecture. They are very receptive to what I have to say. But at the same time they are quite distant from me, for the presence of God is alien to them."[81]

While affirming Israel's importance and permanence, Dubois, especially in his last years, grew increasingly more concerned about the situation of the Palestinians under Israeli rule. His encounters with the hierarchy and laity of the Palestinian Christians, an encounter facilitated by the leaders of St. George's Cathedral, the Anglican Church in Jerusalem, made Dubois more sympathetic to the Palestinian cause.

Dubois also wrote that "the mystery of Israel is the key to all Christian self-understanding."[82] This is a position that Dubois shared with James Carroll and others: the church cannot effectively reform without confronting its treatment of the Jews. Two prominent American Catholic theologians, Elizabeth Schussler Fiorenza and David Tracy, wrote in the mid-1980s of the need to integrate an understanding of the Shoah into contemporary theology: "If Christian theology is to enter history, surely this interruption, of the Holocaust, is a frightening disclosure of the real history within which we have lived. The theological fact is that Christian theology cannot fully return to history until it faces the Holocaust. It cannot face that interruption in history without facing as well the anti-Semitic effects of its own Christian history."[83]

Although Maritain supported Israel, he was careful to qualify its theological significance:

> I did not mean to declare the state of Israel a state by divine right—as has been suggested by some. The state of Israel as a state is like all other states. But the return of part of the Jewish people to the Holy Land, and its reestablishment there (of which the existence of the state is a sign and guarantee), is the refulfillment of the divine promise which is not withdrawn. One remembers that which was said to Abraham, Jacob, and Moses, and that which Ezekiel proclaimed. . . . Not that we should consider the establishment of the state of Israel to be a kind of prelude to the realization of the prophecy. I know nothing about this, although it is not impossible. But surely we should keep in mind our respect for the ways of God? And I have no doubt that this event, mysterious as it is for Jews and Christians alike, bears the sign of God's faithful love for the people which is ever His. It therefore seems to me that once the Jewish people have set foot again on the land which God has given them, nobody can take it away from them again. To wish for the disappearance of the state of Israel is to want the nullification of that return which has at least been granted to the Jewish people and which allows it to have a shelter of its own in this world . . . anti-Israelism is not much different from anti-Semitism.[84]

Maritain, the great Catholic philosopher, considered one of those who inspired Vatican II and regarded by Pope John Paul VI as "his master," was able to influence Fathers Marcel Dubois and Bruno Hussar on the issue of the church's relationship to the Jewish people. He also influenced the bishops of France. In April 1973, a few weeks before Maritain's death, a document published by the French Bishops Committee for Relations with the Jews revealed how much his thought found an echo in the French Catholic clergy. In step with the argument articulated by Maritain, the French church continued to affirm its long-maintained distinction between Christian antipathy to Judaism and murderous anti-Semitism. Its March 1988 document "We Remember: A Reflection on the Shoah" claimed that "the Shoah was the work of a thoroughly modern neo-pagan regime. Its anti-Semitism had its roots outside of Christianity."[85]

~

A Variety of American Catholic Opinions

Up to this point, I have focused on popes and influential Catholic theologians. For a wider view of Catholic opinion, let us look at the American Catholic press. Before the establishment of Israel, the tone of many articles and editorials on the situation in Palestine was hostile to Zionism. The Jesuit journal *America*, in 1936, commented on Zionism in relation to the Arab revolt in Palestine. The British Mandate, the editorial contended, had failed because British policymakers were caught up in the liberal idea "that one religion is as good as another." The editorial went on to argue that "the overpowering interest in the future and welfare of the Holy Land is neither Jewish nor Islamic. It is Christian. And as its soil was trodden by the Incarnate Word who founded His church there, the welfare of Palestine is inextricably bound up with the Catholic and Apostolic Church of Christ."[86] After World War II and the revelations about the murder of the Jews of Europe, a more sympathetic tone entered into articles in the Catholic press. Among American Catholic public intellectuals of the period between the establishment of the State of Israel in 1948 and the establishment of Vatican-Israeli diplomatic relations in 1993, there was a wide variety of opinion expressed about the State of Israel. Among the most passionate supporters of the Jewish state was Robert Drinan, a Jesuit priest who served in the U.S. House of Representatives from 1971 to 1981. Drinan's 1977 book *Honor the Promise: America's Commitment to Israel* chastised the church hierarchy for not giving full diplomatic support and recognition to Israel. Drinan recognized Zionism as "the only escape from anti-Semitism," and he argued that "Christians must confront the question of the meaning of the state of Israel and what Christians should do for that country in reparation or restitution for the genocide of Jews carried out in a nation whose population was overwhelmingly Christian."[87]

Drinan's liberal political positions, including support of abortion rights—although he was personally opposed to abortion—incurred the wrath of many conservative Catholics, and as a result of reactions to Drinan and other liberal priests involved in politics, Pope John Paul II demanded in 1980 that all ordained Catholic priests withdraw from elected office. During his ten years in the House of Representatives, Father Drinan made human rights the center of his work, and he saw his advocacy for Israel as first and foremost a human rights issue. Drinan first visited Israel in 1963, eight years before he was elected to the House of Representatives. He was moved, as were many visitors to the young state, by the rehabilitation of the survivors of the Shoah. Subsequent visits to Israel led Drinan to accept "the momentous and monumental importance of Israel as the dominant existential reality in Jewish self-consciousness today." For that reason, Drinan argued, "It seems clearer each day that the land of Israel is the supreme testing ground for the Jewish-Christian relationship."[88] Drinan set himself the task of improving that relationship by educating American Catholics about the centrality of Israel for American Jews.

For Drinan, and later for James Carroll, author of *Constantine's Sword: The Church and the Jews*, the need of the church to confront its relationship with Jews was unavoidable and essential. Without coming to terms with its earlier attitudes toward Jews and Judaism, the church could not modernize or reform. The process that had begun with Vatican II had to continue. The State of Israel, now understood by many in the church as representative of all Jews, thus became the center of the new narrative. For reformers within the church who supported the changes brought about by Vatican II, the Jewish issue became symbolic of the need to confront modernity in its many forms. Opponents of those changes, who dubbed themselves "traditionalists," often focused on this same issue. In some cases, such as the church supported by Hutton Gibson, father of the actor Mel Gibson, resistance to change within the church was couched in anti-Semitic attitudes and actions. Hutton Gibson wrote that the reforms of Vatican II were "a Masonic plot backed by the Jews." Inspired by the excommunicated demagogue Father Leonard Feeney, Gibson and other Catholic "integrists" have a growing following in many American cities. The American Catholic bishops, loyal to the teachings of Vatican II, continue to condemn these groups and work to marginalize them.[89]

While American Catholics of the 1950s to the 1980s were to some extent influenced by the Vatican's antagonism to Zionism, they were by no means uniform in this regard. As on many other issues, there were differences and disagreements between the Vatican and the American church hierarchy, and even more pronounced differences between the hierarchy and the laity. A key factor was post–World War II improvement in Catholic-Jewish relations within the United States. Will Herberg's mid-1950s classic study *Protestant, Catholic, Jew* reflected America's new religious reality. Jews and Catholics were now considered full participants with Protestants in American religious life. As historian Jenna Joselit has noted, "American Jewry took Herberg and his book to its bosom. . . . Its impact on American Jews cannot be underestimated. . . . Integrating Judaism into the body politic and, better yet, placing it on a par with the nation's two major Christian denominations, Herberg made the case that this old-time religion was here to stay."[90] In this atmosphere, Catholic-Jewish dialogue flourished in the United States. Inevitably, the question of Vatican recognition of Israel arose in that dialogue, but the issue was not to be resolved for close to half a century.

At times, the Vatican had to remind those American Catholics who were supportive of Zionism of the official church position on relations with the proposed—and later actual—State of Israel. After Vatican II, opposition to Vatican recognition of Israel came primarily from the conservative wing of the church. These Catholics saw reconciliation with the Jews and Judaism as a betrayal of the church doctrine. *Nostra Aetate* was one of Vatican II's innovations that deeply disturbed conservatives. Opposition also came from prelates of Middle Eastern countries with substantial Catholic populations. These prelates feared that any reconciliation with Jews and Israelis would be seen as supportive of Zionism and thus place Catholics in Arab lands in jeopardy. These fears were heightened by the difficult situation of Catholics among the Arabs of Palestine.

Soon after the publication of *Nostra Aetate*, the prelate Cardinal Augustin Bea distinguished clearly between improving Catholic-Jew relations and furthering Vatican-Israel relations. "There is no national or political question here," he declared. "In particular, there is no question of the recognition of the state of Israel."[91] This distinction had been highlighted in Cardinal Bea's 1964 communiqué about *Nostra Aetate*. Now Bea was assuring the many Middle Eastern prelates at the conclave that no pro-Israeli statement would emerge from its deliberations. During and after Vatican II, American bishops were enthusiastic about improving the Catholic relationship with Jews and Judaism—and they were often affirming of the growing American Jewish support of Zionism.[92]

The American bishops at Vatican II were generally more liberal than their European and Middle Eastern counterparts. On the issues of Jews and Judaism the Middle Eastern prelates were the most reactionary. As David Singer noted, "Among the Episcopal delegations to Vatican II, the American Bishops played a particularly important role in winning the Council's approval of *Nostra Aetate*."[93]

But within American Catholic life there were some virulent opponents of both Catholic-Jewish rapprochement and improved Vatican-Israel ties. Father Leonard Feeney's newsletter, *The Point*, returned again and again to Israel's— both the people and the state—modern sins: "It is not yet ten years since Missouri Jew Eddie Jacobson saw his former clothing-store partner, Harry

Truman, commit the United States of America to formal recognition of a Jewish state in Palestine. In less than a decade, we have watched the bloody beginnings and aggressive growth of the Jewish nation's first political sovereign ghetto in nineteen centuries." Feeney concludes his screed with an observation tying the State of Israel's sins to those imputed to the people of Israel: "The evils which the Catholic editors see in the Zionists are not peculiar to Jews in Palestine . . . those traits are the common property of all Jews."[94] Among the generality of American Catholics these views would not prevail. Rather, Leonard Feeney was excommunicated by Cardinal Richard Cushing of Boston for his statements, and his anti-Jewish and anti-Israeli teachings were discredited.[95]

In the spring of 1967, a year and a half after the publication of *Nostra Aetate*, American bishops under the leadership of Cardinal Lawrence Shehan published guidelines on Catholic-Jewish relations in the United States. According to Cardinal Shehan's 1969 statement, "Christians, whatever the difficulties they may experience, must attempt to understand and respect the religious significance of the link between the people and the land. The existence of the state of Israel should not be separated from this perspective; which does not in itself imply any judgment on historical occurrences or on decisions of a purely political order."[96]

One indication of Catholic thinking on Zionism and Israel was the range of opinion expressed in the American Catholic press. Articles in publications like *The Catholic World*, *America*, and *Commonweal* posed this question: Does the emergence of the State of Israel have theological meaning for Catholics? Perusing the Catholic press of the period up to the mid-1970s, historian David Singer noted that there were three categories of opinions expressed. First, the state had no meaning for Catholics. Second, it had great meaning—as it presented an opportunity for Catholics to examine their attitudes toward Jews and Judaism. And a neutral third position: some Catholics, while open to dialogue with Jews on the question of Israel, saw no religious significance in this question.[97]

~

Pope John Paul II's 2000 Visit to Israel

The Madrid Peace talks of 1991 led to the Oslo Accords of 1993, in which Israel and the Palestine Liberation Organization (PLO) granted each other diplomatic recognition. The public sign of this accord was the Rabin-Arafat handshake on the White House lawn. It was only after these accords were signed that the

Vatican established full diplomatic relations with Israel. Aharon Lopez, Israeli ambassador to the Vatican, quoted a church diplomat as saying, "If the Palestinians can sit down formally with the Israelis, why can we not do it?"[98] In 2000 the Vatican finalized its agreement with the PLO only a few days before the pope's visit to Jordan, Israel, and the Palestinian territories. Thus the pope's visit to Israel—part of his millennium pilgrimage to the lands of Christian origins—was preceded by and enabled by the Vatican-Israel Accords of 1993 and the Oslo Accords of the same year.

When in 1994 the first Israeli ambassador to the Vatican, Shmuel Hadas, met the pope, John Paul II told him of his long-standing wish to visit Israel. John Paul II had first mentioned his wish to visit the Holy Land sixteen years earlier, in 1978. In 1994, as he anticipated marking the beginning of the third Christian millennium six years later, the pope envisioned a pilgrimage that would follow biblical chronology and geography in the footsteps of Abraham, Moses, Jesus, and St. Paul: "It is my fervent wish to visit the places on the road taken by the people of God of the Old Covenant starting from the places associated with Abraham and Moses, through Egypt and Mt. Sinai as far as Damascus, the city that witnessed the conversion of St. Paul."[99] Ideally, the pilgrimage would have started in Iraq, the land of Abraham's origins. In 2000 this proved impossible to arrange—the Iraqi government did not issue an invitation; therefore, the pope's pilgrimage started in Egypt, in the Sinai Desert, a month before his journey to Jerusalem. In March 2000, John Paul II flew to Jordan, and from there he went to Israel and the Palestinian territories. The plan was that this trip would be followed by a later pilgrimage in the footsteps of St. Paul—to Greece, Turkey, and Syria.[100] This was John Paul II's first visit to Israel as pope, but he had been there a number of times before his election to the papacy. As an active participant in Vatican II, he was moved to visit the Holy Land and to engage in conversations with Jewish scholars in Israel. He first visited in 1963 and 1964, followed by subsequent pilgrimages.

Paul VI, on his January 1964 pilgrimage to the Holy Land, had spent only eleven hours in the State of Israel. Thirty-six years later, John Paul II extended his stay in Jordan, Israel, and the Palestinian territories to six days, each of which was tightly scheduled and filled with diplomatic meetings and religious ceremonies. Technology enabled John Paul II's visit to the Holy Land to be broadcast all over the world, and the mass he held at the Mount of Beatitudes was viewed by millions. While in Jerusalem, the pope met with leaders of the Orthodox churches. He told the assembled church dignitaries that "this meeting reminds me of the historic meeting here in Jerusalem between my predecessor Pope Paul VI and the Ecumenical Patriarch Athenagoros I, an event which laid the foundations of a new era of contacts between our churches. In the intervening years we have learned that the road to unity is a difficult one. This should not discourage us."[101]

This comment was an oblique reference to discord during the pope's pilgrimage to Mt. Sinai a month earlier. The Greek Orthodox monks of the Monastery of St. Catherine, which sits at the foot of the mountain identified in Christian traditions as Sinai, refused to join the pope and his entourage in prayer. Their monastic rules prohibited them from praying with those outside of the Orthodox faith. On this issue they refused to make any concession to the pope. Similarly, the monastery's leaders refused the pope's request to use St. Catherine's to convene an interfaith meeting where Christians, Muslims, and Jews could meet at the site that tradition affirms God revealed himself to Moses and the Israelites.[102]

In contrast to the brief, uneasy 1964 meeting between Paul VI and Israel's leaders, John Paul II was greeted at Ben-Gurion Airport by Prime Minister Barak and President Weizman. The pope arrived on a Royal Jordanian airline jet from Amman. This detail, like the rest of the pope's visit to the Middle East, would have been impossible without the 1994 Israeli-Jordanian Peace Accords, which followed soon after Vatican recognition of Israel in December of 1993, and the Oslo Accords that preceded them.

While Paul VI had refused to meet with Israel's two chief rabbis, the Sephardic and the Ashkenazic, John Paul II went to the seat of the Israeli chief rabbinate, Jerusalem's Hechal Shlomo, to pay his respect to the rabbis. The Ashkenazi chief rabbi, Rabbi Israel Lau, a Holocaust survivor, understood the pope's visit as an affirmation of Israeli sovereignty in Jerusalem. Rabbi Lau had first met the pope in Rome in 1993. Of the 2000 visit he said: "When he was in the Chief Rabbinate office in West Jerusalem, as well as when he was at the Western Wall and the house of Notre Dame in East Jerusalem, the pope always appeared under the Israeli flag. . . . In my eyes, it was if the pope was giving his stamp of approval to the Israeli authority over its eternal capital, Jerusalem."[103] But the chief rabbi's perception was not the political reality. For Palestinians, too, felt affirmed by the pope's visit. Equally significant to Palestinians was the recognition that the pope granted to the Palestinian Authority and to its head, Yasir Arafat. Arafat accompanied the pope on a visit to the Dehaishe refugee camp in Bethlehem. In his speech there, the pope expressed deep sympathy for the plight of the refugees.

It needs to be emphasized that just as the Vatican and Israel—and by extension, Catholics and Jews—understood the Vatican-Israel Accords of 1993–94 differently, John Paul II's 2000 visit to Jerusalem held very different meanings for Catholics and Jews. For the Vatican and Catholics worldwide, the visit to Israel was part of the millennium pilgrimage, a pilgrimage in which the pope had requested Catholics join him. One hundred thousand participants, including many pilgrims from overseas, participated in the pope's mass at Corazim/Mount of Beatitudes on the Sea of Galilee. The rapprochement with Jews and Israel did not change the church's understanding of the Holy Land as *Christian* sacred space. Nor did it change the wide historical and geographic meaning with which the pope infused his millennium pilgrimage. It was a Christian pilgrimage to the places that marked the history of the faith, not an interfaith meeting.

In Israel the Jewish population understood the pope's visit as aimed specifically at Jewish relations with the church. Three months before the pope's visit, Chief Rabbi Lau told Israeli state radio: "I expect that this visit will have positive results. Indeed it could open a new page in the relations between our peoples and our faiths. The pattern of our relations . . . for a long time was filled with agony and suffering and drenched in blood—in a one-sided fashion. This pope has followed in the footsteps of Pope John XXIII. . . . The present pope is, I believe, one of the best to ever rule the church."[104] For the Vatican, the State of Israel was an important element of the visit, but it was only one of a number of elements. The visits to Jordan and the Palestinian Authority were of equal importance to the Holy See. Just as Jews and Catholics were divided in their perception of the pope's visit, Israelis and Palestinians were divided. The Palestinian government, recently established, saw the pope's visit as affirming their legitimacy and sovereignty. The Vatican's often expressed sympathy for and support of the Palestinian refugees, support first articulated in 1949, was reinforced and reiterated during this pilgrimage.

Pope Benedict XVI, too, has announced his intention to visit Israel. As Cardinal Ratzinger he has been to Israel previously. In 1994 as prefect of the Congregation for the Doctrine of Faith he addressed a Christian-Jewish interfaith meeting in Jerusalem. He opened the meeting by stating, "The history of the relations between Israel and Christianity is saturated with tears and blood." According to Dan Segre of the Jerusalem Center for Public Affairs, "A call by Jerusalem Chief Rabbi Kolitz to boycott the Congress was sufficient to stop any significant Orthodox rabbinical attendance."[105] Ratzinger used his Jerusalem visit to address Catholic clergy and "articulate the correct catechism for the churches in Africa, Asia, and Latin America."[106]

For Catholics, John Paul II's pilgrimage reaffirmed the importance of Christian origins in the historic Middle East. Old Testament and New Testament stories were evoked in the places in which these miracles and narratives took place. The Catholic Church's sense of continuity with the historical past was extended beyond and before St. Peter's journey to Rome. In this formulation, the pope is not only the 268th heir to St. Peter but the heir to and spokesman for Abraham's monotheistic message. For Catholics resident in the Palestinian Authority, Israel, Jordan, and Egypt, the pope's visit had especially powerful resonances. It strengthened their standing as a Christian minority both in the Muslim states of the Arab Middle East and in the Jewish state of Israel.

For Israeli Jews, the pope's mastery of religious symbolism both Christian and Jewish was remarkably effective. There were highly positive reactions to the mass at Corazim/Mount of Beatitudes, an event broadcast on television in Israel and around the world. During the pope's sojourn in Israel, according to Dan Segre, "Forty-two percent of Israeli Jews told pollsters that they liked the pope more than they did former Sephardi Chief Rabbi Ovadiah Yosef, the spiritual leaders of the largest religious party, Shas. No less significant is the fact that throughout his visit, the pope was referred to in Hebrew, as 'His Holiness.' "[107]

Most effective and masterful was the symbolism that attended the pope's visit to the Western Wall, where he placed a written prayer in a crack in the wall. The note that the he offered as a prayer read as follows:

> God of our fathers,
> You chose Abraham and his descendants
> To bring your Name to the Nations:
> We are deeply saddened
> By the behaviour of those
> Who in the course of history
> Have caused these children of yours to suffer,
> And ask your forgiveness.
> We wish to commit ourselves
> To genuine brotherhood
> With the people of the Covenant.
>
> Jerusalem 25, March 2000
> Signed: John Paul II[108]

The deep impression that this act of the pope's made on many Jews was paralleled by the effect it had on those Catholic thinkers—"Maritain's disciples"—who had been grappling with the meaning of the Jewish experience for Catholics. James Carroll saw the pope's visit to the Western Wall as a great historical moment:

For the pope to stand in devotion before that remnant of the Temple, for him to offer a prayer that did not invoke the name of Jesus, for him to leave a sorrowful *Kvitel*, a written prayer, in a crevice of the wall, in Jewish custom, was the single most momentous act of his papacy. . . . The pope's unprecedented presence in Jerusalem has said, in effect, that the Catholic Church honors Jews at home in Israel—a rejection of the ancient Christian attachment to the myth of Jewish wandering, even if Catholic ambivalence about the Jewish state seems less than fully resolved.[109]

Conclusions

Two of the most influential Catholic thinkers of the twentieth century, G. K. Chesterton and Jacques Maritain, were deeply engaged in the question of the Catholic Church's relationship to Zionism. These writers and others helped the church and the Zionist leadership arrive at an uneasy but slowly evolving understanding—one that would lead, at the end of the twentieth century, to full Vatican diplomatic relations with the State of Israel. The meaning of the transformation of the Vatican's attitudes toward and relationship with the State of Israel is not easy to unravel or decipher. Jewish and Catholic responses to that transformation differ so widely that we might be speaking of two different processes, one between the Vatican and Israel, and one between Catholics and Jews. But these processes have now become inextricably linked.

In the realm of Catholic understandings of Judaism perhaps the most astounding change is the result of recent papal pronouncements that Judaism is the church's "elder brother." Church spokesmen have interpreted this pronouncement to mean that Catholics should no longer strive to bring Jews into the church. In a 2002 lecture, Cardinal Walter Kasper, president of the church's Commission for Religious Relations With Jewry, stated: "Jews in order to be saved do not have to become Christians; if they follow their own conscience and believe in God's promises as they understand them in their religious tradition, they are in line with God's plan, which for us came to its historical completion in Jesus Christ."[110] Christianity, then, is for Christians and Judaism is for Jews. A straightforward statement, but, considering the history of the church's relationship with the Jews, an astounding one nevertheless.

Rabbi Abraham Joshua Heschel, who was so instrumental in advancing Catholic-Jewish dialogue, employed a different metaphor for the relationship.

For Heschel, Judaism was not Christianity's "elder brother" but, rather, its mother. And, as Judaism's daughter, Christianity should follow the Ten Commandments and honor its parent. Only then, according to Heschel, could the two religions enter into a relationship in which both parties gained the other's respect.[111]

In 1996, close to a century after Theodor Herzl's 1897 audience with the papal nuncio in Vienna, a meeting at which the nuncio articulated the Vatican's vigorous opposition to Zionism, the archbishop of Vienna spoke at that city's Theodor Herzl Symposium. In 1897 Herzl had been bitterly disappointed by the nuncio's negative response to his request for Vatican support for the idea of a Jewish state. Could Herzl, who "imagined" the Jewish state, have imagined that a century later the archbishop of Vienna would honor Herzl's memory and state that "the return to the land of Israel is a sacred commandment that follows from the continuing covenant . . . the return to the land is a sign of hope, though not yet its full realization"?[112] Could Herzl, who visited the Western Wall on his 1898 pilgrimage to Ottoman-ruled Palestine, have imagined that in 2000 the pope would visit the Western Wall as the official guest of the Jewish state? Even Herzl, the inveterate dreamer whose most quoted phrase is "If you wish it, it is not a dream," would have been astounded by the transformation of Roman Catholic attitudes toward Jews and Judaism.

In the next chapter we move from the realms of theology and interfaith relations to the realm of literary creativity. Three literary masters of the twentieth century, Jorge Luis Borges, Robert Graves, and Vladimir Nabokov, each developed his own unique form of literary Christian Zionism, a Zionism expressed in their art, politics, and personal commitments.

Twentieth-Century Literary Pilgrims to Zion
Jorge Luis Borges, Robert Graves, & Vladimir Nabokov

∽

Borges: "A Jew in His Mind" (1899–1986)
"I believe that we are all Hebrews and Greeks."—Borges

LISTENING TO BORGES

In 1969 I was living in Jerusalem, waiting to be inducted into the Israeli army, for which I had volunteered a few months earlier. From friends at the Hebrew University I learned that Jorge Luis Borges was visiting Jerusalem and that he would be speaking that evening at the university. I arrived at a packed lecture hall at the university's Givat Ram campus. Borges spoke in slightly accented English, softly but very clearly. There was the aura of the blind seer about him, and his audience was clearly entranced. In his opening remarks he made it clear that he felt privileged to be in Jerusalem, a city on which so much attention had been focused over the millennia. He was particularly fascinated by Israel's mixture of the old and the new. Listening to his lecture, I realized that his view of Jerusalem was related to his literary ideas on eternity and time. This mixing of the ancient and the modern was at the center of Borges's technique as a storyteller. On that visit, Borges spent ten days in Israel. He returned for a second visit, of shorter duration, two years later. He often reflected on these Jerusalem journeys in subsequent poems, stories, and essays.

Borges's journeys to Jerusalem in 1969 and 1971 were the outcome of his life-long interest in the Jewish people and Jewish texts—especially, but not exclusively, in Kabbalistic texts. These two journeys—and particularly his meetings with Gershom Scholem, professor of Jewish mysticism at Hebrew University—further influenced his literary work. From his early adolescence until his death in 1986, Borges was drawn to matters Hebrew and Jewish. His journeys to Israel were the result of that interest, and these visits, in turn, further strengthened it.

Two other twentieth century literary masters, Robert Graves and Vladimir Nabokov, shared Borges's fascination with Jews and Judaism. Borges, Graves, and Nabokov were three radically different writers from three very different national literary traditions. They shared a fascination with religious expression, especially with mysticism. Each writer demonstrated an abiding interest in Jewish texts, and in the welfare of the Jewish people. Jewish characters and themes were often featured in their work. They also shared an admiration for the aspirations and achievements of Zionism.

Borges, Graves, and Nabokov disdained the reactionary politics of many modernist writers, including T. S. Eliot and Ezra Pound. These reactionary politics often were tainted by anti-Semitism. These three were among the writers opposed to clemency for Ezra Pound when he was accused of treason for broadcasting for the Axis powers during World War II. Borges had considerable disdain for Pound, "whose scholarship he thought ludicrous and his poetry not worth mentioning. I have one word for Pound: '*Fraud.*' "[1]

From the 1930s to the 1970s, Borges fought against the Argentinean reactionary Right, Nabokov declared himself an adversary of European anti-Semites of the Right and Left, and Robert Graves was a staunch liberal who spoke up against human rights violations wherever they might be. Graves, Nabokov, and Borges each took a moral and political stand against totalitarianism and for minority rights, with an emphasis on Jewish rights. We can understand these positions in the context of post–World War II philo-Semitism and support for the 1948 establishment of Israel. Liberal enthusiasm for Israel would wane after the 1967 war. It was then that Israel's treatment of the Palestinians became an international issue. But while the pre-1967 enthusiasm for Israel lasted, the Jewish state was a favorite cause of liberal intellectuals.

Robert Graves and Vladimir Nabokov both expressed an interest in learning Hebrew and, with Borges, were intrigued by the revival of Hebrew in modern Israel. But unlike their colleague critic Edmund Wilson, they did not apply themselves to the systematic study of the sacred tongue; rather, they each relied on translations from the Hebrew. Borges found the mystical in Judaism, Robert Graves found the mythic, and Nabokov found a sustained and resounding affirmation of the traditions of learning and liberalism. For Borges, the most compelling Jewish texts were those of the mystics, the Kabbalists. For Robert Graves, the Hebrew Bible and the rabbinic legends woven around biblical narratives represented the height of Hebraic achievement. Nabokov drew on Jewish literature and history and was compelled by Jewish responses to persecution.

Each of these three literary masters was invited to Israel by government officials. They exemplified one process in the history of Christian engagement with Judaism: the Bible as the door to positive interest in Jewish texts and Judaism. But it was *not* a door that all readers of the English Bible opened. Some readers of the Bible developed an antipathy toward Jews and Judaism; these three did not. During the first decades of Israeli statehood Prime Minister David Ben-Gurion and his advisers tapped into this Christian enthusiasm for Jewish culture and wisely invited authors of international stature to Jerusalem as guests of the government. For the most part, these writers' responses to Israel were very positive—it affirmed their already held philo-Semitic worldview. In 1969 former prime minister Ben-Gurion invited Borges to Israel. Earlier, in 1959, Ben-Gurion had invited Robert Graves; later, in 1973, former Ben-Gurion aide Jerusalem mayor Teddy Kollek would invite Nabokov. These invitations, and others like them, were directed by Israeli officials to friends and supporters of Zionism, and especially to writers with an international audience.

Borges, Graves, and Nabokov were masters of poetry and prose whose artistry was rooted in a classical past. And each of them excelled in the art of translation. In addition to translating, each of them wrote poetry. Graves was a translator of Greek and Latin and interpreter of the classical world. Nabokov was a master of Russian prose, a teacher of Russian and European literature, and a translator of Pushkin. Borges was an astute literary critic and shaper of Spanish and Latin American literatures. Throughout his long career, he published translations into Spanish of a wide range of materials, ranging from German Expressionist poetry and Kafka's stories to selections from Joyce's *Ulysses*.

BORGES IN JERUSALEM

The audience at Borges's 1969 lecture that evening in Jerusalem was international and included quite a few Argentinean Israelis. Argentinean Jews came in large numbers to Israel in the late 1960s and early 1970s. Some of them joined kibbutzim. Many in the audience had read Borges—either in Hebrew,

Spanish, or English—and were eager to hear him. There was something oracular about his speech, and he had an uncanny ability to quote long selections of poetry and prose from memory. His smile was warm and at times joyful. He took questions from the audience and he made us laugh. It surely wasn't a "lecture" as we knew them at the Hebrew University, an institution often dubbed "the last nineteenth-century German university." Most Hebrew University lectures were Germanic in style and delivered with considerable academic reserve. Borges's talk was a nuanced performance delivered with a light touch. It was more like a lively poetry reading than a lecture, and the audience that evening was reluctant to let Borges leave the stage.

We had hoped that Borges would speak of his interest in the Kabbalah, and he did not disappoint us. We thought of Borges as a literary mystic. Among the questions addressed to him were: Did he see affinities between his specu- lative, questioning stories and the tales of the Hasidim? Did he feel a kinship with Kafka? Were his *ficciones* influenced by the mystical tales of the Jewish tradition? He answered these queries in the affirmative. He said that Kabba- lism formed a "technique" in his art, an idea at which he had hinted in his 1931 essay "Vindication of the Cabala."

On that Jerusalem evening in 1969, Borges was still in the middle of his journey through the Hebraic, the Kabbalistic, and the mystical, a journey that would continue until his death in 1986. In his lecture he returned again and again to the figure of the golem, the artificial being brought to life by wonder- working rabbis of Jewish folklore. The power to create a golem was God-like; it was a power that adepts both coveted and feared. Borges had read widely in the golem material and had discussed these tales with Professor Gershom Scholem of Hebrew University.

Like Robert Graves in his talks to Jewish audiences in Tel Aviv (1960) and London (1959), Borges enjoyed lecturing about Jewish topics to Jewish au- diences. Other philo-Semitic Christian literati of the period shared this plea- sure. John Dos Passos wrote to Edmund Wilson in the early 1950s that he hoped Wilson was enjoying the role of "uncircumcised rabbi" as he published his essays on the Dead Sea Scrolls and taught the *New Yorker* readership about Israel, the Bible, and the revival of the Hebrew language.[2]

This was Borges's first visit to the Holy City; he would return again two years later, in 1971. On that second visit he was awarded the Jerusalem Prize. In his 1969 Jerusalem lecture Borges made clear his enthusiasm for both the idea and the reality of a Jewish state. Yes, he was blind, but he could "see" Jerusalem, and was deeply moved by it. He spoke of his deep personal interest in Jewish texts in general and in the Kabbalah in particular. Borges then presented his meditations on Kabbalah, a system he thought relevant to the spiritual and literary concerns of modern life. "I am not dealing with a museum piece from the history of philosophy," he said. "I believe the system has an application: it can serve as a means of thinking, of trying to understand the universe."[3] Although Borges's lecture expressed unqualified admiration for the Jewish state, in his writings he was less celebratory and somewhat more ambivalent. Edna Aizenberg speaks of Borges's "mixture of excitement and misgiving about the Jewish homeland."[4] This ambivalence sprang from his sense that the Jewish function in society was to be a catalyst for innovation, change, and conscience. He feared that if the Jews were gathered in one land they would lose that universal function. As Borges saw it, the Jewish role was to act as "the conscience of humanity" and "a light unto the nations," and they had filled that role for centuries. But then came the moment in European history, the mid-1930s, when Jewish life in Europe was endangered. Like many other European Christian liberal intellectuals, Borges, when confronted with the perilous situation of European Jewry in the 1930s and their murder by the Nazis in the 1940s, supported postwar Zionist aspirations.

In this new Zionist situation, how can one understand the catalyzing function of the Jews among the Gentiles? Was it to be lost? Or could it be preserved in a Jewish state? Borges had given considerable thought to this question, one that concerned many Jewish thinkers of the time as well. Thus, when Borges visited Jerusalem in 1969, he had behind him a half century of engagement with Jewish themes. He was enthusiastic about the State of Israel, but the Judaism that interested him was the culture of the Diaspora. For Borges, the Jew in European culture was an intellectual; he was multilingual; he was an outsider and a persistent critical voice. "The thought that Israel might eradicate these almost archetypal Jewish characteristics . . . did not sit well with Borges," writes Aizenberg.[5] Despite this ambivalence, Borges supported the Israeli cause, especially when international opinion began to turn against Israel after the 1967 war. By the time he visited Israel in 1969, he was far less ambivalent about Israel and the Jewish role in history. He celebrated the "new Jew" and was less interested in the role of the "old," pre-Israel Jew.

Borges's Zionism, like that of Graves and Nabokov, was pragmatic; it was based on the history of European anti-Semitism and the post–World War II need for a Jewish refuge. Their support of Zionism was not based on millennialist expectations. These three writers did not share the End Time ideas of some Christian Zionists in England and the United States. Rather, their support of Zionism was linked to their liberal worldviews. Borges had been an

Borges at the Dead Sea with a tour guide (Galaxia Gutenberg)

antifascist in Argentina—witness his many run-ins with the Perón regime—and he had sympathy for liberal causes. (His politics would turn rightward in the 1970s.) The "need for refuge" was by no means the only reason for Borges's Zionist sympathies. His Zionism was close to that of Robert Graves and Vladimir Nabokov; all three writers shared a common Anglo-Saxon cultural heritage and an attraction to the idea of Zion, both as metaphor and as actuality. In Mathew Arnold's formulation, the Hebraic and the Hellenic traditions were the pillars of Western culture. "Athens" and "Jerusalem" were thus seen as the sources of the humanities, and of humanism. Affection for the ideas of "Athens and Jerusalem" predisposed many European literary figures to accept and promote the Jewish return to the Holy Land. Now, in 1969, Borges, like Robert Graves a decade earlier, had come to Jerusalem to further demonstrate his interest in and support of the Jewish state.

In "An Autobiographical Essay," written in the mid-1970s, Borges recalls,

Early in 1969, invited by the Israeli government, I spent ten very exciting days in Tel Aviv and Jerusalem. I brought home with me the conviction of having been in the oldest and the youngest of nations, of having come from a very living, vigilant land back to a half-asleep nook of the world. Since my Genevan days, I had always been interested in Jewish culture, thinking of it as an integral element of our so-called Western civilization, and during the Israeli-Arab war of a few years back I found myself taking immediate sides. While the outcome was still uncertain, I wrote a poem on the battle. A week after, I wrote another on the victory. Israel was, of course, still an armed camp at the time of my visit. There, along the shores of Galilee, I kept recalling these lines from Shakespeare: "Over whose acres walk'd those blessed feet, / Which, fourteen hundred years ago, were nail'd, / For our advantage, on the bitter cross."[6]

For Borges, Jesus's story is Jewish, and the New Testament is a Jewish text. "Christianity is an offshoot of Judaism" was an aphorism he often affirmed. In the tradition that imbibed from his English grandmother Fanny Haslam, both the Old and New Testaments were "Jewish books." Borges reimagined Jesus as a Jew—as did Robert Graves in *King Jesus* and in *The Nazarene Gospel* written with Joshua Podro. These writers were working against the "Aryan Christ" view of Jesus, which sought to divorce Christianity from its Jewish background. Borges, Graves, Edmund Wilson, and other Christian writers were thus constructing a "Jewish Jesus." In the same period, the mid-twentieth century, we see a parallel move in Israeli scholarship and fiction to reexamine Jesus's Jewish background. In Borges last book of poems, he penned these lines:

Christ on the Cross. His feet touch the earth.
The three beams are the same height.
Christ is not in the middle. He's the third one.
His black beard hangs over his chest.
His face is not the face of engravings.
He is harsh and Jewish.[7]

Jesus, then, was "harsh and Jewish"—not the blond, gentle Jesus of European art. Borges rejected the "Aryan Christ" in favor of a more "authentic" Semitic Jesus.

For Borges, "the Bible was one of the first things I read or heard about. And the Bible is a Jewish book,"[8] and the root of all that is valuable in Western culture. This attitude was the legacy of his greatest childhood influences, his father and his maternal grandmother. With the rise of fascism in Europe and Argentina, the Bible assumed even greater importance in his mind. The Bible stood for morality, justice, and the prophetic voice. Fascism, with its hostility toward the religion and the people of the Bible, was the enemy of culture and personal morality. This "biblical" antifascist cultural attitude was exemplified in a well-known literary project, the 1944 publication of *The Ten Commandments: Ten Short Novels of Hitler's War Against the Moral Code.*[9] Among the writers who contributed to the volume were many Borges greatly admired: Thomas Mann, Rebecca West, Franz Werfel, and Sigrid Undset. The book was published in Spanish and other European languages and had wide distribution through the Americas.

Borges's philo-Semitism and familiarity with Jewish texts led him to examine Christianity's Jewish roots, and to emphasize the similarities and differences between the two religious systems. Borges thus emerges as a late figure in the long history of Christian Hebraism and Christian Kabbalism. His early reading in Jewish texts was in the context of mastering European literature. Dante's *Divine Comedy* was a pivotal text in Borges's development as a writer.[10] He first heard of Kabbalah in an unlikely source: "I found it in Longfellow's translation of *The Divine Comedy.* . . . There is a three-page appendix in that translation that Longfellow took from a book—I believe it was *Rabbinical Literature*—by J. P. Stehelin."[11] Borges viewed both the Old Testament *and* the New Testament as "Jewish Literature." The "Old Testament," for Borges, was not subsumed into either Jewish or Christian categories, but rather, the Bible in its entirety was a *Jewish* document. Borges saw both a mystical and a historical connection between Western culture and Hebrew texts.

Hearing Borges that night in 1969 was a turning point in my intellectual development. For the five years before coming to Israel in 1968 at the age of twenty one, I had read widely in world literature, hungry for a wider view of culture after total immersion in the world of rabbinic texts. Reading and hearing Borges introduced me to the presence of the Hebraic in world literature, a presence I was barely aware of.

BORGES'S EARLY YEARS: ARGENTINA AND EUROPE

Borges was born in Buenos Aires in 1899. His maternal grandmother, Frances Haslam, was an English Protestant woman well versed in the Bible—which she read often to her precocious Argentinean grandson. While his parents spoke to him in Spanish, his grandmother spoke to him in English. The young boy read avidly in the English classics. In much the same way, Nabokov, in St. Petersburg, was reared on the English classics and learned to speak English as a child. Robert Graves, grandson of an Anglican cleric, was reared on the English Bible and the Greek and Roman classics.

At eighty, Borges was asked about his early years. He recalled having to hide on the roof of his house in order to peruse Burton's *Arabian Nights* undisturbed.[12] Asked which books he enjoyed reading as a young man, Borges replied: "Those books are the books I enjoy now. I began reading Stevenson, reading Kipling, reading the Bible, reading the Arabian Nights in the Edward William Lane translation, and later the Burton version, and I am still rereading those books." Asked about why he became interested in Judaism, he replied: "I suppose there are many reasons. Firstly, my grandmother was English, from a stock of preachers. So I was brought up, let's say, hearing the English Bible over and over again."[13]

Borges's father was a successful Buenos Aires lawyer. He was also a minor literary figure. He wrote a novel called *El Caudillo*, which was published in 1920.[14] "If I were asked the chief event in my life, I should say: my father's library," said Borges in his 1969 autobiographical essay.[15]

Thus Borges's real education took place at home, in his father's library. He did not go to school until he was nine years old, and as an adult he described his formal education as "scattershot." In the family library he gravitated toward works of the imagination. Borges said, "I have always come to things after coming to books."[16] When finally he was sent to school, it was to a state institution, where he suffered at the hands of bullies who could not abide the bookish, bespectacled, and unathletic youngster. His parents soon removed him from the school, and he returned to his beloved library.

When he was fifteen years old, Borges's parents took him to Europe, where the family spent the next seven years. In Europe, Borges's father hoped to find treatment for the hereditary eye disease that had left his own father blind and would later blind himself and his son Jorge Luis. The young Borges went to school in Geneva and quickly mastered French. He taught himself German, studied Latin in school, and continued his wide reading in European literature. It was during these seven years that Borges transformed himself from an Argentinean provincial youth into a European intellectual.

Many of the European writers who influenced Borges in his years in Geneva were Jewish. Among them were Franz Kafka, Max Brod, Leon Feuchtwanger, Franz Werfel, and Felix Mauthner. The first novel that Borges read in German was a retelling of a Jewish legend, Gustave Meyrinck's *The Golem*, a Kabbalistic tale with a theosophical bent. His first excursions into European poetry were through the works of Heinrich Heine, which moved him deeply. Thus the famed German-Jewish cultural symbiosis of the late nineteenth and early twentieth centuries had a profound effect on the young aspiring Argentinean writer.

Even before the family voyage to Europe, while at school in Buenos Aires, the young Borges began writing and publishing poems with his father's encouragement. The elder Borges, a lawyer by profession, was an aspiring writer who was frustrated by his inability to make a life as a literary figure. He urged his son Jorge Luis to devote himself to poetry. "From the time I was a boy, when blindness came to my father," wrote Borges, "it was tacitly understood that I had to fulfill the literary destiny that circumstances had denied my father. This was something that was taken for granted. I was expected to be a writer."[17]

In Buenos Aires and later in Europe, he sought out avant-garde poets and writers. Speaking of friendships forged in Geneva, Borges recalled in his old age: "The Swiss are rather proud and standoffish. My two bosom friends were of Polish-Jewish origin—Simon Jichlinski and Maurice Abramowicz. One became a lawyer and the other a physician."[18] With both Abramowicz and Jichlinski Borges forged lifelong friendships, and through them maintained his ties to Geneva. At the end of his life, Borges chose to die and be buried in Geneva, a city he identified with culture and civilization.

In his late teens, Borges traveled to Madrid to meet the poets and novelists of the literary avant-garde. In Madrid, the twenty-year-old aspiring literateur came under the influence of Spanish writer Rafael Cansinos-Assens. According to Borges, Cansinos-Assens "insisted on his alleged Jewish ethnic-cultural ancestry." Some Spanish associates of his claimed that the writer had himself circumcised because of his identification with the Jewish people. From Cansinos-Assens and other European writers Borges imbibed both political radicalism and sympathy for Jewish culture. Decades later, Borges would assert, somewhat playfully, that he himself had Jewish ancestors.[19]

His years in Europe transformed Borges into a serious literary figure. He was eager to bring "new" European literary culture to Argentina. Returning to Buenos Aires at age twenty-two, Borges promoted the poets of the Spanish avant-garde; and he soon established himself as a leader in emerging Argentinean literary culture. Borges's political radicalism would wane over time; his interest in Jewish culture would grow. This was especially true of his fascination with Kabbalah. Unlike many other Christian writers who sought to divorce Kabbalism from the Jewish tradition, Borges sought to affirm that connection.

Although he mastered French, German, and Latin, Borges did not study Hebrew or Aramaic; his introduction to the Bible was through English, and his introduction to rabbinic Jewish literature was through German. "Borges approached Judaism as a creative writer," says writer Alberto Manguel, "not as a professor of Semitics. If the Jewish material he required for his purposes was available in a form already accessible, there was no urgency to acquire the original linguistic codes."[20] A gifted multilingual reader in his teens, Borges continued to master new languages in adulthood. In this he was like Vladimir Nabokov, who became a master of American prose in his fifties after moving to the United States, and Robert Graves, master of the Greek and Latin classics. Borges began to study Old English in his fifties and Old Norse in his sixties.[21]

For Borges, the tradition of reading and rereading was a mainstay of his life; in a sense, reading became his life: "Reading books, writing about books, talking about books: In a profound manner, Borges was conscious of continuing a dialogue begun thousands of years ago and which, he believed, would never end."[22] A pivotal aspect of this cultural dialogue across time was his affinity with the Bible and postbiblical Jewish literature. Borges's sense of literature as a dialogue across time mirrors the concept of Kabbalah, "tradition"—in both its exoteric and esoteric senses.

Borges's interest in the Bible, Jews, and Judaic culture, including Kabbalism, started in his father's library. The English Bible was a formative influence in his early years in Argentina. His seven-year sojourn in Europe, particularly his time in Geneva, brought him into contact with Jewish intellectuals; two of these associates remained lifelong friends. Thus it was in his adolescence that Borges began a lifelong interest in Jews and Jewish texts. That Borges's work is suffused with Kabbalistic spirit and references is well known. What is not as well known is that his engagement with Kabbalism emerged from a deep interest in Judaism.

Borges eyesight, weak in his youth, diminished over the subsequent decades and failed him in his midfifties. "My eyesight left me for reading purposes in 1955," said Borges, "and since then I have attempted no contemporary reading." Borges eyes failed as the result of a rare hereditary disease inherited from the English side of the family. His father, too, lost his eyesight.[23] The fact that he could no longer read or write was a cruel blow for a man whose entire life had been devoted to books. According to translator Eliot Weinberger, after Borges lost his sight, he wrote no more essays and few stories. He devoted himself largely to poetry.[24] In an essay titled "On Blindness" in his collection "Seven Nights," Borges compares his situation to those of Samson and Milton. Blindness reinforced his mystical tendencies. According to Borges, the blind poet often "sees" more than those with sight.

It is striking that from his English ancestors, Borges inherited his eye disease, his love of English literature, and his familiarity with the Bible in

English. "The world of the blind is not the night that people imagine," Borges commented. "I should say that I am speaking for myself, and for my father and my grandmother, who both died blind—blind, laughing, and brave, as I also hope to die."[25]

From Borges's "Poem of the Gifts":

No one should read self-pity or reproach
into this statement of the majesty
of God; who with such splendid irony
granted me books and blindness at one touch.[26]

BORGES AS ANTI-FASCIST AND PHILO-SEMITE

Borges was in his thirties when Argentinean politics turned to the right. That political shift was preceded by decades of anti-Semitic agitation and legislation, including restrictive immigration laws aimed at Jews. The relationship between Borges's philo-Semitism and his antifascism was openly expressed in some of his short fiction and poetry, especially in his story "Deutsches Requiem." The story's narrator is a convicted Nazi war criminal writing on the eve of his execution for war crimes. Formerly subcommandant of a concentration camp, Otto Dietrich Zur Linde is not repentant. He sprang from a family of German military men and intellectuals and is proud of his actions during the war. He proclaims, "As for me, I will be executed as a torturer and a murderer." He speaks of the purifying effects of violence and claims in his last testament that "essentially, Nazism is an act of morality, a purging of corrupted humanity, to dress him anew." Zur Linde considers himself an unrepentant fascist intellectual. For Zur Linde, the murder of Europe's Jews was justified, for "the world was dying of Judaism and from that sickness of Judaism, the faith of Jesus: we taught it violence and the faith of the sword."[27]

In Borges's story, David Jerusalem, a renowned German-Jewish poet, is a prisoner in Zur Linde's camp. The Nazi officer admires the poet's work and knows much of it by heart; all the more reason, then, to drive the poet to suicide. For mercy is a quality the officer wishes to destroy. "I do not know whether Jerusalem understood that, if I destroyed him, it was to destroy my compassion," says Zur Linde. The truly frightening aspect of this story is that this unrepentant Nazi is convinced that the Nazi cause will not die with the defeat of the Third Reich: "Many things will have to be destroyed in order to construct the New Order; now we know that Germany also was one of these things."[28]

In Buenos Aires newspaper articles of the 1930s and 1940s, Borges relentlessly attacked the Nazis and their many Argentinean sympathizers, and he did this with an edge of sadness that only a lover of the German language and German culture could manifest. In 1937 Borges reviewed a new German book for children, *Don't Trust any Fox from a Heath or any Jew on His Oath*: "Its goal is to instill in the children of the Third Reich a distrust and animosity towards Jews. . . . What can I say about such a book. Personally I am outraged, less for Israel's sake than for Germany's, less for the offended community than for the offensive nation. I don't know if the world can do without German civilization, but I do know that its corruption by the teachings of hatred is a crime."[29]

To contextualize Borges's attack on Nazi sympathizers and his defense of Europe's Jews: Borges's articles were "part of the tug between pro-Allied and pro-Axis forces then raging in a not-so-neutral Argentina. Borges despised the Anglophobia, the anti-Semitism, and, not the least, the authoritarian tendencies that were threatening to turn Argentina into a fascist dictatorship."[30] In Argentina, as in Germany, pro-Nazi political sentiment was intimately linked to anti-Semitism. In a 1940 Buenos Aires newspaper editorial, Borges mocked Argentinean pro-German sentiment: "The Germanophile is anti-Semitic as well: he wishes to expel from our country a Slavo-Germanic community in which names of German origin predominate (Rosenblatt, Gruenberg . . .) and which speaks a German dialect, Yiddish."[31]

In the Buenos Aires of the 1930s, Borges was a member of the Committee Against Racism and Anti-Semitism. His antifascist and philo-Semitic stance generated accusations that he was of Jewish origin. In 1934 the right-wing journal *Crisol* made the accusation. In the context of the magazine's anti-immigration and anti-Semitic stance the article spoke of Borges's "Jewish ancestry maliciously hidden." Borges countered with the brilliant satire "I, a Jew" ("Yo, Judeo"), published in the literary journal *Megáfono*. He mentions some ancestors who may have come from "Judaeo-Portuguese roots," but he had not found any evidence to support the assertion:

> Two hundred years without being able to discover the Israelite, two hundred years without managing to set my hands on this ancestor. I am grateful to *Crisol* for having impelled me to pursue these investigations, but I have less and less hope of ever ascending to the Altar of the Temple, to the Bronze Sea, to Heine, to Gleizer [the Argentine publisher], and to the Ten Righteous Men, to Ecclesiastes, and Charlie Chaplin. . . . Who has not one day played at searching for his ancestors, imagining the prehistory of his race and blood? I have

often played at that myself, and it has not displeased me to imagine myself often as a Jew. It is a matter of a simple hypothesis, a sedentary and modest adventure that can harm no one—not even the good repute of Israel—in view of the fact that my Judaism, like the songs of Mendelssohn, is without words."[32]

While indulging in a fantasy of Jewish origins Borges also satirizes it. He is aware of how persistent and common a Christian fantasy it is, and he is also aware of how Jews are singled out for persecution. "Statistically speaking," he wrote, "the Jews were very few. What would we think of someone in the year 4000 who discovers everywhere descendants of the inhabitants of the San Juan province [one of the least populated in Argentina]? Our inquisitors are seeking Hebrews, never Phoenicians, Numidians, Scythians, Babylonians, Huns, Vandals, Ostrogoths, Ethiopians, Illyrians, Paphlagonians, Sarmatians, Medes, Ottomans, Berbers, Britons, Libyans, Cyclops, or Lapps. The nights of Alexandria, Babylon, Carthage, Memphis have never succeeded in engendering one single grandfather; it was only to the tribes of the bituminous Dead Sea that such power was granted."[33]

As I mentioned earlier, Borges introduction to German literature was through Heine's poetry and Gustav Meyrink's Kabbalistic novel *The Golem*. Thus a German-Jewish poet and a novel on a Jewish theme were the first books he read in German. Twenty years later, when the Nazis rose to power and burned the works of these and other "decadent" authors, Borges wrote of Germany: "We feel devastated by its chaotic descent into darkness."[34] By 1941 Borges was "thrust into the public eye as one of the leading representatives of the anti-nacionalista and anti-Nazi intellectuals in Argentina."[35] In Argentina Borges's anti-Nazism was remembered, for good and for ill, during and after World War II.

For his antifascist stance Borges was "more or less blacklisted by the official Argentine press" during the 1940s and 1950s. This was during the dark days of Perónist rule in Argentina.[36] Borges hated and opposed Perón, and he suffered because of that opposition.[37] Famously, Borges was fired from his civil service librarian's position and made a poultry and rabbit inspector for the city of Buenos Aires. Not, he reminded interviewer Dick Cavett on American television, "a poetry inspector but a *poultry* inspector." According to Argentinean novelist and Borges confidant Estela Canto, it was a bitter right-wing intellectual loyal to Evita Perón who decided on this insult to Borges: "This man wanted to make a heavy joke at the expense of a political enemy."[38] Borges biographer James Woodall points out that "chickens and rabbits are in Spanish, as in English, synonyms with cowardice."[39] When Borges asked a government clerk why he had been so ungraciously demoted, he was told, "You were on the side of the Allies, what did you expect?"[40] Without his job at the library, Borges slipped into a genteel poverty from which he emerged by entering the Argentinean lecture circuit, on which he became quite popular. With the fall of the Perónist government, Borges was honored with an appointment as head of the National Library. He was by that time almost completely blind. Borges wrote of "God's splendid irony in granting me at one time 800,000 books and darkness."[41]

Though he remained staunchly antifascist he did not support the Latin American leftist and Communist movements of the 1950s and 1960s. Borges became rigidly anti-Communist; he supported the Bay of Pigs invasion of Cuba and simplistically interpreted the war in Vietnam as a conflict between "Western culture and Soviet Imperialism."[42] His support of the Argentinean military junta of 1976, led by General Videla, caused a complete break between Borges and the Latin American left. Many Latin American intellectuals attacked Borges for this rightward shift. Borges was not awarded the Nobel Prize for literature, a prize for which he was nominated and considered in the 1970s. Some claim that it was because he was vociferously anti-Communist and because he met with General Pinochet of Chile; others thought that it was because of his unflinching and uncritical support of Israel.[43]

Today's neoconservatives might classify Borges's political stand as "antiauthoritarian"—resisting the dictatorships of both the right and the left. But a more widespread view was that Borges's literary writing was apolitical and devoid of any consideration of morality. In his influential 1964 essay "A Modern Master," Paul de Man wrote of Borges's stories, "They are about the style in which they are written."[44] This view of Borges, in which his style is said to overshadow the content of his writing, portrays the Argentine master as a great writer, but one whose oeuvre is detached from worldly concerns and decidedly apolitical. This is similar to some critical views of Vladimir Nabokov, views I argue against in the Nabokov section of this chapter.

BORGES'S KABBALISM

Speaking to an Argentinean Jewish audience in 1967, Borges said: "Despite your hospitality I consider myself something of a stranger here. But two reasons mitigate that impression. The first is that I was brought up as a Christian, within Western cultures. Christianity—beyond our personal beliefs or doubts—is an amalgam of two nations that have been essential for the

Western world: Israel and Greece. I believe that we are all Hebrews and Greeks, by the mere fact of belonging to Western culture . . . beyond any vicissitudes of our blood, our multiple blood."[45]

Some earlier researchers saw Borges's interest in Kabbalah as primary and his sympathy for Jewish causes as secondary to that interest, but the truth is quite the contrary. From his early youth he was sympathetic to Jewish causes, and that sympathy led him to an intellectual and spiritual interest in Kabbalistic Jewish texts. Borges's interest in Jewish texts was related to his Anglican background and to a philosophical crisis in his youth. His grandmother, he wrote, knew her Bible "so much so that if somebody quoted a verse, any verse, she would reply: yes, Job, such and such chapter and verse. So there was that side. And then, since I have not been able to believe in a personal God, the idea of a vast and impersonal God, the *en-sof* of the Kabbalah, has always fascinated me."[46] Borges's Kabbalism was gnostic and "heretical," not traditional, and it stemmed from a crisis of belief. It did not reject the biblical but, rather, fused it with the mystical.

The texts and ideas that inspired many of Borges's fictional works, poems, and essays were culled from the writings of religious mystics, foremost among them the Kabbalists. Borges opens his essay "The Kabbalah" with the observation that the teachings of the Kabbalah "derive from a concept alien to the Western mind, that of the sacred book." In Borges's analysis, influenced by Spengler's *Decline of the West*, the West venerates the classics, but both Judaism and Islam venerate the sacred book. In it "not only the words but the letters in which the words are written are sacred . . . in that book, nothing can be accidental. In human writing there is always something accidental."[47] Borges concludes his essay with a meditation on the tale of the golem. In Jewish legend the golem was the creature made by wonder-working rabbis, among them Rabbi Judah of Prague. Rabbi Judah's golem was created to protect the Jews of Prague; but he soon went beyond the rabbi's control and threatened to destroy those he was created to defend. Rabbi Judah had to destroy the golem using the same technique he used to create him—the manipulation of Hebrew letters. As Borges noted, the Jewish mystical tradition believes "that the letters came first, that they were the instrument of God, not the words signified by the letters." The golem story, which may have inspired Mary Shelley's *Frankenstein*, held a lifelong fascination for Borges. Its theme haunted him all his creative life.

In 1958 Borges published "The Golem," a poem of eighteen stanzas. In interviews, he noted that this was his favorite published poem.[48] The poem builds on the idea presented in its first stanza, that "a name is the archetype of a thing." With knowledge of the divine name, humans can create life. The example Borges provides is that of Rabbi Judah of Prague. The rabbi shaped a clay figure, the golem, and animated it with the power of the divine name. But the golem lacks human intelligence, and the rabbi wonders "who could bring such a sorry creature into the world." In the last stanza, we find the humorous touch that made this poem Borges's favorite:

> In his hour of anguish and uncertain light,
> Upon his Golem his eyes would come to rest.
> Who is to say what God must have been feeling,
> Looking down and seeing His rabbi so distressed.[49]

As with Mary Shelley's *Frankenstein*, the reader of golem stories is led to religious questions presented by the dilemma of the out-of-control creator of life. Might God's relationship to humankind be similar to Rabbi Judah's relationship to the golem? Might God use the power of the word to waken or destroy humanity? For the Kabbalists, the world is a text, and the text is a world. Creation and destruction of both texts and worlds are in the hands of those who know the secrets of the tradition. In Borges's mystical speculations and allusions—expressed in his short fictional works, poems, and essays—Jewish esoteric ideas are presented in the context of general esotericism. For Borges, Kabbalistic ideas are part of a larger system that includes concepts and practices originating in other religious and cultural traditions. For Borges was also inspired by other occult teachings—including Vedanta, Buddhism, and Christian mysticism. He utilized these teachings in his public lectures and later in constructing his *ficciones*. Early in his literary career, in 1926, Borges wrote an essay called the "History of Angels," in which he describes the doctrine of the Sefiroth and its relationship to the Hebrew alphabet: "To each one of the ten *Sefiroth*, or eternal emanations of the godhead, corresponds a region of heaven, one of the names of God, one commandment of the Decalogue, a part of the human body, and a class of angels."[50]

In 1971, in the sixth of a seven lecture series delivered in Buenos Aires, Borges presented the Kabbalah in a much more accessible and informed manner. He had recently read Scholem's *On the Kabbalah and Its Symbolism*. Scholem had presented him with a copy of the book during their meeting in Jerusalem.[51] Borges, informed by Scholem's scholarship, now delivered a more historically accurate account of Jewish mystical thought.

Borges's immersion in the Kabbalah left a powerful mark on his short stories. His fiction can be read as a universalization of Kabbalistic ideas. Just as Moses de Leon, the author of *The Zohar*, invented books that he then proceeded to quote from, so Borges invented books and quoted from them. Borges, however, lets us in on his secret, unlike de Leon, who keeps the secret to himself. Critic George Steiner has written of three modern masters who were deeply influenced by Kabbalism: Walter Benjamin, Franz Kafka, and Borges. Steiner notes that Borges's poetry and prose reflect multiple Kabbalistic motifs. Among them are "the image of the world as a concatenation of secret syllables, the notion of an absolute idiom or cosmic letter—alpha and aleph—which underlies the rent fabric of human tongues, the supposition that the entirety of knowledge and experience is prefigured in a final tome containing all conceivable permutations of the alphabet."[52]

Other critics and readers see the vague, the indeterminate, and the ethereal in Borges's stories; they overlook Borges's obsession with specificity and precision. In *Books and Bombs in Buenos Aires*, Edna Aizenberg notes that "scholars have finally (at the end of the twentieth century) begun to question the long-regnant tenet of extreme unreality" in Borges stories.[53] In "A Vindication of the Cabala" (1931), published in *Discusión*, Borges wrote: "That God dictated the Scriptures would make of them an absolute text where the collaboration of chance can be calculated at zero. . . . I do not wish to vindicate the doctrine, but rather the hermeneutical or cryptographic procedures which lead to it."[54] This was a speculative, meditative, article; in the early 1930s Borges was experimenting with various forms of writing. In the 1940s his *ficciones* form emerged. In the early 1960s those *ficciones* would earn him international renown. When he was asked in a 1967 *Paris Review* interview if he had tried to make his own stories Kabbalistic, Borges answered, "Yes, sometimes I have." In his 1970s essay "The Kabbalah," Borges wrote of Kabbalism's "doctrine that seems to me so worthy of attention. In each of us there is a particle of divinity. This world, evidently, cannot be the work of an all powerful and just god, but it depends on us. This is the lesson the Kabbalah gives us—beyond being a curiosity studied by historians or grammarians."[55]

BORGES AND ZIONISM

As mentioned earlier, Zionism presented a challenge to Borges's view of the Jewish intellectual as the universalist, cosmopolitan chronicler of exile. The Jewish works he read and the writers he befriended in his youth exemplified this detached, *luftmenschlich* quality—beginning with his Polish-Jewish friends

Marcus Abramowicz and Simon Jichlinski and extending to his reading of Kafka, Brod, and Werfel. In short, it was the Diaspora Jew that Borges grew to admire. Zionism's rejection of the Diaspora struck him as problematic and disorienting. According to Edna Aizenberg, Borges adjusted eventually to the Zionist idea and came to admire Zionism and to support the campaign for a Jewish state.[56] After 1967, as we have seen, Borges's Zionism became more militant and less ambivalent. David Ben-Gurion was aware of Borges's solidarity with Israel and invited Borges to visit the country. Similarly, Ben-Gurion invited Robert Graves, and Jerusalem mayor Teddy Kollek invited Vladimir Nabokov. "The creation of a Jewish state in Palestine made Borges downright uncomfortable," wrote essayist Ilan Stavans, "although he did not oppose the idea; in fact, he admired the valor of the Jews fighting to establish the State of Israel. Still, he wondered why such an ethereal people, perfectly at home with its homelessness, would dare dream of being ordinary."[57]

Borges, as early as the 1920s, "imagined" Jewish ancestors. He did so playfully, in response to "accusations" that he was from a Jewish family. Robert Graves, also playfully, put forth—and then rejected—the notion that he had Jewish ancestors. He told his Tel Aviv audience that he was content to define himself as "a goy," while at the same time situating himself within the English Hebraist tradition. Nabokov could claim philo-Semitic ancestors. His father and grandfather had made sacrifices for liberal causes and fought Russian anti-Semitism, but Nabokov never claimed Jewish ancestors. Rather, he found a connection to the Jewish people through his wife, Vera Slonim, and their many Jewish friends. Edmund Wilson, Nabokov's close friend and critic, was a student of Hebrew, the Bible, and the Dead Sea Scrolls. He placed himself squarely in the American Hebraist tradition. Wilson's grandfather had studied Hebrew at Princeton Theological Seminary. Wilson, like Borges, visited Israel twice, in 1954 and 1967, and, like Borges, delighted in the Israeli mix of the old and the new. In Borges's fiction and essays, that mix of the old and the new is a central theme. To many mid-twentieth-century Western intellectuals, "Reborn" Israel represented the ideal fusion of the old and the new. This fusion appealed, for different reasons, to both liberals and conservatives.

In addition to bringing modernist European writing to Argentinean culture, "Borges also rediscovered the importance of the Jewish and Arab traditions in Hispanic literary culture."[58] Borges's childhood readings of *The Arabian Nights* in their various translations influenced him deeply. Timothy Weiss makes the case for Borges's engagement with an Oriental literary tradition: "Borges' Oriental tales generally operate according to two basic principles:

things are never what they seem, and there is no eluding things as they are."[59] In an essay titled "On Poetry" Borges said, "I ought to have studied the Oriental languages: I have only glanced at them through translations. But I have felt the punch, the impact of their beauty."[60]

Borges was an incredibly prolific writer. His famous short *ficciones* are a small fraction of his literary output, which runs to many volumes. But it is through these *ficciones*, first published in 1944 in Spanish and translated in 1962 into English, that Borges influenced world literature, especially in the United States and Latin America. Before his work was published in English in the early 1960s, Borges toiled in relative obscurity, and lived a modest life. He was well known in Argentina and elsewhere in the Spanish-speaking world, but until the mid-1960s Borges's influence did not extend beyond that world.

JEWISH ASSOCIATES

As in the cases of Vladimir Nabokov and Robert Graves, Borges's sympathy for and interest in Jewish culture was facilitated by personal relationships with Jewish friends, interlocutors, and intellectual partners. Nabokov had his wife, Vera, and his many Jewish friends; Graves had his colleagues Raphael Patai and Joshua Podro. Similarly Borges's friendships with Jews were a reflection of his philo-Semitism. A case in point was his friendship with Dr. Miguel Kohan-Miller of Buenos Aires, a psychiatrist with a practice in the Plaza de Mayor. Kohan-Miller, a Jewish physician whose orientation was psychoanalytic, helped Borges overcome two severe crises that beset him in his mid-forties. These crises arose from problems relating to sex and work.

The first crisis was precipitated by the loss of his job at the Buenos Aires library. Borges had been a vocal opponent of Perón; when Perón was elected in early 1946, Borges lost his position. Demoted to "inspector of chickens and rabbits," he was both unemployed and publicly insulted by the demotion. Offered part-time teaching jobs at two institutes, Borges was reluctant to accept because of his fear of public speaking. Dr. Kohan-Miller coached Borges, helped him to master his phobia, and recommended that he memorize all of his lectures. This method worked, and with subsequent coaching by Kohan-Miller, Borges embarked on a successful teaching career. For the rest of his long life, Borges lectures were carefully prepared performances. I witnessed this in Jerusalem in 1969, and this same careful preparation can be heard in Borges's 1967 Charles Eliot Norton lectures at Harvard, now available on compact disk.

The other problem that Dr. Kohan-Miller helped Borges with was sexual, a "performance" problem that seemed tied to his fear of public speaking. As the psychiatrist said in a 1990 interview: "Above all, Borges was greatly inhibited. The patient who suffers from this condition doesn't only suffer from an inhibition over speaking. . . . I could alleviate the verbal impotence, but could not finish treating him for sexual impotence, although I could help to a point."[61]

In his career as lecturer Borges kept returning to Kabbalah. Yes, Kabbalah was but one of his many literary interests, but it was the interest that bound many others together. He enumerated some of these topics in his account of his late-1940s career as public lecturer: "I traveled up and down Argentina and Uruguay, lecturing on Swedenborg, Blake, the Persian and Chinese mystics, Buddhism, Gaucho poetry, the Icelandic sagas, Heine, Dante, Expressionism and Cervantes."[62] And this was only a partial list of Borges "areas of expertise."

Mysticism and the exotic, both in religion and literature, were at the center of Borges's presentations. Perónist reaction had forced him from his safe, private library job into public life; it also enabled and encouraged him to make contact with the wider world, including Jewish cultural institutions and individuals. In the early 1950s, Borges became a regular contributor to *Davar*, the Argentine-Jewish literary journal. In the 1960s Borges became even more explicit about his connection to Jewish communities and concerns. As Edna Aizenberg has noted, many Jewish themes emerged in his writings of the period; exile, alienation, and the crisis of belief among them. She noted that "Borges wanted to be perceived as a writer shaped by Scripture and Kabbalah."[63] The 1967 war, which galvanized the Argentinean Jewish community, had a profound effect on Borges. Two years after the war, in 1969, he accepted David Ben-Gurion's invitation to visit Jerusalem. The profound impression that Israel made on Borges is reflected in his poem "Israel 1969":

I feared that in Israel there might be lurking,
sweetly and insidiously,
the nostalgia gathered like some sad treasure
during the centuries of dispersion
in cities of the unbeliever, in ghettoes,
in the sunset of the steppes, in dreams,
the nostalgia of those who longed for you,
Jerusalem, beside the waters of Babylon.
What else were you, Israel, but that wistfulness,
that will to save
amid the shifting shapes of time

your old magical book, your ceremonies,
your loneliness with God?
Not so. The most ancient of nations
is also the youngest.
You have not tempted men with gardens or gold,
and the emptiness of gold
but with the hard work, beleaguered land.
Without words Israel has told them:
Forget who you are
Forget who you have been
Forget the man you were in those countries
which gave you their mornings
and evenings and to which
you must not look back in yearning.
You will forget your father's tongue
and learn the tongue of Paradise.
You shall be an Israeli, a soldier,
You shall build a country on wasteland,
making it rise out of deserts.
Your brother, whose face you've never seen,
will work by your side.
One thing only we promise you:
your place in the battle.[64]

LAST YEARS AND LAST WISHES

With the return of Perónist right-wing dictatorship to Argentina of the early 1970s, Borges spent a good deal of the last decade of his life in foreign travel. He knew that this new government disliked him, but he also knew that they did not dare harm him. "Borges was quite right in 1973 when he said that no Argentine government would dare harm him—the most famous man in the country—for fear of worldwide repercussions."[65] During the last fifteen years of his life he was almost constantly in motion from country to country. *Atlas*, published in 1968, details Borges's travels throughout the world.

From the early 1970s until his death in 1986 Borges spent much of his time in travel abroad. Accompanied by his young companion, Maria Kodama, he visited the United States and Spain most frequently, making at least ten trips to each country. The couple also visited Israel, Egypt, Morocco, and Japan.

On each visit, there would be lectures, readings, honorary degrees, and receptions. Often Borges would meet with his translators. At this point in his life, Borges was an old man enjoying a prolonged, if not overproductive, Indian summer. He was well aware, though he claimed to find the notion puzzling, that he was one of the world's most famous writers. And, unlike many other writers of his age, he was a famous writer who kept writing and publishing. The short stories, poems, and essays of his last two decades were published first in their original Spanish and then in many translations. His last story, "Shakespeare's Dream," was published when he was eighty-two years old. The year before he died, Borges and Maria Kodama, who had been his constant companion for fifteen years, decided to marry.

In 1986, at age eighty-six, feeling that his end was near, Borges settled in Geneva. He even made enquiries about becoming a Swiss citizen. It was in that city that he first absorbed European culture, and it was there that he wished to die and be buried. Borges did not wish to return to Buenos Aires, and felt that Argentinean writers and intellectuals would reject him if he did. Among the friends who visited him during his long hospital stay in Geneva was his childhood friend Simon Jichlinski.[66] Borges died in June of 1986.

Both Protestant and Catholic clergymen visited Borges in the last days of his life. At the funeral no speaker alluded to the fact that Borges, throughout his long life, never professed any denominational religious belief and often wrote of his inability to believe in a personal God. Two eulogies were delivered at the funeral, one Catholic and one Protestant. The first was by the Catholic priest who officiated, the second by a Calvinist minister. That minister represented the legacy of Swiss Calvinist tradition and of Borges's grandmother, Fanny Haslam. It was in her home that Borges was born, and she had read to him from the King James Bible and other classics of English literature, preparing him for a life in books. Borges had been impressed that Fanny Haslam had remained faithful to her traditions in Catholic Argentina. In requesting a Protestant presence at his funeral, Borges honored her legacy and the legacy of Geneva, which for him epitomized the finest in European culture.

In the life and works of Borges's contemporary, English poet Robert Graves, we will witness a very different, but equally powerful, fusion between the cultures of Hellenism and Hebraism. How this conditioned Robert Graves's attitudes toward Jews and Zionism will be the subject of the following section.

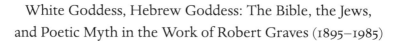

White Goddess, Hebrew Goddess: The Bible, the Jews, and Poetic Myth in the Work of Robert Graves (1895–1985)

"What does it feel like to be a goy? Embarrassing, for careful students of religious history."—Robert Graves

ROBERT GRAVES'S LITERARY REPUTATION

In the mid-1990s the English literary world celebrated the centennial year of Robert Graves. By 2000 Graves's reputation as a major English poet, a reputation that had diminished in recent decades, had been somewhat restored and a new edition of his collected poetry and prose was being readied. Graves's justly celebrated historical novels, most successful among them *I Claudius*, remain in print. His two-volume work *The Greek Myths* is still popular. His most enigmatic, and in some ways most influential book, *The White Goddess*, continues to challenge and inspire readers.[67] The book's subtitle, *A Historical Grammar of Poetic Myth*, well describes its daring leaps of imagination across cultures and times. As is now clear, *The White Goddess*, first published over fifty years ago, had an enormous influence on generations of British and American poets, musicians, visual artists, and novelists, particularly American artists associated with Black Mountain College. In England and the United States, the book became something of a talisman for young poets. It was a volume that poets gave to other aspiring poets in the hope that they, too, would be inspired by its combination of erudition, myth, and creative speculation. As Miranda Seymour, Graves's biographer noted, "Ted Hughes and Sylvia Plath were among the young poets who acknowledged the book as a formative influence; Hughes won *The White Goddess* as a school poetry prize and read it when he was in Cambridge in the early fifties. When he met Sylvia Plath, this was one of the first books he wanted her to read."[68] That *The White Goddess* influenced cultural icons of the following generation is evident in Bob Dylan's memoir *Chronicles* published in 2004. In the book's evocative opening chapter, Dylan recounts early influences on his thought and music, particularly the great books that moved him most deeply, including *The White Goddess*.

Quite significant in modern cultural history is the book's role in promoting the view that a prehistoric matriarchy ruled early human societies, and that a return to matriarchy would have a beneficial effect on our troubled modern world. Though these ideas are not the central focus of Graves's book, they are related to its argument that true poetry is inspired by an actual, living muse, a "goddess" with aspects both mythic and personal. According to Graves, each true poet must find his own muse in a person who embodies, for a time, the attributes and power of the goddess, a figure that Graves identifies with the great Mother Goddess of antiquity.

Also influential, though directed toward a different cultural audience, were the ideas Graves presented in his lectures on poetry given during his tenure as professor of poetry at Oxford from 1960 to 1964. Like *The White Goddess*, which had been published twenty years earlier, these lectures influenced a generation of writers, critics, and teachers of English literature. In the intervening decade, in the mid-1950s, Graves, on one of his rare visits from Spain to England, lectured at Cambridge, where he delivered the Clark Lectures on poetry. One of the lectures, "These Be Your Gods O Israel"—the phrase that the Israelites yelled when worshipping the Golden Calf—was a daring attack on the "cult of modernism." The "idols" whose careers Graves attempted to debunk included Yeats, Pound, and Eliot. In that lecture Graves examined the reactionary politics that informed the poetry of Eliot and Pound and pointed out the anti-Semitic elements of their work. Graves was one of the few English literary figures to make these accusations public. Only George Orwell preceded him. Related to his dim view of Pound and Eliot was Graves's refusal after World War II to sign a petition organized by T. S. Eliot urging clemency for Ezra Pound, who had been convicted of treason for his pro-fascist radio broadcasts from Italy during the war.[69]

Not noted in the Graves centennial celebrations and not fully recognized by contemporary students of Gravesiana, including his three biographers, is Graves's enormous enthusiasm for matters biblical and Hebraic, an enthusiasm that was coupled with an assertive philo-Semitism that later manifested itself in a spirited defense of Zionism and the State of Israel. Contrary to the claims of some scholars, this Hebraism was not merely a curious vestige of Graves's Anglican upbringing and his interest in the biblically inspired classics of English literature, although these factors may have influenced his sympathies. Nor can his modern Christian Hebraism, which Graves celebrated and made explicit in an essay titled "To Be a Goy" (1955), be dismissed as the product of a once-vibrant poet's doddering old age. Rather, his Hebraism and philo-Semitism reflected a lifelong interest in the Bible, Hebrew, and the Jews, an interest that matured in late middle age to great enthusiasm for modern Israel, its language and culture. When Graves lectured in Israel in the late 1950s, he told his Tel Aviv audience that the invitation was the greatest honor ever paid him and that he was in awe of the accomplishments of the new state:

"My sense of awe has been heightened by the realization that Hebrew is again a living spoken language, the same Hebrew from which our vernacular Old Testament was translated at third hand, through Latin and Greek."[70]

I will trace the Hebraic and Judaic themes in Graves's literary works, a vast oeuvre that includes poetry, essays, historical novels, children's books, and studies of mythology, both Greek and Hebrew. For this progression, from an interest in the biblical and Hebraic to sympathy for the Judaic and Zionist is surely not inevitable. Often an opposite and unequal reaction to Jews and Judaism ensues; the Hebraist and philo-Semite may turn into a virulent anti-Semite.

In *Patriotic Gore*, the American critic Edmund Wilson pointed this out in a chapter on John Jay Chapman, the nineteenth-century American novelist and essayist. A more extreme case of interest in the Jews turning into antipathy toward them is that of the late-nineteenth-century French scholar Paul La-garde, author of a dozen books on Hebrew and other Semitic languages, a man who was a pathological anti-Semite and whose philological work was used in the 1930s by the Nazi propagandists. Alternately, a Christian Hebraist may never pass through a stage in which the Jews are admired. For interest in the Hebrew language may be the result of hostility to the Jewish understanding of the Bible, and may stem from a wish to refute Jewish beliefs and arguments through a selective reading of Jewish texts. Graves, in sharp contrast to scholars who displayed indifference, ambivalence, or hostility toward Jews and Judaism, had an early positive interest in Hebrew and its effect on Western culture, and this Hebraic interest later shaped his attitudes toward Zionism and the State of Israel. I will focus on the relationship between Graves's intuitive, poetic reading of ancient myth, especially the myth of the goddess, and his interest in Judaica and sympathy for the Jews. This interest and sympathy influenced Graves's prose and poetry and it led to the creation of a body of work that has contemporary literary and scholarly relevance.

Born into a distinguished English literary family, Robert Graves was reared in the English public school system and he planned to attend Oxford University. But his education was interrupted, and the world as he knew it shattered, by the advent of the First World War. He was nineteen years old when the war began. Soon he found himself at the front. He saw many of his friends die; he himself was wounded and left for dead. Graves's recovery, which he called his "rebirth," is vividly described in *Goodbye to All That*, his classic account of the upper-class English life that he left behind at the war's end. From that account and from Graves's letters to friends and family we learn of the poet's prewar education. At Charterhouse, Graves's public school, the Bible and the Greek and Roman classics were at the core of the curriculum. Graves displayed an early affinity for the ancient texts and a facility for Greek and Latin. Many years later, his adaptation of the *Iliad*, told for children in *The Fall of Troy*, was presented as a reflection of his childhood love of the classics. His full translation of the *Iliad*, *The Anger of Achilles*, was not as well received. But one senses that for the young Graves the Old Testament held greater fascination and personal relevance than the Greek epics. As Graves's friend and biographer Martin Seymour-Smith noted, "Graves not only knew his Bible, but also believed in it."[71] This knowledge of and belief in the Bible gave him sources for literary expression and a source of spiritual strength when confronted with the horrors of war. But the strength and consolation he drew from the Bible was not of the conventional variety, that of consolation through identification with biblical figures. Rather, Graves's early poetry at times subverts the possibility of consolation by offering the unsuspecting reader alternative outcomes of familiar stories. In his 1916 war poem "Goliath and David," it is the young David, not the powerful giant, who is vanquished. The "Goodly-faced boy so proud of strength" stands his ground before the advancing scornful giant. But "God's eyes are dim, His ears are shut," and David the young warrior is killed.

That poem, written in memory of Graves's close friend and fellow officer David Thomas, was one of his earliest published poems and the title poem of Graves's second volume of verse. For Graves, there was more at stake here than allusion to biblical themes. The outcome of the biblical tale is reversed, and that reversal accomplishes two tasks. It leaves the reader within a belief system that still sees God acting in history, but it asserts that God has withdrawn his hand from the young David and favored the giant Goliath.

Graves's use of biblical themes was not limited to poetry; his first novel retold a biblical tale. *My Head, My Head* (1925) was based on an incident in the Book of Kings. Thus Robert Graves's earliest published works, both in prose and poetry, engaged and highlighted biblical themes. Among them was his early poem "Jonah," which, like "Goliath and David," reverses the outcome of the biblical story and thereby subverts the reader's expectations. As readers of the Bible know, the great fish saves Jonah from the waters of the deep by swallowing him. Though Jonah's sojourn in the fish is terrifying, the fish is an instrument of redemption. The prophet is given another chance and can now go to Nineveh. In Graves's poem the fish is an agent of destruction, the people of Nineveh fear it. Will it destroy their city? Just as God abandoned David in "Goliath and David," God abandons Jonah. The whale betrays him and threatens the very city that the reluctant prophet has been sent to save. This daring inversion of the biblical tale was quite startling to early-twentieth-century British readers. Surprise alternate endings to biblical tales were considered audacious and attention getting, and Graves used them to great effect. I have mentioned two of many such Gravesian "inversions" of biblical stories. The power of these inversions is predicated on the assumption that the stories are familiar to all readers. This assumption, coupled with the assumption that his readers are familiar with Greek and Roman myth, underlies the appeal of much of Graves's early poetry and prose.

In *The White Goddess*, written thirty years after "Goliath and David," Graves writes of the radical shift away from the classics of Western culture and laments the loss of these great stories to the reading public: "The myths too are wearing thin. . . . Only a severe classical education can impress them on a child's mind strongly enough to give them relevance, and the classics no longer dominate the school curriculum either in Britain or the United States."[72] Elsewhere he suggests that a basic, 200-book reading list should be our shared body of common knowledge. But, according to Graves, not all of the ancient myths can be recovered through the ancient texts; some have been lost or suppressed. In *The White Goddess* Graves claims to recover a lost ancient myth, that of the mother goddess. That recovered story, suppressed by Christianity, could enable the modern reader to grapple with the harshness of modern life, and it would enable the modern poet to call on the muse of poetry, a muse that, for Graves, was both an abstraction and a reality.

POETRY AND POLITICS

As a student of the Bible and the classical world, Graves was aware of Jewish history and of the varieties of modern Jewish national aspirations. The development of modern Jewish nationalism was not a surprise to him. As a young man he sympathized with some of these aspirations and was especially indignant about the presence of anti-Semitism in British life. Zionism seemed to him a natural solution to the persistent problem of anti-Semitism.

Robert Graves's ties to Middle Eastern issues in general and to the question of Zionism in particular developed under the influence of three of his older half brothers and sisters. Journalist Philip Graves worked closely with T. E. Lawrence and later gained fame when he exposed *The Protocols of the Elders of Zion* as a forgery. Another brother, Richard Graves, was also a journalist and author. His 1924 book, *Palestine: Land of Three Faiths*, was widely read in England and influenced the British debate about Palestine.[73] Richard entered the British foreign service and over twenty years later was appointed the last administrator of Jerusalem under the British Mandate. Sympathetic to Zionism,

Richard Graves was instrumental in drawing Robert Graves to Zionism. Additional information and influence came from Graves's half sister Clarissa, who had settled in Palestine during the British Mandate. She was in charge of BBC broadcasts in Palestine and corresponded with Robert about developments in both the Arab and the Jewish communities under the British Mandate.

Curiously, Robert Graves had a brush with anti-Semitism long before his brother Philip exposed the forgery of the most influential anti-Jewish tract of modern times, *The Protocols of the Elders of Zion*. At Charterhouse, Graves was "accused" of being a German Jew. This accusation was an illustration of the anti-German sentiment rampant in England in the years before the outbreak of World War I. When one of the schoolboys found out that Graves was registered as "Robert Von Ranke Graves"—his mother was a von Ranke—he spread the rumor that Graves was an enemy alien, and a Jew. To deal with the worsening situation at school, Graves, who knew his Bible well, adopted the biblical David's strategy and "feigned madness." By going out of his way to alienate and distance his classmates, Graves prepared the way for his role as the possessed young poet of Charterhouse School. As Martin Seymour-Smith noted, "His feigned madness worked wonders. He was shunned, which was just what he wanted. When he started writing poetry his fellow pupils regarded this as confirmation of his insanity."[74] The incident left Graves with a heightened sensitivity to the irrationality of anti-Semitism. Throughout his long life he demonstrated considerable sympathy for the victims of that prejudice. During World War II he wrote of the plight of the Jews and exerted considerable effort on behalf of his German-Jewish amanuensis, Karl Goldschmidt, who was threatened with deportation from England as an enemy alien. In addition, Graves cultivated relationships with Jewish scholars and writers, collaborations that yielded remarkable scholarly and literary results.

Even before he "feigned madness" to escape persecution at school, Graves, at age fifteen, had dedicated himself to poetry. His experiences as an officer in the British army were later integrated into his poetic project, and his near-death on the battlefield altered his perception of life's meaning. Graves delighted in telling of how he read his own obituary in the London *Times* while languishing in a British field hospital. His recovery from shellshock after the war was linked in his mind to the power of the muse. From the time of his recovery onward he defined himself ever more assertively as a poet, and he was determined to avoid the constraints of conventional workaday existence. He would support himself and his family by writing; even teaching was rejected by Graves as too conventional. After one term as a professor of English in Cairo, Graves decided never to take a regular teaching job again.

ON MAJORCA

Graves moved from England to Majorca in 1929, and except for the nine years between the start of the Spanish Civil War and the end of World War II (1936–45), when he lived in England, he made his home in Majorca until his death in 1985. Majorca, a refuge from conventional and stifling England, was recommended to Graves by Gertrude Stein, who had an uncanny ability to match writers and artists with locales that would inspire and welcome them. (Stein, some two decades later, suggested to Paul and Jane Bowles that they try settling in Morocco. They both spent the rest of their very productive lives there.) Stein and Alice B. Toklas had lived in Majorca in 1914–15. They left it for Paris and tended to joke about Majorca's "backwardness." Hence, Gertrude Stein's 1928 comment to Graves and Laura Riding, "Majorca is paradise —if you can stand it!"[75]

Over the decades of his sojourn on the Spanish island, Graves, his family and friends, achieved a remarkable degree of integration into the communal life of Majorca. He supported himself through writing, translating, and editing, working on many projects at once. Graves often said that he wrote prose to support his family and poetry to honor his muse. Accepted as an honorary citizen of the island, and active in the cultural and economic life of Deya, his own village, and of the Majorcan capitol, Palma, Graves became a kind of Majorcan aristocrat. Despite his nine-year absence from Majorca Graves was able to reestablish himself quickly on the island after World War II, so thoroughly had he achieved "permanent citizen" status. Here he would write his many novels, poems, and translations, undisturbed by the outside world.

On Majorca, Graves's long-standing interest in Jewish history was awakened by his discovery of the presence of the hidden Jews of Majorca, the Chuetas. In "A Dead Branch of the Tree of Israel," Graves traces the origins of the merchant families of Majorca, who "are of unmixed Jewish stock, but strict Catholics," to the victims of the Spanish Inquisition. He notes that a group of these Majorcan Marranos wrote the Israeli government in the 1950s requesting books on Judaism and information on the possibility of immigrating to Israel. This demonstration of belief in the restoration of a long-exiled people and the possibility of their return to Israel touched Graves deeply. Noteworthy in Graves's essay on the Chuetas are his translations of sixteenth-century Inquisition documents that provide grisly evidence of the Spanish Crown's cruelty to the New Christians and Jews of their domain. Here Graves touches on one of his favorite historical themes: that Christianity, sprung from Jewish roots, was intent on extirpating Jewish beliefs and rituals and the way that this persecution was conducted was often "justified" by biblical texts appropriated from Jewish tradition.[76]

Once settled in Majorca, Graves was an indefatigable worker; he worked at his desk every morning of the year and wrote until the late afternoon. He worked in solitude and brooked no interruptions. His literary output was quite remarkable. The money he earned from his many and varied literary projects enabled Graves to support his family for the decades they lived on the Spanish island. Occasionally, Graves collaborated on books with academic scholars; he compiled three books with Alan Hodge, among them a writer's manual, *The Reader over Your Shoulder*.[77] His two other collaborators were scholars of Judaica. The first was Joshua Podro, a Yiddish journalist with whom Graves wrote *The Nazarene Gospel Restored* (1953).[78] In a 1944 letter to Alan Hodge, Graves wrote, "I have written three introductory chapters of the Jesus book and had them vetted by Joshua Podro, a marvelous little Hebrew and Aramaic scholar who manages a press-cutting bureau at Paddington and has all God's words in his left-hand coat pocket, and all the comments in his overcoat and trouser pockets."[79] Graves is at times humorously deprecating about Podro but otherwise very respectful. As Miranda Seymour noted, Podro was the source for much of the raw subject matter of Graves's work in the mid-1940s. Graves and Podro "talked for hours about myth, ritual and pre-Christian history." A good deal of what was discussed with Joshua Podro found its way, although in a rather different form, into *The White Goddess*, which Graves wrote, and rewrote, alongside *King Jesus*, in 1943–44.[80]

Another Judaica scholar that Graves collaborated with was Raphael Patai, the Hungarian-born anthropologist. Patai was trained at the Hebrew University and was editor of the Herzl Press in New York and a prolific author. Patai's *Man and Temple* (1947), in which he argued for an anthropological approach to the rituals of the Second Temple, caught Graves's attention. His 1947 letter to Patai opened this way: "I have just read your beautifully argued but all too brief *Man and Temple*." Graves then launched into a list of his own observations on affinities between Temple rituals and their Greek and Celtic parallels, and closed the letter saying, "I wish all ethnologists wrote as well as you do."[81] This very complimentary letter, to which Patai promptly responded, was the beginning of a highly productive twenty-five-year collaborative relationship between the English poet and the American Jewish scholar. Together they wrote *Hebrew Myths: The Book of Genesis* (1964). The story of their collaboration is told and documented in Patai's *Robert Graves and the Hebrew Myths* (1992). Patai's later book, *The Hebrew Goddess*, was profoundly influenced by Graves's ideas. Patai wrote of Graves: "Robert Graves nonfiction writing is a unique combination of great erudition and poetic insight cum license. When-ever erudition is about to shackle him he breaks loose. . . . The mix of fact, reinterpretation, and fiction is in itself fascinating."[82]

Graves's relationship with Patai had its unlikely and surprising aspects. Patai was a professional scholar who allowed himself occasional imaginative forays into the mythic. Graves was an inspired poet who lived in a "mythic present." In a 1961 letter to Graves, Patai summed up their collaboration. He gratefully acknowledged the receipt of Graves's *Collected Poems* and noted that reading the poems "brought into sharp focus the difference between you and me in relation to myth: I may have an understanding of myth and be able to write about them; but you live and breathe them. In view of this, it is quite remarkable that we have so few differences about our *Hebrew Mythology*."[83]

Graves's work with Patai took on a larger cultural and poetic meaning for the poet, a meaning beyond the collaborative effort on this specific book. It spoke to Graves's lifelong interest in the Jews and Judaica, and it confirmed his long-held views on the relationship between Hebraic culture and Western culture. In a June 1962 letter to Patai, Graves tells of his hopes for their joint project, *Hebrew Myths*:

> I want this book to be as serviceable and readable and perfect as
> possible: an example of how a Jew and a Gentile can work together and
> produce something that just won't be another book about the Bible;
> but something new and exciting and useful for the general reader,
> regardless of his religious (or non-religious) upbringing. What first
> encouraged me to work with you was your fearlessness in your pursuit
> of truth; and I hope that the readers will realize that I am not merely
> not anti-Semitic but very much at home in Jewry, however little respect
> I may seem to pay the chroniclers of Genesis.[84]

Graves's "little respect" for the Bible is also at work in his remarkable 1955 volume, *Adam's Rib*. It pays homage to the creation narrative in Genesis but reworks that narrative and rearranges the sequence of events, much as they were rearranged and challenged in Graves's biblical poems of the 1920s, "Jonah" and "Goliath and David."[85]

HEBRAIC THEMES AND *THE WHITE GODDESS*

Robert Graves's first novel, *My Head, My Head*, was a literary refashioning of an episode in the life of the biblical prophet Elisha. Published in 1925, it retells the story (II Kings 4) in which Elisha revives the son of the Shunamite woman. According to Miranda Seymour, Graves "got the idea for it after reading Isaac Rosenberg's poem about Moses, and added his own thoughts about a golden age when 'woman' was held to be of the gods and sacred."[86] Recognizing the Hebraic underpinnings of the young English poet's verse, Graves wrote about Rosenberg's poetry in a *Survey of Modernist Poetry*, a volume he coauthored with Laura Riding. For that same volume Riding wrote an homage to Gertrude Stein.

At this early state of Graves's development as a writer we can see a fusion of two of his interests: the resonance of biblical tales and the question of woman's role in antiquity and prehistory. *My Head, My Head* was the book in which Graves set out the ideas that were later developed and expounded in *The White Goddess*. Graves's last prose work, published forty-eight years after *My Head, My Head*, was his translation of *The Song of Songs*. And this work was preceded by *Adam's Rib*. Thus Graves's prolific writing career was bracketed by biblically inspired works.

Despite his interest in the Bible and the Jews, Graves did not take up the study of Hebrew. Latin and Greek were the languages in which he excelled. In 1947, when he began working with Joshua Podro, his interest in the Hebrew language was kindled. His scholarly relationship with Podro influenced *The White Goddess* and *King Jesus* and led to their collaboration on *The Nazarene Gospel Restored*. Podro attempted to teach Graves Hebrew, but Graves's commitment to finishing his many writing projects took precedence over learning a new language. But this did not stop the author of *The White Goddess* from using Hebrew philological evidence to validate his theories on goddess worship and the centrality of the muse. In a long excursus on the Jewish mystical tradition and the *Maaseh Merkabah* (the chariot imagery of Ezekiel's vision), Graves, citing rabbinic sources, emphasizes the "forbidden knowledge" aspect of the mystical path. In quoting a Talmudic story that emphasizes that Merkabah speculation is forbidden or dangerous territory, Graves makes some astute points about modern Hebrew usage as opposed to biblical Hebrew usage. We can assume that this information, and the supporting Talmudic citations, came from Podro, although the use to which they were put was uniquely Gravesian.

In his earlier books, Graves had made use of and challenged some academic scholarship on the classics; conversely, many university scholars expressed skepticism about Graves's use of classical sources. Some academicians were hostile to Graves's "pretensions to scholarship" and were dismissive of his conclusions. One eminent Oxford classicist expressed skepticism about

Graves's theories on the origins of poetic myth. When he and Graves met, the scholar was thoroughly charmed by Graves, and he later grew to appreciate the poet's intuitive approach to the ancient texts. Raphael Patai, academic anthropologist and Hebraist, was quick to appreciate Graves's perspicacity and intuition. He recognized that Graves's poetic imagination could not be fettered by the bounds of conventional scholarship. Other scholars, but not all, were similarly impressed by the literary results of Graves's "intuitive readings" of ancient texts. No doubt many academicians were jealous of Graves's ability to write for the general public. Their disdain for the poet's "popular entertainments" may have served as a mask for envy.

The theme of the "Goddess ascendant," which for Graves is fused with the idea that all true poets must be inspired by the muse, is a cornerstone of Graves's work, both in poetry and in prose. Though some recent feminist scholarship claims that Laura Riding, who Graves met in 1926, was the source and catalyst for this idea, Graves's biographer Miranda Seymour has demonstrated that the idea dominated Graves's thinking long before Laura Riding and her poetry did. More importantly for our subject, the goddess idea is, for Graves, inextricably linked to his understanding of biblical religion and the question of the status of women in the ancient Near East. James Frazer's *The Golden Bough* was Graves's source for information on ancient myth and its interpretation. Graves's early reading of Frazer bore fruit in *The White Goddess*. But, as John B. Vickery noted in the early 1970s, Frazer is not simply a source of in *The White Goddess*. Actually, Graves's book is a kind of displacement and rearrangement of the central themes of *The Golden Bough*. Perhaps we could think of it as a "midrash" on Frazer's monumental and highly influential work. It is significant that T. S. Eliot, who enthusiastically published *The White Goddess* at Faber and Faber, was himself deeply influenced by Frazer, but in a radically different manner. Twenty-five years before *The White Goddess* was published, Graves was writing poems with motifs borrowed from Frazer. He was playful and irreverent with these ancient myths, many of which concern themselves with vegetative fertility and human sexuality. This provides a sharp contrast to Eliot, who used *The Golden Bough* for "purposes of symbolic profundity and religious solemnity."[87] Graves also read deeply and closely in Frazer's *Folklore in the Old Testament*, a volume neglected by many of the writers influenced by *The Golden Bough*. Thus Graves's understanding of the Bible's place in Western culture was an inclusive one. His view of the Bible was surprisingly "modern" in that he read the Bible in its ancient Near Eastern context.

Graves's "creative inversion" of biblical stories can be linked to his later interest in the creativity inherent in the project of Midrash. He delighted in the rabbis' reshaping of biblical narratives and noted structural similarities between Midrash and the many renditions of the Greek myths. In a review of *Legends of the Bible*, the one-volume condensation of L. Ginzberg's *Legends of the Jews*, Graves contrasts the "heroic aspect of Roman myth with the didactic moral intent of aggadah, which is concerned with the Jews' obligation to truth, mercy, humility, and the love of God."

Graves placed biblical motifs at the center of his early poetry; similarly, he placed biblical prose at the center of his history of English prose. In *The Reader Over Your Shoulder: A Handbook for Writers of English Prose* (1943), Graves surveys the role that the King James Bible played in shaping English literary style. The citation of a long section from Isaiah illustrates the author's point that "the incantatory device of repetitive phrasing was well suited to the now copious English vocabulary. . . . The rhetorical exquisiteness of such writing encouraged those who heard the Bible read in church to read it aloud at home."

In a footnote to this observation, Graves evokes the Jewish background of Old Testament content and style. Explaining the "incantatory device of repetitive phrasing," Graves notes, "In the synagogues of Palestine the first phrase of a pair was sung by a hazzan, the second round by the congregation as a sort of confirmatory echo."[89]

KING JESUS AND THE RABBINIC IMAGINATION

Graves's first novel, *My Head, My Head*, was a retelling—and a daring interpretation—of the biblical tale of II Kings 4, in which the child of the woman of Shunem is revived by the prophet Elisha. As Martin Seymour-Smith observed: "*My Head, My Head* exemplifies Graves's lifelong fascination with the Bible— his passion for 'restoring' ancient and sacred texts . . . along matriarchal rather than patriarchal lines; and his conviction that the key to truth lies in woman and her mysteries."[90]

Robert Graves returned to a biblical setting in his 1944 novel *King Jesus*, perhaps his most enigmatic and challenging work of fiction. More than yet another attempt to set Jesus's life in its historical context, the book is a reinterpretation of Jesus's mission and an affirmation of the Jewishness of Jesus's life and message. In this way, the novel was daring and innovative in that it anticipated a later trend in scholarship that sought to recover the Jewish elements in early Christianity. In *King Jesus*, Jesus clashes with those who worship the fertility goddesses of the ancient Near East. His project is to challenge her authority and the hold she has over Israelite religion. In one sense *The White Goddess* and *King Jesus* are complementary works in dialectical conversation. The first work asserts the historical presence of a mother goddess; the second presents the founder of Christianity as a challenger to her rule. Graves's Jesus, the child of a secret marriage between King Herod's son Antipates and Miriam, a woman of the Israelite aristocracy, is the rightful heir to the throne of Israel. But earthly kingship is not his aspiration. He yearns for the spiritual power that kingship over Israel confers. For temporal authority, he has only disdain. Rejecting the goddess and her fertility cults, Jesus demands a pledge of chastity from his followers. His death comes about because of his opposition to the goddess and because he wants to replace her worship with worship of God the Father.

Just as Graves anticipated and precipitated modern interest in the idea of the mother goddess and the call for her return to power, he also anticipated modern scholarly reexaminations of Jesus's Jewish background. To what degree Graves influenced the zeitgeist on these issues is an important question, and one which merits further examination. But it is clear that he intended to challenge Christian doctrine. Earlier in his life, Graves's connection to his strict Protestant religious upbringing prevented him from tackling Christianity as a topic of inquiry. In the mid-1940s, after a long period of immersion in reading anthropological theory, the great influences on Graves's thinking in the areas of religion and culture were Frazer's *The Golden Bough* and Jane Harrison's *Prolegomena to the Study of Greek Religion*. He then felt ready to take on the thorny issue of Christian origins. In Graves's view, the classical and biblical myths no longer spoke to people; this made the work of poets and novelists all the more difficult. Myths needed to be reinterpreted and presented anew to this generation. Further complicating the cultural situation was the fact that the Bible's stories were not as well known as they once were. "The growth of rationalism since the Darwinian controversy," Graves wrote, "has so weakened the churches that biblical myths no longer serve as a secure base of poetic reference."[91]

To *King Jesus*, which treads on sensitive ground and whose speculations some readers might find offensive, Graves appended a short, five-page "Historical Commentary." It covers in discursive fashion the central arguments of the book, but it is not comprehensive or exhaustive. Graves wrote, "A detailed commentary written to justify the unorthodox views contained in this book would be two or three times as long as the book itself, and would take years to complete; I beg to be excused the task." But despite the absence of notes or a bibliography, which would be more impressive than helpful, Graves assures his readers that "every element in my story is based on some tradition, however tenuous."[92]

But even more intriguing than its willingness to challenge conventional ideas of Christian origins, *King Jesus* reveals a method of reading history that is integral to Graves's larger project. This is the examination of the origins of poetic inspiration, a project that culminated in the writing of *The White Goddess*. In *King Jesus*, Graves presented a statement about his techniques and aims in which he further refines this intuitive technique of reconstructing the past: "To write a historical novel by the analeptic method—the intuitive recovery of forgotten events by a deliberate suspension of time—one must train oneself to think wholly in contemporary terms." He goes on to compare the method best suited for this act of imagination—"impersonating the supposed author of the story"—to the use of figures drawn into the foreground of architectural drawings.[93]

King Jesus was influenced by *The Brook Kerith*, George Moore's early-nineteenth-century novel.[94] But *King Jesus* was also a reaction against Moore's book, which was given to Robert Graves by his friend poet Siegfried Sassoon. "The imaginative findings of *King Jesus* were a necessary step towards the formulation of the poetic theory embodied in *The White Goddess*," says Martin Seymour-Smith.[95] Both works are based on the assumption that there was an ancient matriarchy and that its vestiges are still operating and apparent to the intuitive poet.

King Jesus was the product of long and intensive work, including both historical research and acts of historical imagining. Immersing himself in the study of Roman Palestine and the development of Christian doctrine, Graves fastened on Paul as the villain of the piece. As Graves saw it, Paul bore responsibility for the rejection of the Law and the separation of the church from the Jews. Paul then began to take his revisionist project so seriously that he lost all sense of proportion.

T. S. Matthews, the *Time* magazine editor who was a lifelong friend of Graves, recalled a conversation he had with Graves in the early 1950s, when Graves was writing *The Nazarene Gospel Restored*. On a walk with Matthews, Graves said that working on the book frightened him. "I have a kind of sentimental attachment to the church I was brought up in, and this book will destroy the church," he said. "It's like having the responsibility for dropping the atom bomb. . . . The Catholics will go on telling themselves fairy stories— it may not affect them much. But Protestant Christianity will be wiped out. The only refuge Protestants can find will be to become Jews—and Pharisees at that."[96] At the end of the 1950s, Graves continued to hold this exaggerated view of the effect of his theories. Responding to his brother Richard's invitation to visit Israel, Graves assured him that the *Nazarene Gospel* book had gained him many supporters and adherents in Israel—for he had "demonstrated Christianity's Jewish roots and rescued the Pharisees from the ignominy to which Christianity had condemned them."[97]

ROBERT GRAVES AND THE ZIONIST IDEA

Graves's half brother Richard Graves served as the last administrator of British Mandate Jerusalem. In letters from Richard, Robert Graves was kept informed of developments in Palestine as seen through the eyes of a resident British official. Richard Graves was considered sympathetic to the Zionist cause, or as sympathetic as a British official of the time might be. He saw some legitimacy in Jewish claims to the land, but he also envisioned problems emerging from the implementation of those claims.

In a December 1947 letter to Joshua Podro, Robert Graves commented on the Palestine Partition Plan recently debated at the United Nations: "About Partition: speaking from the point of view of religious tradition, I should say that 'he who holds Hebron (rather than Jerusalem) holds Palestine.' I think it's a silly partition. The Jews should have all the South, including Jerusalem and Hebron, and share the North with the Arabs (also Sons of Abraham) if the fifteen relevant texts in the (Pentateuch) Scriptures are to be fulfilled, as they have a habit of being in the long run. But better something than nothing."[98] Many of the people closest to Graves were of Jewish descent, and this may have something to do with his Zionist leanings and philo-Judaism. To the list of Graves's Jewish associates we can add the two scholars who co-wrote books with Graves: Joshua Podro and Raphael Patai. Others on the list would also have to include Laura Riding (born Laura Reichenthal),[99] Graves's lover and companion from 1926 to the late 1930s and the inspiration for much of his early love poetry; and Kenneth Gay (born Karl Goldschmidt), for many years Graves's personal secretary, editor, and companion on Majorca. Graves is rightfully credited with saving Goldschmidt from deportation and probable death during World War II. And we cannot forget Gertrude Stein—it was Stein who suggested to Graves and Riding that they try living on Majorca. These three figures, Laura Riding, Kenneth Gay, and Gertrude Stein, were deeply ambivalent about, or hostile to, their Jewish origins. But this would not prevent Graves from having a Protestant view of them as people of "biblical stock."

ROBERT GRAVES IN ISRAEL

A year after the end of World War II, Graves and his family returned to Majorca from their nine-year sojourn in England. Graves's work habits were legendary, and he kept to them while he traveled. On his infrequent trips away from Majorca he would carry his writing notes with him and devote the early part of every day to his current project. Nights were devoted to socializing, drinking, and conversation. The afternoons, bracketed by writing and socializing, were devoted to lectures, interviews, and meetings with publishers, editors, and admirers. The exception to this routine was his January 1959 visit to Israel. Richard Graves was instrumental in coordinating the visit with Prime Minister Ben-Gurion's office. The occasion was the tenth anniversary celebration of Israeli independence. Graves's itinerary, as he described it, was "a taxing month of meetings, discussions and expeditions around a country he had only imaginatively explored in his researches."[100] This trip so excited him that he relinquished his usual work schedule and spent his mornings in Israel taking notes on all he had seen and learned the previous day. Other writing projects could wait until he returned to his desk on Majorca.

Some of the high points of this visit were Graves's meeting with Ben-Gurion (he accompanied the prime minister on his famous morning walk), his conversations with Foreign Minister Golda Meir, Graves's lecture at the ZOA House in Tel Aviv—a lecture playfully titled "To Be a Goy," and his trip to Eilat, where he visited King Solomon's Mines. The first of these events, the visit with Ben-Gurion, revealed some startling connections between the two men, then both in their sixties. On this walk, the two men shared their mutual enthusiasm for the Greek classics. At the time, Ben-Gurion was deeply engaged in the study of classical Greek philosophy and literature and, of course, shared Graves's enthusiasm for matters biblical. An unexpected connection between the two men was that during World War I both Ben-Gurion and Graves had been members of the Royal Welsh Fusiliers, the famous British regiment whose courage in battle was legendary.

In 1959 at the time of Graves's visit, Ben-Gurion's attachment to the Greek classics raised the hackles of some Israel intellectuals. The prime minister had alienated Israeli poets and writers when he stated in a *Ma'ariv* interview that he "did not read poetry and fiction in general or Hebrew literature in particular." When asked what three books he would choose to save from oblivion, he selected the Bible, the works of Plato, and the writings of the Buddha.[101] In Ben-Gurion's estimation, the classics of postbiblical literature or the works of the Hebrew revival were not worth saving.

Both Ben-Gurion and Graves were lifelong students of ancient languages and texts. Ben-Gurion knew Hebrew and was then studying classical Greek. Graves knew classical Greek, but not Hebrew. Graves saw his ignorance of Hebrew as a serious problem, something he failed to accomplish. A year before his trip to Israel, on a lecture tour in the United States, Graves opened a lecture on poetry with this remark: "There comes a time when a man realizes that it is too late to start doing a lot of things he half-wishes he had done years ago. Learning Hebrew, for instance, or becoming a champion figure-skater."[102] As mentioned earlier, Joshua Podro had tried to teach Graves Hebrew in the late 1940s, but he soon gave up the effort. It was one aspiration that Graves was never to fulfill.

During his trip to Israel, Graves spoke to a number of Israeli audiences. In his wonderfully witty Tel Aviv lecture, he made clear at the outset that, unlike some British and American writers "who ransack their yellowing archives in search of a Jewish great-great-grandmother," he made no claim to Jewish ancestry. "I am a goy and the son of goyim: several generations at least on both sides of the family." Expanding on his family history, he told of his Anglican forebears and their Catholic ancestors, and in the process let it be known that he was still in rebellion against the family of "divines" from which he emerged, "a long line of Anglo-Irish Protestant rectors, deans and bishops, until I broke the sequence."[103]

After winning over his Jewish audience with this description of himself as an admiring outsider, Graves quickly moved to the heart of his talk: his view of Christianity's historical relationship to Judaism and Jewish texts. He presented a sympathetic and engaging analysis, one that is at its heart quite profound. One can think of Graves's lecture as a distillation of his "iconotropic" insights into the relationship between myth and ritual. Hearkening back to the themes of *King Jesus*, he placed the blame for early Christianity's rejection of Mosaic law and its subsequent hostility to Judaism on St. Paul. "When Judaism had been proscribed and nearly battered out of existence," he said, "the Christians escaped by joining the hue and cry against their parent faith, accusing the Jews of Jesus' murder, and rewriting the Gospels to present him as an original thinker who detested the Pharisees, knew better than Moses, and was honourably treated by Pontius Pilate, the Roman Procurator."[104]

Skillfully evoking the Anglican atmosphere of his bucolic childhood in a small English parish, Graves recalled his bewilderment that the local gentry and commoners sang King David's Psalms at Sunday services: "How unconvincing the psalm of the Babylonian captivity sounded from those bucolic Gentile lips!" A survey of England's relation to the Bible followed—with many witticisms throughout. Pulling the lecture together and drawing the talk to a close, Graves used the image of the Babylonian captivity to great effect: "Ten years after the Lord turned again the captivity of Zion, your Government invited me to visit Israel. I answered in hot sincerity that it was the greatest honour ever paid me."[105]

In 1985, toward the end of his life, Graves was visited at his Majorcan refuge by Jorge Luis Borges and his companion Maria Kodama. Borges had long admired Graves's prose and poetry and, like Graves, had been an honored guest of the Israeli government. Like Graves, Borges believed that a writer's inspiration was dependent on an actual living muse. In Spain to receive the Cervantes Prize, the premier literary award in the Spanish-speaking world, Borges traveled to Deya, Majorca, to visit Graves and his wife. Sadly, Borges and Kodama found Graves incapacitated: "Blind and deaf, Graves had plainly not long to live, and Borges was not even sure that the English poet had actually registered their presence, since he uttered not a word during the entire visit. But when they took their leave, Graves shook Borges's hand and kissed Maria's."[106]

Vladimir Nabokov, the subject of our next section, was, like Robert Graves, a lifelong philo-Semite and an ardent Zionist. Unlike Graves, he was never able to make the actual pilgrimage to Israel. The story of his romance with Jews, Zionism, and Israel is told in the following section.

～

"Nabokov's Minyan": A Study in Philo-Semitism

Classification did not exist for you—Armenian, Jew, German. You distinguished
people only by their individual characteristics and not by labels of any kind.
—Samuel Rosov to Vladimir Nabokov

I can only extend my heartfelt congratulations to your young ancient
great little country.—Vladimir Nabokov to Yitzhak Livni

There are moral principles passed down from father to son,
from generation to generation.—Vladimir Nabokov

Vladimir Nabokov (1899–1977) was a master of prose in both his native Russian and American English. His reputation and influence have grown considerably since his death. *Lolita*, a brilliant satire on mid-twentieth-century mores, is Nabokov's most famous novel. Though he wrote many other novels both before and after the publication of *Lolita*, it is this book with which he is most frequently associated. In terms of literary reputation, he has now achieved the status of an immortal. As critic Brian Boyd has noted, "By the beginning of the 1990s, after a posthumous lull, a resurgence of interest in Nabokov was clearly in evidence . . . and more are now ready to name him the foremost writer of the mid-twentieth century, and one of the greatest of all times."[107]

Despite his fame, one does not readily think of Nabokov in relation to social or political issues; his self-portrayal as an aesthete works against it. He often criticized those who use literature for political ends. The Soviet example served as a dire warning against the use of art for political purposes, and he mocked Socialist Realism. But Nabokov had firm ethical and moral commitments, foremost among them a concern for the oppressed, and this concern motivated him to speak out on certain political issues. One of the few issues on which he would comment publicly was the persistence of anti-Semitism. In his later life and work, Nabokov moved beyond opposition to anti-Semitism to an assertively philo-Semitic stance, which would be most clearly expressed in his high regard for the State of Israel. As we shall see, Nabokov first learned of Zionism in his St. Petersburg grammar school; one of his closest childhood friends, Samuel Rosov, was even then an enthusiastic Zionist.

Many of Nabokov's books have been translated into Hebrew, and he has had a powerful influence on Israeli writers and critics. Still, Jewish themes and characters have remained a largely unrecognized aspect of his remarkable art and remarkable life story. But is there more here than the proverbial "elephant and Jewish question," or the "butterfly and the Jewish question," to substitute a Nabokovian symbol? To explore the Jewish aspects of Nabokov's life and work forces us to examine afresh the complex aesthetic and moral dimensions of this master's oeuvre.

NABOKOV AS MORALIST

For many students of twentieth-century literature, Nabokov's work is understood as purely aesthetic, both in content and concern. He is a master of language and technique in both Russian and English, but his work is not viewed as having a moral dimension. For those who do not know his work well, who may be familiar with the reputation of *Lolita* (but may not have read that novel), the name Nabokov conjures up the image of an aging roué, perhaps a cleaned-up Charles Bukowski, an aging litterateur inexorably drawn to prepubescent girls. This view was enshrined in the Police song *Don't Stand So Close to Me*: "It's no use, he sees her, he starts to shake and cough / Just like the, old man in, that book by Nabokov." Careful scrutiny of Nabokov's life and work, however, reveals a deeply moral man and a profoundly moral body of work. Nabokov noted in his journal: "There are moral principles passed down from father to son, from generation to generation."[108] He strove to express these moral principles in his fiction—and in his life.

The first critical studies of Nabokov's novels focused on the aesthetic dimensions of his prose. They emphasized wordplay and internal literary references as important keys to solving the puzzles presented by his work. But in the early 1980s, a shift in Nabokov studies allowed for a more philosophical, even religious, reading of his novels, stories, and poems. As Samuel Schuman pointed out in 2000, Nabokov was long identified with the "art for art's sake" movement. For his early critics, ideas mattered little in his oeuvre. Schuman, however, concluded that "a more reflective contemporary overview of Nabokov's life and work gives the lie to such an impression: it is very evident that he was very deeply serious about a great many things."[109] Among those "many things" about which Nabokov was deeply serious was the fate of persecuted minorities in general and the fate of the Jews in particular. An integrated, holistic view of Nabokov's fiction requires that we read the aesthetic and moral dimensions of his work as delicately intertwined. And an interest in and concern for Jews and Jewish culture was one focus of his moral concern that we must consider.

Before we discuss Nabokov's concern for Jewish matters, however, let us look at Nabokov as both an aesthete and a moralist. He was a novelist known for his aesthetic refinement and sensibility and not for his commitment to any ideology. He opposed the harnessing of literature for social ends, and mocked those writers whose political commitments were transparent. As he said in the introduction to his novel *Bend Sinister*, "There exist few things more tedious than a discussion of general ideas inflicted by author or reader upon a work of fiction." Soviet Socialist Realism he treated dismissively, and Pasternak's *Doctor Zhivago* came in for special derision. The notion of literature as a "tool of the State" seemed to him particularly dangerous. His disdain for agitprop was not limited to Russian literature; he also dismissed the work of Thomas Mann, especially after he won the Nobel Prize. Nabokov conveyed his opinions on literature most forcefully in his popular lectures at Cornell University. For the great novelist was also a great college teacher. His lectures were later published as *Lectures on Literature*, *Lectures on Russian Literature*, and *Lectures on "Don Quixote."*

At the conclusion of his famous Cornell course, Literature 311–12, Nabokov advised his students, "The novels we have imbibed will not teach you anything that you can apply to the obvious problems of life. . . . In fact, the knowledge I have been trying to share with you is pure luxury. . . . It may help you, if you have followed my instructions, to feel the pure satisfaction which an inspired and precise work of art gives."[110] For Nabokov, art was inspiration, not instruction.

If Nabokov was an aesthete, however, he was not an amoral aesthete. For him morality was intimately linked to the idea of beauty: "For me a work of fiction exists only insofar as it affords me what I shall bluntly call aesthetic bliss, that is a sense of being somehow, somewhere, connected with other states of being where art (curiosity, tenderness, kindness, ecstasy) is the norm."[111] Foremost in his moral universe were the concepts of commitment, fidelity, equality, and freedom of expression. He saw a great threat to these principles in the rise of authoritarian regimes—particularly Stalin's Russia and Hitler's Germany. In *Bend Sinister*, written in 1947, Nabokov conflates the histories and crimes of the two dictatorships to create a terrifying dystopia. Though he denied that *Bend Sinister* was a political novel ("I am neither a didacticist nor an allegorizer"), he did note that it reflected his brushes with "idiotic and despotic regimes that we all know . . . worlds of tyranny and torture, of Fascists and Bolshevists, of Philistine thinkers and jackbooted 'baboons.' "[112] In both the German and Russian social experiments, minorities presented a challenge to the hegemonic totalizing energy of authority, with Jews serving as a very special case in both regimes. In a 1972 essay, Robert Alter compared and contrasted Nabokov's art with the works of German novelist Hermann Broch and Hebrew poet Saul Tchernichowsky: "I want to be so bold as to say that a lively consciousness of history shapes Nabokov's artistic endeavors. . . . The artist resists totalitarianism . . . he is the most powerful representative of the human race. The act of the imagination, which is much more than an aesthetic luxury, is the way that the human race manifests its humanity."[113]

Nabokov's favorite of his novels, *Invitation to a Beheading*, published in 1935, is deeply concerned with political and moral issues. In the opening pages, Cincinnatus, a prisoner of an unnamed totalitarian state, is condemned to death by decapitation, and he is made to cooperate, or collaborate, in his own execution. On the day of Cincinnatus's execution, the representatives of the state are indeed cruel and capricious:

> "Well, and how is our doomed friend today?," quipped the elegant, dignified director, compressing in his meaty purple paws the cold little hand of Cincinnatus. "Is everything all right, no aches or pains?"[114]

Invitation to a Beheading tells of one man's imprisonment in a fortress from which there seems no escape. Like Kafka's work, it presaged a world in which millions of people would be enslaved and tortured by the agents of totalitarian regimes. In the introduction to the 1959 English translation, Nabokov noted, "I composed the Russian original exactly a quarter of a century ago in Berlin, some fifteen years after escaping from the Bolshevist regime, and just before the Nazi regime reached its full volume of welcome."[115]

These novels of the 1930s and 1940s have a moral/political dimension, but what of Nabokov's work of the 1950s and 1960s? Many readers think of *Lolita*, Nabokov's most famous novel, as an amoral book, but like many challenging erotic classics, it is in fact deeply moral. In the novel, Humbert Humbert, who is in jail for murder, recounts his adventures and misadventures, including his pursuit of his twelve-year-old step-daughter Lolita and his successful plan to murder Clare Quilty, a competitor for Lolita's affection. Humbert describes his erotic interests as a "humiliating, sordid, taciturn love life." Humbert's obsession with and exploitation of Lolita is portrayed in the darkest manner and condemned in the strongest terms possible. Nabokov, while brilliantly depicting erotic obsession and exploitation, shows us their often murderous consequences. What *Lolita* exposes is America's sexual confusion and hypocrisy. As the American poet Howard Nemerov noted: "*Lolita* is . . . a moral work, if by morality in literature we are to understand the illustration of a usurious rate of exchange between our naughty desires and virtuous pains, of the process whereby pleasures become punishments, or our vices suddenly become recognizable as identical with our sufferings."[116]

In the late 1950s when *Lolita* was published, the general public saw Nabokov as a "dirty-old-man." In actuality, the novelist was as truly "moral" as his novel. According to his biographers, the erotic adventures of Nabokov's youth culminated in his courtship of and marriage to Vera Slonim, to whom he would remain married, most happily and faithfully, it seems, for more than forty years, until his death in 1977. Nabokov may have "strayed" from the marriage, but only with a woman of his own age. He was *not* attracted to young girls of Lolita's age. Nabokov's lovingly described Lolita was an artistic creation, but she was not the object of the novelist's erotic reveries. Rather, she was the object of the fantasies of his creation, Humbert Humbert. In a 1956 letter to Edmund Wilson, Nabokov made this request of the eminent critic: "When you do read *Lolita*, please mark that it is a highly moral affair."[117]

In Nabokov's personal life, conventional morality was the standard; in his novels and stories, the unconventional reigns. Humbert's obsession with Lolita and his lyrical, lingering descriptions of her resemble nothing so much as detailed anatomical descriptions of pinned butterflies. Thus the descriptions of her anatomy, the erotic obsession of Humbert, reflect the scientific obsession of her pursuer, and by extension, the author. Nabokov, of course, had a scientific interest in and an aesthetic passion for lepidopterology, the study and description of butterflies. "[I]n *Lolita*," writes one scholar, "Nabokov has transposed his own passion for butterflies into his hero's passion for nymphets."[118]

How might we connect this to Nabokov's philo-Semitism (Here we might speak of "the Butterfly and the Jewish Question")? Brian Boyd, Nabokov's biographer, notes that Nabokov "was deeply serious as a thinker—an epistemologist, metaphysician, moral philosopher, and aesthetician." The image many readers come away with, that Nabokov is somehow identified with his characters, is far too facile. Nabokov writes convincingly of the extremes of human obsession and behavior, but, says Boyd, "he was also quite 'normal,' lucidly sane, outraged by cruelty, committed to faithful love after a youth of energetic sexual adventure."[119] One could say that Nabokov's normality and sanity led him to portray unconventional stances in a world gone mad. He was a witness to both the Russian Revolution and the rise of European fascism. Unlike many European intellectuals, he rejected both the Bolshevik and Fascist alternatives and remained steadfast in his liberalism. Philo-Semitism was one of the most enduring aspects of this liberalism. Nabokov and his wife, Vera, exemplified this moral stance at a time and place in which it was rare. Some of Nabokov's admirers have recognized this. Martin Amis spoke of Nabokov's "unwavering though riskily stretched . . . moral concern."[120] And Azar Nafisi, in *Reading Lolita in Tehran*, makes the case that *Lolita* goes "against the grain of all totalitarian perspectives." Nafisi cites Vera Nabokov's own appraisal of the Lolita character. She is not, as most critics would have, a "spoiled brat" but, rather, a child who is helpless, dependent on "monstrous HH," and possessed of "heartrending courage."[121]

JEWISH ISSUES

After the 1917 Russian Revolution, many Russian exiles in Germany, France, the United States, and elsewhere blamed a "Jewish conspiracy" for the revolution. (This conspiracy theory was one factor linking the White Russians and European fascists during the Second World War.) Nabokov distanced himself from this stance. He was unusual in that he did not turn to the right politically but persisted in his liberalism and resisted scapegoating Jews or other minorities. Because of his liberalism he was ostracized and attacked during his Berlin years (1922 to 1937)—despite writing novels and stories in Russian and having his work published by émigré presses. His politically reactionary fellow émigrés claimed that he was not "really Russian." This language was code for his being a liberal "tainted" by Jewishness, especially as he was married to a Russian Jew. Here we would do well to remember Stephen Eric Bronner's point that "anti-Semitism was never simply an independent impulse. It was always part of a broader project directed against the civilizing impulse of reason and the dominant forces of modernity."[122]

Nabokov's sensitivity to anti-Semitism is evident in his *Lectures on Literature*, distilled from his lectures at Cornell from 1948 to 1958. His great set of lectures on Joyce's *Ulysses* ended the series. At the beginning of the introductory lecture on that novel, Nabokov notes that both Leopold and Molly Bloom are of Jewish origin: "Bloom is of Hungarian Jewish origin. . . . Molly is Irish on her father's side and Spanish-Jewish on her mother's side."[123] Leopold Bloom is an outsider, "the wandering Jew, the type of the exile." With his usual attention to detail, Nabokov points out that Virag, Bloom's father's Hungarian family name, means "flower." And "Henry Flower" is the secret name Bloom uses in his correspondence with his lover. Yes, Nabokov notes, Leopold Bloom's mother is Irish Protestant and his father Jewish. Thus, he remains an outsider in a Catholic country. "Despite these complications," comments Nabokov, "Bloom considers himself a Jew, and anti-Semitism is the constant shadow hanging over him throughout the book."[124]

His American friends related many stories in which Nabokov stood up to anti-Semitism. In the early 1950s, during a vacation in New England, Nabokov, with his son Dmitri and Dmitri's school friend, stopped in a local inn for lunch. The menu had a "Gentiles only" notice on its cover. "He called over the waitress and asked her what the management would do if there appeared at the door that very moment a bearded and be-robed man, leading a mule bearing his pregnant wife, all of them dusty and tired from a long journey. 'What . . . what are you talking about?' the waitress stammered. 'I am talking about Jesus Christ!' exclaimed Nabokov, as he pointed to the phrase in question, rose from the table, and led his party from the restaurant."[125]

What, then, are we to make of this set of interests, associations, and sympathies, and what is the meaning of these associations in a comprehensive understanding of Nabokov's art? Nabokov surrounded himself with Jewish and philo-Semitic associates; we might contextualize this by looking at the general sympathy for Jews among European liberals during the 1930s and

1940s. As a persecuted minority, threatened with extermination, Jews evoked sympathy. This sympathy persisted in the postwar period, though it was by no means universal. With the establishment of the State of Israel in 1948, some of the sympathy of liberal intellectuals was lost—and it virtually disappeared after Israel's victory in the 1967 war. Disillusionment with Israel set in; the Jewish state, whatever its self-presentation, was, as far as many American and European liberals were concerned, now a victor, not a victim.

Vladimir Nabokov's intellectual trajectory, in Jewish matters as in all others, was uniquely individualistic. On the establishment of Israel he became an ardent Zionist, and remained so until his death in 1977. Like his onetime friend Edmund Wilson, he often found himself defending Israeli policies when many in the American literary world, Jews among them, found these policies indefensible. Like Wilson, Nabokov denounced anti-Semitism. They both objected to the campaign for clemency for Ezra Pound and argued against the awarding in 1950 of the prestigious Bollingen Prize for Poetry to Pound. As Nabokov's Cornell colleague Alfred Appel noted, "Doubtless Nabokov's detestation of Ezra Pound—'that total fake'—was based on the poet's fascist and anti-Semitic opinions, as well as on the artistic clutter and confusion of the Cantos."[126]

For many readers it comes as something of a surprise to find that throughout his long and illustrious life Nabokov displayed an uncommon interest in, and deep concern for the welfare and fate of the Jews. He seldom commented on public affairs; his concerns tended to be literary and aesthetic, not political. He did incorporate his interest in and concern for the Jews in some of his stories and novels, and he expressed his principled opposition to all forms and expressions of anti-Semitism in the interviews he reluctantly granted. (Nabokov rarely granted spontaneous interviews. Questions had to be submitted to him in writing in advance. He would then answer them in writing, occasionally reading the answers aloud to his interviewer.)

By declaring himself to be a philo-Semite (not just declaring, but living out the role), Vladimir Nabokov was taking an ultimate moral stance for his time and place, and this stance profoundly influenced his life and art. Critic Michael Wood noted that Nabokov's life was a tale of "courage and dignity, discreet concern for members of the family and for history's victims, and almost incredible amounts of hard unseen labor."[127] One might say that Nabokov's view of the relationship between art and morality was the classical Western view—"true art is moral: it seeks to improve life, not debase it."[128] Art instructs. Nabokov's philo-Semitism and his opposition to totalitarianism were for him moral imperatives.

NABOKOV'S LIFE AND HIS "MINYAN"

Vladimir Nabokov's life story has both an elegant beginning and an elegant ending, with much displacement in between. He began life in an upper-class home in St. Petersburg, and it was in that city and on the nearby Rozhestveno Estate that he and his family lived until they were dispossessed and displaced by the Russian Revolution. The family then moved to Berlin. The young Vladimir, who had learned English as a child, attended Cambridge University from 1919 to 1922. When Vladimir was in his last year at Cambridge, White Russian fascists assassinated his father, V. D. Nabokov, in Berlin. The effects of this great trauma would be reflected in many of Nabokov's novels and stories. From 1922 to 1937, Nabokov lived in Berlin, where he met and married Vera Slonim, daughter of an upper-class Russian Jewish family. During his fifteen years in the German capital, he wrote six novels, and it was there that his wife gave birth to their son, Dimitri. With the Nazi rise to power and the enforcement of the Nuremberg Laws, the Nabokovs moved to Paris, where they lived until the fall of France to the Nazis in 1940. From 1940 to 1960 they lived in the United States, spending most of that time at Cornell University in Ithaca, New York. When the financial success of *Lolita* in the late 1950s freed Nabokov from having to earn his living as a professor of literature, he and Vera moved in 1960 to Switzerland, where they spent the rest of their lives ensconced in an elegant hotel in Montreux.

In Switzerland in his early sixties, Nabokov was free to pursue his literary work without teaching responsibilities and other intrusions, and he could indulge his other remarkable career—as a lepidopterist, or butterfly scientist. He made major contributions in this field. There are several species of butterfly named after him, and two books on his butterfly research have been published.[129] He also continued to write new novels and stories—and to translate into English his earlier German and Russian novels, most often assisted in this translation work by his son, Dmitri. During this second European period of their lives, after a twenty-year sojourn in the United States, the Nabokovs began to reestablish connections with old European and Russian friends, among them, Jews and Israelis. They developed close relationships with individuals, Jewish and non-Jewish, that played an important part in the twentieth-century saga of European, American, and Israeli Jewry. Toward the end of his life, Nabokov expressed a strong wish to pay an extended visit to Israel, a state he had long supported and whose writers he deeply influenced.

I think of Nabokov's group of intimates as "Nabokov's Minyan," and here I am playing on the title of his first English-language collection of short stories,

Nabokov's Dozen (1958). First in importance in this "minyan" was Nabokov's wife, Vera Slonim, daughter of a distinguished Russian Jewish family (she traced her lineage to a renowned rabbinical family). Critic Maxim Shrayer has noted, "Following his marriage to Vera Slonim, opposition to anti-Semitism became a leitmotif of Nabokov's life."[130] In fact, the twenty-six-year-old Nabokov had recorded his contempt for anti-Semitism before he met Vera in Berlin in 1925—and, according to Vera Nabokov's biographer, Stacy Schiff, he had demonstrated his philo-Semitism in that "his previous conquests included a disproportionate number of Jewish girlfriends."[131] While Vera was assertively proud of her Jewish heritage, she did not think of herself as religious. She "remained as areligious all her life as her family appeared to be in Russia, but knew well that her existence was predicated on a hard-won—and flimsy—right."[132] As Schiff has noted, "honesty very nearly constituted a religious principle for her." Throughout her life she continually reminded her interlocutors that she was Jewish. This honesty and moral courage were qualities that both Nabokovs shared and endeavored to pass on to their son. There was an amusing and fascinating dynamic in the Nabokov marriage: Vladimir was more sensitive than Vera to anti-Jewish comments, though she did not shrink from expressing herself on this issue.

Despite Vera's influence, Nabokov's moral stance, especially as regards Jewish issues, did not begin with his marriage but had a long family history. More to the point, his philo-Semitism predisposed him to overcome prejudices in the Russian émigré community and marry her. Nabokov's parents and grandparents were prominent liberals and advocates of Jewish rights in tsarist Russia. The story of Vladimir Nabokov's interest in Jews and Jewish themes cannot be told without telling the stories of his father's and grandfather's engagement with liberal politics and Jewish issues. Both men were Russian liberal jurists, academicians, and politicians. The fight against anti-Semitism, a persistent problem in Russian public and intellectual life, served as the cornerstone of their political and intellectual lives.

Nabokov devotes chapter 3 of his acclaimed memoir *Speak, Memory* to his ancestors, of whom he is fiercely proud. He traces his father's family to the late-fourteenth-century Tatar prince Nabok Murza, noting that from the sixteenth century onward the family men were government officials and military officers. His paternal grandmother was of German origin, daughter of a German general who served under the tsar. Vladimir's mother was a daughter of the Russian aristocracy, her father a famous industrialist and landowner. Toward the end of Nabokov's loving, yet acerbic survey of the Nabokov family history, he forcefully makes the point that the nostalgia he feels for the

Russia of his youth, "a hypertrophied sense of lost childhood," is at the core of his "quarrel with Soviet dictatorship." The quarrel is "wholly unrelated to the question of property . . . it is not sorrow for banknotes."[133] Here, too, Nabokov chose to take a moral and personal stand rather than stake out a political or personal position on Bolshevik rule.

Vladimir's grandfather, Dmitri Nabokov (1826–1904), had served as minister of justice under Tsar Alexander II. With the accession of Alexander III, who became tsar following the assassination of his father in 1881, reaction and anti-Semitic legislation set in. Nabokov's grandfather became an advocate for Jewish rights and an outspoken opponent of Konstantin Pobedonostev, Alexander III's reactionary adviser.[134] The notoriously anti-Semitic Pobedonostev, who said of Russian Jews that "one third will be baptized, one third will starve, and one third will emigrate . . . then we shall be rid of them," vilified Dmitri Nabokov for his objections to the persecution of Russian Jews.

Dmitri's son, Nabokov's father, condemned the publication of the *Protocols of the Elders of Zion*, a notorious pamphlet first circulated in 1903, which soon became the manifesto of the proto-fascist Black Hundreds.[135] V. D. Nabokov understood the power of anti-Semitism as a tool of political reactionaries. When he condemned the Kishinev pogrom of 1903 and pointed the finger of blame at the politicians and policemen who enabled the attacks to take place, he suffered the consequences of taking a principled stand.

In the spring of 1903 V. D. Nabokov wrote and published a powerful newspaper article condemning the Kishinev pogrom. According to Vladimir Nabokov's biographer Brian Boyd, "This unrhetorical, coolly analytical article, considered one of the most dazzling productions of Russian public debate under censorship, set the whole capital buzzing."[136] The major point of "The Bloodbath of Kishinev" was that anti-Semitism was a "disease" that not only was harmful to its immediate victims, the Jews, but was equally harmful to the Russian body politic. According to the elder Nabokov, the real responsibility for the pogroms rested with the police and the tsarist government, not with the mob who perpetrated them. Similarly, in the younger Nabokov's stories and novels—like "Signs and Symbols"—we see an unmasking, or uncovering, of anti-Semitic canards, especially those promulgated in the *Protocols*.

In *Speak, Memory* Vladimir Nabokov relates that with the publication of "The Bloodbath of Kishinev" the Russian government deprived his father of his court title. His father became known as "the most outspoken defender of Jewish rights among all Russian gentiles trained in the law."[137] The Kishinev pogrom of 1903, which the elder Nabokov was one of the first Russian intellectuals to condemn, was a pivotal event in modern Jewish history—a catalyst for change that lit a fire under the emergent Zionist movement. The pogrom inspired the Hebrew poet Hayyim Nahman Bialik to write one of his greatest poems, a poem that in turn inspired a whole generation of Zionists. V. D. Nabokov's part in condemning this and other pogroms became a major influence on his son Vladimir's life and work.

Eight years later, when he was working as a journalist, V. D. Nabokov condemned the show trial of Mendel Beylis, a Russian Jew accused of kidnapping a Christian child and using his blood for ritual purposes. The Beylis case, Russia's equivalent of the Dreyfus affair, aroused indignation around the world.[138] Out of sympathy for the accused Jewish defendant, V. D. Nabokov attended the trial as a reporter for a liberal newspaper. Though Beylis was eventually acquitted, liberal reporters who questioned the Russian government's motives in the case were punished. Some journalists were given prison sentences, others, V. D. Nabokov among them, were heavily fined.

From his parents and grandparents the young Vladimir absorbed a tradition of liberalism. His father and grandfather represented between them a century of principled opposition to Russian anti-Semitism and its blood brother, reactionary politics. From the very beginning of Nabokov's life as a writer, we see a "minyan" forming: two committed liberal philo-Semites—his father and grandfather, his Jewish wife, Vera Slonim, and their son, Dmitri. (If we include Vladimir himself, we already have half of the "minyan.") Beyond the immediate family there would be other philo-Semites and Jews.

As Nabokov moved to Berlin, Paris, and then the United States, the "minyan" grew. Concerned with Jewish issues, he was drawn to intellectuals of Jewish origin. In Berlin and Paris, among the Russian émigrés, many of whom were reactionaries, Nabokov was drawn to the critics Ilya Fondaminski and Yuli Aikhenwald, two Russian Jewish liberal intellectuals. To the "minyan" we might also add the names of three American Jewish academicians who befriended the Nabokovs during their American sojourn. These were Harry Levin of Harvard University and Herbert Gold and Meyer Abrams, both of Cornell University. Thus we reach a count of ten even before Nabokov encountered Edmund Wilson, a fellow philo-Semite who was, in the 1940s, Nabokov's friend and supporter, though the two literary titans eventually became estranged. We could easily double the size of this "minyan" with Nabokov's other Jewish and philo-Semitic associates.

Another central figure in "Nabokov's Minyan" was a friend from his childhood. At the Tenishev School, "one of the best Russian secondary institutions of the time . . . emphatically liberal, democratic, and nondiscriminatory in terms of rank, race, and creed,"[139] Vladimir Nabokov's closest friend was

Samuel Rosov, one of the many Jewish students in the school. Tenishev, liberal and privately run, was not bound by the Russian state quota system, which limited Jewish enrollment in Russian schools to five percent. At this remarkable school, Vladimir first learned of Zionism, an ideology then making powerful inroads among Russian Jewish youth. Rosov, in early adolescence, declared himself a Zionist and eventually moved to Palestine. Writing to Nabokov decades later, Rosov reminisced about their years together at school: "Classifications did not exist for you—Armenian, Jew, German. You distinguished people only by their individual characteristics and not by labels of any kind."[140]

Rosov would cross paths with Nabokov a decade later. When Vladimir was enrolled as a student at Cambridge University (1919–22), Samuel Rosov was studying at University College London.[141] The two school friends sought each other's company in their new English environment, and from Rosov Nabokov learned about the various forms of emergent Jewish nationalism. Rosov, who was to spend a good part of his life in Haifa, would again renew his friendship with Nabokov many years later.

While in his last year at Cambridge, Nabokov began to publish his first poems. Another member of the "minyan," Aleksander Glikberg, was instrumental in launching Nabokov's writing career.[142] Glikberg, whose pen name was Sasha Chorny, founded a Russian press in Berlin to publish émigré writers. Under the pen name "Sirin," Nabokov began to publish his first work.

Vladimir Nabokov's lifelong liberalism, philo-Semitism, and antiracism were no doubt strengthened by the great trauma of his life: a White Russian terrorist shot his father while he was giving a speech in Berlin in 1922. Chapter 9 of *Speak, Memory* is devoted to his father's life and death. At the time of the assassination in March of 1922, Vladimir, a student at Cambridge, was spending Easter vacation at his parents' apartment in Berlin. Vladimir's father was active in émigré politics, working to establish a united political front against the Bolshevik regime. At a mass meeting in support of this cause, V. D. Nabokov was shot when he tried to protect Pavel Milyukov, former Kerensky government minister, from an assassin's bullet. Nabokov died; Milyukov survived. In his diary Vladimir recorded his reactions to the news of his father's murder: " 'Father is no more.' These four words hammered in my brain and I tried to imagine his face, his movements. The night before he had been so happy, so kind."[143] Vladimir's response to this tragedy was to immerse himself in his work—studying for his Cambridge exams and producing new fiction and poetry.

The Nabokovs' concern for the treatment and fate of European Jewry was part and parcel of their liberalism. Vladimir's son, Dmitri, spoke of his father's "utter freedom from anything cruel, cheap, or mean . . . (he had) a menacing tone he used only when defending the weak and blameless."[144] This serves to remind us that Nabokov's concern for the underdog was not limited to Jews. The persecution of minorities anywhere aroused his interest and indignation. As critic L. L. Lee noted in the mid-1970s, "Racism, in life or in fiction, is abhorrent to Nabokov."[145]

In the 1930s, Nabokov realized that his fate was linked to the fate of European Jewry and European Jewish refugees. He left Berlin in 1937—as an antifascist, and as the husband of a Jew. He spoke of the "nauseous dictatorship" of Hitler. When France fell to the Germans, the Nabokovs were able to gain passage to the United States through the offices of the Union of Russian Jews, a Jewish refugee organization in Paris. "In gratitude for his father's resolute attacks almost four decades before on Russia's officially sanctioned anti-Semitism," the organization provided the Nabokovs with first-class tickets from France to New York in mid-May 1940.[146]

When Nabokov immigrated to the United States in 1940, he became very aware of American racial discrimination. In 1942, he was invited to lecture at Spelman College in Atlanta, Georgia. He spent five days at the historically black women's college. The students and faculty responded to his lectures on Pushkin, in which he stressed Pushkin's Ethiopian heritage (Pushkin's grandfather was a freed Ethiopian slave who had been brought to the royal court in St. Petersburg), "with wild enthusiasm."[147] Each day of his visit, Nabokov met with Florence Read, Spelman's president, and with other African American intellectuals.[148] As a result of this visit, Florence Read became a lifelong friend of the Nabokovs.

JEWS IN NABOKOV'S FICTION

Overtly Jewish characters are infrequent in Nabokov's fiction. One important exception is the short story "Signs and Symbols," a much beloved and often anthologized story. Nabokov called this tale "my story about the old Jewish couple."[149] The couple's ethnicity, however, is only implied, not made explicit in the story, which makes the tale all the more powerful.

The New Yorker published "Signs and Symbols," one of Nabokov's first stories written in English, in 1948, and the story later appeared in *Nabokov's Dozen* (1958). (Here "Nabokov's Dozen" and "Nabokov's Minyan" converge.) In the story, the elderly protagonists, whose only son is mentally ill and confined to a psychiatric hospital, are accepting of the pain that the world metes out to them. We learn that they and their son were refugees from occupied Europe. As a child, their son was "prodigiously gifted," but in adolescence his gift degenerated into " 'referential mania' . . . [he] imagines that everything happening around him is a veiled reference to his personality and existence."[150] The shift in their lives came with immigration to the United States, when the boy was only ten years old, and he has never adjusted to American life. Acceptance of pain is ingrained in the parents, "for after all living did mean accepting the loss of one joy after another." After a disastrous trip to visit their son at the psychiatric hospital, the mother thinks of "the endless waves of pain that for some reason or other she and her husband had to endure."[151]

The son's madness and the helplessness of his parents result from their European experiences. As critic Leona Toker said of this "mad Jewish boy": "His acute paranoia, his sense of the systematic hostility of the world, is a morbidly condensed literalization of the Jewish experience in Europe at the time of the Holocaust."[152] Writing of Nabokov's dark portrayal of totalitarianism in his novel *Bend Sinister*, critic Michael Wood has noted: "The Holocaust itself . . . is figured in Nabokov as a recurring massacre or mutilation of the innocent; it is what cannot be borne, let alone performed, except by moral monsters; what cannot be spoken of, except by the monster's witting or unwitting allies. But it is also what must be borne, because it is what there is, and culture and the mind are not entirely helpless."[153]

The most direct reference in Nabokov's fiction to Jewish victims of the Nazis comes in his 1957 novel *Pnin*. The protagonist, an émigré Russian intellectual teaching at a small American liberal arts college, is reminded, through a chance encounter, of a young Jewish woman with whom he had had a brief affair. He knows that she did not survive the Second World War but died in a German concentration camp. "In order to exist rationally," writes Nabokov, "Pnin had taught himself, during the last ten years, never to remember Mira Belochkin—not because, in itself, the evocation of a youthful love affair, banal and brief, threatened his peace of mind . . . but because, if one were quite sincere with oneself, no conscience, and hence no consciousness, could be expected to subsist in a world where such things as Mira's death were possible." Pnin imagines the various ways Mira might have died in Buchenwald, the camp that is "an hour's stroll from Weimar, where walked Goethe, Herder, Schiller."[154]

As his biographers have noted, Nabokov's evocation of loss is both without sentimentality and without cruelty.[155] Brian Boyd writes of the novel *Pnin* that Mira Belochkin stands "at the moral center of the novel . . . [as she was] put to death in Buchenwald simply because she was Jewish and therefore less than human to those who accepted a millennium of derisive dismissals. She comes to represent humanity at its best and most vulnerable."[156]

In his fiction, Nabokov links the persistence of anti-Semitism to the rise of totalitarian regimes. Two short stories written in the 1930s, "Cloud, Castle, Lake" and "Tyrants Destroyed," express the writer's contempt for the Stalinist and Hitlerite regimes. In "Tyrants Destroyed," the narrator imagines the successful assassination of a dictator who has ruled and ruined a country for decades. The protagonist is obsessed with the tyrant; his hatred for "the leader of the people" is mixed with a twisted love. Brian Boyd notes that in this story, "Nabokov exposes with devastating accuracy the inanity of hero worship, and statist planning."[157] Just as Vladimir's father fought anti-Semitism as an aspect of state oppression and tyranny, his son Vladimir condemned anti-Semitism as a persistent aspect of totalitarianism.

The persistence of anti-Semitism, even after the Nazi crimes against the Jews have been revealed, is the theme of another Nabokov short story, "Conversation Piece." The protagonist, a thinly disguised young Nabokov, who has recently arrived in Boston after fleeing Europe in 1938, finds himself confused with another Russian émigré of the same name. As it turns out, this is not the first time that the protagonist has been confused with his unwanted "double." Ten years earlier, while living in Prague, a right-wing organization demanded that he return their copy of *The Protocols of the Elders of Zion*. As Vladimir Nabokov describes it in this story, "This book, which in the old days had been wistfully appreciated by the Tsar, was a fake memorandum the secret police had paid a semiliterate crook to compile." The library, of course, sees it differently; it demands the return of a "popular and valuable work." "Conversation Piece" was the first Nabokov story to appear in *The New Yorker*. Brian Boyd notes, "What seems to me most striking about the story is its immense shadowy background of pain and frightening possibility; not its secret but its silence."[158]

NABOKOV AND KAFKA

The Jewishness of Joyce's protagonist in *Ulysses* is but one of a number of astute Nabokovian observations about Jewish writers and characters in the Modernist canon. Nabokov notes in his lectures on Kafka's "The Metamorphosis" that the writer "came from a German-speaking Jewish family in Prague, Czechoslovakia. He is the greatest German writer of our time. Such poets as Rilke or such novelists as Thomas Mann are dwarfs or plaster saints in comparison to him."[159] He considered *The Metamorphosis* one of the four great novels of the twentieth century. The others were *Ulysses*, Proust's *Remembrance of Things Past*, and Andrey Bely's *Petersburg*.[160] Here Nabokov disagreed with Edmund Wilson, whose opinion of Kafka's talents was rather low. Nabokov goes into great detail to prove that Gregor Samsa was not transformed into a "cockroach," as some translators would have it, but into a monstrous beetle. Nabokov's training as a lepidopterist came into play here, complete with blackboard sketches of beetles. What Nabokov does not mention in the lectures is his personal obsession with Kafka. During the first months of his stay in Berlin in 1922, Nabokov imagined that he often saw Kafka riding the Berlin streetcar system.[161] "Often he sat across from me. Of course I didn't know it then, but I am certain it was Kafka. One could not forget that face, its pallor, the tightness of the skin, those most extraordinary eyes, hypnotic eyes glowing in a cave."[162] When told in the 1960s that it was unlikely that he ever saw Kafka, Nabokov nevertheless continued to speak of his "theoretically possible glimpse of Kafka."[163]

While Nabokov notices and highlights Kafka's Jewish origins, he does not see—as Max Brod did—the Jewish religious implications of Kafka's writings. For Nabokov, Kafka was ethnically Jewish but not spiritually Jewish. This view is in keeping with Nabokov's tendency to concentrate on the realistic detail of even the most fantastic fiction. In his Cornell lectures on literature, Nabokov hammers home the observation that Gregor Samsa was turned into a beetle, not a cockroach. Nabokov, as a critic, was reluctant to see "spiritual meaning" in an author's work, much as he was reluctant to endorse the social utility of literature.

How might one explain Nabokov's affection for Kafka? Let us return to the conclusion of Nabokov's Cornell lectures on *The Metamorphosis*: "You will mark Kafka's style. Its clarity, its precise and formal intonation in such striking contrast to the nightmare matter of his tale. No poetical metaphors ornament his stark black and white story. The limpidity of his style stresses the dark richness of his fantasy. Contrast and unity, style and matter, manner and plot are most perfectly integrated."[164] Was Nabokov himself aspiring to such integration? Are we to take Nabokov's *Lectures on Literature* as a casebook of his personal aspirations as a novelist and short story writer? Despite Nabokov's professed admiration for Kafka, he at times goes out of his way to distance his work from any similarities to Kafka's. For, when reflecting on his own writings, Nabokov insisted that they were free of outside influence. In the introduction to the English-language version of *Invitation to a Beheading*, Nabokov comments on the Russian émigré response to the 1935 Russian original of the novel: "Émigré reviewers, who were puzzled but liked it, thought they distinguished in it a 'Kafkaesque' strain, not knowing that I had no German, was completely ignorant of modern German literature, and had not yet read any French or English translations of Kafka's works."[165] Contrast Nabokov's Kafka with Robert Alter's: "What is peculiar and, I would say, peculiarly Jewish in all this is Kafka's textualization of the truth[;] . . . the distinctive strength as well as the drastic limitation of the Hebrew orientation, with a belief in revelation as its point of departure, was its commitment to deriving everything from the text rather than from the circumambient world."[166]

NABOKOV, CHRISTIANITY, AND JUDAISM

Nabokov's lifelong commitment to Jewish causes and his consistent pro-Zionist stance define him as a "Christian Zionist" of sorts. But his Christian Zionism was unique, idiosyncratic, and bears little resemblance to the right-wing Christian Zionism of today. Unlike the Robertsons, Falwells, and Ralph Reeds of Evangelical Zionism, Nabokov supported liberal causes within Israel, and he was dismayed by encroachment on civil liberties by Israel's Jewish religious authorities. In the 1970s Nabokov sent money to the League for the Abolition of Religious Coercion in Israel, a group that advocated the promotion of civil institutions (in place of religious ones) in Israeli society. Nabokov's Zionism was more akin to Reinhold Niebuhr's liberal Protestant Zionism than to the right-wing Zionism of today's Evangelical Christians.[167]

Nabokov was brought up in the Russian Orthodox Church and never formally left it, which raises an important question: Up to now I have traced Nabokov's relationship to Jewish issues in the sense of ethnic issues, but what of religious questions? First, can we speak of Nabokov as a "religious" writer? What is his understanding, and use, of his Russian Orthodox upbringing? Does he display religious sensibilities, or use religious themes or tropes? Second, what was his understanding of Judaism as a religious system? I noted that he was reluctant to see religious elements in the writings of others. What of his own fiction? Was he aware of their religious implications? In "Death, Immortality, and Nabokov's Jewish Theme," Maxim Shrayer traces Jewish themes in Nabokov's fiction. He sees *Pnin*, Nabokov's 1957 novel of a Russian academic misfit's misadventures in the American academy as "the pinnacle of Nabokov's Jewish theme," a theme Shrayer identifies as a qualified belief in a "reciprocal relationship" between this life and the afterlife. "Pnin's awareness amounts to an understanding, prominent in Judaism, that life in the other world is only significant insofar as it affects those living in this world."[168] This seems to me too vague a definition of a "Jewish theme." Rather, it would be more productive to consider Nabokov's religiosity within the framework of the church in which he was raised—the Russian Orthodox Church. Samuel Schuman, in a very insightful article makes the case that Nabokov's visual acuity and memory and his 'painterly' writing style are linked to an "iconic impulse."[169] Nabokov grew up surrounded by the icons of the Russian Orthodox Church. Their spiritual power shaped his view of the arts—of painting, poetry, and prose. I agree with Schuman that "formal religion, as well as intimations of a world beyond our everyday reality figures importantly in Nabokov's art."[170] In his novels, earthy as their surface might seem, there is deep religious sensibility. In his stories of Jews and other non-Christians we see this sensibility at work; it is not limited to the Russian Orthodox sphere.

One aspect of Russian Orthodox life that Nabokov rejected was a tendency toward anti-Semitism. His lifelong admiration of both individual Jews and Jews as a collective led him, as it led many midcentury intellectuals, to sympathy for the idea of a Jewish state. Unlike many of his fellow artists, Nabokov's commitment to Israel strengthened, rather than diminished, over time. He wanted to see and experience the Jewish state firsthand.

NABOKOV AND ISRAEL

Letters in the Nabokov Archives demonstrate the novelist's interest in and connection to Israel, and tell of Nabokov's attempt to arrange a sojourn in Jerusalem. In a letter dated 31 December 1970, Nabokov responded positively to Israeli ambassador to Switzerland Arye Levavi's invitation to visit Israel: "I wish to thank you and your Government very warmly for inviting my wife and me to visit Israel. We shall be delighted to do so. Would April 1972 be an acceptable time? The reason we must wait till 1972 is that we have to go this spring on a business trip to New York for the opening of a musical made of one of my novels. I would be happy to give one or two readings of my works, I would enjoy visiting museums, libraries and universities, and I would like to take advantage of this wonderful occasion to do some butterfly hunting." Three years later, in a letter dated 12 February 1973, Nabokov congratulates Yitzhak Livni on the twenty-fifth anniversary of Israel: "I don't have to tell you what ardent sympathy marks my feelings toward Israel and her twenty fifth anniversary. . . . I can only extend my heartfelt congratulations to your young ancient great little country." In a letter to Ambassador Levavi, dated 9 October 1973, and written on the outbreak of the 1973 Arab-Israeli War, Nabokov offers "a small contribution to Israel's defense against the Arabolshevist aggression. May I beg you to forward the enclosed check. I am leaving the name blank because I don't know to what organization exactly it should go."[171]

In the following year, Nabokov's wish to visit Israel was rekindled when he received a letter of invitation from Mayor Teddy Kollek of Jerusalem. Nabokov replied politely but firmly that "a man seventy-five years old really couldn't embark on a Middle Eastern adventure." He needed the tranquility of Switzerland to continue working steadily. Kollek persisted and sent Nabokov another invitation in late 1974, assuring the writer that he would be guaranteed tranquility and privacy. He could stay at the municipality's guesthouse at Mishkanot Shaananim.[172] In a January 1975 response to Kollek, Nabokov decided that he and Vera would accept the invitation but could not say precisely when they would arrive. Nabokov, assisted by his son Dmitri, was busily working on translating and writing and could not free himself for a trip.

Over the following two years (1975–77), many friends of the Nabokovs, including English publisher George Weidenfeld, urged the couple to make more definite plans to stay at Mishkanot Shaananim. Weidenfeld was Nabokov's English publisher, a loyal fan and friend, and yet another member of Nabokov's "minyan." In the spring of 1976 Nabokov wrote to the director of Mishkanot, Peter Halban, and accepted the invitation: he and Vera would spend the spring of 1977 in Jerusalem. In his letter, Nabokov wrote, "Few things could tempt me more than a trip to Israel, especially in the conditions that you so kindly offer." Among the pleasures that Nabokov looked forward to in Israel was a reunion with his childhood friend Samuel Rosov. Rosov was living in Haifa and had corresponded with Nabokov through the years. Nabokov also wanted to collect and study the butterflies of the Holy Land.

But, alas, the visit was never to take place. Nabokov fell ill in late 1976. From his sickbed, he persisted in planning his visit to Israel. He wrote Teddy Kollek, describing the pneumonia that had put him in the hospital and expressing disappointment that "a trip to which we had long looked forward to" would again have to be postponed. A few months later, in a March 1977 letter to Teddy Kollek, Nabokov apologized for having "again to forego a trip to which we had long looked forward." In April, Kollek replied, wishing Nabokov a speedy recovery, and expressing the hope that he would soon be able to visit Jerusalem. This wish was not to be fulfilled: Nabokov died on 2 July 1977.

Though Vladimir and Vera Nabokov never made it to Israel, their son eventually did. Trained as an opera singer, Dmitri was invited to sing with the Tel Aviv Opera during the 1970s. But for various reasons, including his father's illness, the arrangements with the opera company were postponed. It was not until 1987 that Dmitri performed in Israel; he sang as a bass soloist in the

Dvořák Requiem. "Some years ago," Dimitri wrote, "my parents and I were invited by Mayor Teddy Kollek to visit at an artist's colony here, but Father's illness made that trip impossible. Now I am finally in Israel, to sing with Aronovitch, the most brilliantly original conductor I have ever encountered, in the Dvorak Requiem."[173]

Vladimir Nabokov was the ultimate cosmopolitan. His lifelong advocacy of and identification with the Jewish people has been little recognized. Nabokov never reached Israel, but one could see why the drama of Israel's "restoration" would appeal to him. As Alfred Kazin put it, "Nabokov stands out just now because he has no country but himself. He is the only refugee who could have turned statelessness into absolute strength."[174] Israel offered a solution to one case of statelessness, that of the Jews. The establishment of Israel, facilitated by a resurgence of Jewish culture, brought about a Hebrew literary and cultural renaissance. This cultural rebirth caught Nabokov's attention and fired his imagination. Though he saw himself as cosmopolitan, he was nevertheless a Russian cosmopolitan, whose work valorized and analyzed Russian culture. Therefore, he could appreciate the link between Jewish culture, Israel, and the Diaspora.

6

Jewish Settlers and Christian
Zionists (1967–2007)

*If you want to know where history is headed, simply keep your
eye on what God is doing with Israel.*[1]

A Remarkable Partnership

Since the mid-1970s a number of American Christian fundamentalists have
forged a remarkable and unexpected partnership with the Israeli settler movement. Those fundamentalists most deeply influenced by dispensationalist
ideas have been at the forefront of this alliance. Though some admirers of the
alliance have dubbed it "a match made in heaven," more skeptical observers
have cast a jaundiced eye on this most unexpected marriage of convenience.
As many fundamentalists feel obligated to "bring Jews to Christianity," and
orthodox Jews consider Christianity an alien, competing, and hostile religion,
one might ask how these very different religious groups have managed to
affiliate and cooperate over the past thirty years. This chapter will tell that
remarkable tale.

As we have seen in previous chapters, American Christians of various
denominations had long been enamored of the Jewish return to Zion. Belief
in the historical accuracy of the biblical narratives influenced public opinion and helped make the case for a Jewish state. But in the first two decades
of Israeli history (1948–68) fundamentalist Christians had few direct allies
among either Israeli or American Jews. For both of those Jewish groups were
overwhelmingly secular and politically liberal. Neither Israelis nor American
Jews evinced much interest in working with conservative Christians, some of
whom were active in missions to the Jews. Why then should Jewish groups
ally themselves with Christians seeking to convert them?

The military and political outcome of the 1967 war changed that situation radically. As Israeli journalist Gershom Gorenberg has noted: "The Six-Day War did more than create a new political and military map in the Middle East. It also changed the mythic map, in a piece of the world where myths have always bent reality."[2] One drastic change in the mythic maps of some Jews and Christians was the establishment of an alliance between the Israeli Right and the American Christian Right. The architects of this alliance were American church leaders influenced by dispensationalist ideas and Israeli politicians of the Likud bloc.

Since 1967, this alliance has had a polarizing effect on American public discourse. The Israeli Right–Christian Right alliance was favored and facilitated by the George W. Bush administration and its supporters. Opponents of Bush administration policies in the Middle East tended to demonize this alliance, blaming it for the intractability of the Israeli-Palestinian conflict and the neoconservative push to "democratize" the Middle East, a push that has led to an open-ended American occupation in Iraq and the threat of an American attack on Iran.

In earlier chapters we traced the very long development of Christian Zionist thought and action. Jewish messianism, from which the Israeli settler movement draws its inspiration, has, of course, an even longer history. Jewish and Christian messianisms, at odds for two millennia, have now, in the beginning of the twenty-first century, begun to converge. As historian of religion Yaakov Ariel noted, this is a most unexpected development, one that would have been inconceivable a few decades ago.[3] Despite their seemingly irreconcilable religious differences, over the last few decades conservative Christians and religious Zionist Jews have forged a powerful and effective relationship, one with wide-ranging geopolitical ramifications.

~

Zionism and Jewish Messianism

How, then, did political Zionism understand and utilize traditional Jewish messianism? In a secularized and generalized form Jewish messianism played a large part in the early development of secular Zionist thought. Messianic expectation was an abstract, symbolic idea in a movement dominated by men who had rebelled against rabbinic authority and the strictures of Orthodox religious practice. In the words of Max Nordau (1849–1923), Theodor Herzl's close associate, "Political Zionism distinguishes itself from the old, religious, messianic form, in that it disavows all mysticism and no longer identifies itself with messianism. It does not expect the return to Palestine to be brought about by a miracle, but rather seeks to accomplish it by its own efforts."[4] Nordau articulated this position in 1902, two years before Herzl's untimely death.

Despite this conscious, deliberate distancing from expectations that an actual messianic leader would appear through divine intervention, Herzl himself was imagined by many of his followers to be the "messiah." Herzl was acutely aware of this projection, and he was careful not to discourage the view that he and the Zionist movement he led represented the fulfillment of messianic expectations.[5] At the time of his death at age forty-four, Herzl was mourned by many as a messianic figure. Rabbi Abraham Isaac Kook (1865–1935), chief rabbi of British Mandate Palestine, eulogized Herzl as the Messiah son of Joseph, the figure from rabbinic legend imagined as the military hero of the Lost Tribes who would prepare the way for the Messiah son of David.[6]

In the Zionist movement during the first half of the twentieth century, Nordau's secular understanding of messianism dominated the movement. Jewish leaders were acutely aware of the disaster wrought by the messianic claims of Sabbatai Sevi, the mystical messiah of Izmir. In the mid-seventeenth century, the Sabbatian movement attracted a large part of the Jewish people. Many gave up their homes and jobs in the expectation that they would soon follow the Messiah to Palestine. When Sabbatai Sevi apostatized to Islam in 1666, a crisis of belief erupted with effects that were felt for the following two centuries. Thereafter, rabbis throughout the Jewish world warned even more stringently against messianic claims. One prominent eighteenth-century European rabbinic scholar, Jacob Emden, "found" secret Sabbatians everywhere, and worked to unmask them. He felt that the heresy had to be extirpated completely. Emden accused some prominent rabbis of his day, among them the renowned Talmudist Yonatan Eibschutz, of being secret Sabbatians.

For this reason, and because of the secularism of the Zionist leadership, the emergence of political Zionism in the late nineteenth century generated much criticism on the part of Orthodox rabbis; many condemned the new movement as the revival of the Sabbatian heresy. The most eminent Orthodox rabbis of the first decade of the twentieth century, among them the Lubavitcher rebbe Sholom Dov Ber Schneersohn, issued powerful condemnations of political Zionism. Schneersohn, in 1903, warned that the Zionists "have made nationalism a substitute for the Torah and the commandments. . . . After this assumption is accepted, anyone who enters the movement regards himself as no longer obliged to keep the commandments of the Torah, nor is there any hope consequently that at some time or another he will return, because, according to his own reckoning, he is a proper Jew in that he is a loyal nationalist."[7] From the vantage point of the first decade of the twenty-first century there are two great ironies here: the first is that, unlike almost all other Hasidic movements, Habad/Lubavitch now supports the religious Zionist settler movement, and the second is that the seventh Lubavitcher rebbe, who died in 1994, has been declared the Messiah by his followers.

Both Hasidim, such as Rabbi Schneersohn of Lubavitch, and Mitnagdim (the opponents of the Hasidim), such as Rabbis Yosef Baer and Hayyim Soloveitchik, of Brisk, condemned political Zionism. Over a decade before Rabbi Schneersohn's edict, the Soloveitchiks proclaimed that the Lovers of Zion were "a new sect like that of Sabbatai Sevi, may his name be blotted out."[8] (Like Habad some of the heirs of this Orthodox movement are also settler supporters.) These early-twentieth-century rabbis did not condemn all attempts to settle in Palestine, but they wanted the pioneering settlers to maintain Jewish law, not flaunt it. Sabbatai Sevi's doctrine was antinomian; he had rebelled against Jewish law and instituted new and innovative religious practices. The new enthusiasts for the return to Zion, many of whom were assertively secular, would have to follow halacha, Jewish law, insisted Europe's rabbinic authorities. Otherwise they could offer no support for the nascent Zionist movement. As a result of this powerful Orthodox critique of the Zionist movement, Orthodox Jews eager to join the movement had to formulate a religious response to the anti-Sabbatian and antisecularist critique.

Among the two hundred delegates to the First Zionist Congress of 1897, there were no Orthodox rabbis from Eastern Europe, and only three from Central and Western Europe.[9] In 1901, four years after the First Zionist Congress, Rabbi Yitzhak Reines (1839–1915) founded Mizrahi, the European religious Zionist movement, as a political faction within the larger Zionist movement. "Rabbi Reines," writes Gideon Shimoni, "was at pains to deny that the Zionist Organization had any messianic pretensions or significance."[10] He sought to bring Orthodox Jews into the activist Zionist fold, without compromising on matters of ritual or faith and without identifying Zionism with messianism.

Rabbi Reines's denial of a messianic basis for Zionism served to counter the argument of some of his Orthodox rabbinical colleagues that Zionists sought to "force the End of Time" through political action and emigration to Palestine. Long before the reaction to Sabbatai Sevi, the rabbinic tradition had discouraged messianic speculation and condemned messianic claims. Both Christianity and the Bar Kochba Rebellion of 135 C.E. were cited as messianic movements that had harmed the Jewish people. Therefore, Orthodox Jews who were moved to support political Zionism sought an organizational framework that could accommodate both their religious and political beliefs, that is, a Zionism that was neither secular nor messianic. Mizrahi enabled them to do this. For decades Mizrahi remained a small, peripheral party within the Zionist movement. With the development of Zionist institutions in Palestine, Mizrahi, too, claimed a part in the emerging structures of the state-in-the-making: it founded schools, kibbutzim, and a political party—all within the structures of the Yishuv. Thus, from the 1920s through the 1960s, Mizrahi was politically and culturally influenced by secular Zionism. Religiously, it remained independent. Its kibbutzim, founded in the 1930s and 1940s, were described as "religious Kibbutzim." The conventional wisdom of the pre-1967 period dubbed them "90 percent Kibbutz and 10 percent religious."[11]

Rabbi Kook the Father and Rabbi Kook the Son

The ideological vanguard of the post-1967 settler movement, spearheaded by Gush Emunim (the Bloc of the Faithful), grew out of the ranks of the religious Zionists of Mizrahi, but it challenged that movement's earlier nonmessianic, socialist, and pragmatist philosophy. The founders of Gush Emunim were students of Rabbi Zvi Yehuda Kook (1891–1982), and they considered themselves the spiritual heirs of Kook's father, Rabbi Abraham Isaac Kook, first Ashkenazi chief rabbi of British Mandate Palestine. The Mizrahi movement's relationship to the Rabbis Kook had always been somewhat ambivalent. The two rabbis were revered, but their theologies proved problematic to their more pragmatic and less mystically inclined rabbinical colleagues.

Short biographies of these two rabbinic luminaries follow, for without their stories, the history of the State of Israel and the saga of the West Bank settlers is incomplete. Rabbi Abraham Isaac Kook, educated in the 1880s in a bastion of Eastern Europe Orthodoxy, the Yeshiva of Volozhin, spoke up in support of political Zionism at a time when many of his rabbinical colleagues were condemning the movement as a heresy. His approach to the renewal of Jewish life in Palestine was redemptive and mystical. In Kook's view, the "new Jews" of Palestine, although assertively secular, would be transformed eventually into "God fearers" by the inherent spirituality of the Land of Israel. He predicted that these rebels against Jewish law would soon return to lives ruled by Torah.

In 1904 Kook accepted an offer to become rabbi of Jaffa in Ottoman Palestine. A few weeks after Kook's arrival in Palestine, Theodor Herzl died in Vienna. Rabbi Kook was invited to deliver the eulogy at the memorial meeting in Jaffa. Invoking rabbinic teachings on the two messiahs, Kook referred to the fallen Zionist leader as "Messiah the son of Joseph." This Messiah, representing the physical realm, is destined to prepare the way for the Davidic Messiah, who represents the spiritual realm. The reason for the early death of Herzl, claimed Kook, was the deep split among Jews about matter and spirit, land and Torah. To bring about the coming of the Davidic Messiah, Jews had to join matter and spirit, and integrate Zionism and Jewish religious practice.

With an extended interruption during World War I, Kook spent the rest of his life in Palestine. From 1904 to 1914 he lived in Jaffa, ministering to all sectors of the Jewish population and serving as a bridge between the various and contentious Jewish groups. In his writings of this period he fused nationalism and messianic expectations. For Kook, all of the Jews of Palestine were actors in the redemptive process, a process of which they were not fully aware, but one whose full meaning would be revealed in messianic times.

One of Rabbi Kook's most elegant expositors, Arthur Hertzberg, analyzed Kook's view of the "new Jews" of early-twentieth-century Palestine: "Jewish secularism, Kook wrote, is a form of self delusion: the spirit of Israel is so closely linked to the spirit of God that a Jewish nationalist, no matter how secularist his intention might be, must, despite himself, affirm the divine. An individual can sever the tie that binds him to life eternal, but the House of Israel as a whole cannot. All of its most cherished national possessions—its land, language, history and customs—are vessels of the spirit of the Lord."[12]

We noted earlier that when Rabbi Reines founded Mizrahi as an Orthodox faction within the Zionist movement, he distanced his faction from messianic ideas and expectations. Like the more secular Herzl, Rabbi Reines focused on Christian persecution of Jews as the reason for a Jewish state: "For not a day has passed in all the days of the *galut* (exile) on which there has not been spilled Jewish blood, and there is not one inch of the globe wherever the Jews have trodden that was not marked by the blood of Israel."[13] To escape persecution, Reines and other Zionist thinkers claimed, Jews had to have their own independent state. To achieve this, they had to be able to defend themselves. On this issue Reines was more prescient than Herzl, who did not foresee armed conflict with the Arabs of Palestine and the neighboring lands.

Rabbi Kook, in contrast, asserted that Zionism was an inherently religious idea—even though Zionism's proponents, whether secular, Orthodox, or somewhere in between, claimed otherwise. In time, said Kook, secularists will repent the error of their ways, and embrace the halacha, Jewish law. In his mystical view of Jewish history and peoplehood, Kook predicted that "the arousal of desire in the whole nation to return to its land, to the essence of its spirit and character, reflects the glow of repentance."[14]

To demonstrate both his loyalty to rabbinic tradition and his ardent support for the secular Zionist pioneers, Kook embarked on a tour of Jewish colonies soon after he arrived in Palestine in 1904. In contrast to most European rabbis of the Yishuv, who spoke in Yiddish, Kook addressed the pioneers in Hebrew and won them over with his obvious concern for their physical and spiritual welfare. For some Zionist pioneers, Kook came to represent the possibility of a bridge between the Orthodoxy of the Old Yishuv and the assertive secularism of the New Yishuv.

For Kook, the militantly antireligious pioneers might not be aware that they were God's agents, but his agents they were. In 1913 he wrote that "there is no doubt that this return to Zion is the beginning of redemption. Its conclusion will come soon."[15] Sixty years later, in 1973, this phrase, "the beginning of redemption," a phrase popularized in the Israeli chief rabbinates' "Prayer for the State of Israel," became the mantra of the leaders of Gush Emunim, the movement that Kook's teachings inspired and that his son Zvi Yehuda Kook led.

A 1914 visit to Europe on the eve of the First World War left Rabbi Kook stranded in Switzerland unable to return to Ottoman Palestine. The enforced separation from his public duties gave him ample time to think and write. In 1916 he moved to London, where he served as a congregational rabbi until he could return to Palestine in 1919. In London when the Balfour Declaration was issued in 1917, Kook was overjoyed at the proclamation of British intent to support the establishment of a Jewish homeland in Palestine. He understood the publication of the declaration in theological terms: "On the great and enlightened British Kingdom has fallen the divinely ordained fate to be first in this sacred endeavor: to build a holy nation on holy land." To a large public assembly of British Jewry Rabbi Kook said, "I haven't come here to thank the British government, but rather to bless it for being the instrument of God to fulfill his promise that we will return to the Land of Israel."[16] Here we can see similarities to Rev. Hechler's reaction to the declaration. Hechler, while pleased with the substance of the document, was disappointed by the Balfour Declaration's secular, diplomatic tone and its lack of a religious dimension.

Intellectually, these five years away from Palestine were very productive for Rabbi Kook. He had time to record his reflections on the grand historical events of his time. Kook understood the results of World War I, among them the Balfour Declaration and the British Mandate in Palestine, as divinely ordained. These events pointed toward what Rabbi Kook called "the ingathering of the exiles," an ingathering that might manifest itself in secular garb, but one that had religious roots and an eventual religious outcome.

In a letter to the Mizrahi delegates to the Eleventh Zionist Congress in 1913, Rabbi Kook rejected the then dominant understanding of Zionism as necessitated by anti-Semitism. As he wrote, "The passing fancy that a despised people is in need of a secure refuge from its persecutors will not be sufficient to vitalize this earth-shaking movement; rather, it is that a holy people, unique among nations, the lion cub of Judah, is stirring from its long slumber, returning to its inheritance, to the pride of Jacob whom he loved."[17]

Returning to British-ruled Palestine in 1919, Kook was appointed chief Ashkenazi rabbi of Jerusalem, and in 1922 Ashkenazi chief rabbinic judge of Palestine, making him the chief rabbi of the British Mandate. But not all Orthodox Jews agreed to his appointment. The non-Zionist and anti-Zionist Orthodox Jews of Jerusalem set up their own rabbinate. In one form or another, this alternative rabbinate still exists today, and still refuses to accept the authority of the government-sanctioned rabbinate. These rabbis of the Orthodox opposition to Zionism disdained Kook's mystical interpretations of current events. Kook spoke of the Balfour Declaration and the British victory in World War I as acts of God, stages in the imminent redemption of Israel and its return to its land. According to Kook, "When there is a great war in the world, the power of the messiah awakens."[18] Rabbis opposed to Kook's view invoked the Talmudic dictum of the Three Oaths. These oaths seemed to forbid all human efforts to redeem the Land of Israel. Rabbi Kook responded respectfully but forcefully to his many ultra-Orthodox critics among the rabbis of the Old Yishuv. In contrast to their blanket condemnation of Zionism, Kook asserted that "the light of holiness dwells also in secular Zionism which is founded upon the love of Israel and of its land."[19]

During the interwar period of great growth in the Yishuv, when the institutions of the Jewish state-in-the-making were shaped, Rabbi Kook's teachings had enormous appeal and influence among many sectors of the Yishuv. He established a Talmudic academy in Jerusalem in the 1920s, a school later known as "Merccaz Harav." His many students would go on to lead the religious Zionist movement in the Mandate and state periods.

In 1920 Kook foresaw a Jewish state that "would be in its essence the expression of an ideal, it would stand at the highest rung of the ladder of fulfillment . . . a throne of God on earth."[20] A half century later, after the 1967 war, this abstract, mystical language would be interpreted by Kook's son and his son's followers in the most concrete fashion. For them, Jewish messianism had to move from speculation to activism. The military conquest of Jerusalem in 1967 was understood by Kook and his followers as a sign of divine intervention in history. The actual restoration of biblical Israel, centered on the revived Temple ritual, became this movement's goal. The elder Rabbi Kook, as a Cohen, descendant of the Temple priesthood, had made the reestablishment of that priesthood a cornerstone of his redemptive plan. On this basis Kook started an institute, "Torat Cohanim," in which students would study the laws of the Temple service. As Kook wrote in 1921: "In this time of our national reawakening, with all of the secularism that surrounds us, preparation (for restoring the priesthood) is incumbent upon us. The eternal anticipation to see priests at worship and Levites at service and Israelites in attendance, that is the essential point of the reawakening. That day is coming near and we have to be prepared for it in all ways."[21]

By the time Rabbi Kook died in 1935 the Jewish population of Palestine had grown to over 300,000. In the period between 1919 and his death in 1935, Kook attempted to create a way for the heads of the Zionist movement and the ultra-Orthodox Jews of Jerusalem to cooperate. Through personal intervention he lessened but could not dissolve the tension between these two seemingly irreconcilable groups. Kook had impeccable rabbinic credentials, and these bolstered his standing in ultra-Orthodox circles. He had long maintained contact with various factions among the secular Jewish pioneers of Palestine as well. Equally significant in the history of the Yishuv was Kook's ability to serve as a bridge between socialists of Ben-Gurion's party and the more socially conservative Revisionists of Jabotinsky's party. Both sides respected Rabbi Kook, although his political sympathies were more aligned with those of the Revisionist Right. When in 1933 the socialist leader Haim Arlosoroff was assassinated on a Tel Aviv beach, Rabbi Kook defended the three accused Revisionist activists accused of the shooting. Kook's campaign to free the accused suspects, a campaign he carried on both within the Yishuv and with the authorities of the British Mandate, was successful. But the release of the suspects further deepened the enmity between Labor and the Revisionists, and it diminished the ability of Rabbi Kook to act as an impartial broker between the Jewish Left and the Jewish Right. Kook and his students, in their insistence that the Revisionists accused of murdering Arlosoroff could not have done so because "one Jew could not kill another," deeply alienated the Labor Party and its followers. As we shall see, these same issues and themes would arise six decades later, in the aftermath of the 1995 assassination of Yitzhak Rabin by Yigal Amir, a fanatical supporter of the settler movement.[22]

Though religious Zionism later found its place within the state-in-the-making of the 1930s and 1940s and in the emerging State of Israel, it did not have the effect on Israeli culture that the elder Rabbi Kook had anticipated. Most Israelis did not "return" to rabbinic law; rather, they became more alienated from it. An assertive secularism was the hallmark of the first decades of Israeli statehood.[23] David Ben-Gurion, Israel's first prime minister, was fond of flaunting his secularism. He delighted in telling and retelling the story of Friday, 14 May 1948, when, after a public reading of Israel's Declaration of Statehood he was invited by his adviser, Rabbi Maimon, to pray at Tel Aviv's Great Synagogue: "I told Rabbi Maimon that it would be the first time I visited a synagogue since I came to Palestine thirty-nine years earlier, in 1909."[24]

The religious Zionist Mizrahi movement developed into a movement thoroughly Israeli in character and style, but like the Revisionist movement it was denied access to the corridors of political power. The first thirty years of Israeli statehood were dominated by the socialist policies of Ben-Gurion's Labor Party, Mapai. Religious matters—Jewish, Muslim, and Christian—were in the hands of officials of the Ministry of the Interior, which was controlled by the National Religious Party.

Unlike his father, who was considered a bridge figure for the Jews of British Mandate Palestine, the younger Rabbi Kook, Zvi Yehuda, ministered to a smaller constituency, the community of young religious Zionists who attended his lectures at the Rav Kook Yeshiva in Jerusalem. In response to the triumph of Israeli secularism, the younger Rabbi Kook, who eventually assumed the leadership of his father's yeshiva, focused his energies on building an alternative Israeli Jewish community, one that was orthodox, activist, pioneering, and politically influential.

In 1948, thirteen years after his father's death, the younger Kook spoke of the recently established Israeli state as divinely ordained and inevitably triumphant: "The divine historical imperative of the purified and revealed end of exile cannot be altered in any way. Neither by the evil machinations of the Gentiles or our own internal deviations. These may cause delays and short detours, but they cannot turn back our progress—which advances with absolute certainty."[25] Kook's pronouncements were considered unusual and, some would claim, heretical. To identify with absolute certainty God's hand in history seemed to the younger Rabbi Kook's Orthodox critics a claim to prophecy, a claim that far exceeded the norms of rabbinic authority. In the classical rabbinic view, prophecy had ceased with the destruction of Jerusalem and the First Temple. There were no more prophets in Israel after the prophets of the Bible. A Talmudic saying noted, "Since the destruction of Jerusalem, prophecy is the province of children and fools." To claim that prophecy had now been revived was theologically daring, and it raised the specter of heresy. Sabbatai Sevi's messianic claims were the most notorious immediate precedent. Jesus's claim to prophecy, a claim that became one of the great dividing lines between Judaism and Christianity, was an earlier example.

~

Rabbi Zvi Yehuda Kook

The younger Rabbi Kook, who continued his father's tradition of interpreting great historical events as signs of Israel's redemption, understood World War II and the birth of the State of Israel in theological terms.[26] This in itself was not unusual. In the aftermath of World War II, many Jewish thinkers, both secular and religious, saw a direct relationship between *Shoah* (destruction) and *Tekumah* (national rebirth) and expressed this relationship in both political and theological terms. Kook's religious interpretation of the Shoah was more daring: for him the murder of Europe's Jews was "a type of heavenly surgery . . . a deep and hidden purification from the impurity of exile."[27] After the 1967 war, Kook called on his yeshiva students to be activists in the unfolding drama of the gradual liberation of the Greater Land of Israel. Now that Israel had returned to its biblical borders, he told his students, they were obligated to settle in the "liberated" territories.

In the younger Kook's thinking, the "liberated territories"—Gaza, the West Bank, and the Golan—had to be incorporated into the State of Israel; the state had to grow into the biblical Land of Israel, from which it had been separated during the years between 1948 and 1967.[28] In this ahistorical conceptualization, the Land of Israel existed in a platonic ideal state, awaiting redemption. The Palestinian inhabitants of the territories were seen as outsiders and interlopers, not as claimants to the land they lived on. They were "strangers living in our land." If the Israeli government of the late 1960s and early 1970s and many of its citizens did not sanction such settlement, the government and those citizens had to be opposed; if necessary, they had to be opposed by force. Religious Zionists were called upon to follow a higher law; Israel's democratic institutions were thus called in to question by this new theological imperative.

For Rabbi Kook and his followers, the meaning of the 1967 war was that God had intervened in history to grant Israel its full biblical heritage. The process of redemption, which had begun in 1948, had accelerated. Israeli political and military leaders had no right to delay this process. To the contrary, they should do their utmost to support it. A few hours after the Old City

Mount Zion, Jerusalem (photograph by Dov Goldman)

of Jerusalem fell to the Israelis, Rabbi Kook was taken to the Western Wall by a group of his students who had served with the paratroopers who fought in the area. To the Israeli and international journalists who soon gathered at the wall, Kook announced: "We have returned home by divine command . . . to the city of our Temple. From today onwards we will not move from here."[29] When within a few weeks of the end of the war the Israeli government backed Minister of Defense Moshe Dayan's decision to leave control of the Temple Mount/Haram al-Sharif in the hands of the city's Muslim religious authorities, Kook and his followers were outraged. As far as religious Zionists were concerned, Dayan had betrayed the divine call to return to the Temple Mount. Dayan's decision was one of a series of disappointments that led the nascent settler movement into antagonistic confrontation with the Israeli authorities.

Another influential rabbi who was outraged by Dayan's decision was Shlomo Goren, chief rabbi of the Israeli army during the 1967 war. Speaking to army officers soon after the war, he related a conversation he had with Moshe Dayan. Goren condemned the Israeli government's decision to leave the Temple Mount under Muslim religious control: "I told this to Dayan and he said 'I understand what you are saying, but do you really think we should have blown up the mosque?' and I said 'Certainly we should have blown it up.

It is a tragedy for generations that we did not do so. I myself would have gone up there and wiped it off the ground completely so that there was no trace that there was ever a Mosque of Omar there.' "[30] Only a few years later, these sentiments would have wide resonance among the ideological vanguard of the settler movement. For it was a faction of that movement that in the early 1980s conspired to blow up the mosques. In 1984, twenty-five members of the "Jewish Underground" were apprehended by the Israeli security services and convicted of conspiring to destroy the mosques on the Temple Mount/ Haram al-Sharif.

The seven years between the wars of 1967 and 1973 set the stage for the growth of Kook's political-religious movement—Gush Emunim (the Bloc of the Faithful). After years of political gestation, Gush Emunim was founded in February of 1974.[31] It provided the settler movement, which had begun immediately after the 1967 war, with a messianic, religious underpinning. In its early secular manifestation, the settler movement had been small and not very effective, but with the addition of the religious Zionist dimension, it would become an unstoppable political force. Settlement of the West Bank and Gaza, supported by a succession of Israeli governments, would transform the State of Israel. In 1998, on the state's fiftieth anniversary, *Ha'aretz*, Israel's newspaper of record, listed the younger Rabbi Kook as one of the ten people who had shaped the destiny of the State of Israel.[32]

The catalyst for this outburst of messianism was the new geopolitical situation. Areas of the biblical Land of Israel that before 1967 had been under Jordanian control were now under Israeli military control. For many religious Zionists, the concepts of the State of Israel and the Land of Israel converged. Many secular Israelis were similarly moved. This was especially true of Revisionists, who had coalesced into the Likud Party, but enthusiasm for a new territorial maximalism was not limited to them. Labor Party supporters also were drawn to the idea that Zionism was in need of a rebirth and that rebirth would be provided by settling the territories. Yearning for these "unredeemed" areas of the land had been expressed in Israeli poetry and song, most famously in Naomi Shemer's popular song "Jerusalem of Gold," written and popularized a few months before the 1967 war. Now redemption, made possible through military conquest, could be actualized through settlement.

Between 1948 and 1967 yearning for and anticipation of the "Greater" or "Complete" Land of Israel were powerful themes in Israeli culture. For many Israelis of the pre-1967 era, the geographical and spiritual promise of Israel had not yet been fulfilled. For example, the Old City of Jerusalem, in Jordanian hands, was visible but inaccessible to Israelis. For religious Zionists, this yearning for "as yet uncovered" sacred spaces had a spiritual dimension. They saw the 1967 war as an act of God moving in history to bring about the full redemption of the Land of Israel. With the Israeli victory in the war dubbed by Israel "The Six-Day War," many Israelis were swept away by secularized forms of religious enthusiasm. The designation "The Six-Day War," first coined by Minister of Defense Moshe Dayan, was itself an evocative phrase. It evoked the biblical idea of the six days of creation, the creation of a new world, or in this specific case, a new political, and for some, new religious, reality.

Whether the territories were "occupied" or "liberated" was hotly debated by Israeli Jews, but for the Palestinians living in those territories (one million people in 1967, over three million in 2000) the situation was quite clear: the Israelis, who had sent many of them into exile following the 1948 war twenty years earlier, were now their occupiers. As Israeli scholar Baruch Kimmerling noted, "In contrast with the well-planned war, the Israeli leadership and political elite had no idea what to do with the occupied territories and especially not with the people who suddenly fell under Israeli control."[33] This vacuum of leadership enabled the emerging settler movement, and its champions within the political and military establishment, particularly Ariel Sharon, to move ahead and establish "facts on the ground." The "great leap forward" of settlement activity in the West Bank and Gaza took place in the 1970s and 1980s with Ariel Sharon's considerable assistance.

Opposition to the settler movement, and to the messianist ideology it espoused, was led by the Peace Now movement, Gush Emunim's nemesis on the political Left. Since the 1970s, the conflicting ideologies of Gush Emunim and Peace Now have expressed most forcefully a profound division within Israeli Jewish society. Peace Now has taken on the job of monitoring settlement activity, including the documentation of government and military support for the settlers. Gush Emunim, fueled by religious enthusiasm, is the more active and assertive of the movements; Peace Now, demonstrating against settler activity, is the more reactive movement.

<hr />

Religious Zionism and the Settlers

Religious fervor was not the only element in the move to establish Jewish enclaves in the territories. Among the first post-1967 settlers were secularists associated with the kibbutz movement. Their rationale for establishing new settlements was the contention, shared then by most Israelis, that Israel's security was at stake; settling Israeli citizens in the new territories would protect Israel's new borders from attack. Between 1967 and 1973 small groups of settlers established outposts in relatively empty areas of the territories. These settlements, approved by the government and peopled with soldiers and civilians, were organized under military supervision and protection. The Israeli government and military, wanting to avoid conflict between Israeli settlers and Palestinians, outlawed Israeli settlement within Palestinian cities and towns. This restriction angered some of the more militant settlement advocates. It particularly outraged Rabbi Kook's students, as it left Hebron, Shechem/Nablus, and other sites with biblical associations out of bounds to Israelis who wanted to put down roots there.

Some secular Israeli intellectuals were also attracted to a mystical interpretation of Israeli conquest of the territories and therefore advocated rapid Israeli annexation. Most prominent among them was Ben-Gurion's confidante Nathan Alterman, the widely read poet and literary critic. A few days after the conclusion of the 1967 hostilities, Alterman wrote, "This victory not only returned to the Jews the most ancient and sanctified of its places, those places inscribed in its memory more than any other. It also erased the difference between the State of Israel and the Land of Israel. From now on the state and land are one entity."[34] But these pronouncements by secular intellectuals did not galvanize a significant ideological movement. That task would fall to the religious Zionists of Gush Emunim. "With God on their side," they were able to sway both religious Zionists and some secular Israelis to join or at least support the settler cause.

Among the leaders of the religious settlers was Rabbi Moshe Levinger, student of Rabbi Zvi Yehuda Kook. On Passover of 1968, ten months after the end of the 1967 war, Levinger and sixty followers checked into the Palestinian-owned Park Hotel in the West Bank city of Hebron. As Israeli citizens, they were forbidden to spend the night in West Bank cities, but Levinger and his followers had been granted an exemption to the law. Their reasoning was that they wanted to celebrate the Passover Seder in the city of the Patriarchs. The sixty guests never left. They and their supporters and their descendants are still there today, four decades later. They used their 1968 Passover sojourn as a way to reestablish a Jewish presence in Hebron. That the birth of this settlement was on Passover, the Festival of Freedom, lent further symbolic weight to the event.[35] This event laid the groundwork for the establishment of Kiryat Arba, a large settlement overlooking Hebron, as well as the establishment of a Jewish presence within the Arab city itself. In 2007, forty years after the 1967 war, Kiryat Arba had 7,000 inhabitants. Within the Arab city of Hebron, there were 700 additional Israeli settlers. These Israeli citizens were living among a Palestinian population of hundreds of thousands. The settlers in Kiryat Arba Hebron are among the most militant and violent of the Israelis living in the territories. It was in Kiryat Arba that Baruch Goldstein, an American-born physician and follower of radical cleric Meir Kahane, lived. In 1994, on the Festival of Purim, which celebrates the deliverance of the Jews from their enemies, Goldstein entered the Ibrahimi Mosque in Hebron's Tomb of the Patriarchs and opened fire with an automatic weapon. He killed twenty-nine worshippers in the mosque before he was beaten to death by the crowd. The more militant settlers soon declared him a martyr. His tomb, in Kiryat Arba, has become a place of pilgrimage for members of the radical Israeli Right.

The conflict between Levinger's group and Hebron's Palestinians soon took on a religious character. Before the 1967 war, Rabbi Zvi Yehuda Kook had said of the Arabs, "They are a pure, monotheistic people who are closer to God than the idolatrous Christians; the conflict with them is temporary."[36] For in classical rabbinic thought, Christianity was seen as a heretical sect that rebelled against rabbinic Judaism. According to Maimonides and other medieval rabbinic authorities, Christianity is not a monotheistic religion; Islam is. Thus the earlier stage of conflict with the "Arabs of the Land of Israel," the stage before the 1967 war, was understood by the Rabbis Kook, father and son, as ethnic, not religious. In the late 1970s, with the settlement of the territories, the rhetoric became more polemical. Palestinians who protested and resisted the Israeli occupation were soon dubbed "Amalekites" by the settlers. Designated with the biblical appellation for the eternal enemies of Israel, the Palestinians were thus placed outside of the realm of negotiation and settlement. They and the Arabs of the surrounding states were thought of as implacable enemies, foes with whom one could never live in peace. To negotiate with them would be folly and a betrayal of the divine imperative to possess the land.

A similar attitude toward Arabs and Muslims was expressed in the writings of some Fundamentalist Evangelicals. Dean Charles Feinberg of the Bible Theological Seminary of Los Angeles wrote in a 1968 article that the Ishmaelites sought "the complete extinction and annihilation of God's people Israel. . . . Today these sons of Ishmael are among the greatest adversaries of the Gospel."[37] These observations drew on a long history of American Evangelical antipathy to Islam.

In the eyes of its secular critics, the radical shift in religious Zionist attitudes toward the Arabs of the territories signaled the rejection of the humanist ideals of the Hebrew prophets as they were understood by the great Jewish philosophers. As Tsvi Raanan noted in his 1980 study of Gush Emunim, "The prophetic vision of the messianic era, a vision which Jews and non-Jews have long-understood as a universal vision of peace, is reduced in the Gush Emunim ideology to a tale of nationalist redemption, an account which encourages hostility toward all outsiders."[38] Here we can see a kinship to the dispensationalist-influenced *Left Behind* series. In that incredibly popular series of apocalyptic fiction, only "Born Again Christians" are saved. Some Jews also will be saved, but only those that embrace Christ in the End Time. Those not saved will suffer eternal damnation.

Gush Emunim's understanding of Zionist history and politics is rooted in a redemptive, messianic ideology. In contrast, political Zionism of the first half of the twentieth century based its appeal for a sovereign Jewish state on universal principles of human rights and minority rights. Making an appeal on this basis implies acceptance of the general principle that all peoples are entitled to political freedom and independence. But the Gush Emunim version of religious Zionist claim to the Land of Israel is exclusive; it is based on the idea of the divine promise of the Land of Israel to the Children of Israel. Thus religious Zionism in the Gush Emunim formulation is the rejection of Jewish humanism and universalism and thus expresses a bitter antagonism to the universalist strain in earlier forms of Zionist discourse. How, then, can we explain its appeal to the many secular Israeli supporters of the settler movement? Baruch Kimmerling's astute observation provides one answer to the question: "Although Gush Emunim's brand of 'Jewishness' was dominated by religious elements, its pioneering spirit, renewed activism, and commitment to the security of the Settlements charmed many elite groups, even secular ones."[39] For members of Israel's founding generation, settler activity in the territories was reminiscent of their own pioneering activities in British Mandate Palestine, activity justified by the need for security.

From the 1970s onward, the political conflict between Israel and the Palestinians took on a more religious aspect. As Gush Emunim's rabbinic leadership, composed of students of the younger Rabbi Kook, formulated the movement's attitude toward the Arabs of Palestine, their rhetoric became more radical and exclusionary. Arabs ("Amalek," "Goyim"), according to these rabbis, had no place in the Land of Israel. Concepts of equality and human rights, concepts long espoused if not put into practice by Israeli political and cultural figures, were rejected by this new form of religious Zionism. The settlers condemned Western humanism and called for a return to biblical standards of punishment, revenge, and justice.[40] Two quotes from prominent Gush Emunim rabbis writing in the 1990s make the point. According to Rabbi

Shlomo Aviner, "Settlement of the land outweighs any moral consideration one might have for the national rights claims of the *goyim* in our land." Even sharper and more directly to the point was Rabbi Yaakov Madan's dictum that "in the Six-Day War God obligated us to cleanse the inheritance of Abraham, Isaac and Jacob of the evil rule that had dominated it."[41]

The younger Rabbi Kook, espousing his view that "the footsteps of the Messiah" could be heard clearly in the aftermath of the 1967 war, was careful to distinguish between his own Bloc of the Faithful and the Sabbatai Sevi movement of the seventeenth century. His critics noted that both the Sabbatian heresy and early political Zionism rebelled against rabbinical authority and the strictures of Jewish law. Were not Gush Emunim and Sabbatianism similar? No, said Rabbi Kook. Sabbatianism was led by an imposter, a man who made false messianic claims. It was a top-to-bottom social movement with an imposed ideology. Sabbati's apostasy to Islam brought down the movement. For Kook, religious Zionism and the settlement of the territories were a bottom-to-top movement; the Jewish masses were disgusted with exile and yearned for redemption. Their vanguard ascended to the Land of Israel to settle it and thus hasten the messianic redemption. In Kook's eyes, their yearning and action had brought about "the beginning of the redemption," a process that now had to be further catalyzed by the settlement of the territories.

Between Gush Emunim's founding in 1974 and Rabbi Zvi Yehuda Kook's death in 1982, the settler movement achieved truly remarkable success. By creating "facts on the ground," it swayed the Israeli government and a large swathe of the Israeli public to its program. In his oration at Zvi Yehuda Kook's funeral in 1982, Kook's disciple Haim Druckman called Kook "the one person in his generation who understood fully the messianic manifestation that is the State of Israel . . . and who identified totally with this truth: that the state of Israel, with all of its problems, is a divine state . . . the fulfillment of the prophecies of redemption."[42]

In 1981, a year before the younger Rabbi Kook's death, the settler movement experienced its first great setback. As a result of the Egyptian-Israeli Peace Agreement of 1979, Israel agreed to evacuate the city of Yamit and return the Sinai to Egyptian control. The settler movement was determined to resist the evacuation, and resist it did. The dramatic scenes of Israeli soldiers forcibly evicting the settlers and their many supporters from their homes, and the subsequent decision by Ariel Sharon to destroy the coastal city's buildings and infrastructure—both in order to discourage the settler's return and to deny the city to the Egyptians—were experienced by the settlers and their many supporters as a national and spiritual trauma. The leadership of Gush Emunim felt betrayed by the Begin government and particularly by Ariel Sharon, who, prior to the Egyptian-Israeli peace accords, had been the movement's champion.

The drama of the Sinai evacuation was repeated in the 2005 Israeli evacuation of the settlers from Gaza. Paradoxically, Ariel Sharon, now prime minister, ordered the evacuation of Gaza. In the twenty-four years between the two withdrawals, the settler movement became both more powerful and more alienated from the established governmental structures of power. In the light of what was perceived as lessening government support for movement endeavors, some of its more extreme elements spoke of the need to establish a "Kingdom of Judah" in the West Bank. But as the numbers of settlers grew exponentially, the extremism of the movement was mitigated. Many Israelis moved into the territories for reasons both economic and ideological. In the economic sphere, government-guaranteed mortgages were cheaper and easier to obtain in the West Bank and Gaza than in Israel proper, and the quality and standards of living, before the Palestinian insurrections, were quite high. The very success of the movement in attracting, with government help, middle-income families to the territories undercut somewhat Gush Emunim's ideological purity. By the 1990s, the ideological vanguard of the movement, led by the original settlers of the 1970s, was still influential but not as powerful as it once had been.

Thus in religious Zionism, which had developed as a response to ultra-Orthodox critiques of Zionist secularism, messianism was suppressed until 1967. Then, with the conquest of the hitherto inaccessible sections of the Land of Israel, this messianism erupted.[43] As Gideon Shimoni noted, "Gush Emunim vigorously expounded an ideology based on a fundamentalist interpretation of divinely endowed right to the whole of Eretz Israel, according to which it was halakhically impermissible to give up an inch of land now providentially restored to Israel."[44] Concepts such as redemption and Jewish destiny, ideas that secular Zionism had long understood metaphorically, were now understood concretely.

The Rabbis Kook, father and son, transformed religious Zionism into an activist movement inspired by messianic expectations. These expectations were latent until the 1967 war. With the Israeli victory and the de facto annexation of the territories, these expectations erupted.[45] All religious Zionists, however, did not support Gush Emunim. A small but vocal opposition emerged in their ranks. Some of Gush Emunim's critics compared them to the Zealots of the Second Temple period. Others warned against a "new Sabbatianism."[46] According to this view, Jews had suffered in the past because of the claims of false messiahs and the activism that those messianic movements generated. They were liable to suffer again if these modern Zealots got the upper hand. The most trenchant of Gush Emunim's critics was the late Hebrew University professor Y. Leibowitz, an Orthodox Jew who was Israel's most prominent and articulate political gadfly. Leibowitz argued that "anyone who points to a specific historical event as the 'beginning of redemption' is one of two types of people. Either they are claiming that they are in communication with God and know the future, which would make them false prophets. Or they constitute a modern form of the Sabbatai Sevi heresy. . . . Some Jews in our time, caught in a web of nationalism and patriotism, see military victories and territorial conquests as signs of redemption. Both groups—the 'prophets' and the new Sabbatians—ignore the true content of the Jewish messianic idea, the return to the Torah."[47]

⁓

Fundamentalists and the History of Modern Israel

During the first half of the twentieth century, some fundamentalist Christians read unfolding historical events in a manner remarkably similar to the way that religious Zionists read them. For these Christians, defeat of the Ottomans was a triumph of Christendom over Islam, and the occupation of Palestine by Great Britain a sign that the Holy Land liberated from the Turks could now return to Christian hands. For many Christian observers, the end of Muslim control was a necessary prelude to the Second Coming and the conversion of the Jews. In England this idea was promoted as early as the Albury Conferences of the 1820s and in the teachings of John Nelson Darby, teachings that influenced American Evangelical Christians in the second half of the nineteenth century. From the 1820s to the 1920s and beyond, dispensationalist ideas influenced many Evangelical Christians. For many Jews, and particularly for the followers of the Rabbis Kook, events in the Holy Land were understood similarly, as steps in the redemptive process, "the beginning of the flowering of our redemption."

When the British defeated the Ottoman Turks and conquered Jerusalem in 1917, many in England saw the hand of God at work. Before World War I, the Catholic and Eastern Orthodox presence in Jerusalem was considerable; the Anglican Church had been at a distinct disadvantage. With the British victory, Anglicans now had a claim to the Holy City. For the previous century, British missionaries in Jerusalem had tried to convert Eastern Christians and Jews to Anglicanism. Attempts to convert Muslims were more circumspect, as the

Ottomans forbade missions to Muslims. With the British victory and the establishment of the Mandate, some English and American Christians felt that God was acting to bring Muslims, Jews, and Eastern Christians under the wing of the Anglican Church. British control of Palestine took on a larger meaning. As John Moscrop has noted: "Although the British Empire had no religion, the Mother Country, so to speak, did. It had a Protestant state church. As the Empire began to unfold, and to weave Anglican Christian principles and practices into the fabric of imperial awareness, as bishops began to be appointed to diocese outside England, and as missionaries began to follow the flag, it became important to show that the nation that ruled a considerable amount of the world's landmass controlled the land of its own religious origins."[48]

Lord Balfour, the British foreign secretary, was a firm believer in the divinely ordained restoration of the Jews to their land.[49] The Balfour Declaration of 1917, facilitated by Balfour's Christian Zionist leanings, elicited great enthusiasm from dispensationalist preachers. For, in their thinking, humanity was now approaching the final dispensation, the one in which the world as we know it would end and the redemptive process would begin. We have seen that Herzl's associate William Hechler was disappointed that the Balfour Declaration was not couched in religious language. When the British defeated the Turks and occupied Jerusalem, many dispensationalist preachers saw the "signs of the times" in current events. Their responses were similar to those of Rabbi Kook, who spoke of Great Britain's "divinely ordained fate" to be the instrument of the fulfillment of God's promise. In the United States, many Christians were enthusiastic about the British victory. Prominent American dispensationalist W. Fuller Gooch summed up the American evangelical reaction to the Balfour Declaration in a March 1918 sermon: "Palestine is for the Jews. The most striking sign of the times is the proposal to give Palestine to the Jews once more. They have long desired the land, though as yet unrepentant of the terrible crime which led to their expulsion there from. . . . There is a mass of Prophetic Scripture yet to be accomplished until Palestine is again in Jewish hands. Prophecy revolves around the despised Jew; and if Jewish restoration is imminent (as it appears to be), how near we must be to the fulfillment of every vision!"[50]

Thirty-one years later, fundamentalists saw the establishment of the State of Israel in 1948 as a further "sign of the times," a fulfillment of the promise inherent in the events of 1917. This reading of unfolding events recalls Rabbi Zvi Yehuda Kook's 1948 pronouncement on the "divine historical imperative of the purified and revealed end of exile." This prophetic understanding was especially relevant for dispensationalists, followers of nineteenth-century British preacher John Nelson Darby. During the early to mid-twentieth century this view of history came to dominate some American churches. In the mid-nineteenth century Darby brought his ideas to the United States, where they were spread to seminary students by the Moody Bible Institute of Chicago and, later, in the twentieth century, by Dallas Theological Seminary. Even more effective in spreading Darby's ideas was the Scofield Reference Bible, which became the Bible of American fundamentalism. Published in 1909 by Oxford University Press, this bible assigned specific dates to all of the biblical narratives, thus buttressing dispensational claims of the fulfillment of biblical prophecy in modern times. The Scofield Bible's successor, the Ryrie Study Bible, makes specific and pointed reference to the story of modern Israel, treating it as a continuation of the biblical narrative. For dispensationalists, the process of redemption had stopped long ago; with the return of the Jews to their land, the process had started again. From the vantage point of 1948, the First World War had been an earlier "sign of the time," one that had prepared the way for British Christian rule in Palestine, rule that enabled a Jewish return. The similarities between this dispensationalist view and the elder Rabbi Kook's view is quite striking, but before the 1970s neither Jewish religious Zionists nor Christian Zionists paid much attention to these similarities. Rather, they ignored them. Evangelical Christians saw Israelis as "unknowing" instruments of a divine process that would bring about a Jewish acceptance of Jesus. Jews saw fundamentalist Christians as potential missionaries, and therefore distanced themselves from them.

For Christian Zionists of the period 1948–67, as for religious Zionists, one essential element of prophecy had yet to be fulfilled—the extension of Israeli rule to East Jerusalem's Temple Mount. Once that rule was established, Israel could proceed with the rebuilding of the Temple and the revival of the Temple sacrifices, essential steps in the process of redemption and the ushering in of the millennium. Like many religious Zionists, some fundamentalist Christians saw "the hand of God" in the Israeli victory of 1967. They endorsed the view of the settlers and the Israeli Right that the creation of a Greater Israel was Israel's destiny. Any peace effort, therefore, would be an act against God. Advocates of a negotiated settlement, among them the activists of Peace Now, were deemed traitors. In the 1990s such accusations were hurled at Israeli prime minister Yitzhak Rabin. Calls for him to resign because of his "treachery" were common in Israeli political rhetoric of the mid-1990s. In November 1995 Rabin was assassinated by Yigal Amir, a staunch supporter of the settlers and an adversary of a negotiated settlement. A year earlier, *Nekuda*, the journal of the settler movement, had published an article descrying any "so-called peace efforts." Viewing efforts to achieve a negotiated settlement with the Palestinians as a form of "Jewish assimilation into the goyim," the journal stated: "We freed ourselves from exile and came here to live not to seek peace, but to fulfill our national rebirth. That there are strangers living in our land is one of the problems we will have to solve in a Jewish way, and not by giving up on the whole national project."[51]

Similar calls came from the American Christian Right. Soon after the end of the 1967 war, the American evangelical journal *Christianity Today* published an article by Nelson Bell, editor of the journal and father-in-law of Billy Graham. Bell wrote, "That for the first time in more than two thousand years Jerusalem is now completely in the hands of the Jews gives a student of the Bible a thrill and a renewed faith in the accuracy and validity of the Bible."[52] If the hand of God was visible in history as it unfolded, it would be presumptuous and rebellious to try and negotiate between the hostile nations and peoples. Negotiation was not seen as part of the divine plan. Rather, it was viewed as inimical to the divine will.

A few years later, Hal Lindsey, in his best-selling book *The Late Great Planet Earth*, spelled out more fully the dispensationalist understanding of God's plan for Israel and the world. Describing the capture of Jerusalem in 1967, Lindsey wrote, "Again, against incredible odds, the Jews had unwittingly further set up the stage for their final hour of trial and conversion."[53] Lindsey, educated at Dallas Theological Seminary, a bastion of dispensationalist thought, called the State of Israel "the fuse of Armageddon." The Jewish state, in fulfillment of New Testament prophecy, would rebuild the Temple and usher in the Second Coming. Lindsey claimed, "There remains but one more event to completely set the stage for Israel's part in the last great act of her historical drama. This is to rebuild the ancient Temple of Worship upon its old site."[54] Since its publication in 1971, more than twenty million copies of *The Late Great Planet Earth* have been sold and it has influenced generations of evangelical Christians and some Jews. It had vast appeal for American college youth of the early 1970s, particularly in the South. In the words of an American student of the early 1970s: "As a college freshman in 1971, I brought a copy of *The Late Great Planet Earth* with me to Auburn University. Everyone on my wing of the dormitory, Christian and non-Christian alike, read the book that year. It scared us to death. We thought the end was near."[55] In subsequent books, Hal Lindsey has further developed his eschatology to incorporate a view of Islam as demonic. He portrays Islam as the greatest threat to world survival and describes that religion as inherently hateful.

David Ben-Gurion, living in retirement in the Negev when *The Late Great Planet Earth* was published, took a lively interest in the book and its popularity in the United States. In the late 1950s and early 1960s he had welcomed prominent American churchmen to Israel, among them Oral Roberts, who visited Israel in 1959. In 1971 Ben-Gurion hosted a conference of American evangelical clergy at Jerusalem's Binyanei Haumah. This conference on biblical prophecy was a great success. On Ben-Gurion's desk at his home at Kibbutz Sde Boker in the Negev, now a museum, there is a copy of Lindsey's book. Recently, a British journalist reported that Menachem Begin, Israeli prime minister from 1977 to 1983, also took a lively interest in Lindsey's book.[56]

The Late Great Planet Earth, the great publishing phenomenon of the 1970s, inspired the even more successful *Left Behind* series of the 1990s and early 2000s. More than sixty-five million copies of *Left Behind*—in twelve volumes—have been sold to date. One of the authors of *Left Behind*, Tim LaHaye, has said that "God has chosen to bless this series. In doing so, He's giving the country and maybe the world one last, big wake-up call before the events transpire."[57] In a companion volume, *Are We Living in the End Times?*, LaHaye and his coauthor, Jerry Jenkins, focus on the rebuilding of the Temple. Writing in 1999, they noted, "Fifty years ago we would not have been discussing the possibility of reconstructing the Jewish Temple. For the first time since the destruction of the Second Temple in A.D. 70, we are on the verge of seeing a third temple built in fulfillment of prophecy—another powerful evidence that we have more reason to believe Christ could return in our lifetime than any generation before us."[58]

The Israeli government's decision, soon after the 1967 war, to grant Jerusalem's Muslim Religious Council the authority to continue its prewar administration of the Temple Mount/Haram al-Sharif demonstrated to the settler movement and its Christian Zionist supporters that Jerusalem was not yet "completely in the hands of the Jews." The blame for this political decision was placed squarely on the shoulders of Defense Minister Moshe Dayan. The Israel government's decision to share responsibility for the Temple Mount with Palestinian religious authorities was profoundly disturbing to both Christian Zionists and Jewish religious Zionists, especially to the followers of Gush Emunim. Did the Israeli government not realize that Israel, in "liberating" East Jerusalem, was acting as God's agent?

Gershon Salomon, founder of the small but influential advocacy group The Temple Mount Faithful, lamented the Israeli government's decision of 1967. He reiterated his dismay in an article written in the 1990s: "As the result of the miraculous events of the Six-Day War of 1967, God brought Israel back to the Temple Mount . . . to build His House and to open another end-time era in the life of Israel. The terrible, sinful mistake of the Defense Minister, Moshe Dayan, did not cancel God's plans but they were merely delayed to that generation. Now a new generation has emerged and the time is ripe for the Temple to be rebuilt."[59] In the United States, Salomon found many more Christian supporters for his cause than Jewish supporters. Within Israel for decades after the 1967 war, only a small number of Israeli Jews called for the rebuilding of the Temple. Yet during the last decade the number of "Third Temple supporters," both in Israel and in the United States, has increased dramatically.

~

Jerry Falwell's Zionism

The 1967 war was the catalyst for the Reverend Jerry Falwell's "conversion" to Zionism. For Falwell and for others influenced by dispensationalism, the Israeli conquest or "liberation" of Jerusalem was the fulfillment of millennial-ist expectation. As Timothy Weber has noted: "For well over a century, pre-millennialists had been anticipating the time when Jerusalem would return to Jewish control after centuries of Gentile dominance. The capture of the Old City pointed to the prophecy of Luke 21:24: 'Jerusalem shall be trodden down of the Gentiles, the times of the Gentiles be fulfilled.' "[60] Rev. Falwell, who identified himself as a premillennialist, first visited Israel soon after the 1967 war. He has since visited dozens of times, often leading large groups of Christian pilgrims. In the mid-1980s these groups included as many as 600 American pilgrims at a time. Among them were large groups of students from Liberty University, the school that Falwell founded. He told an inter-viewer in 1984 that "the destiny of the State of Israel is without question the most crucial international matter facing the world today. I believe that the people of Israel have not only a theological but also a historical and legal right to the land. I am personally a Zionist, having gained that perspective from my belief in Old Testament Scriptures."[61]

In that interview, Falwell expanded on his understanding of Israel's theo-logical meaning: "I am convinced that the miracle of statehood in 1948 was providential in every sense of the word. God promised repeatedly in the Old Testament that He would re-gather the Jewish people unto the land which He had promised—namely, the Land of Israel. He has kept his word."[62] Aware that the question of Israeli rule over the territories was widely debated both internationally and within Israel itself, Falwell placed himself squarely in the settler camp: "Biblically, prophetically, and ultimately, 'the land' will include the area promised to Abraham in Genesis 15:18."⁶³ Asked about his views on the eventual political fate of the West Bank and Gaza, Falwell answered using the biblical names of the areas: "There is no question that Judea and Samaria should be part of Israel."⁶⁴ The Israeli government adopted the use of these biblical names for the areas of the West Bank when the Likud government of Menachem Begin took power in 1977. Falwell, like Pat Robertson and Billy Graham, preached the dispensationalist doctrine that the Second Coming, to be preceded by the great tribulation, is imminent. This view is supported by a strict biblical literalism. Israel's expansion in 1967 to include biblical areas and the rise of a pro-settler government in 1977 were interpreted by dispensationalists as the fulfillment of prophecy.

The radical change in Israel's political leadership—in which the rightist Likud Bloc led the governments of the late 1970s and the 1980s—strengthened the emerging Israeli alliance with American Christian Zionists. Falwell's religious and political stance endeared him to Menachem Begin. Begin invited Falwell to Israel and treated him with great respect. Begin and Falwell soon developed both a political alliance and a close personal friendship. Falwell visited Israel frequently and was welcomed at the prime minister's office and residence and, in 1980, was honored with the Jabotinsky Prize, named for Begin's mentor, Revisionist Zionist leader Vladimir Zev Jabotinsky. When Israel bombed the Iraqi nuclear facility Osirak in 1981, Falwell called on Americans to support Israel at a time when the state was being condemned by many in the international community. Some liberal Jewish spokesmen descried the emerging alliance between the Israeli Right and the Christian Right. Rabbi Alexander Schindler, head of Reform Judaism, said: "When the Jabotinsky Foundation presents its award to Jerry Falwell for his support of Israel . . . it is madness and suicide. . . . Can someone really be good for Israel when everything else he says and does is destructive of America and undermines the Jewish community?"⁶⁵ But Rabbi Schindler's warning went unheeded. By the first few years of the twenty-first century, the great majority of American Jewish organizations welcomed the Christian Zionist embrace of Israel. The 2007 annual meeting of the American Israel Public Affairs Committee (AIPAC) featured a keynote address by dispensationalist preacher Rev. John Hagee, founder of Christians United for Israel (CUFI), the "Christian AIPAC." In his enthusiastically received speech, Hagee told the conference's 6,000 delegates: "Think of our future together. Fifty million evangelicals joining in common cause with five million Jewish people in America on behalf of Israel is a match made in heaven. Let the word go forth from Washington, D.C., tonight that there is a new beginning in America between Christians and Jews."[66]

Hagee had been building a constituency for this alliance over the past three decades. Like his colleague Jerry Falwell, he was vocal in support of the Israeli bombing of the Iraqi nuclear reactor in 1981. In his books addressed to Christian audiences, Hagee has written of God's plan for the Jews: "From the time of Joseph in Egypt to Einstein in America, God has placed Jewish people at the major intersections of history to bless the world. And I've got news for you— God isn't finished. The people of Israel and their Holy City will soon fill the major role in a coming world drama."[67]

When, in November 1995, Yitzhak Rabin was assassinated by Yigal Amir, an extreme nationalist who was trying to prevent the Rabin government from agreeing to any withdrawal from the West Bank, evangelical Christian Zionists seemed neither surprised nor disturbed. Of the Rabin assassination John Hagee wrote: "The shot that killed Yitzhak Rabin launched Bible prophecy onto the fast track."[68]

When Jerry Falwell died in May 2007, his passing was mourned by the heads of American Jewish organizations, including Abraham Foxman of the Anti-Defamation League. Though Foxman had criticized Falwell in the 1990s, by 2007, Falwell's support for Israeli policies trumped all other considerations. He was eulogized as "a dear great friend of Israel."[69] As with the relationship between G. K. Chesterton and prominent Jewish leaders of the 1920s, and as in the stories we recounted of Rabbi Stephen Wise and his "Jesus Sermon" in 1925, support for Zionism outweighed all other considerations.

~

The 1973 War and the Rise of the Israeli Right

If the Israeli victory of 1967 was seen by many Christians and Jews as the fulfillment of prophecy, the 1973 war, in which Israel, attacked on two fronts by Egypt and Syria, suffered considerable losses, presented a theological challenge of considerable proportions. Israel lost almost three thousand soldiers in a war that began with a surprise attack on Yom Kippur, the Jewish Day of Atonement. Though Israel eventually won the war, its citizens emerged from it bloodied and demoralized. If history was moving toward the culmination of a redemptive messianic process, what to make of a seeming setback in that process? If God was acting in history by having the Israelis conquer their biblical inheritance, including Jerusalem, what was his intent in having them battered in the 1973 war?

One of Rabbi Zvi Yehuda Kook's senior students, Yehuda Amital, articulated the postwar questions then raging among the religious Zionist soldiers who had served in the war. Amital asked: "What was the purpose of the war? The Land of Israel was already ours, why did we need another war? A sharper question: Is the war a sign of regression, God forbid? Did the very outbreak of the war, with all its tragic consequences, raise the possibility that there is a retreat from the divine process of the beginning of redemption?"[70]

All of Israeli society was deeply shaken by the large number of Israeli casualties in the 1973 war. Religious Zionists participated in the national trauma; unlike secular Israeli Jews, they also had to confront a theological challenge. Among the dead and wounded were many soldiers affiliated with B'nai Akiva, the religious Zionist youth movement. Religious Zionist thinkers raised theological questions about the war. But for secular Israelis, the burning postwar questions were political, not theological. Why had Israel's political and military leadership failed to prepare the country for a surprise attack? And why had the army's lack of preparedness enabled the Egyptian and Syrian armies to surprise the Israeli forces and batter them? Israelis referred to these events as "Hamechdal," the "national blunder."

Within a few years, this internal Israeli debate about government responsibility for the security and intelligence failures of the 1973 war would lead to the "mahapach," the political revolution of 1977 in which the Labor Party fell from power and the Revisionist Zionists led by Menachem Begin assumed the mantle of leadership. For the first time, Israel was governed by a right-wing party. From 1977 until 1992, these Likud governments, at times in partnership with the Labor Party, greatly expanded settlements in the territories.

For religious Zionists, the post–1973 war questions were both political *and* theological, and the answers they arrived at addressed both spheres. For religious Zionists, the lesson of the Yom Kippur War was that Jewish settlement activity in the territories had to be increased. This conclusion flew in the face of the military and political evidence. The settlements had proven to be a liability in the 1973 war, not an asset. Settlers in the Golan Heights had to be evacuated on the first day of the war, delaying the Israeli army's military response to the Syrian attacks. But this objection to the settlements was the opinion of military analysts and strategists, not that of the theologians.[71] Religious Zionists were sure that God was sending them a message that they had to persevere in their dedication to the cause of Greater Israel, an Israel that incorporated the "biblical heartland," Judea and Samaria, as well as the

Sinai Desert and the Golan Heights. They were convinced that they should not betray the cause of Greater Israel by supporting negotiations with the Egyptians and the Syrians.

Gush Emunim, formed in response to the negotiations that ended the Yom Kippur War and brought about the negotiated return of the Sinai Desert to Egypt, anticipated and feared further negotiations that would endanger Israeli control over the other territories captured in the 1967 war—the Golan Heights, the West Bank, and the Gaza Strip. To forestall the implementation of any further negotiations or peace agreements that would require Israeli territorial concessions, they decided to create "facts on the ground" and populate the territories with Israeli Jews. This strategy proved remarkably effective. They created these "facts" with the complicity of many in the Israeli government and military.

The founding document of Gush Emunim states the movement's objectives: "We hope to bring about a great revival in the nation, a revival that will fulfill the Zionist vision to its greatest extent. We embark on this task fully aware that the root of the Zionist vision is in the traditions of Israel and in the root and purpose of Judaism—the full redemption of the people of Israel and of the whole world."[72]

Thus the negotiations with Egypt after the 1973 war, negotiations that were conducted by U.S. secretary of state Henry Kissinger, were the immediate catalyst for the formation of Gush Emunim. That the Israeli government would consider returning the captured Sinai Peninsula to Egyptian control disturbed the settlers deeply. That the American negotiator, Henry Kissinger, was a Jew further raised the ire of the settlers. Rabbi Zvi Yehuda Kook condemned the negotiated peace agreement with Egypt as an act of "governmental treason." His followers subjected Kissinger to considerable vilification. The religious Zionist response to the possibility of withdrawal from the Sinai was to call for increased Jewish settlement in the West Bank and Gaza. Since 1968 the Golan Heights had been actively settled by secular kibbutzniks and some religious Zionists. The time had come for the settler movement to confront opponents in the Israeli government and military head on. To forestall any negotiations, as many settlements as possible had to be established. The 1967 war demonstrated that God was working in history; now, after the 1973 war, God's faithful had to move the messianic process forward. The faithful would not be discouraged by an apparent setback. Neither would proponents of new settlements who worked within the Israeli government.

Although condemned by Gush Emunim for sharing rule of the Temple Mount with the Muslim religious authorities, Moshe Dayan remained an advocate of building Israeli settlements in relatively unoccupied areas of the territories. One of his pet projects was Yamit, a seaside town on the Sinai coast just south of Gaza. Yamit, which was built in 1974 and 1975, was quickly settled by hundreds of Israelis. But with the American-brokered Israeli-Egyptian negotiations that followed Egyptian president Anwar Sadat's 1977 visit to Jerusalem, Dayan supported the return of all of the Sinai, including Yamit, to Egypt. When in 1982 Yamit was evacuated and destroyed, the settlers became even more determined to prevent further evacuation of settlements in the territories. Their new American Christian fundamentalist allies supported them in this struggle. When Sadat made his surprising announcement that he would visit Jerusalem, a group of prominent Christian Zionists, anticipating the possibility of a "land for peace" agreement between Israel and Egypt, placed this advertisement in the *Washington Post*: "As evangelicals we affirm our belief in the promise of the land to the Jewish people. . . . We would view with grave concern any effort to carve out of the historic Jewish homeland another nation or political entity, particularly one which would be governed by terrorists whose stated goal is the destruction of the Jewish state."[73]

Among Israeli Jews the debate over the security value of the settlements continued through the 1970s, 1980s, and 1990s. The fate of the territories became the central issue in Israeli politics, and it soon became an issue taken up by the Arab citizens of Israel. Many of *these* Israelis were radicalized by the Palestinian insurrections of 1987 and 2000. This exacerbated tensions between Jewish and Arab citizens of Israel, tensions that have flared up in violent encounters in the last years of the twentieth century and the first years of the twenty-first.

Converging Jewish and Christian Views

Within this maelstrom of political and military activity, Gush Emunim achieved truly remarkable success in moving Israeli Jews into the West Bank and Gaza—what the movement termed Judea, Samaria, and Gaza—whose Hebrew acronym "Yesha" also meant salvation. (It did not escape Gush Emunim's Christian supporters that "Yesha" was the Hebrew root of the name "Yeshua," the Hebrew name of Jesus, according to Evangelical Christians.) During the 1970s and 1980s a remarkable transformation in Christian attitudes toward Israel was in the making. For centuries, the Holy Land's sanctity was linked to the life of Jesus, and pilgrims to the Holy Land had sought to "walk in Jesus' footsteps." In the view of post-1967 Christian Zionists, the sanctity of the land was now linked to the Old Testament as well as the New. For almost two millennia, Christians had understood the Holy Land as sanctified by Jesus's life, not by its association with the narratives of the Hebrew Bible. Now, this understanding had changed. The imminent Second Coming was now overshadowing the first coming. For the Temple to be rebuilt, the State of Israel had to retain its "biblical heritage," and Israeli Jews had to be encouraged and supported in their efforts to carry out this project. Thus the theologies and plans of both religious Zionist Jews and Christians Zionists converged. Political and economic support, maximalist territorial claims, and the work of the settler movement became central causes of the American Christian Right.

The Israeli army had conquered the territories in 1967. Over the next seven years, there was a small but steady growth of settlements in the territories. Why, then, did it take seven years for the settler movement to organize and take on a religious orientation? According to Hanan Porat, one of Gush Emunim's founders: "Until the Yom Kippur War our understanding was that the return to Zion would be led by the government. After the war, amid the great general crisis in government leadership, it dawned on us that we could no longer depend on the government."[74] From 1974 onward, the settlers and their ideological leaders placed themselves in opposition to their own government. Through adroit political maneuvering they influenced a series of Israeli governments to follow their dictates.

Gush Emunim's struggle with a succession of Israeli governments had a profound, catalyzing effect on the Israeli body politic. As the spearhead of the settler movement, Gush Emunim, the Bloc of the Faithful, galvanized considerable public opinion in its favor. Their appeal operated on a number of levels—emotional, religious, and political-military. Peace Now, the movement that took upon itself to monitor settler activity, appealed to a radically different Israeli constituency. Secular in its orientation, it, too, had a powerful emotional appeal. For Peace Now, settlement activity, which enraged and unsettled the Palestinians in the territories, was a threat to Israel's security. If security and self-defense were the ultimate Israeli values, the settlers, by exacerbating the already intractable Israeli-Palestinian struggle, were threatening the state's future. The numbers of settlers in the territories increased from a mere fifteen hundred before 1973 to over a quarter of a million by 2005. Their presence became an international issue in the dispute with the Palestinians and often raised the ire of the U.S. State Department.

As the fate of the "occupied," "liberated" (or simply "administered") territories became the central issue in Israeli politics, evangelical Christian supporters of Israel felt compelled to take a stand on the territorial issue. With few exceptions, their stand was that Israel should retain the territories at any cost. Had not the Bible mandated the full extent of Israel's borders? Jerry Falwell told the *Jerusalem Post* in 1978, "The United States government should not be a party to any pressure that would create a peace that is not lasting, equitable and scriptural."[75] Jan Willem van der Hoeven, the head of the International Christian Embassy of Jerusalem (ICEJ), said that an Israeli agreement to return the territories would constitute "a second betrayal of Jesus."[76] The ICEJ is a Christian Zionist advocacy group that was established in 1980. The impetus for its founding was the Jerusalem Law of 1980 in which the Israel government declared all of Jerusalem, including the eastern parts of the city, annexed. Most countries, in protest, moved their embassies to Tel Aviv (or, in the case of the United States, refused to move its already established embassy from Tel Aviv to Jerusalem). To demonstrate their approval of these and other Israeli government policies, the Christian Embassy opened its doors and quickly became the darling of the Jerusalem municipality under the leadership of Mayor Teddy Kollek.[77]

Surprisingly, many religious Zionists began to speak favorably of the Christian Embassy and its many overseas supporters. At end of the 1980s the romance between the ICEJ and the settler movement became more open and explicit. In *Nekuda*, the bi-monthly journal of Gush Emunim, Tzipora Luria published an enthusiastic article about the ICEJ and Jan Willem van der Hoeven. What Van der Hoeven has to say about Israel and Jews met Ms. Luria's enthusiastic approval. The Dutch pastor condemned the tendencies of some Israelis to self-criticism: "Many Israelis speak as if their enemies are justified, and then the Western world thinks: if Israelis are so hard on themselves, then we can criticize them too." Rather than indulge in self-criticism, said Van der Hoeven, Israelis should proclaim the biblical basis of the claim to the land, and especially of the claim to Jerusalem.[78]

Orthodox Jews, both American and Israeli, were more comfortable interlocutors for Christians Zionists than "secular Jews." This locution made no sense to evangelicals: for what would "secular Christian" mean? From the late 1940s to the late 1970s secular Jews were the public face of American and Israeli Jewry. With the rise of the (Revisionist) Likud government of the late 1970s and the empowerment of its supporters in the United States, this situation would change. Revisionists and religious Zionists moved into positions of influence, and Zionist organizations that previously had a secular orientation now became more "religious" in their self-presentation.

Christian Zionist unease with secular Israeli culture was reflected in many pronouncements by prominent churchmen. As Walter I. Wilson wrote, "The nation of Israel has been formed, they have all the likeness of one of the nations of the earth; they have their government, their postal, coinage, and banking system, but there is no God. They have come together as a nation of Israelites, without the God of Israel."[79]

To address the issue of American Christian unease with Israeli secularism, newly elected Prime Minister Menachem Begin in 1977 sent his friend Shmuel Katz to the United States. Katz, Revisionist ideologue author of the right-wing chronicle *Battleground Palestine*, was, like Begin, sentimentally attached to the Jewish religious tradition. *Battleground Palestine* claimed that there were no Palestinians; those Arabs living within the State of Israel were Arabs from neighboring countries who were attracted to Mandate Palestine because of the prosperity generated by the Jewish presence. With its "blood and soil" ideology and its denial of any Palestinian claims, Revisionism appealed to Conservative Christians in the Bible Belt and elsewhere. Though Revisionist politicians may not have been any more ritually observant than their Labor Party counterparts, they were more respectful of rabbis and the rabbinic tradition. Surely they were not hostile to that tradition, as many secular Israelis were. Therefore they were less threatening, and more appealing, to American evangelicals.

We spoke of the cultural and religious consequences of the 1973 war. The accompanying political change was equally dramatic. Yitzhak Rabin became prime minister in 1974 and immediately faced a challenge from the settler movement. The movement's ideological vanguard, Gush Emunim, initiated a series of challenges to the Israeli government and army. The most dramatic and conclusive was the December 1975 demonstration at Sebastia in the West Bank. Over the previous two years, the settlers had made six attempts to settle at this site. Each time, they were repelled by the Israeli army. Some two thousand settlers and supporters took over Sebastia, an abandoned train station near Nablus, and vowed to stay until the government approved the establishment of a new settlement in the immediate area. After a tense series of negotiations, a compromise with the authorities was worked out. Thirty families would be allowed to move into a nearby Israeli army installation. In time, this group of thirty would grow to include hundreds in the settlement of Elon Moreh. Gush Emunim's victory over the Israeli government was a turning point in the history of Israel. The disparate elements who advocated for settlement of the territories now had an ideological vanguard, and that vanguard had led them to victory over the state's elected government.

When Menachem Begin's Likud Party won the elections in 1977 and ended thirty years of Labor Party rule, the Bloc of the Faithful were triumphant. Now the government would be on their side, or so they hoped. After the 1977 elections, the settlers thought of themselves as bridegrooms under the Likud bridal canopy of Menachem Begin, a man beloved of the believers in Greater Israel.[80] Ariel Sharon, one of the architects of the Likud victory, was soon appointed minister of agriculture, a post that gave him authority over the establishment of settlements in the territories. He quickly became the darling of the leaders of the Bloc, working with the leadership of the settler movement to establish "facts on the ground"—new settlements in the territories.

The settlements issue was a point of contention in the first meeting between Prime Minister Begin and President Jimmy Carter in July 1977. Carter noted that the American government, as it had since 1967, objected to Israeli settlement in, and annexation of, the territories. Begin's response, of which he was very proud, was that the American objections were of ten years standing, but the Jewish connection to biblical Israel was three thousand years old. As Begin said to Carter, "In the United States, there are eleven places named Hebron, five places named Shiloh, and another seven named Bethlehem or Bethel. Can you imagine one of the governors of these American states forbidding Jews from settling in these places. Similarly, the Israeli government can't forbid Jews from living in the original Hebron, Bethlehem, Bethel, or Shiloh."[81] This was a brilliant rhetorical move on Begin's part. He knew that Carter was a devout Baptist who had taught the Bible in Sunday school for many years. But at this point in 1977, Begin and his advisers did not understand the political differences among American evangelicals. Jimmy Carter was not Jerry Falwell. He was a progressive Southern Baptist, not a conservative one. And he was not a dispensationalist. Rather than convince him, Begin's rhetoric repelled him. When Begin, ignoring Carter's request, refused to freeze settlement activity in the territories, there were some seven thousand Israeli settlers. Fifteen years later, in 1992, when Likud fell from power, there were seventy-five thousand settlers. By 2007 there were a quarter of a million Israelis in the territories. The number rises to four hundred thousand if one includes the areas of Jerusalem annexed by the Israeli government after the 1967 war.

Throughout the 1980s and 1990s, Likud politicians continued to cultivate the support of the American Christian Right. The most effective and forceful of these political figures is Benjamin Netanyahu. In 1985, when he was the Israeli ambassador to the United Nations, Netanyahu addressed a "National Prayer Breakfast to Honor Israel." The event was held during the National Religious Broadcasters annual convention in Washington, D.C. In an impas-

The Old City, Jerusalem (photograph by Dov Goldman)

sioned speech, Netanyahu told the hundreds of attendees that "it was the impact of Christian Zionism that helped modern Jewish Zionism achieve the rebirth of Israel."[82] Netanyahu, scion of one of the most prominent Revisionist Zionist families, rose to the leadership of the Likud Party and served as Israeli prime minister from 1996 to 1999. A decade later, in 2009, he again occupied that office.

The Temple Mount

Since the political empowerment of the American Christian Right in the 1980s, the settler-evangelical alliance has experienced remarkable growth. The shift of American Jews to the political Right—on both Israeli and American issues—has expanded the settlers' base of support, a base that now includes many churches, particularly in the Bible Belt. This development has to be seen in the context of the American government's military, political, and economic support of the State of Israel from the 1960s to the present. During the Cold War and in its aftermath, American and Israeli interests converged. Conservative Protestants were more supportive of post-1967 Israeli policies than their liberal counterparts. U.S. policy toward the settlements often reflected this difference of opinion. The Carter, Clinton, and the first Bush administrations tended to criticize settlement activity; the second Bush administrations have lent this activity their tacit approval, and after 9/11 this approval became quite explicit. In 2004 President George W. Bush spoke of the need to shift Israel's borders to include "already existing major Israeli population centers" in the West Bank.[83]

Although the settler movement experienced remarkable success in the late 1970s and early 1980s, its ideological vanguard was frustrated by its inability to change Israeli government policy concerning the Temple Mount/Haram al-Sharif. The most radical expression of that frustration was the hatching of a number of plots to blow up the mosques on the Temple Mount, thus "liberating" the space for the building of the Third Temple. By this point in the mid-1980s, the great majority of settlers had moved away from the early militancy of the movement. Along with most Israelis, this settler silent majority was shaken by the uncovering in 1984 of a Jewish underground plot to blow up the mosques. The plot thus moved the settler population away from the political extremism of the Jewish underground. Decades earlier, American Fundamentalists had called for the removal of the mosques on the Haram. In a 1938 tract titled *The Battle of Armageddon*, dispensationalist Charles S. Price laid out this scenario: "When the Jew under the protection of some great power (for they could not do it alone) tears down the Moslem Mosque of Omar and builds his temple, then the Moslem world will gnash its teeth in rage."[84]

Long before extremist religious Zionists plotted to "hasten the end" by destroying the mosques, a disturbed young Australian Christian attempted to burn down al-Aqsa, the great mosque that faces the Dome of the Rock on the Haram. Dennis Michael Rohan set fire to the *minbar* (the oration pulpit) of al-Aqsa in August of 1969. Israeli firefighters extinguished the fire, but the southeast section of the mosque was damaged. There was an outcry in the Muslim world, with charges that the fire was the first stage of an Israeli plan to take over the Temple Mount/Haram al-Sharif and rebuild the Temple. That the fire had been set by a Christian did not mitigate reaction in the Muslim world; rather, Rohan was described in the Arab press as a Christian agent of the Israelis.

Rohan, a volunteer worker on a kibbutz, was arrested two days after he had set the fire at al-Aqsa. He lit it, he claimed, to destroy the mosque and to enable Israel to rebuild the Temple. His direct inspiration was the teaching of American evangelist Herbert W. Armstrong, head of the Worldwide Church of God. Rohan was a regular reader of Armstrong's prophecy magazine *Plain Truth*, a journal distributed in millions of copies worldwide. *Plain Truth* had on many occasions predicted the rebuilding of the Temple. In early 1967 Armstrong wrote: "There will be a Jewish Temple built in Jerusalem, with

animal sacrifices once again being offered."[85] Along with other dispensationalist teachers, Armstrong had been preaching this doctrine since the mid-1950s,
over a decade before the 1967 war. When he was captured, Rohan told the
Israeli police, "God wanted me to build this Temple. . . . Therefore if I am the
chosen one to do this, then I would have to prove this by destroying the
mosque."[86] Rohan was declared insane, hospitalized in Israel, and later de-
ported to Australia.

From the 1970s onward, dispensationalist writers and preachers enthused
about full Israeli control over the Temple Mount. Their churches have contributed large sums of money for Israeli organizations dedicated to this purpose. The restoration of the Temple is seen by messianic groups Jewish and
Christian as an absolute necessity. Rather than fearing the outcome of such
action, these groups welcome it. Hal Lindsey predicted that "the dispute to
trigger the war of Armageddon will arise between the Arabs and Israelis over
the Temple Mount and Old Jerusalem (Zechariah 12:2–3), the most contested
and strategic piece of real estate in the world."[87]

Forty years earlier, in the mid-1930s, "Evangelist Charles Price contended
that the Arab's removal from Palestine was biblically ordained, and that the
Jews would receive temporary protection from European powers to tear
down the Dome of the Rock and rebuild the Temple."[88] Price made this
argument in 1938, a decade before the establishment of the State of Israel, and
decades before any Jewish spokesperson articulated such a plan.

In the settlers' emerging ideology, the struggle for the Temple Mount was
intimately tied to the political and military struggle against the Palestinians. In
the late 1970s, a decade after the 1967 war, some of the leaders of the settler
movement formed underground cells and organized armed groups to attack
Palestinians. Their first actions were attacks on West Bank mayors, two of
whom were maimed in bombings. Some members of this underground were
members of the group that conspired to blow up the mosques on the Temple
Mount. Israeli intelligence officers infiltrated this cell, and in 1984 twenty-five
members of the group, all affiliated with Gush Emunim, were arrested and
put on trial. They quickly became known as the "Jewish Underground." They
were formally charged with the attacks on the West Bank Arab mayors—two
of whom had their legs blown off—and plotting to blow up the mosques. The
leaders of the plot received long prison sentences, but their sentences were
later commuted.[89]

Davar, the newspaper of the Labor Party, reflected the views of many
Israeli Jews when it outlined the probable consequences of blowing up the
mosques, foremost among them a regional war: "To blow up the Temple

Mount would be to blow up Zionism. It would mark the end of the historic State of Israel and the beginning of the Messianic land of Israel."[90] To some in their own religious Zionist community, the members of the Jewish underground were heroes; few had expressed any remorse. In the eyes of the supporters of Peace Now, they were unrepentant villains.[91] Some Christian Zionists in the United States championed the cause of the Jewish Underground. Jerry Falwell and other television evangelists protested to the Israeli government about their imprisonment and helped raise money for their defense. American Jewish supporters of the settlers set up a similar campaign, a campaign endorsed by some of the more rightist "pro-Israel" organizations in the United States.

In the 1980s and early 1990s the ties between evangelical Christian Zionists and Israel deepened. One of the prime movers in this alliance was Rabbi Yechiel Eckstein, whose International Fellowship of Christians and Jews raises large sums of money for Israel in American churches. These funds are used in Israel for charitable causes—particularly in the territories—and for support of immigration to Israel of Jews from the former Soviet Union. Orthodox Jews in Israel and the United States are uneasy with Eckstein's close relationship with Christian fundamentalists, a relationship that they contend aids Christian missionary aims.

American fundamentalist tour groups to Israel are sure to include a visit to the Temple Mount in their pilgrimage plans. At churches in the Bible Belt and elsewhere, large sums are collected for purchase of land and buildings in the territories, particularly in Jerusalem's Old City, where Jewish settlers are buying all available real estate. Particularly fascinating to these Christian pilgrims is the Temple Institute in Jerusalem's Jewish Quarter.

The Temple Institute was founded by Rabbi Yehuda Ariel, one of the leaders of Yamit, the Sinai settlement evacuated in 1982 after the Egyptian-Israeli Peace Agreements. Known in Hebrew as Machon Hamikdash, the institute is devoted to recreating the ritual objects and priestly garments of the Temple service. The unstated implication of this project is that the objects are being prepared for use in the soon-to-be-built Third Temple. From its inception, Christian fundamentalists have been among the institute's most enthusiastic supporters, donating large sums of money to its upkeep and expansion. Among the projects associated with the institute is the attempt to breed a pure red heifer, a cow whose ashes, prepared according to biblical ritual, can purify the ritually impure. With these ashes, Kohanim, members of the priestly caste, can be prepared for service in the rebuilt Temple. After an unsuccessful series of attempts to raise a red heifer on a farm in Mississippi, the project moved to Israel. Breeding a red heifer and using its ashes in a purification ritual would remove the rationale for the current rabbinic injunction against entering the Temple Mount for fear of polluting it.

The dispensationalist expectation that the Temple would be rebuilt by Jews has many a variation and an unexpected twist. The new Third Temple would, according to some Christian "prophecy experts," stand for only three and a half to four years—to be destroyed at the great battle that would begin at Armageddon.[92] After Armageddon, those Jews who accepted Jesus would then build a fourth Temple, which would stand for eternity as the place where God would be worshipped. But whether it is a third or fourth Temple that is envisioned, the return of the Temple is eagerly anticipated by many Christians. And it seems that the numbers of these adherents and their influence are growing quickly.

That Israel's leaders recognize the power of Israeli territorial claims on the imagination of the Western world is clear from Prime Minister Ehud Barak's comments at the United Nations Millennium Summit in September 2000: "I believe that the very words 'Temple Mount,' in every Western language, carry the real story of this place. When we think of Jesus walking in the streets of Jerusalem, what he saw there was not a mosque, nor even a Christian church. What he saw was the Temple—the Second Temple of the Jews."[93] Barak, military hero, leader of the Labor Party, and exemplar of Israeli secularism, was as ideologically distant from his Jewish coreligionists of the Temple Mount faithful as he was from Christian Zionists. It may have struck some in his United Nations audience as strange that the Israeli prime minister was invoking the name of Jesus. But like all Israeli leaders from Ben-Gurion onward, Barak recognized the power exerted by ancient images and ideas on the religious and political imaginations of Christians the world over.

Notes

INTRODUCTION

1 Israel Ministry for Foreign Affairs, "Zionism."

2 Popkin, "Christian Roots of Zionism," 114.

3 Babylonian Talmud, Tractate Gittin, 55–56.

4 Halevi, *The Kuzari*, 97.

5 Ravitsky, *Messianism, Zionism and the Jewish Religious Radicalism*, 211–34.

6 Wilken, *Land Called Holy*.

7 Ibid.

8 Carpenter, *Revive Us Again*, 247.

9 Bain, *March to Zion*.

10 Ben-Artzi, "Traditional and Modern Rural Settlement Types," 140.

11 Robinson and Smith, *Biblical Researches*.

12 Quoted in Nachman Ben-Yehuda, *Masada Myth*.

13 T. Marsden, "Zionism," 1626.

14 On these books for young people, see Shadur, *Young Travellers to Jerusalem*.

15 For the background of Bush's comment, see Goldman, *God's Sacred Tongue*, 204.

16 Long, *Imagining the Holy Land*, 43–70.

17 Ibid.

18 Sykes, *Two Studies in Virtue*.

19 Malachy, *American Fundamentalism and Israel*.

20 Ewbank, *National Restoration of the Jews*.

21 Sokolow, *History of Zionism*.

22 Friesel, "Zionism and Jewish Nationalism," 306 n. 3.

23 Popkin, "Christian Roots of Zionism," 113.

24 Shimoni, *Zionist Ideology*, 64.

25 Carmel, "Christlicher Zionismus."

26 Ibid., 135.

27 Eliot, *Daniel Deronda*, 485.

28 Eliezer Ben-Yehuda, *Dream Come True*, 26–27.

29 Joseph Patai, *Star Over Jordan*, 98.

30 Lustick, *For the Land and the Lord*, 120.

31 Zangwill, "Return to Palestine," 627. For a history of this phrase, see Garfinkle, "On the Origin, Meaning, Use and Abuse of a Phrase."

32 Shlaim, *Iron Wall*.

33 Epstein, "Hidden Question," 561.

34 Currie, "God's Little Errand Boy," 6.

35 For the text of the Memorial, see Moshe Davis, *Christian Protagonists*.

36 Ibid.

37 Ariel, *On Behalf of Israel*, 70.

38 Quoted in Florence, *Lawrence and Aaronsohn*, 80.

39 Goldman, *God's Sacred Tongue*, 208.

40 Ariel, *On Behalf of Israel*, 62.

41 Currie, "God's Little Errand Boy," 9.

42 Merkley, *Christian Attitudes*, 44.

43 On the *Christian Century* and Zionism, see Fishman, *American Protestantism*, 53–99.

44 McCullough, *Truman*, 596.

45 Benson, *Harry S. Truman*, 189.

46 Ganin, *Uneasy Relationship*, 184.

47 Uris, *Exodus*, 371.

48 Herzl, *Old-New Land*, 124.

49 Mosley, *Gideon Goes to War*, 34.

50 Ibid., 61.

51 Ibid., 63.

52 Ibid., 216.

53 Institute for the Study of American Evangelicals, "Defining Evangelicalism."

54 Dayton and Johnson, eds., *Variety of American Evangelicalism*, 12–14.

55 Pew Research Center, "Trends, 2005."

56 Carpenter, *Revive Us Again*, 7.

57 Marsden, *Fundamentals*, 9:43.

58 Ibid., 8:76.

59 Carpenter, *Revive Us Again*, 97.

60 Wolfe, "Opening of the Evangelical Mind."

61 Hofstadter, *Anti-Intellectualism*.

62 *New York Times*, 8 April 2008.

63 Boyer, *When Time Shall Be No More*, 185.

64 Ibid., 391.

65 LaHaye, *Revelation Unveiled*, 15.

66 Ariel, *Philosemites or Antisemites?*

67 Boyer, *When Time Shall Be No More*.

68 Naor, "Behold Rachel, Behold."

69 Boyer, *When Time Shall Be No More*, 246.

70 The Barna Group, "Barna Updates: Left Behind," <www.Barna.org>.

71 Israel Gutman, "Jewish-Presbyterian Ties."

72 Wallis, *God's Politics*, 186.

73 National Council of Churches, "Why We Should Be Concerned about Christian Zionism."

74 Sykes, *Crossroads to Israel*, 6.

75 Ariel, *On Behalf of Israel*, 97–117.

76 Walt and Mearsheimer, *Israel Lobby*, 6.

77 Tessler, *History of the Israeli-Palestinian Conflict*.

78 Goldman, "Christians and Zionism."

CHAPTER ONE

1 Lawton and Schneider, *Prophet and a Pilgrim*, 366; Henderson, *Life of Laurence Oliphant*, 222.

2 Kabakoff, *Master of Hope*, 12, 20.

3 Rogel, *Imber File*, 10; Leon, "What Hope for *Hatikvah*." Although *Hatikvah* has long been described as the "Israeli National Anthem," it did not have that official status until recently. It was only on 10 November 2004 that the Knesset moved to declare it the *official* national anthem.

4 For a description of the meeting, see Blumenthal, "Birth Pangs."

5 Five years earlier, Joseph Smith had studied Hebrew with Joshua Seixas, a Jewish teacher from New York. Smith acknowledged Seixas's help in "mastering the ancient languages," and scholars have pointed out the influence that Seixas had on Mormon teachings and attitudes toward Jews and Judaism. In this and many other ways, Christian Hebraism prepared the way for Christian Zionism. See Goldman, *God's Sacred Tongue*, 176–98.

6 Only three years after Orson Hyde's "blessing of Jerusalem," the American Presbyterian clergyman and scholar George Bush predicted in his *Valley of Vision* (1844) that the Jews would return to their ancient home. This would not occur, he wrote, in one miraculous movement but as part of a gradual global transformation. Although Bush was a gradualist, his millennialist contemporaries expected the imminent return of the Jews to their land, an event that would signal the beginning of the End Time. See Goldman, *God's Sacred Tongue*, 199–207.

7 Laqueur, *History of Zionism*, 41–46.

8 Ariel, *On Behalf of Israel*, 1–10.

9 Kabakoff, *Master of Hope*, 92.

10 Oliphant had slid into obscurity, from which he has emerged only recently as a character in William Gibson and Bruce Sterling's very popular 1990s sci-fi fantasy *The Difference Engine*.

11 Kabakoff, *Master of Hope*, 92.

12 De Haas, *Theodor Herzl*.

13 One of the attendees at the first Albury Prophecy Conference reported in a letter to a friend that Edward Irving was "regularly preaching of the Advent as at hand, and preparing the minds of their people for the coming judgment." See Whitley, *Blinded Eagle*, 42.

14 Anne Taylor, *Laurence Oliphant*, 3, 28, 122; Davenport, *Albury Apostles*, 18–19.

15 Whitley, *Blinded Eagle*, 41; Davenport, *Albury Apostles*, 18.

16 Dallimore, *Life of Edward Irving*, 94; Margaret Oliphant, *Life of Edward Irving*.

17 In 1828, at the third conference, Henry Drummond told the assembled participants that "the Ten Lost Tribes have been discovered, twenty millions in number, inhabiting the region north of Cashmere and towards Bohara, in the great central plain of Asia." A short while later, however, one of Irving's followers declared that the American Indians were the ten lost tribes and that they would all immigrate to Palestine. See Tudor, *Morning Watch*.

18 Taylor, *Laurence Oliphant*, 2.

19 Quoted in Henderson, *Life of Laurence Oliphant*, 5.

20 Louis Loewe, *Diaries of Sir Moses and Lady Montefiore*, 64.

21 Lawton and Schneider, *Prophet and a Pilgrim*, xiv.

22 For a comprehensive study of Harris and his teachings, see Lawton and Schneider, *Prophet and a Pilgrim*.

23 Anne Taylor, *Laurence Oliphant*, 91.

24 See Anne Taylor, *Laurence Oliphant*.

25 Ibid., 123.

26 Laurence Oliphant, *Episodes*, 342.

27 Ibid., 343.

28 Melton, "Harris, Thomas Lake," 105–6.

29 In a delightful essay titled "Quacks and Alchemists," English poet Dame Edith Sitwell chronicled the ideas of Harris and other eccentrics of the era. She dubbed them "those who would cure the ills of this world." Thomas Lake Harris, Sitwell was convinced, was a sexual adventurer who encouraged his acolytes to find as many partners as possible in the Brotherhood. Sitwell quotes Mrs. White's *Religious Fanaticism*: "Thus, it was the duty of the true believer to love, and approach as close as possible to any and every other human being (if of the opposite sex), so as to be united to that part of their own counterpart which was mirrored within; and the more often the experiment was repeated with a different partner the more thorough the approximation would become" (Sitwell, *English Eccentrics*, 107).

30 Laurence Oliphant, *Episodes*, 343.

31 Henderson, *Life of Laurence Oliphant*.

32 Anne Taylor, *Laurence Oliphant*, 233.

33 Lawton and Schneider, *Prophet and a Pilgrim*, 359–64.

34 Presbyterian clergyman and scholar George Bush was a nineteenth-century Swedenborgian and American translator of Swedenborg's writings. See Goldman, *God's Sacred Tongue*, 199–207.

35 Duker, "Swedenborg's Attitude towards the Jews," 274.

36 Laskov, *The Biluim*, 56.

37 S. Imber, *Complete Poems of Naphtali Herz Imber*, 19.

38 Ibid., 20.

39 Ibid., 15.

40 Kabakoff, "N. H. Imber in the Eyes of His Generation," 9. The bohemian artist as child prodigy and the child prodigy as bohemian are familiar themes in literary biography.

41 Kabakoff, *Master of Hope*, 92.

42 Ibid., 58–59.

43 Lipsky, *Memoirs in Profile*, 179–80.

44 In the century since Lipsky met and immediately disliked Imber, a wide range of strategies has developed for negotiating the ambivalent relationship between the American Jewish community and the nearly 700,000 "non-resident Israelis" in the United States. This is five times the most generous estimate of the number of American Jews who have emigrated to Israel. Furthermore, the estimate does not take into account the large percentage of those American *olim* who have returned to the United States.

45 Segev, "Illuminating Gesture," 6.

46 See Sadan's introduction in S. Imber, *Complete Poems of Naphtali Herz Imber*.

47 S. Imber, *Complete Poems of Naphtali Herz Imber*, 20.

48 See the Hebrew dedication in *Barkai*, with its misspelled English-language dedication.

49 Kabakoff, *Master of Hope*, 58–59.

50 Kabakoff, *N. H. Imber, "Baal Hatikva,"* 7–10.

51 See the letter quoted in Moruzzi, "Strange Bedfellows," 60.

52 They shared this "safe" quality with their contemporary novelist George Eliot, who approvingly mentions Oliphant's proto-Zionism in her correspondence. See Shimoni, *Zionist Ideology*.

53 S. Imber, *Complete Poems of Naphtali Herz Imber*, 20–21.

54 Kabakoff, *Master of Hope*, 59.

55 Rogel, *Imber File*, 42; Kabakoff, *N. H. Imber, "Baal Hatikva,"* 78.

56 Nedava, *Haifa, Oliphant, and the Zionist Vision*, 18.

57 Laurence Oliphant, *Land of Gilead*, xxiii.

58 See Vital, *Origins of Zionism*, 94–97.

59 Isaiah 45:1: "Thus says the Lord to Cyrus his anointed, whom he has taken by the right hand."

60 Ilan, *Plans for Jewish Settlement East of the Jordan*, 29.

61 Ibid., 38; Polowetsky, "Chapter 5: Laurence Oliphant Offers His Leadership," 135.

62 Ilan, *Plans for Jewish Settlement East of the Jordan*, 40.

63 Rogel, *Imber File*, 41; Anne Taylor, *Laurence Oliphant*, 225.

64 Anne Taylor, *Laurence Oliphant*, 190, 278.

65 Laurence Oliphant, *Land of Gilead*, xviii.

66 Ibid., 285.

67 Ibid., 284.

68 Laurence Oliphant, *Episodes*, 289.

69 N. M. Gelber, *Zur Vorgeschichte des Zionismus*, 114.

70 Nedava, *Haifa, Oliphant, and the Zionist Vision*, 29.

71 Laqueur, *History of Zionism*, 78.

72 Salmon, *Religion and Zionism*, 174–75.

73 Nedava, *Haifa, Oliphant and the Zionist Vision*, 30 (emphasis added).

74 Laurence Oliphant, *Haifa*, 69–71.

75 Ibid., 69–70.

76 Ibid., 109–11.

77 Laurence Oliphant, *Haifa*.

78 See Laurence Oliphant, "New Discoveries," *Palestinian Exploration Fund Quarterly* (1886): 73–81.

79 Kabakoff, *Master of Hope*, 65.

80 From Mrs. Smith's *Religious Fanaticism*, quoted in Sitwell, *English Eccentrics*, 112.

81 Kabakoff, *Master of Hope*.

82 Yardeni, "N. H. Imber and Laurence Oliphant."

83 Kabakoff, "N. H. Imber in the Eyes of His Generation."

84 Kabakoff, *Master of Hope*.

85 S. Imber, *Complete Poems of Naphtali Herz Imber*, 27.

86 Mendes-Flohr and Reinharz, *Jew in the Modern World*, 54–56.

87 Yardeni, "N. H. Imber and Laurence Oliphant," 42, n. 10.

88 S. Imber, *Complete Poems of Naphtali Herz Imber*.

89 Wilk, "Bohemian Who Wrote *Hatikvah*," 55.

90 Zangwill, *Children of the Ghetto*, 137.

91 Ibid.

92 Ibid., 265–68.

93 Anne Taylor, *Laurence Oliphant*, 230.

94 Ibid.

95 Lawton and Schneider, *Prophet and a Pilgrim*, 381.

96 Henderson, *Life of Laurence Oliphant*, 260.

97 Lawton and Schneider, *Prophet and a Pilgrim*, 412 n. 19.

98 Ibid., 359, 424.

99 Kabakoff, *Master of Hope*, 35.

100 Imber commented, "I have just been to take the last look at my dear friend and benefactor. He lies, as peacefully asleep, in his bed and the house of Sir Mounstuart Grant Duff" (ibid., 37).

101 Yardeni, "N. H. Imber and Laurence Oliphant," 50.

102 Kabakoff, *Master of Hope*, 21–22.

103 Uriel, "Magazine of Cabbalistic Science."

104 S. Imber, *Complete Poems of Naphtali Herz Imber*, 29; Silberschlag, "Naphtali Herz Imber," 156.

105 Silberschlag, "Naphtali Herz Imber," 156.

106 Naphtali Imber, "To Ivan the Terrible."

107 Silberschlag, "Naphtali Herz Imber," 157.

108 On Imber's reburial in Jerusalem in 1953, see Rogel, *Imber File*, 32–34.

109 Wilk, "Bohemian Who Wrote *Hatikvah*," 60; Lawton and Schneider, *Prophet and a Pilgrim*, 414.

110 Lawton and Schneider, *Prophet and a Pilgrim*, 108.

111 Ibid., 417.

112 Tuchman, *Bible and Sword*, 270; Lawton and Schneider, *Prophet and a Pilgrim*, 417–19; Henderson, *Life of Laurence Oliphant*, 270.

113 Anne Taylor, *Laurence Oliphant*, 252.

114 Lawton and Schneider, *Prophet and a Pilgrim*, 418 n. 41.

115 Owen, *My Perilous Life in Palestine*, 300.

116 Henderson, *Life of Laurence Oliphant*, 270.

117 Owen, *My Perilous Life in Palestine*, 242; Lawton and Schneider, *Prophet and a Pilgrim*, 418.

118 See Revelation 20:7–10.

119 Owen, *My Perilous Life in Palestine*, 249.

120 Quoted in Cline, *Battles of Armageddon*, 177.

121 Matthews and Winters, *Israel Handbook*, 573, 585.

122 Ze'evi, *L. Oliphant's Haifa*.

123 Ilan, *Plans for Jewish Settlement East of the Jordan*, 41.

CHAPTER TWO

1 Bein, *Theodor Herzl*, 232.

2 Ibid., 221.

3 Ibid.

4 Pawel, *Labyrinth of Exile*, 327.

5 Ibid., 242.

6 Herzl, *Diaries*, 215.

7 Ibid., 103.

8 Quoted in Y. Salmon, "Herzl and Orthodox Jewry," in Shimoni and Wistrich, *Theodor Herzl: Visionary*, 299.

9 Friedman, "The Political Activity of Theodore Herzl," in Shimoni and Wistrich, *Theodor Herzl*, 185.

10 Ibid., 213.

11 Bein, *Theodor Herzl*, 232.

12 Kertzer, *Popes Against the Jews*, 142, 175.

13 Pawel, *Labyrinth of Exile*, 215.

14 J. Katz, "Zionism," 1033.

15 De Haas, *Theodor Herzl*, 1:30.

16 Bein, *Theodor Herzl*, 3.

17 De Haas, *Theodor Herzl*, 1:182.

18 Bein, *Theodor Herzl*, 90.

19 On Hans Herzl, see Sternberger, *Princes Without a Home*.

20 Bein, *Theodor Herzl*, 94.

21 Ibid., 490.

22 Sokolow, *History of Zionism*.

23 De Haas, *Theodor Herzl*, 1:31; Bein, *Theodor Herzl*, 15.

24 Herzl, *Diaries*, 11.

25 Bein, *Theodor Herzl*, 18.

26 Ibid., 78–92.

27 Haramati, *Leviyim Bamikdash Haivrit*, 215.

28 Bein, *Herzl*, 80.

29 Haramati, *Leviyim Bamikdash Haivrit*, 213.

30 Bein, *Theodor Herzl*, 80–82.

31 Beller, *Herzl*, 16.

32 Haramati, *Leviyim Bamikdash Haivrit*, 216–17.

33 Hechler, *Restoration of the Jews*, 1.

34 Zohn, "Herzl, Hechler and the Grand Duke," 234.

35 Ibid.

36 Sokolow, *History of Zionism*, 270.

37 Ben-Gurion, *Memoirs*, 34.

38 Laqueur, *History of Zionism*, 98.

39 Goldberg, *To the Promised Land*, 53, 263.

40 Berkowitz, *Zionist Culture*, 135.

41 De Haas, *Theodor Herzl*, 1:100.

42 Ibid.

43 See S. Mandelbrote, "Isaac Newton and the Exegesis of the Book of Daniel."

44 Duvernoy, *Prince and the Prophet*, 15.

45 Pawel, *Labyrinth of Exile*, 279.

46 Herzl, *Diaries*, 195; Pawel, *Labyrinth of Exile*, 280; Bein, *Theodor Herzl*, 191–97.

47 Herzl, *Diaries*, 105–7.

48 Ibid., 107.

49 Ibid.

50 Ibid., 118.

51 Ibid., 123.

52 Ibid., 124–25.

53 De Haas, *Theodor Herzl*, 2:104.

54 Kobler, *Vision Was There*, 108.

55 Herzl, *Diaries*, 198.

56 Ibid., 200.

57 Ibid., 200.

58 Ibid., 23.

59 Zohn, "Herzl, Hechler and the Grand Duke."

60 Ibid., 233.

61 See Röhl, "Herzl and Kaiser Wilhelm II," 29–30; and Zohn, "Herzl, Hechler and the Grand Duke," 232.

62 Zohn, "Herzl, Hechler and the Grand Duke."

63 Röhl, "Herzl and Kaiser Wilhelm II," 32–33.

64 Herzl, *Diaries*, 266–75.

65 Ibid., 268.

66 See Röhl, "Herzl and Kaiser Wilhelm II," 136.

67 Ibid., 36.

68 Bein, *Theodor Herzl*, 342.

69 Fleischer, "Vambery."

70 Vambery, *His Life and Adventures*, 25; Mandler, "Vambery."

71 Vambery, *His Life and Adventures*, 8.

72 Vambery, *Struggles*, 18.

73 Ibid., 198.

74 Ibid., 21.

75 Ibid., 23.

76 Ibid., 36.

77 Ibid., 42.

78 Ibid., 48.

79 Ibid., 50–51.

80 Ibid., 58.

81 Ibid., 121.

82 Vambery, *His Life and Adventures*, 10, 325; Vambery, *Struggles*, 88, 94.

83 Vambery, *Story of My Struggles*.

84 Vambery, *His Life and Adventures*, 28–29.

85 Adler and Dalby, *Dervish of Windsor Castle*, 490.

86 Landau, "Arminius Vambery," 96.

87 Pawel, *Labyrinth of Exile*, 426; Vambery, *His Life and Adventures*.

88 See Vambery, *Struggles*, 263.

89 Adler and Dalby, *Dervish of Windsor Castle*, 345–66.

90 On the Armenians see ibid., 359–62, 423.

91 Kramer, *Jewish Discovery of Islam*.

92 De Haas, *Theodor Herzl*, 1:352; Pawel, *Labyrinth of Exile*, 427.

93 Pawel, *Labyrinth of Exile*, 42.

94 Herzl, *Diaries*, 327–28; Pawel, *Labyrinth of Exile*, 427; Adler and Dalby, *Dervish of Windsor Castle*, 368.

95 De Haas, *Theodor Herzl*, 1:7, 352.

96 Herzl, *Diaries*, 327–28.

97 Ibid., 333.

98 Adler and Dalby, *Dervish of Windsor Castle*, 371, 263.

99 Herzl, *Diaries*, 55–56; Pawel, *Labyrinth of Exile*, 242.

100 Stanislawski, *Zionism and the Fin de Siècle*, 19–20.

101 Pawel, *Labyrinth of Exile*, 434.

102 Duvernoy, *Prince and the Prophet*, 78–79; Beller, *Herzl*, 65.

103 Pawel, *Labyrinth of Exile*, 287.

104 Feldenstein, "Fulfilling Theodor Herzl's Last Will and Testament."

105 Ravitzky, *Messianism, Zionism, and Jewish Religious Radicalism*, 98.

106 See ibid., 99, and Shimoni and Wistrich, *Theodor Herzl*, 336–37.

107 Ravitzky, *Messianism, Zionism, and Jewish Religious Radicalism*, 100.

108 Hertzberg, *Zionist Idea*, 46.

109 Ibid., 48.

110 Ravitzky, *Messianism, Zionism, and Jewish Religious Radicalism*, 85.

111 Ibid., 51, 93, 256.

112 Yahuda, "Hechler," 2.

113 Ibid., 3.

114 Sternberger, *Princes Without a Home*, 491.

CHAPTER THREE

1 Danby, *Jew and Christianity*, 17.

2 Reinharz, *Chaim Weizmann*, 18.

3 Farah, *In Troubled Waters*, 73.

4 Lidberg, *Hundred Years*.

5 Shepherd, *Ploughing Sand*, 44.

6 Danby, *Gentile Interest*, 1–2.

7 Biographical materials on Danby are limited. See R. Loewe, "Herbert Danby."

8 Archival Records: St. George's Cathedral, 4 September 1893, Jerusalem.

9 Cohn-Sherbok, *Politics of Apocalypse*, 127–28.

10 Ibid., 142, 202.

11 The *Journal of the Palestine Oriental Society* was published from 1920 to 1948.

12 According to Nick Mays in "The *Times* in Palestine": "Until 1945 *The Times* employed British residents to report on events in Palestine—from 1921 to 1936, the Rev. Doctor Herbert Danby, Librarian of St. George's Cathedral in Jerusalem."

13 Yellin, "Eliezer ben Yehuda," 194.

14 Albright, "Presidential Address."

15 Danby, "Book Review."

16 Danby, *Studies in Judaism*, 12, 30.

17 Klausner, *Jesus of Nazareth*; Ruzer, "David Flusser," 126.

18 See Klausner, *Darki*, 1:90–92.

19 Danby, *Studies in Judaism*, 28–29.

20 Asher Ginzberg, *Essays on Zionism and Judaism*, 223–53.

21 Danby, *Jew and Christianity*, 82.

22 Klausner, *Darki*, 2:83.

23 Danby, *Jew and Christianity*, 100.

24 Wise, *Challenging Years*, 281.

25 Voss, *Rabbi and Minister*, 225–26.

26 Ibid.

27 Kabak, *Narrow Path*; Flusser, *Jesus*.

28 Ben Siegel, *Controversial Sholem Asch*.

29 Schoffman, "Herbert Danby," 44.

30 Klausner, *Darki*, 2:53.

31 Deinard, *Herev La Hashem Uleyisrael*; Danby, *Gentile Interest*, 2.

32 Danby, *Studies in Judaism*, 6–7.

33 Ibid., 31.

34 Ibid.

35 Sonaberg, *Ambivalent Friendship*, 69.

36 Scott, "Jewish Interpretation of Jesus."

37 Danby, "Budapest and Warsaw Conferences," 1.

38 Klausner, "Herbert Danby."

39 Danby, *Jew and Christianity*, 89.

40 Ibid., 100.

41 Ibid., 101.

42 Ibid., 2, 4.

43 Klausner, *Darki*, 1:154.

44 Klausner, *History of Hebrew Literature*.

45 Bialik, *And It Came to Pass*.

46 For an insightful Hebrew essay on this book see Yehezkel, "Vayehi Hayom."

47 Lahover, *Bialik*, 690–706.

48 Yehezkel, "Vayehi Hayom," 340.

49 Bialik, *Knights of Onion and Garlic*.

50 Maimonides, *Commentary on the Mishnah*, Toharot, cited in *The Book of Cleanliness XXXIX*; Hagigah 14a.

51 Neusner, *Mishnah*, x.

52 R. Loewe, "Herbert Danby," credits him with contributions to modern Hebrew lexicography.

53 Editor's note, *Bible Lands* 9, no. 19 (July 1936): 749–50.

54 Shepherd, *Ploughing Sand*, 46–47.

55 Danby, "Church in Jerusalem."

56 Gill, "Jews in Palestine," 1255.

57 Sloan, "Problems and Prospects." Sloan delivered this address at Tallin, Estonia, on Tuesday, 23 July 1935, before a United Conference of the Churches of Estonia and Finland.

58 "Professor Herbert Danby," *Palestine Post*, 30 August 1937.

59 Rosenberg, *Immorality in the Talmud*, 6.

60 Ibid.

61 Ibid., 8.

62 Obermann, *Code of Maimonides*.

63 Ibid., v.

64 Danby, *Gentile Interest*, 14.

65 Danby, *Jew and Christianity*, 17.

66 Chertok, *He Also Spoke as a Jew*, 185.

67 Ibid., 452.

68 Klausner, "Herbert Danby," 504.

CHAPTER FOUR

1 Frankel, *Damascus Affair*, 285.

2 Herzl, *Diaries*, 593–94.

3 Introvigne, "Catholic Church and the Blood Libel Myth," 4.

4 Dubois, "Theological Implications of the State of Israel," 168.

5 See Kertzer, *Popes Against the Jews*; Carroll, *Constantine's Sword*; Minerbi, "Pope John Paul II and the Jews" and *Vatican and Zionism*.

6 Hudson and Mancini, *Understanding Maritain*, 21.

7 J. Cohen, *Friars and the Jews*.

8 Ibid., 97.

9 Minerbi, "Vatican and Zionism," 96.

10 Kertzer, *Popes Against the Jews*, 135.

11 Herzl, *Diaries*, 132; Minerbi, "Vatican and Zionism," 96.

12 Newman, *Apologia Pro Vita Sua*, 143.

13 Turner, *John Henry Newman*, 396.

14 Minerbi, *Vatican and Zionism*, 95–96.

15 Ibid., 100.

16 Ibid., 181.

17 Allit, *Catholic Converts*, 160.

18 Ibid., 173.

19 Boyd, Caldecott, and Mackey, "Chesterton's Alleged 'anti-Semitism.'"

20 Orwell, "Anti-Semitism in Britain," 65.

21 Chesterton, *New Jerusalem*, 284.

22 Ibid., 276.

23 Ibid., 284.

24 Ibid., 44, 46, 49.

25 Ibid., 289.

26 Belloc, *Jews*, 159; Royal, *Jacques Maritain and the Jews*, 219.

27 Minerbi, "Pope John Paul II and the Jews," 179.

28 Schulman, "Chesterton's *The New Jerusalem* and His Jew Baiting," 3; "Rabbis Denounce Chesterton Book."

29 Coren, *Gilbert*, 210–11.

30 Ibid., 208.

31 Pearce, *Wisdom and Innocence*, 449–50.

32 Ibid.

33 Royal, *Jacques Maritain and the Jews*, 105; Hudson and Mancini, *Understanding Maritain*, 22.

34 Hudson and Mancini, *Understanding Maritain*, 63.

35 Ibid., 74.

36 Ibid., 119.

37 Royal, *Jacques Maritain and the Jews*, 72, 93–98.

38 Ibid., 257.

39 De Lubac, *Christian Resistance to Anti-Semitism*, 15.

40 Royal, *Jacques Maritain and the Jews*, 63.

41 Maritain, *Christian Looks at the Jewish Question*.

42 Bruteau, *Merton and Judaism*; Flannery, *Anguish of the Jews*, 275.

43 Flannery, *Anguish of the Jews*, 275.

44 Kertzer, *Popes Against the Jews*, 15–16.

45 Royal, *Jacques Maritain and the Jews*, 60, 263–64, 321; Flannery, *Anguish of the Jews*, 271.

46 Feldblum, *American Catholic Press and the Jewish State*, 62.

47 De Lubac, *Christian Resistance to Anti-Semitism*, 28.

48 Ibid., 29.

49 Ibid., 26–27.

50 Bruteau, *Merton and Judaism*, 47–48.

51 Royal, *Jacques Maritain and the Jews*, 119.

52 Carroll, *Constantine's Sword*, 632.

53 Dalin, *Pius War*, 23.

54 Hudson and Mancini, *Understanding Maritain*, xiii.

55 Merkley, *Christian Attitudes towards the State of Israel*, 21.

56 Minerbi, *Vatican and Zionism*, 155.

57 From "Commonweal" 47, 2/27/48, cited in Feldblum, *American Catholic Press and the Jewish State*, 66.

58 Hershcopf, "Church and the Jews," 116.

59 Bruteau, *Merton and Judaism*, 223–24.

60 Banki, "Interfaith Story Behind Nostra Aetate."

61 Donnelly and Pawlikowski, "Lovingly Observant."

62 Flannery, *Vatican Council II*, 7:738–42.

63 Flannery, *Anguish of the Jews*, 268.

64 Kimberly Katz, "Legitimizing Jordan," 182.

65 Rynne, *Second Session*, 306.

66 BBC News, Middle East: "Flashback—1964 Papal Visit," <www.bbc.co.uk>.

67 Signer, "John Paul II."

68 Bialer, *Cross on the Star of David*, 188–91.

69 Kimberly Katz, "Legitimizing Jordan," 184.

70 *New York Times*, 2 January 1964.

71 Meir, *My Life*, 406.

72 Breger, *Vatican-Israel Accords*, 175.

73 Bialer, *Cross on the Star of David*, 90.

74 Drinan, *Honor the Promise*, 39–40.

75 Signer, "John Paul II," 3.

76 Pawlikowski, "Re-Judaization of Christianity," 60.

77 Bernstein and Politi, *His Holiness*, 443.

78 Ibid., 444.

79 Cantalamessa, "Preacher of the Papal Household," 4.

80 Zeldin, *Catholics and Protestants in Jerusalem*, 237.

81 *Ha'aretz*, 10 October 1982, quoted in ibid., 127.

82 Weiman, "From Recognition to Reconciliation," 198.

83 Fiorenza and Tracy, *Holocaust as Interruption*, 85.

84 Maritain, *Christian Look at the Jewish Question*.

85 Minerbi, "Visit of the Pope to the Holy Land," 5.

86 *America*, 30 May 1936, quoted in Feldblum, *American Catholic Press and the Jewish State*, 51.

87 Drinan, *Honor the Promise*, 1.

88 Ibid., 204.

89 Beirich, "Where Mel Gibson Got His Anti-Semitism."

90 Joselit, "Wonders of America."

91 Augustin Cardinal Bea, *The Church and the Jewish People* (London, 1966) as quoted in Feldblum, *American Catholic Press and the Jewish State*, 114.

92 Feldblum, *American Catholic Press and the Jewish State*, 110–19.

93 Singer, "American Catholic Attitudes," 716.

94 Feeney, "Unholy People," 1.

95 Beirich, "Where Mel Gibson Got His Anti-Semitism," 5.

96 *The Catholic Review*, 12 December 1969, as quoted in Feldblum, *American Catholic Press and the Jewish State*, 115.

97 Singer, "American Catholic Attitudes," 715.

98 Lopez, "Israel's Relations with the Vatican," 3.

99 Pope John Paul II, Apostolic Letter, *Tertio Millennium Adveniente (The Beginning of the Third Millenium)*, 10 November 1994, available at <http://www.vatican.va/holy_father/john_paul_ii/apost_letters/documents/hf_jp-ii_apl_10111994_tertio-millennio-ad veniente_en.html>.

100 Merkley, *Christian Attitudes towards the State of Israel*, 157.

101 "Visit of His Holiness Pope John Paul II to the Holy Land," <www.opuslibani.org.lb>.

102 Walsh, "Two Cheers for the Pilgrimage," 4–5.

103 Rabbi Israel Lau, quoted in "Pope in Jerusalem," <www.ijn.com/archive>.

104 *Christians and Israel* 8, no. 2 (Winter 1999–2000).

105 On this meeting see Allen, *Rise of Benedict XVI*, 250–52, and Segre, "Pope's Millennium Visit to Israel."

106 Weiman, "From Recognition to Reconciliation."

107 Segre, "Pope's Millennium Visit to Israel," 4–5.

108 Carroll, *Constantine's Sword*, 109.

109 Ibid., 110.

110 Rosen, " 'Nostra Aetate.' "

111 Bruteau, *Merton and Judaism*, 277 n. 24.

112 Quoted in Merkley, *Christian Attitudes towards the State of Israel*, 156.

CHAPTER FIVE

1 Barnstone, *With Borges*, 23.

2 Goldman, *God's Sacred Tongue*, 276.

3 Borges, *Seven Nights*, 101.

4 Aizenberg, *Aleph Weaver*, 55–58.

5 Ibid., 58.

6 Borges, "Autobiographical Essay," 183.

7 Borges, *Selected Poems*.

8 Aizenberg, *Aleph Weaver*, 66.

9 Robinson, *Ten Commandments*.

10 Williamson, *Borges*, 240–55.

11 Alazraki, *Borges and the Kabbalah*, 5; Borges, *Seven Nights*, 43; Williamson, *Borges*, 240–55.

12 Woodall, *Borges*, 13.

13 Barnstone, *Borges at Eighty*.

14 Williamson, *Borges*, 29.

15 Borges, "Autobiographical Essay," 140.

16 Woodall, *Borges*, 13.

17 Borges, "Autobiographical Essay," 146.

18 Ibid.

19 Bell-Villada, *Borges and His Fiction*, 17.

20 Alberto Manguel, quoted in Weiss, *Translating Orients*, 20.

21 See Woodall, *Borges*, and Williamson, *Borges*.

22 Barnstone, *Borges at Eighty*, 7.

23 Bell-Villada, *Borges and His Fiction*, 23.

24 Borges, *Selected Non-Fictions*, xiv.

25 Borges, *Seven Nights*, 108.

26 Monegal and Reid, *Borges*, 279; Williamson, *Borges*, 341.

27 Borges, *Labyrinths*, 146.

28 Ibid., 147.

29 Borges, *Selected Non-Fictions*, 200.

30 Aizenberg, *Books and Bombs*, 131.

31 Monegal and Reid, *Borges*, 128.

32 Ibid., 64.

33 Ibid., 65.

34 Borges, *Selected Non-Fictions*, 201; Woodall, *Borges*, 28.

35 Williamson, *Borges*, 261.

36 Ibid., 286; Bell-Villada, *Borges and His Fiction*, 5.

37 Williamson, *Borges*, 292–93.

38 Ibid., 292.

39 Woodall, *Borges*, 149.

40 Williamson, *Borges*, 292.

41 Borges, *Seven Nights*, 110.

42 Bell-Villada, *Borges and His Fiction*, 41.

43 Ibid., 11; Borges, *Selected Non-Fictions*, xi; Woodall, *Borges*, 251–52. On Borges and the Nobel Prize, see Woodall, *Borges*, 251–52.

44 de Man, "Modern Master," 55.

45 Aizenberg, *Books and Bombs*.

46 Alazraki, *Borges and the Kabbalah*, 17. This essay is discussed in Aizenberg, *Books and Bombs*, 128.

47 Borges, *Seven Nights*, 95–97.

48 Aizenberg, *Books and Bombs*.

49 Borges, *Selected Poems*, 197.

50 Alazraki, *Borges and the Kabbalah*, 17.

51 For references to Scholem's work, see ibid., 54.

52 Steiner, *After Babel*, 67.

53 Aizenberg, *Books and Bombs*, 132.

54 Monegal and Reid, *Borges*, 22–24.

55 Alazraki, *Borges and the Kabbalah*, 39; Borges, *Seven Nights*, 106.

56 Aizenberg, *Books and Bombs*.

57 Stavans, "Why Borges Wished He Was an Israelite."

58 Woodall, *Borges*, 259.

59 Weiss, *Translating Orients*, 32.

60 Borges, *Seven Nights*, 91.

61 Woodall, *Borges*, 292.

62 Ibid., 155.

63 Aizenberg, *The Aleph Weaver*, 66.

64 On this poem, see Stavans, "Borges's Zionist Bent," 15.

65 Woodall, *Borges*, 251.

66 Ibid., 257.

67 Graves, *White Goddess*.

68 Seymour, *Robert Graves: Life on the Edge*, 328.

69 O'Prey, *In Broken Images*, 341–42.

70 Graves, *Food for Centaurs*, 159.

71 Seymour-Smith, *Robert Graves: His Life and Work*.

72 Graves, *White Goddess*, 459.

73 Richard Graves, *Palestine*; on Philip Graves's exposure of the *Protocols*, see Bronner, *Rumor About the Jews*, 78. Philip Graves's article on the *Protocols* was published in the London *Times*, 16, 17, 18 August 1921.

74 Seymour-Smith, *Robert Graves: His Life and Work*, 15.

75 Seymour, *Robert Graves: Life on the Edge*, 185.

76 "A Dead Branch of the Tree of Israel," in Graves, *Food for Centaurs*.

77 Graves and Hodge, *Reader over Your Shoulder*.

78 Graves and Podro, *Nazarene Gospel Restored*.

79 Graves, *In Broken Images*, 326.

80 Seymour, *Robert Graves: Life on the Edge*, 315–17.

81 Graves and Patai, *Hebrew Myths*; Patai, *Robert Graves and the Hebrew Myths*.

82 Patai, *Hebrew Goddess*.

83 Graves and Patai, *Hebrew Myths*; Patai, *Robert Graves and the Hebrew Myths*.

84 Patai, *Robert Graves and the Hebrew Myths*, 290.

85 Graves, *Adam's Rib*.

86 Seymour, *Robert Graves: Life on the Edge*, 122.

87 Vickery, *Robert Graves and the White Goddess*, 1.

88 Graves, "Review of Legends of the Bible."

89 Graves and Hodge, *Reader over Your Shoulder*.

90 Seymour-Smith, *Robert Graves: His Life and Work*, 111.

91 Graves, *White Goddess*, 459.

92 Graves, *King Jesus*.

93 Ibid.

94 George Moore, *The Brook Kerith*.

95 Seymour-Smith, *Robert Graves: His Life and Work*.

96 T. S. Matthews, *Jacks or Better*, 281.

97 Seymour, *Robert Graves: Life on the Edge*, 376.

98 Graves and O'Prey, *Between Moon and Moon*, 50–51.

99 For a strange exchange of letters with Gertrude Stein on Laura Riding's "Jewish Characteristics," see ibid., 336–40.

100 Seymour, *Robert Graves: Life on the Edge*, 376.

101 Shapira, "Ben Gurion and the Bible."

102 Graves, *Food for Centaurs*, 97.

103 Ibid., 149.

104 Ibid., 155.

105 Ibid., 159.

106 Williamson, *Borges*, 447.

107 Boyd, *Vladimir Nabokov: The American Years*, 656.

108 Goldman, "Nabokov's Minyan," 1.

109 Schuman, "Beautiful Gate," 48.

110 Nabokov, *Lectures on Literature*, 381.

111 See "Author's Note," in Nabokov, *Annotated Lolita*.

112 Nabokov, *Bend Sinister*, xii–xiii.

113 Alter, "Literature of the Age," 190.

114 Nabokov, *Invitation to a Beheading*, 38.

115 Ibid., 5.

116 Howard Nemerov as quoted in Page, *Vladimir Nabokov*, 92.

117 Karlinsky, *Dear Bunny, Dear Volodya*.

118 Butler, "Lolita Lepidoptera," 60.

119 Boyd, *Vladimir Nabokov: The Russian Years*, 4.

120 Amis, "Sublime and the Ridiculous," 73.

121 Nafisi, *Reading Lolita in Tehran*, 35, 40.

122 Bronner, *Rumor about the Jews*, 2.

123 Nabokov, *Lectures on Literature*, 285.

124 Ibid., 301, 316.

125 Boyd, *Vladimir Nabokov: The American Years*, 107.

126 Appel, "Remembering Nabokov," 33.

127 Wood, *Magician's Doubts*, 1.

128 Gardner, *On Moral Fiction*, 5.

129 Nabokov, *Nabokov's Butterflies*; Johnson and Coats, *Nabokov's Blues*.

130 Shrayer, "Death, Immortality, and Nabokov's Jewish Theme," 18.

131 Schiff, *Vera (Mrs. Vladimir Nabokov)*, 26.

132 Ibid., 25.

133 Nabokov, *Speak, Memory*.

134 Boyd, *Vladimir Nabokov: The Russian Years*, 21.

135 Bronner, *Rumor about the Jews*, 76.

136 Boyd, *Vladimir Nabokov: The Russian Years*, 21.

137 Nabokov, *Speak, Memory*, 174–75.

138 Boyd, *Vladimir Nabokov: The Russian Years*, 104.

139 Ibid., 86.

140 For the source and context of this letter, see Goldman, "Nabokov's Minyan," 1.

141 Ibid., 166.

142 Ibid., 186–89.

143 Ibid., 192.

144 Quennell, *Vladimir Nabokov*, 128.

145 Lawrence Lee, *Vladimir Nabokov*, 25.

146 Boyd, *Vladimir Nabokov: The American Years*, 11.

147 Boyd, *Vladimir Nabokov: The Russian Years*, 50.

148 Ibid.

149 Goldman, "Nabokov's Minyan."

150 Nabokov, *Stories of Vladimir Nabokov*, 37.

151 Ibid., 601.

152 Toker, *Nabokov*, 69.

153 Wood, *Magician's Doubts*, 65.

154 Nabokov, *Pnin*.

155 See Wood, *Magician's Doubts*, 168; Shrayer, "Death, Immortality, and Nabokov's Jewish Theme," 25.

156 Boyd, *Vladimir Nabokov: The American Years*, 279.

157 Boyd, *Vladimir Nabokov: The Russian Years*, 487.

158 Boyd, *Vladimir Nabokov: The American Years*, 85–86.

159 Nabokov, *Lectures on Literature*, 225.

160 Boyd, *Vladimir Nabokov: The Russian Years*, 149.

161 Ibid., 202.

162 Ibid.

163 Appel, "Remembering Nabokov," 19–20.

164 Nabokov, *Lectures on Literature*, 283.

165 Nabokov, *Invitation to a Beheading*, 6.

166 Alter, *Necessary Angels*, 72.

167 Goldman, *God's Sacred Tongue*, 263–67.

168 Shrayer, "Death, Immortality, and Nabokov's Jewish Theme," 25.

169 Schuman, "Beautiful Gate."

170 Ibid., 64.

171 Goldman, "Nabokov's Minyan."

172 Zavylov-Leving, "Phantom in Jerusalem."

173 Dimitri Nabokov, "Close Calls."

174 Kazin, "Nabokov," 364–65.

CHAPTER SIX

1 LaHaye and Ice, *Charting the End Times*, 87.

2 Gorenberg, *End of Days*.

3 Ariel, "How Are Jews and Israel Portrayed in the Left Behind Series?"

4 Shimoni, *Zionist Ideology*, 102.

5 Herzl, *Old-New Land*, 82–83.

6 Gorenberg, *End of Days*, 87; Ravitzky, *Messianism, Zionism, and Jewish Religious Radicalism*, 98–101; Rozenak, *Harav Kook*, 45–47.

7 Shimoni, *Zionist Ideology*, 138.

8 Salmon, *Religion and Zionism*, xxxi, 177–78.

9 Ibid., 170.

10 Shimoni, *Zionist Ideology*, 141–43.

11 On religious Zionism and the religious kibbutzim, see Aran, "Jewish Zionist Fundamentalism," 274.

12 Hertzberg, *Zionist Idea*, 43.

13 Shimoni, *Zionist Ideology*, 144.

14 Ibid., 148.

15 Amnon Rubinstein, *Zionist Dream Revisited*, 24.

16 Rozenak, *Harav Kook*, 175.

17 Ravitzky, *Messianism, Zionism, and Jewish Religious Radicalism*, 100; Agus, *High Priest of Rebirth*, 86–87.

18 Gorenberg, *Accidental Empire*, 91.

19 Rozenak, *Harav Kook*.

20 Eldar and Zertal, *Lords of the Land*, 257.

21 Ravitzky, *Messianism, Zionism, and Jewish Religious Radicalism*.

22 Berkowitz, *Zionist Culture*, 120, 211; Peri, *Brothers at War*, 238–42.

23 Rabkin, *Threat from Within*, 52.

24 Segev, *1949: The First Israelis*.

25 Eldar and Zertal, *Lords of the Land*, 264.

26 Ibid., 261.

27 Segal, *Dear Brothers*, 28.

28 Shimoni, *Zionist Ideology*, 151, 343.

29 New, *Holy War*, 140.

30 On Rabbi Goren and the Temple Mount, see Lustick, *For the Land and the Lord*, 170.

31 Eldar and Zertal, *Lords of the Land*, 250.

32 "The Ten Who Made Israel What It Is," *Ha'aretz*, 5 June 2005, <http://www.haaretz.com/hasen/>.

33 Kimmerling, *Politicide*, 63.

34 Shragai, *Temple Mount Conflict*, 51.

35 Eldar and Zertal, *Lords of the Land*, 30–45.

36 Friedman, *Zealots for Zion*, 119.

37 Kidd, *American Christians*, 93.

38 Raanan, *Gush Emunim*, 100.

39 Kimmerling, *Politicide*, 38.

40 Eldar and Zertal, *Lords of the Land*, 283–84.

41 Dov Schwartz, *Challenge and Crisis in Rabbi Kook's Circle*, 42.

42 Eldar and Zertal, *Lords of the Land*, 263.

43 See Shimoni, *Zionist Ideology*, 151; quoted in Salmon, *Religion and Zionism*, 19.

44 Shimoni, *Zionist Ideology*, 151; Rubenstein, *On The Lord's Side*, 25.

45 Shimoni, *Zionist Ideology*, 151–53, 343.

46 For a critique of Gush Emunim's appropriation of the elder Rabbi Kook's ideas, see Zvi Yaron and Eliezer Goldman as quoted in Raanan, *Gush Emunim*, 68–70.

47 See Leibowitz, *Judaism, Human Values, and the Jewish State*, 106–27.

48 Moscrop, *Measuring Jerusalem*, 1–2.

49 Sykes, *Two Studies in Virtue*.

50 Weber, *On the Road to Armageddon*, 112.

51 Peri, *Brothers at War*, 287.

52 L. Nelson Bell, "Unfolding Destiny," quoted in Weber, *On the Road to Armageddon*, 184.

53 Lindsey, *Late Great Planet Earth*.

54 Ibid., 45.

55 J. Daniel Hays, quoted in Sutherland, "Apocalypse Now," 7.

56 On Begin and the Christian Right, see Shindler, "Likud and the Christian Dispensationalists," 160–65.

57 Sutherland, "Apocalypse Now."

58 LaHaye and Jenkins, *Are We Living in the End Times?*, 129.

59 "Voice of the Temple Mount" Newsletter, 17 May 1998, quoted in Price, *Temple and Bible Prophecy*, 435.

60 Weber, *On the Road to Armageddon*, 185–86.

61 Simon, *Jerry Falwell and the Jews*, 62.

62 Ibid., 43.

63 Ibid., 62.

64 Ibid., 81.

65 Quoted in Friedman, *Zealots for Zion*, 144.

66 Hagee, Speech at AIPAC Policy Conference, 2007.

67 Hagee, *Final Dawn over Jerusalem*, 33.

68 Ibid.

69 Kampeas, "Pro-Israel Founder of Moral Majority."

70 Eldar and Zertal, *Lords of the Land*, 267. For more on Amital's lecture, see Gorenberg, *Accidental Empire*, 260–62.

71 Morris, *Righteous Victims*, 406.

72 On the founding of Gush Emunim, see Aran, "Jewish Zionist Fundamentalism."

73 Quoted in Shindler, "Likud and the Christian Dispensationalists," 164.

74 Y. Sheleg, "From Sebastia to Migron," *Ha'aretz*, 2004.

75 *Jerusalem Post*, 24 November 1978, quoted in Shindler, "Likud and the Christian Dispensationalists," 177.

76 On Van der Hoeven, see Ariel, "Unexpected Alliance," 84–86.

77 Ibid.

78 See Luria, "Are These People Christians?"

79 Walter I. Wilson quoted in Malachy, *American Fundamentalism and Israel*, 148.

80 Eldar and Zertal, *Lords of the Land*, 83.

81 Gorenberg, *Accidental Empire*.

82 Wilkinson, *For Zion's Sake*, 221.

83 R. Cohen, "Her Jewish State."

84 Quoted in Kidd, *American Christians*, 84–85.

85 Ariel, "Unexpected Alliance," 92.

86 Gorenberg, *End of Days*, 109.

87 Lindsey, *Late Great Planet Earth*, 155.

88 Kidd, *American Christians*, 84–85.

89 Lustick, *For the Land and the Lord*, 166.

90 Segal, *Dear Brothers*, 248.

91 See chapter 3 in Lustick, *For the Land and the Lord*, and Eldar and Zertal, *Lords of the Land*, 108–32.

92 Shragai, *Temple Mount Conflict*, 250–57.

93 See the journal *Christians and Israel* 8, no. 4 (2000).

Bibliography

Abbot, Abiel, William Gordon, and Samuel Langdon. *The American Republic and Ancient Israel*. America and the Holy Land. New York: Arno Press, 1977.

Abrahams, Israel, and C. G. Montefiore, eds. *The Jewish Quarterly Review*. Vols. 1–20. Philadelphia: University of Pennsylvania Press, 1888–1908.

Adler, Joseph. *Restoring the Jews to Their Homeland: Nineteen Centuries in the Quest for Zion*. Northvale, N.J.: J. Aronson, 1997.

Adler, L., and R. Dalby. *The Dervish of Windsor Castle: The Life of Arminius Vambery*. London: Bachman and Turner, 1979.

Agus, Jacob B. *High Priest of Rebirth: The Life, Times, and Thought of Abraham Isaac Kuk*. New York: Bloch Publishing Company, 1972.

Ain, Stewart. "Point Man on Pullout Cites Risks." *The Jewish Week*, 27 May 2005.

Aizenberg, Edna. *The Aleph Weaver: Biblical, Kabbalistic and Judaic Elements in Borges*. Potomac, M.D.: Scripta Humanistica, 1985.

——. *Books and Bombs in Buenos Aires: Borges, Gerchunoff, and Argentine-Jewish Writing*. Hanover, Mass.: Brandeis University Press, 2002.

——, ed. *Borges and His Successors: The Borgesian Impact on Literature and the Arts*. Columbia: University of Missouri Press, 1990.

Alazraki, Jiame. *Borges and the Kabbalah: And Other Essays on His Fiction and Poetry*. Cambridge: Cambridge University Press, 1988.

——, ed. *Critical Essays on Jorge Luis Borges*. Boston: G.K. Hall, 1987.

Albright, W. F. "Presidential Address." *Journal of the Palestinian Oriental Society* 3 (1923): 93–107.

Alkalai, Judah, Yitzhak Raphael, and Nathan Shelem. *Kitve Ha-Rav Yehudah Alkalai*. Jerusalem: Mosad ha-Rav Kook, 1974.

Allen, John L. *The Rise of Benedict XVI: The Inside Story of How the Pope Was Elected and Where He Will Take the Catholic Church*. New York: Doubleday, 2005.

Allit, Patrick. *Catholic Converts: British and American Intellectuals Turn to Rome*. Ithaca, N.Y.: Cornell University Press, 1997.

——. "Navigating the Future." *Commonweal*, 15 August 2003, 27–28.

Alter, Robert. "The Literature of the Age and the Literature of Literature: Hermann Broch, Vladimir Nabokov, Saul Tsernihovski." *Hasifrut* 3 (1971): 187–95.

——. *Necessary Angels*. Cambridge: Harvard University Press, 1991.

Amis, Martin. "The Sublime and the Ridiculous: Nabokov's Black Farces." In *Vladimir Nabokov: His Life, His Work, His World*, edited by Peter Quennell, 73–87. London: Weidenfeld and Nicolson, 1980.

Anderson, Irvine H. *Biblical Interpretation and Middle East Policy*. Gainesville: University Press of Florida, 2005.

Appel, Alfred. "Remembering Nabokov." In *Nabokov: Criticism, Reminiscences, Translations and Tributes*, edited by Alfred Appel Jr. and Charles Newman, 33. Evanston, Ill.: Northwestern University Press, 1970.

Aran, G. "Jewish Zionist Fundamentalism." In *Fundamentalisms Observed*, edited by Martin E. Marty and R. Scott Appleby, 265–344. Chicago: University of Chicago Press, 1991.

Ariel, Yaakov S. "How Are Jews and Israel Portrayed in the Left Behind Series?" In *Rapture, Revelation, and the End Times*, edited by Bruce David Forbes and Jeanne Halgren Kilde. New York: Palgrave Macmillan, 2004.

———. *On Behalf of Israel: American Fundamentalist Attitudes toward Jews, Judaism, and Zionism, 1865–1945*. Chicago Studies in the History of American Religion. Brooklyn: Carlson Publishing, 1991.

———. *Philosemites or Antisemites?: Evangelical Christian Attitudes towards the Jews*. Jerusalem: Vidal Sasson Center, 2002.

———. "An Unexpected Alliance: Christian Zionism and Its Historical Significance." *Modern Judaism* 26, no. 1 (February 2006): 74–100.

Arkin, William A. "The Pentagon Unleashes a Holy Warrior." *Los Angeles Times*, 16 October 2003, B17.

Aronson, Raney. "The Jesus Factor: America's Evangelicals." Edited by Seth Bomse. WGBH Educational Foundation (29 April 2004), <http://www.pbs.org/wgbh/pages/frontline/shows/jesus/evangelicals>. 1 October 2007.

———. "The Jesus Factor: Interviews." <http://www.pbs.org/whbh/pages/frontline/shows/jesus/interviews>. 1 October 2007.

———. "The Jesus Factor: Readings and Links." <http://www.pbs.org/wgbh/pages/frontline/shows/jesus/readings>. 1 October 2007.

"Backgrounder: Christians and Zionism." *Middle East Digest* 8 (August 1997), <http://christianactionforisrael.org/medigest/aug97/backgrnd.html>.

Badt-Strauss, Bertha. *White Fire: The Life and Works [of] Jessie Sampter*. America and the Holy Land. New York: Arno Press, 1977.

Bain, Kenneth R. *The March to Zion: United States Policy and the Founding of Israel*. College Station: Texas A&M University Press, 1979.

Banki, J. "The Interfaith Story Behind Nostra Aetate." The Center for Advanced Holocaust Studies, <www.ushmm.org>.

Barnstone, Willis. *Borges at Eighty: Conversations*. Bloomington: Indiana University Press, 1982.

———. *With Borges on an Ordinary Evening in Buenos Aires: A Memoir*. Champaign: University of Illinois Press, 1999.

Baron, Salo Wittmayer, and Jeannette Meisel Baron. *Palestinian Messengers in America, 1849–1879: A Record of Four Journeys*. America and the Holy Land. New York: Arno Press, 1977.

Bar-Yosef, Eitan. "Christian Zionism and Victorian Culture." *Israel Studies* 8, no. 2 (Summer 2003): 18–44.

Barzel, Hillel. *A History of Hebrew Poetry*. Vol. 1: *The Chibbat Zion Period*. Tel Aviv: Sifriat Poalim, 1987.

Bayfield, Tony. "We Need a New Kind of Zionism." *The Guardian*, 23 March 2005.

Bednarowski, Mary Farrell. "Harris, Thomas Lake." In *The Dictionary of American National Biography*, edited by John A. Garraty and Mark C. Carnes, PP. Oxford: Oxford University Press, 1998.

Bein, Alex. *Theodor Herzl: A Biography*. Philadelphia: Jewish Publication Society, 1941.

Beirich, Heidi. "Where Mel Gibson Got His Anti-Semitism." <www.alternet.org / story / 46854 / >. 27 January 2007.

Beller, Steven. *Herzl*. New York: Grove Weidenfeld, 1991.

Belloc, Hilaire. *The Jews*. London: Constable, 1920.

Bell-Villada, Gene H. *Borges and His Fiction: A Guide to His Mind and Art*. Austin: University of Texas Press, 1999.

Ben-Artzi, Yossi. "Traditional and Modern Rural Settlement Types in Eretz-Israel in the Modern Era." In *The Land That Became Israel*, edited by R Kark, 133–46. New Haven: Yale University Press, 1989.

Ben-Gurion, David. *Memoirs*. New York: World Publishing Co., 1970.

Bennet, James. "Palestinians Must Bear Burden of Peace, DeLay Tells Israelis." *New York Times*, 31 July 2003, A7.

Benson, Michael T. *Harry S. Truman and the Founding of Israel*. Westport, Conn.: Praeger, 1997.

Ben-Yehuda, Eliezer. *A Dream Come True*. Boulder: Westview Press, 1993.

Ben-Yehuda, Nachman. *The Masada Myth: Collective Memory and Mythmaking in Israel*. Madison: University of Wisconsin Press, 1995.

Ben-Yishai, A. Z. "Parody, Hebrew." In *Encyclopedia Judaica*. 13:124–39. Jerusalem: Keter, 1973.

Ben-Zvi, Abraham. *Decade of Transition: Eisenhower, Kennedy, and the Origins of the American-Israeli Alliance*. New York: Columbia University Press, 1998.

Berkowitz, Michael. *Zionist Culture and West European Jewry Before the First World War*. Chapel Hill: University of North Carolina Press, 1993.

——, ed. *Nationalism, Zionism and Ethnic Mobilization of the Jews in 1900 and Beyond*. IJS Studies in Judaica, vol. 2. Leiden: Brill Academic Publishers, 2003.

Bernstein, Carl, and Marco Politi. *His Holiness: John Paul II and the Hidden History of Our Time*. New York: Doubleday, 1996.

Besser, James D. "New Tack in Divestment War." *The Jewish Week*, 1 April 2005.

Bialer, Uri. *Cross on the Star of David: The Christian World in Israel's Foreign Policy, 1948–1967*. Indiana Series in Middle East Studies. Bloomington: Indiana University Press, 2005.

Bialik, Hayyim N. *And It Came to Pass: Legends and Stories About King David and King Solomon*. New York: Hebrew Publishing Company, 1938.

——. *Knights of Onion and Garlic*. New York: Hebrew Publishing Company, 1939.

Blackstone, William E. "The Blackstone Memorial." Washington, D.C., 5 March 1891.

Blumenthal, Max. "Birth Pangs of a New Christian Zionism." *The Nation*, 8 August 2006, <http://www.thenation.com / doc / 20060814 / new_christian_zionism>. 7 November 2007.

Borges, Jorge Luis. "An Autobiographical Essay." In *The Aleph and Other Stories, 1933–1969*, edited and translated by Norman Thomas di Giovanni, 135–85. New York: E. P. Dutton, 1970.

——. *Labyrinths: Selected Stories and Other Writings*. New York: New Directions, 1964.

——. *Selected Non-Fictions*. Edited by Eliot Weinberger. New York: Penguin, 1999.

——. *Selected Poems*. New York: Penguin, 1999.

——. *Seven Nights*. New York: New Directions, 1984.

Bottum, Joseph, and David G. Dalin, eds. *The Pius War: Responses to the Critics of Pius XII*. New York: Lexington Books, 2004.

Boyd, Brian. *Vladimir Nabokov: The American Years*. Princeton: Princeton University Press, 1993.

———. *Vladimir Nabokov: The Russian Years*. Princeton: Princeton University Press, 1993.

Boyd, I., S. Caldecott, and A. Mackey. "Chesterton's Alleged 'anti-Semitism.'" G. K. Chesterton Institute, <www.chestertoninstitute.org>.

Boyer, Paul S. "John Darby Meets Saddam Hussein: Foreign Policy and Bible Prophecy." *The Chronicle Review* 49 (14 February 2003): B10.

———. *When Time Shall Be No More: Prophecy Belief in Modern American Culture*. Cambridge: Belknap Press of Harvard University Press, 1992.

Breger, Marshall J., ed. *The Vatican-Israel Accords: Political, Legal, and Theological Contexts*. Notre Dame, Ind.: University of Notre Dame Press, 2004.

Brog, David. *Standing with Israel: Why Christians Support the Jewish State*. Charleston: Frontline Press, 2006.

Bronner, Stephen Eric. *A Rumor about the Jews: Reflections on Antisemitism and "The Protocols of the Learned Elders of Zion."* 1st ed. New York: Palgrave Macmillan, 2000.

Brown, Michael. *The Israeli-American Connection: Its Roots in the Yishuv, 1914–1945*. America– Holy Land Monographs. Detroit: Wayne State University Press, 1996.

Bruteau, B., ed. *Merton and Judaism*. Louisville: Fons Vitae, 2003.

Buchanan, John M. "Family Tensions." *Christian Century*, 16 November 2004, 3.

Burge, Gary M. "Christian Zionism, Evangelicals and Israel." *The Holy Land Christian Ecumenical Foundation* (2005), <http://www.hcef.org/index.cfm/ID/159.cfm>. 14 June 2006.

Burge, Gary M., Harry Hagopian, and Donald Kruse. "Growing Legacy of American Christian Zionism, Noted by Kathleen Murphy." *The Holy Land Christian Ecumenical Foundation* (15 January 2001), <http://www.hcef.org/index.cfm/mod/news/id/16/submod/newsview/NewsID/164.cfm>. 14 June 2006.

Burgin, Richard. *Conversations with Jorge Luis Borges*. London. Souvenir Press Ltd., 1973.

Burnet, David S. *The Jerusalem Mission under the Direction of the American Christian Missionary Society*. America and the Holy Land. New York: Arno Press, 1977.

Burton, William L. "Protestant America and the Rebirth of Israel." *Jewish Social Studies* (October 1964).

Buruma, Ian. "How to Talk About Israel." *New York Times Magazine*, 31 August 2003, 28–33.

Butler, Diana. "Lolita Lepidoptera." In *Critical Essays on Vladimir Nabokov*, edited by Phyllis A. Roth, 59–74. Boston: G. K. Hall, 1984.

Byrne, Mary M. "Mythology & Krispy Kreme." *Atlanta Journal-Constitution*, 17 April 2004.

Cantalamessa, Raniero. "Preacher of the Papal Household." *The Tablet*. 12 May 2007.

Carlson, Charles E. "Why Judaized Christians Are Re-Electing George W. Bush." *Scion of Zion Internet Ministry* (12 July 2005), <http://www.scionofzion.com/pw10604.htm>. 8 October 2004.

Carmel, A. "Christlicher Zionismus." *100 Jahre Zionismus*. 127–35. Stuttgart, 2000.

Carpenter, J. *Revive Us Again: The Reawakening of American Fundamentalism*. New York: Oxford University Press, 1997.

Carroll, James. *Constantine's Sword: The Church and the Jews*. Boston: Houghton Mifflin, 2001.

Chabin, Michele. "Grave Site for Arafat Is Another Point of Contention." *USA Today*, 8 November 2004, 7A.

Chafetz, Ze'ev. *A Match Made in Heaven: American Jews, Christian Zionists, and One Man's Exploration of the Weird and Wonderful Judeo-Evangelical Alliance*. New York: Harper Collins, 2007.

Chapman, Colin Gilbert. *Whose Promised Land?: The Continuing Crisis over Israel and Palestine*. Oxford: Lion, 2002.

Charry, Ellen. "On Christ and Judaism: The Other Side of the Story." *The Princeton Theological Review* 8 (Autumn 2001): 24–29.

Chertok, Haim. *He Also Spoke as a Jew: The Life of the Reverend James Parkes*. London: Vallentine Mitchell, 2006.

Chesterton, G. K. *The New Jerusalem*. London: T. Nelson, 1920.

Cline, Eric. *The Battles of Armageddon: Megiddo and the Jezreel Valley from the Bronze Age to the Nuclear Age*. Ann Arbor: University of Michigan Press, 2000.

Coffman, Elesha. "Zion Haste." *Christian History Newsletter* (1 February 2002), <http://www.christianitytoday.com/history/newsletter/2002/feb1.html>. 15 August 2004.

Cohen, Don. "Christian and Zionist." *The Atlanta Jewish Times Online* (28 September 2007), <http://www.jtonline.us>. 2 October 2007.

Cohen, J. *The Friars and the Jews*. Ithaca: Cornell University Press, 1982.

Cohen, R. "Her Jewish State." *New York Times*, 8 July 2007.

Cohn-Sherbok, Dan. *The Politics of Apocalypse: The History and Influence of Christian Zionism*. Oxford: Oneworld Publications, 2006.

Combs, James. "Is Israel's Restoration Still a Sign of the Lord's Return and Can We Still Accept 1948 as a Fulfillment of Ezekiel 36,37?" In *Conference and Colloquium on Bible Prophecy*. Dallas–Fort Worth, 1992.

Conder, Claude R. Vol. 1 of *Tent Work in Palestine. A Record of Discovery and Adventure*. London: R. Bentley & Son, 1878.

Coren, Michael. *Gilbert, The Man Who Was G. K. Chesterton*. London: Cape, 1989.

Cresson, Warder. *The Key of David: David the True Messiah; or, The Anointed of the God of Jacob*. Philadelphia, 1852.

Crossman, R. H. S. "Gentile Zionism and the Balfour Declaration." In *The Commentary Reader*, edited by Norman Podhoretz, 284–94. New York: Atheneum, 1962.

Culver, Douglas J. *Albion and Ariel: British Puritanism and the Birth of Political Zionism*. American University Studies: Theology and Religion, no. 166. New York: P. Lang, 1995.

Currie, William E. "God's Little Errand Boy." *100 Years of Blessing*. Lansing: American Messianic Fellowship International, 1987.

Dalin, D., ed. *The Pius War: Responses to the Critics of Pius XII*. New York: Lexington Books, 2004.

Dallimore, Arnold. *The Life of Edward Irving*. Edinburgh: Banner of Trust, 1983.

Danby, Herbert. "Book Review: A Social and Religious History of the Jews." *Journal of Biblical Literature* 56 (Winter 1937): 395–98.

——. "The Budapest and Warsaw Conferences on the Presentation of the Christian Message to the Jews." Transcript. St. George's Cathedral Archives, A.C.J. Box #131.

——. "The Church in Jerusalem." *Bible Lands* 10, no. 170 (October 1941): 1248–55.

——. *Gentile Interest in Post Biblical Hebrew Literature*. Jerusalem: Syrian Orphanage Press, 1930.

——. *The Jew and Christianity: Some Phases, Ancient and Modern, of the Jewish Attitude toward Christianity*. London: Sheldon Press, 1927.

——. *Studies in Judaism. Two Lectures Delivered at St. George's Cathedral*. Jerusalem: St. George's Cathedral, 1922.

Davenport, Rowland A. *Albury Apostles*. United Writers: Birdlip, 1970.

Davidson, Israel. *Parody in Jewish Literature*. New York: AMS Press, 1966.

Davis, John. *The Landscape of Belief: Encountering the Holy Land in Nineteenth-Century American Art and Culture*. Princeton: Princeton University Press, 1996.

Davis, Moshe, ed. *America and the Holy Land*. Vol. 4 of *With Eyes toward Zion*. Westport, Conn.: Praeger, 1995.

——. *Christian Protagonists for Jewish Restoration*. New York: Arno Press, 1977.

——. *Israel: Its Role in Civilization*. New York: Seminary Israel Institute of the Jewish Theological Seminary of America, 1956.

——. *Themes and Sources in the Archives of the United States, Great Britain, Turkey, and Israel*. Vol. 2 of *With Eyes toward Zion*. New York: Praeger, 1986.

Davis, Moshe, Eli Lederhendler, and Jonathan D. Sarna. *America and Zion: Essays and Papers in Memory of Moshe Davis*. Detroit: Wayne State University Press, 2002.

Dayton, Donald, and Robert Johnson, eds. *The Variety of American Evangelicalism*. Knoxville: University of Tennessee Press, 1991.

De Haas, Jacob. *Theodor Herzl: A Biographical Study with Sixty Illustrations, Index, Chronological Table, Appendices, and Bibliography*. 2 vols. Chicago: Leonard, 1927.

Deinard, E. *Herev La Hashem Uleyisrael*. St. Louis: Moinester Printing Company, 1924.

Deinard, E., and Sigmund Seelingmann. "Herev LeHashem. ule-Yis'ra'el: neged ha-sefer Yeshu ha-Notsri we-torato me'et Yosek Kloyzner." St. Louis: Moinester Printing Company, 1922.

de Lubac, Henri. *Christian Resistance to Anti-Semitism*. San Francisco: St. Ignatius Press, 1988.

de Man, Paul. "A Modern Master." In *Critical Essays on Jorge Luis Borges*, edited by Jiame Alazraki, 55–61. Boston: G.K. Hall, 1987.

Dickter, Adam. "Evangelicals Joining Gaza Pullout Protest." *The Jewish Week*, 27 May 2005.

Domb, Jerahmeel I. I. *The Transformation: The Case of the Neturei Karta*. London: Hamadfis, 1958.

Donnelly, Doris, and John Pawlikowski. "Lovingly Observant." *America* 196 (18–25 June 2007): 10–14.

Drinan, Robert F. *Honor the Promise: America's Commitment to Israel*. New York: Doubleday, 1977.

Dubois, Marcel-Jarques. "Theological Implications of the State of Israel: The Catholic View." In *Encyclopedia Judaica: Year Book 1974*, edited by Cecil Roth, 167–73. Jerusalem: Keter, 1974.

Duker, Abraham G. "Swedenborg's Attitude towards the Jews." *Judaism* 5 (Summer 1956): 272–76.

Duvernoy, Claude. *The Prince and the Prophet*. Paradise, Calif.: Land of Promise Productions, 1973.

Eden, Ami. "9/11 Commission Finds Anger at Israel Fueling Islamic Terrorism Wave." *Forward*, 30 July 2004.

Ein-Gil, Ehud. "Into the Maelstrom." *Ha'aretz*, 20 August 2004, <http://www.haaretzdaily.com>. 12 September 2004.

Eisenberg, Laura Z. "Desperate Diplomacy: The Zionist-Maronite Treaty of 1946." *Studies in Zionism* 13 (Autumn 1992): 147–63.

Eldar, Akiva, and Idith Zertal. *Lords of the Land: The Settlers and the State of Israel.* Or Yehuda: Kinueret, 2004. In Hebrew.

Eliot, George. *Daniel Deronda.* Modern Library Edition. New York: Random House, 2002.

Epstein, I. "The Hidden Question." In *The Jew in the Modern World: A Documentary History,* edited by Paul Mendez-Flohr and Jehuda Reinharz, 558–62. Oxford: Oxford University Press, 1995.

Ewbank, William W. *The National Restoration of the Jews to Palestine Repugnant to the Word of God.* Liverpool: Deighton and Laughton, 1849.

Farah, Rafiq A. *In Troubled Waters: A History of the Anglican Church in Jerusalem, 1841–1998.* Leicester, UK: Christians Aware, 2002.

Feeney, Leonard. "An Unholy People in the Holy Land." *The Point* (September 1957): 1–5.

Feinstein, Sarah. "A Hundred Years Since the Kishinev Pogrom: Literary and Historic Implications." *Hadoar* 82 (Spring 2003): 13–19.

Feldblum, Esther Y. *The American Catholic Press and the Jewish State, 1917–1959.* New York: Ktav Publishing House, 1977.

Feldenstein, Ariel. "Fulfilling Theodor Herzl's Last Will and Testament." *Midstream,* November / December 2007, 9–14.

———. "Textbooks as Memory Shapers: Structuring the Image of Theodor Herzl in Textbooks as Part of Israeli Collective Memory in the 1950s." *Israel Affairs* 13 (Winter 2007): 80–94.

Fiorenza, E. S., and David Tracy, eds. *The Holocaust as Interruption.* Edinburgh: T. C. Clark, 1984.

Fisher, Eugene. "The Holy See and the State of Israel: The Evolution of Attitudes and Policies." *Journal of Ecumenical Studies* 24 (Spring 1987): 191–211.

Fishman, Hertzel. *American Protestantism and a Jewish State.* Detroit: Wayne State University Press, 1973.

Fisk, Pliny, Levi Parsons, Orson Hyde, and Rosa E. Lee. *Holy Land Missions and Missionaries.* America and the Holy Land. New York: Arno Press, 1977.

Flannery, Austin. *Vatican Council II: The Conciliar and the Post Consiliar Documents.* Northport, N.Y.: Costello Publishing, 2004.

Flannery, Edward H. *The Anguish of the Jews.* New York: Macmillan, 1965.

Fleischer, Ezra. "Vambery." In *Encyclopedia Judaica,* 16:65–66. Jerusalem: Keter, 1972.

Flusser, David. *Jesus.* New York: Herder and Herder, 1969.

Florence, Ronald. *Lawrence and Aaronsohn: T. E. Lawrence, Aaron Aaronsohn, and the Seeds of the Arab-Israeli Conflict.* New York: Viking, 2007.

Flores, Angel. "Magical Realism in Spanish American Fiction." In *Magical Realism: Theory, History, Community,* edited by Lois P. Zamora and Wendy B. Faris, 109–16. Durham: Duke University Press, 1995.

Forbes, Bruce D., and Jeanne H. Kilde. *Rapture, Revelation, and the End Times: Exploring the Left Behind Series.* New York: Palgrave Macmillan, 2004.

Frankel, Jonathan. *The Damascus Affair: "Ritual Murder," Politics, and the Jews in 1840.* Cambridge: Cambridge University Press, 1997.

Friedman, Robert I. *Zealots for Zion: Inside Israel's West Bank Settlement Movement.* New York: Random House, 1992.

Friesel, E. "Zionism and Jewish Nationalism." *Journal of Israeli History* 25, no. 2 (September 2006), 285–312.

Fruchtenbaum, Arnold. *Footsteps of the Messiah: A Study of the Sequence of Prophetic Events.* San Antonio: Ariel Press, 1982.

Fuchs, Marek. "Public Lives; Scholar, Matchmaker and Convention Presence." *New York Times*, 31 August 2004.

Gallo, Partrick J., ed. *Pius XII, The Holocaust and the Revisionists.* London: McFarland, 2006.

Ganin, Z. *An Uneasy Relationship: American Jewish Leadership and Israel, 1948–1957.* Syracuse: Syracuse University Press, 2005.

Gardner, Jon. *On Moral Fiction.* New York: Basic Books, 1978.

Garfinkle, A. "On the Origin, Meaning, Use and Abuse of a Phrase." *Middle Eastern Studies* 27, no. 4 (October 1991): 539–47.

Gelber, N. M. *Zur Vorgeschichte des Zionismus.* Vienna: Phaidon-Verlag, 1927.

Gibson, William, and Bruce Sterling. *The Difference Engine.* New York: Bantam Books, 1991.

Gill, C. H. "Jews in Palestine." *Bible Lands* 10, no. 170 (October 1941).

Ginzberg, Asher. *Ten Essays on Zionism and Judaism.* London: G. Routledge and Sons, 1922.

Ginzberg, Louis. *Legends of the Jews.* Translated from the German by Henrietta Szold. Philadelphia: The Jewish Publication Society of America, 1909–38.

Glass, Joseph B. *From New Zion to Old Zion: American Jewish Immigration and Settlement in Palestine, 1917–1939.* America–Holy Land Monographs. Detroit: Wayne State University Press, 2002.

Goell, Yohai, and Chava Dinner. "Zionism: A Bibliography for 1991." *Studies in Zionism* 13 (Autumn 1992): 191–255.

Goldberg, David. *To the Promised Land.* New York: Penguin, 1996.

Goldman, Shalom. "Christians and Zionism: A Review Essay." *American Jewish History* 93, no. 2 (June 2007): 245–60.

———. *God's Sacred Tongue: Hebrew and the American Imagination.* Chapel Hill: University of North Carolina Press, 2004.

———. "Nabokov's Minyan: A Study in Philo-Semitism." *Modern Judaism* 25 (Winter 2005): 1–22.

———. "White Goddess, Hebrew Goddess: The Bible, The Jews, and Poetic Myth in the Work of Robert Graves." *Modern Judaism* 23 (Winter 2003): 32–50.

Goldstein, Evan R. "Churchill—Fairweather Friend of the Jews." *Jerusalem Report*, 15 October 2007, 39–41.

Goodman, Hirsh. "Danger in the Shadows." *Jerusalem Report*, 7 March 2005, 9.

———. "On Top of Everything Else." *Jerusalem Report*, 26 July 2004, 10.

Goodman, Walter. "Israelis vs. Arabs, Arabs vs. Arabs, Israelis vs. Israelis." *New York Times*, 22 January 1999, B31.

Goodstein, Laurie. "Christian Foes of 'Da Vinci Code' Debate How to Fight It." *New York Times*, 11 May 2006, A14.

———. "Schiavo Case Highlights Catholic-Evangelical Alliance." *New York Times*, 24 March 2005, A16.

Gorenberg, Gershom. *The Accidental Empire: Israel and the Birth of the Settlements, 1967–1977.* New York: Times Books, 2006.

———. *The End of Days: Fundamentalism and the Struggle for the Temple Mount*. New York: Free Press, 2000.

———. "The Year in Ideas: Christian-Right Zionism." *New York Times Magazine*, 15 December 2002, 72.

Gottheil, Richard. *Zionism*. Philadelphia: The Jewish Publication Society of America, 1914.

Graves, Philip P. *Palestine, the Land of Three Faiths*. New York: George H. Doran Company, 1924.

Graves, Robert. *Adam's Rib, and Other Anomalous Elements in the Hebrew Creation Myth; a New View*. New York: Thomas Yoseloff, Inc., 1958.

———. *Food for Centaurs: Stories, Talks, Critical Studies, Poems*. New York: Doubleday, 1960.

———. *Goodbye to All That: An Autobiography*. London: Cape, 1929. Revised edition, New York: Doubleday, 1957.

———. "I Discover Israel." *Holiday Magazine*, December 1959.

———. *In Broken Images: Selected Correspondence of Robert Graves*. Edited by Paul O'Prey. London: Hutchinson, 1982.

———. *King Jesus*. New York: Creative Age Press, 1946.

———. "Review of Legends of the Bible." *Commentary* (June 1957).

———. *The White Goddess: A Historical Grammar of Poetic Myth*. New York: Farrar, Straus, and Giroux, 1948.

Graves, Robert, and Alan Hodge. *The Reader over Your Shoulder: A Handbook for Writers of English Prose*. New York: Macmillan, 1943.

Graves, Robert, and Paul O'Prey. *Between Moon and Moon: The Selected Letters of Robert Graves, 1946–1972*. London: Hutchinson, 1984.

Graves, Robert, and Raphael Patai. *Hebrew Myths: The Book of Genesis*. New York: Doubleday, 1964.

Graves, Robert, and Joshua Podro. *The Nazarene Gospel Restored*. New York: Doubleday, 1959.

Greenberg, Eric J. "Controversial Imams Enter Dialogue with Rabbis." *Forward*, 3 December 2004.

———. "Evangelicals Seen Forging Alliance with 'Messianic Jews.'" *Forward*, 6 August 2004.

———. "Feeling Heat, Episcopal Church Backs Away from Divestment." *Forward*, 12 November 2004.

———. "Protestant Group OKs Divestment from Israel." *Forward*, 16 July 2004.

Greenberg, Irving. *For the Sake of Heaven and Earth: The New Encounters Between Judaism and Christianity*. Philadelphia: The Jewish Publication Society of America, 2004.

Grose, Peter. *Israel in the Mind of America*. New York: Knopf, 1983.

Gutman, Israel. "Jewish-Presbyterian Ties at New Low." *Forward*, 27 June 2008.

———. *The Jews in Poland Between Two World Wars*. Hanover, Mass.: Brandeis University Press, 1989.

Guttman, Nathan. "Getting Tight with the Bible Belt." *Ha'aretz*, 16 February 2005.

Hagee, John. *Final Dawn over Jerusalem*. Nashville: Thomas Nelson, 1999.

———. Speech at AIPAC Policy Conference, 11 March 2007. <www.aipac.org / Publications / SpeechesByPolicymakers / Hagee-PC-2007.pdf>.

Halbrook, Stephen. "The Class Origins of Zionist Ideology." *Journal of Palestine Studies* 2 (Autumn 1972): 86–110.

Halevi, Y. *The Kuzari*. New York: Schocken Books, 1964.

Halpern, Ben. *The Idea of the Jewish State*. Cambridge: Harvard University Press, 1961.

Handy, Robert T. *The Holy Land in American Protestant Life, 1800–1948: A Documentary History*. New York: Arno Press, 1981.

Hapgood, Hutchins. *The Spirit of the Ghetto*. Edited by Moses Rischin. Cambridge: Harvard University Press, 1967.

Haramati, Shlomo. *Leviyim Bamikdash Haivrit*. Tel Aviv: Y. Golan, 1996.

Harkavy, S. G. *Vehu Shaul*. Boston: Harkavy, 1911. In Hebrew.

Hazony, David. "Memory in Ruins." *Azure* 16 (Winter 2004): 11.

Hechler, William. *The Restoration of the Jews to Palestine*. London: published by the author, 1884.

Henderson, Philip. *The Life of Laurence Oliphant: Traveller, Diplomat, and Mystic*. London: Robert Hale, 1956.

Herbert, Bob. "Shopping for War." *New York Times*, 27 December 2004, A17.

Hershcopf, Judith. "The Church and the Jews: The Struggle at Vatican Council II." *American Jewish Yearbook* 66 (1965): 99–136.

Hertzberg, Arthur. *The Jews in America: Four Centuries of an Uneasy Encounter: A History*. New York: Simon & Schuster, 1989.

——, ed. "Treifene Medina: Learned Opposition to Emigration to the United States." In *8th World Congress of Jewish Studies*, 1–29. Jerusalem: Magnes Press, 1984.

——. *The Zionist Idea: A Historical Analysis and Reader*. Garden City: Doubleday, 1959.

Herzl, Theodore. *The Diaries of Theodore Herzl*. Edited by M. Lowenthal. London: Gollancz, 1958.

——. *Old-New Land*. New York: Bloch Publishing Company, 1960.

Hitchens, Christopher. "Great Scot: Between Kipling and Fleming Stands John Buchan, the Father of the Modern Spy Thriller." *Atlantic Monthly* 293 (March 2004): 104.

Hodgkin, E. C. "In Memoriam, Emile Marmorstein, 1909–1983." *Middle Eastern Studies* 20, no. 2 (1984): 131–32.

Hoffman, Christhard. "Classical Scholarship, Modern Anti-Semitism and the Zionist Project: The Historian Eduard Meyer in Palestine (1926)." *Studies in Zionism* 13 (Autumn 1992): 133–46.

Hofstadter, Richard. *Anti-Intellectualism in American Life*. New York: Knopf, 1963.

Holmes, John H. *Palestine to-Day and to-Morrow: A Gentile's Survey of Zionism*. America and the Holy Land. New York: Arno Press, 1977.

Hoofien, S. *Report of Mr. S. Hoofien to the Joint Distribution Committee of the American Funds for Jewish War Sufferers*. America and the Holy Land. New York: Arno Press, 1977.

Hudson, D., and M. Mancini, eds. *Understanding Maritain: Philosopher and Friend*. Macon: Mercer University Press, 1987.

Ilan, Zvi. *Plans for Jewish Settlement East of the Jordan, 1871–1947*. Jerusalem: Ben Zvi Institute, 1985. In Hebrew.

Imber, Naphtali H. *Master of Hope: Selected Writings of Naphtali Herz Imber*. Edited by Jacob Kabakoff. Madison, N.J.: Fairleigh Dickinson University Press, 1985.

——. "To Ivan the Terrible." *New York Jewish World*, June 1903.

Imber, S., ed. *The Complete Poems of Naphtali Herz Imber*. Tel Aviv: Newman Publishers, 1950. In Hebrew.

Institute for the Study of American Evangelicals. "Defining Evangelicism," <www.wheaton
.edu / ISAE>. 1 October 2008.

Introvigne, Massimo. "The Catholic Church and the Blood Libel Myth: A Complicated
Story." *Covenant* 1 (April 2007): 1–8.

Irwin, Col. James B. Foreword to *The Holy Land*, edited by George F. Owen, 7–12. Grand
Rapids: Baker Book House, 1977.

Irwin, Robert. *Dangerous Knowledge: Orientalism and Its Discontents*. Woodstock, N.Y.:
Overlook Press, 2006.

Isaac, F. Reid. *Fleshing the Word*. Cincinnati: Forward Movement Publications, 1996.

Israel Ministry for Foreign Affairs. "Zionism," <www.mfa.gov.il / mfa / history>. 6 October
2008.

Janofsky, Michael. "G.O.P. Adviser Says Bush's Evangelical Strategy Split Country." *New York
Times*, 11 November 2004, A23.

Jenkins, Jerry B. "Mel Gibson." *Time*, 26 April 2004, 120.

Johnson, Kurt, and Steven L. Coates. *Nabokov's Blues*. New York: McGraw-Hill Professional
Publishing, 2001.

Johnston, Philip, and Peter Walker, eds. *The Land of Promise: Biblical, Theological, and
Contemporary Perspectives*. Downers Grove, Ill.: Inter-Varsity Press, 2000.

Joselit. "Wonders of America." *Forward*, 2 November 2007.

Kabak, Aaron A. *The Narrow Path: The Man of Nazareth*. Tel Aviv: Massadah, 1968.

Kabakoff, Jacob, ed. *Master of Hope: Selected Writings of Naphtali Herz Imber*. London: Herzl
Press, 1985.

———. *N. H. Imber, "Baal Hatikva."* Lod, Israel: The Habermann Institute, 1991.

———. "N. H. Imber in the Eyes of His Generation." *Hadoar* (1979–81).

Kafkafi, Eyal. "Ben-Gurion, Sharett and the Johnson Plan." *Studies in Zionism* 13 (Autumn
1992): 165–86.

Kaganoff, Nathan M., Menahem Kaufman, and Mira Levine. *Guide to America–Holy Land
Studies*. America–Holy Land Studies. New York: Arno Press, 1980.

Kalmar, Ivan D., and Derek J. Penslar. *Orientalism and the Jews*. Hanover, Mass.: Brandeis
University Press, 2005.

Kampeas, R. "Pro-Israel Founder of Moral Majority." Jewish Telegraphic Agency, 15 May
2007.

Kaplan, Esther. *With God on Their Side: How Christian Fundamentalists Trampled Science, Policy,
and Democracy in George W. Bush's White House*. New York: New Press, 2004.

Kaplow, Larry. "Outnumbered in Mideast." *Atlanta Journal-Constitution*, 2 January 1999, F1, F5.

———. "Few Remain to Speak 'the Lord's Language.'" *Atlanta Journal-Constitution*, 2 January
1999.

Kark, Ruth. *American Consuls in the Holy Land, 1832–1914*. Detroit: Wayne State University
Press, 1994.

———. "The Impact of Early Missionary Enterprises on Landscape and Identity Formation in
Palestine, 1820–1914." *Islam and Christian-Muslim Relations* 15 (Spring 2004): 209–35.

———, ed. *The Land That Became Israel*. New Haven: Yale University Press, 1989.

Karlinsky, Simon. *Dear Bunny, Dear Volodya: The Nabokov-Wilson Letters, 1940–1971*. Berkeley:
University of California Press, 2001.

Katz, J. "Zionism." In *Encyclopedia Judaica*, 7:1033. Jerusalem: Keter, 1972.

Katz, Kimberly. "Legitimizing Jordan as the Holy Land: Papal Pilgrimages—1964, 2000." *Comparative Studies of South Asia, Africa and the Middle East* 23, nos. 1–2 (2003): 181–89.

Kazin, Alfred. "Nabokov." In *Nabokov: Criticisms, Reminiscences, Translation and Tributes*, edited by Alfred Appel Jr. and Charles Newman, 364–65. Evanston, Ill.: Northwestern University Press, 1970.

Keinon, Herb. "French FM says US Jewry Influences Bush." *Jerusalem Post*, 24 April 2002, 1.

Kertzer, David I. *The Popes Against the Jews: The Vatican's Role in the Rise of Modern Anti-Semitism*. New York: Knopf, 2001.

Kessner, Carole. "The Emma Lazarus–Henry James Connection: Eight Letters." *American Literary History* 3 (Spring 1991): 46–62.

Kidd, Thomas S. *American Christians and Islam: Evangelical Culture and Muslims from the Colonial Period to the Age of Terror*. Princeton: Princeton University Press, 2008.

Kimelman, Reuven. "Irving Greenberg, *For the Sake of Heaven and Earth: The New Encounter between Judaism and Christianity*." *Modern Judaism* 27 (Winter 2007): 103–25.

Kimmerling, Baruch. *Politicide: Ariel Sharon's War Against the Palestinians*. London: Verso, 2003.

King, Laura. "Israel Foils Cult's Apocalypse Plot." *Atlanta Journal-Constitution*, 4 January 1999.

Klausner, Joseph. *Darki likrat Hageulah ve-Hatekhiyah*. 2 vols. Tel Aviv: Massadah, 1955.

——. "Herbert Danby." *Davar Annual* 5714 (1954): 497–504.

——. *A History of Modern Hebrew Literature, 1785–1930*. London, M. L. Cailingold, 1932.

——. *Jesus of Nazareth: His Life, Times, and Teaching*. New York: Menorah Publishing Company, 1925.

Kobler, Franz. *The Vision Was There: A History of the British Movement for the Restoration of the Jews to Palestine*. London: Lincolns-Prager, 1956.

Kramer, M., ed. *The Jewish Discovery of Islam*. New York: Moshe Dayan Center for Middle Eastern and African Studies, Tel Aviv University, 1999.

Kreutz, Andrej. *Vatican Policy on the Palestinian-Israeli Conflict: The Struggle for the Holy Land*. Contributions in Political Science, no. 246. New York: Greenwood Press, 1990.

LaHaye, Tim F. *The Popular Encyclopedia of Bible Prophecy*. Eugene, Ore.: Harvest House Publishers, 2004.

——. *Revelation Unveiled*. Grandville: Zondervan, 1999.

LaHaye, Tim F., and Thomas Ice. *Charting the End Times*. Eugene, Ore: Harvest House Publishers, 2001.

LaHaye, Tim F., and Jerry Jenkins. *Are We Living in the End Times?* Wheaton, Ill.: Tyndale House Publishers, 1999.

Lahover, Pinhas. *Bialik, His Life and Works*. Tel Aviv: Bialik Institute, 1944.

Lamm, Norman. "The Ideology of the Neturei Karta According to the Satmarer Version." *Tradition* 13 (Fall 1971): 38–53.

Lampman, Jane. "From Churches, a Challenge to Israeli Policies." *Christian Science Monitor*, 6 December 2004.

Landau, Jacob. "Arminius Vambery." In *The Jewish Discovery of Islam*, edited by Martin Kramer. New York: Moshe Dayan Center for Middle Eastern and African Studies, Tel Aviv University, 1999.

Laqueur, Walter. *A History of Zionism*. New York: Schocken Books, 1976.

Laskov, Shulamit. *The Biluim*. Jerusalem: Hassifriya Haziyonit, 1979.

Lawton, George, and Herbert W. Schneider. *A Prophet and a Pilgrim*. New York: Columbia University Press, 1942.

Lee, Lawrence L. *Vladimir Nabokov*. Twayne's United States Authors, no. 266. Boston: Twayne Publishers, 1976.

Lee, Sidney. "Oliphant, Laurence (1829–1888)." In *Dictionary of National Biography*, 133–37. New York: Macmillan and Co., 1895.

Leff, Laurel. *Buried by the Times*. Cambridge: Cambridge University Press, 2005.

Leftwich, Joseph. *Israel Zangwill*. London: James Clark, 1937.

Leibovich-Dar, Sara. "Do Unto Your Neighbor." *Ha'aretz*, 28 April 2004.

Leibowitz, Yeshayahu. *Judaism, Human Values, and the Jewish State*. Edited by Eliezer Goldman. Cambridge: Harvard University Press, 1992.

Leon, Dan. "What Hope for *Hatikyah*." *Jerusalem Report*, 6 February 2006, 46.

Levi, Amnon. *Haredim*. Tel Aviv: Keter, 1987. In Hebrew.

Levine, Yael. "Borges, Scholem, and the Golem." *Hadoar* (Summer 1987).

Lidberg, Judith M. *A Hundred Years: A Cathedral Presence in Jerusalem*. Jerusalem: St. George's Cathedral, 1998.

Lieber, Sherman. *Mystics and Missionaries: The Jews in Palestine, 1799–1840*. Salt Lake City: University of Utah Press, 1992.

Lindsey, Hal. *The Late Great Planet Earth*. Grand Rapids: Zondervan, 1970.

Lipman, Steve. "Meeting of Minds." *Jewish Week*, 3 December 2004.

Lipsky, Louis. *Memoirs in Profile*. Philadelphia: The Jewish Publication Society of America, 1975.

——. *Thirty Years of American Zionism*. America and the Holy Land. New York: Arno Press, 1977.

Loewe, Louis. *Diaries of Sir Moses and Lady Montefiore*. Chicago: Belford-Clarke Co., 1890.

Loewe, R. "Herbert Danby." In *Encyclopedia Judaica*. Jerusalem: Keter, 1972.

Long, Burke O. *Imagining the Holy Land: Maps, Models, and Fantasy Travels*. Bloomington: Indiana University Press, 2003.

Lopez, Aharon. "Israel's Relations with the Vatican." *Jerusalem Letter*, no. 401 (March 1999): 2–14.

Luria, Z. "Are These People Christians?" *Nekuda*, 17 March 1989.

Lustick, Ian. *For the Land and the Lord: Jewish Fundamentalism in Israel*. New York: Council on Foreign Relations, 1988.

Luz, Ehud. *Parallels Meet: Religion and Nationalism in the Early Zionist Movement (1882–1904)*. Philadelphia: The Jewish Publication Society of America, 1988.

Malachy, Yona. *American Fundamentalism and Israel: The Relation of Fundamentalist Churches to Zionism and the State of Israel*. Jerusalem: Institute of Contemporary Jewry, The Hebrew University of Jerusalem, 1978.

Mandelbrote, S. "Isaac Newton and the Exegesis of the Book of Daniel." In *Die Geschichte der Daniel—Auslegung in Judetum, Christentum und Islam*, edited by K. Bracht and D. S. du Toit, 351–75. Berlin: de Gruyter, 2007.

Mandler. "Vambery." *Shofar* 25, no. 3 (Fall 2007): 1–15.

Maritain, Jacques. *A Christian Look at the Jewish Question*. New York: Longmans, 1939.

Marmorstein, Arthur. *Studies in Jewish Theology; the Arthur Marmorstein Memorial Volume*. Freeport, N.Y.: Books for Libraries Press, 1972.

Marmorstein, Emile. *The Scholarly Life of Elkan Adler*. London: Jew's College, 1962.

Marsden, George M., ed. *The Fundamentals: A Testimony to the Truth*. 12 vols. New York: Garland, 1988.

Marsden, T. "Zionism." Vol. 4 of *The Encyclopedia of Mormonism*, edited by Daniel Ludlow. New York: Macmillan, 1992.

Mart, Michelle. "The 'Christianization' of Israel and Jews in 1950s America." *Religion and American Culture: A Journal of Interpretation* 14 (Winter 2004): 109–46.

Matthews, John, and Dave Winters. *Israel Handbook*. Bath: Footprint Handbooks, 1998.

Matthews, T. S. *Jacks or Better: A Narrative*. New York: Harper & Row, 1977.

Mays, Nick. "The *Times* in Palestine." *The Times Online*, 25 October 2000, <www.timesonline.co.uk>.

McCullough, David. *Truman*. New York: Simon & Schuster, 1993.

McGarvey, Ayelish. "Carter's Crusade." *American Prospect*, 5 April 2004, <http://www.prospect.org/cs/articles?article=carters_crusade>.

———. "Reaching to the Choir." *American Prospect*, 23 March 2004.

Medoff, Rafael. "Communication: The Influence of Revisionist Zionism in America During the Early Years of World War II." *Studies in Zionism* 13 (Spring 1992): 187–90.

Mehr, Kahlie B. "Dreamers of Zion: Joseph Smith and George J. Adams: Conviction, Leadership, and Israel's Renewal by Reed M. Holmes." *Journal of Mormon History* 30 (Fall 2004): 259–62.

Meir, G. *My Life*. New York: G. B. Putnam, 1975.

Mekay, Emad. "Iraq War Was About Israel, Bush Insider Suggests." *InterPress Service*, 29 March 2004.

Melman, Yossi, and Dan Raviv. *Friends in Deed: Inside the U.S.-Israel Alliance*. New York: Hyperion, 1994.

Melton, J. Gordon. "Harris, Thomas Lake." In *Biographical Dictionary of American Cult and Sect Leaders*, 105–6. New York: Garland, 1986.

Mendes-Flohr, Paul, and Jehuda Reinharz. *The Jew in the Modern World: A Documentary History*. Oxford: Oxford University Press, 1995.

Merkley, Paul C. *American Presidents, Religion, and Israel: The Heirs of Cyrus*. Westport, Conn.: Praeger, 2004.

———. *Christian Attitudes towards the State of Israel*. Westport, Conn.: Praeger, 2001.

———. *The Politics of Christian Zionism, 1891–1948*. Portland: F. Cass, 1998.

Minerbi, Sergio I. "Pope John Paul II and the Jews: An Evaluation." *Jewish Political Studies Review* 18 (Spring 2006): 1–14.

———. *The Vatican and Zionism: Conflict in the Holy Land, 1895–1925*. Oxford: Oxford University Press, 1990.

———. "The Visit of the Pope to the Holy Land," Israel Ministry of Foreign Affairs website, <www.mfa.gov.il/mfaarchive>.

Monbiot, George. "Their Beliefs Are Bonkers, but They Are at the Heart of Power." *The Guardian*, 20 April 2004, <http://www.guardian.co.uk/comment/story/0,3604,1195568,00.html>. 15 August 2005.

Monegal, Emir Rodriguez, and Alastair Reid, eds. *Borges: A Reader*. Boston: E. P. Dutton, 1981.

The Morning Watch; or, The Quarterly Journal of Prophecy and Theological Review (1829–32).

Moore, Deborah Dash. "Jewish GIs and the Creation of the Judeo-Christian Tradition." *Religion and American Culture: A Journal of Interpretation* 8 (Winter 1998): 31–53.

Moore, George. *The Brook Kerith; a Syrian Story.* London: William Heinemann, 1929.

Morris, Benny. *Righteous Victims: A History of the Zionist-Arab Conflict, 1881–1999.* New York: Knopf, 1999.

Moruzzi, Norma C. "Strange Bedfellows: The Question of Laurence Oliphant's Christian Zionism." *Modern Judaism* 26 (Winter 2006): 55–73.

Moscrop, John James. *Measuring Jerusalem: The Palestinian Exploration Fund and British Interests in the Holy Land.* New York: Leicester University Press, 2000.

Mosley, Leonard. *Gideon Goes to War.* New York: Scribners, 1955.

Nabokov, Dmitri. "Close Calls and Fulfilled Dreams: Selected Entries from a Private Journal." *Antaeus* 61 (Autumn 1998): 322.

Nabokov, Vladimir. *The Annotated Lolita.* Edited by Alfred Appel Jr. New York: Vintage Books, 1991.

——. *Bend Sinister.* New York: Time Incorporated, 1964.

——. *Invitation to a Beheading.* New York: Capricorn Books, 1959.

——. *Lectures on Literature.* New York: Harcourt, 1980.

——. *Nabokov's Butterflies.* Boston: Beacon Press, 2000.

——. *Pnin.* New York: Doubleday, 1957.

——. *The Real Life of Sebastian Knight.* New York: New Directions, 1959.

——. *Selected Letters: 1940–1977.* New York: Harcourt, 1989.

——. *Speak, Memory: An Autobiography Revisited.* New York: G. P. Putnam's Sons, 1966.

——. *The Stories of Vladimir Nabokov.* New York: Random House, 1996.

Nadel, Ira B. "G. W. Cooke and Laurence Oliphant: Victorian Travellers to the Orient." *Journal of the American Oriental Society* 94 (January–March 1974): 120–22.

Nadler, Allan. "Moshe Idel's Search for the Messiah." *Forward,* 26 March 1999.

Nafisi, Azar. *Reading Lolita in Tehran: A Memoir in Books.* New York: Random House, 2003.

Nahshon, Gad. "The Author of 'Hatikvah' as American Populist." *Molad* 39–40 (1980): 189–96.

——. "Christian Zionism." *Jewish Post,* <http://www.jewishpost.com/archives/news/christian-zionism.html>.

Naor, Arye. "Behold Rachel, Behold: The Six Day War as a Biblical Experience and Its Impact on Israel's Political Mentality." *Journal of Israeli History* 24, no. 2 (September 2005): 229–50.

National Council of Churches. "Why We Should Be Concerned About Christian Zionism," <www.ncccusa.org>.

Nedava, Joseph. *Haifa, Oliphant, and the Zionist Vision.* Haifa: The University of Haifa, 1978.

Neela, Banerjee. "Presbyterians and Jews to Meet on Mideast." *New York Times,* 28 September 2004.

Neiman, Moshe. "More on Borges and the Jews." *Hadoar* (Summer 1988).

Nemerov, Howard. "Lolita." In *Vladimir Nabokov: The Critical Heritage,* edited by Norman Page, 91–92. New York: Routledge, 1982.

Netanyahu, Benjamin. "Christian Zionism and the Jewish Restoration" (6 February 1985), <http://www.internationalwallofprayer.org/A-091-Christian-Zionism-and-the-Jewish-Restoration.html>.

Neusner, Jacob. *The Mishnah: A New Translation*. New Haven: Yale University Press, 1988.

New, David. *Holy War: The Rise of Militant Christian, Jewish, and Islamic Fundamentalism.* Jefferson, N.C.: McFarland and Co., 2001.

Newman, John Henry. *Apologia Pro Vita Sua*. London: Oxford University Press, 1913.

Nicosia, Francis R. "Zionism and Palestine in Anti-Semitic Thought in Imperial Germany." *Studies in Zionism* 13, no. 2 (1992): 115–31.

Noah, Mordecai M. *Call to America to Build Zion*. America and the Holy Land. New York: Arno Press, 1977.

Noble, Shlomo. "The Image of the American Jew in Hebrew and Yiddish Literature in America, 1870–1900." *YIVO Annual of Jewish Social Science* 9 (1954): 83–108.

Northcott, Michael S. *An Angel Directs the Storm: Apocalyptic Religion and American Empire.* London: I. B. Tauris, 2004.

Obermann, Julian, ed. *The Code of Maimonides (Mishneh Torah), Book Ten: The Book of Cleanliness*. New Haven: Yale University Press, 1954.

Oliphant, Laurence. *Altiora Peto*. 2nd ed. London: William Blackwood, 1883.

——. *Episodes in a Life of Adventure; or, Moss from a Rolling Stone*. New York: Harper & Brothers, 1887.

——. *Haifa; or, Life in Modern Palestine*. London: William Blackwood, 1887.

——. *A Journey to Katmandu (the Capital of Nepaul) with the Camp of Jung Bahadoor; Including a Sketch of the Nepaulese Ambassador at Home*. Appleton's Popular Library of the Best Authors. New York: D. Appleton & Company, 1852.

——. *The Land of Gilead, with Excursions in the Lebanon*. London: William Blackwood, 1880.

——. *The Land of Khemi. Up and Down the Middle Nile*. London: William Blackwood, 1882.

——. *Narrative of the Earl of Elgin's Mission to China and Japan in the Years 1857, '58, '59*. London: William Blackwood, 1859.

——. *Piccadilly: A Fragment of Contemporary Biography*. 5th ed. London: William Blackwood, 1875.

——. *The Russian Shores of the Black Sea in the Autumn of 1852, with a Voyage Down the Volga, and a Tour through the Country of the Don Cossacks*. 2nd ed. London: William Blackwood, 1853.

Oliphant, Laurence, Rosamond Dale Owen, and Haskett Smith. *Scientific Religion; or, Higher Possibilities of Life and Practice through the Operation of Natural Forces*. London: William Blackwood, 1888.

Oliphant, Margaret. *Jerusalem, the Holy City; Its History and Hope*. New York: Macmillan & Company, 1891.

——. *The Life of Edward Irving*. 2 vols. London: Hurst and Blackett, 1846.

——. *Memoir of the Life of Laurence Oliphant and of Alice Oliphant, His Wife*. New York: Harper & Brothers, 1891.

O'Prey, Paul, ed. *In Broken Images: Selected Letters of Robert Graves, 1914–1946*. London: Hutchinson, 1982.

Oren, Stephen. "Continuity and Change in Israel's Religious Parties." *Middle East Journal* 27 (1973): 38.

Orwell, George. "Anti-Semitism in Britain." In *The Complete Works of George Orwell*, 17:64–70. London: Secker and Warburg, 1998.

Owen, Rosamond D. *My Perilous Life in Palestine*. London: George Allen & Unwin Ltd., 1928.

Page, Norman. *Vladimir Nabokov: The Critical Heritage*. New York: Routledge, 1982.

Palestine Exploration Fund. *Prospectus of the New Survey of Eastern Palestine, Including Bashan, Moab, and the Land of Gilead: Also Excavations at the Sea of Galilee: With Report of the Meeting Held in the Jerusalem Chamber, on Tuesday, Nov. 30, 1880.* London: Palestine Exploration Fund, 1880.

Palestine Facts Editors. "Who, Besides Jews, Supported the Zionist's Ideas?" *Palestine Facts*, <http://www.palestinefacts.org/pf_early_palestine_zionist_support.php>. 8 December 2006.

Patai, Joseph. *Star Over Jordan: The Life of Theodore Herzl.* New York: Philosophical Library, 1946.

Patai, Raphael. *The Hebrew Goddess.* New York: Ktav Publishing House, 1967.

——. *Robert Graves and the Hebrew Myths: A Collaboration.* Jewish Folklore and Anthropology Series, no. 3. Detroit: Wayne State University Press, 1991.

Pawel, Ernst. *The Labyrinth of Exile: A Life of Theodor Herzl.* New York: Farrar, Straus, and Giroux, 1989.

Pawlikowski, J. "The Re-Judaization of Christianity." *Immanuel* 22/23 (1989): 60–64.

Pearce, Joseph. *Wisdom and Innocence: A Life of G. K. Chesterton.* London: Hodder and Stoughton, 1996.

Peri, Yoram. *Brothers at War.* Tel Aviv: Bavel Publishers, 2005. In Hebrew.

Perko, F. Michael. "Contemporary American Christian Attitudes to Israel Based on the Scriptures." *Israel Studies* 8 (Summer 2003): 1–17.

——. "Toward A 'Sound and Lasting Basis': Relations between the Holy See, the Zionist Movement, and Israel, 1896–1996." *Israel Studies* 2 (Spring 1997): 1–21.

Perlstein, Rick. "Bush White House Checked with Rapture Christians Before Latest Israel Move." *The Village Voice*, 18 May 2004.

Pew Research Center. "Trends, 2005," <www.pewresearch.org>.

Pileggi, David. "The Experiment at Artouf." *Mishkan* 12 (1990).

Pipes, Daniel. "The Clout of Christian Zionism." *American Daily: Analysis with Political and Social Commentary*, 16 July 2003, <http://www.americandaily.com/article/2431>. 15 October 2004.

——. "Review: The Politics of Christian Zionism, 1891–1948." *Middle East Quarterly* (Spring 2000).

Plesur, Milton. "The American Press and Jewish Restoration during the Nineteenth Century." In *Early History of Zionism in America*, edited by Isidore Meyer, 55–76. New York: Theodore Herzl Foundation, 1958.

Polowetsky, Michael. "Chapter 5: Laurence Oliphant Offers His Leadership." In *Jerusalem Recovered: Victorian Intellectuals and the Birth of Modern Zionism*, 119–45. Westport, Conn.: Praeger, 1995.

Popkin, Richard H. "The Christian Roots of Zionism." *Contention* 2 (Fall 1992): 113–24.

Popper, Nathaniel. "Kosher Corporation Releases a Cartoon 'Passion.'" *Forward*, 3 December 2004, 1–2.

——. "PR Group Clashes with Jerusalem on Image of Israel." *Forward*, 12 November 2004.

Portis, Larry. "The Cultural Connection: Zionism and the United States." *Counterpunch* 24/25 (February 2007), <http://www.counterpunch.org/portis02242007.html>. 5 March 2007.

Postal, Bernard, and Lionel Koppman. *American Jewish Landmarks: A Travel Guide and History.* Jewish Landmarks Series. New York: Fleet Press, 1977.

Price, Randall. *The Temple and Bible Prophecy: A Definitive Look At Its Past, Present, and Future.* Eugene: Harvest House Publishers, 2005.

Prothero, Stephen. "The Personal Jesus." *New York Times Magazine,* 29 February 2004, 26–30.

Quennell, Peter, ed. *Vladimir Nabokov: A Tribute—His Life, His Work, His World.* London: Weidenfeld and Nicolson, 1979.

Raanan, Zvi. *Gush Emunim.* Tel Aviv: Sifriat Poalim, 1980. In Hebrew.

"Rabbis Denounce Chesterton Book." *New York Times,* 31 January 1921, 1.

Rabinowicz, Harry. *The Hasidim and Israel.* Madison, N.J.: Fairleigh Dickinson University Press, 1982.

Rabkin, Yakov M. *A Threat from Within: A Century of Jewish Opposition to Zionism.* London: Zed Books, 2006.

Radler, B. "Imber." *Hatekufah* 18: 414–25. In Hebrew.

Ratsabi, Shalom. *Between Zionism and Judaism: The Radical Circle in Brith Shalom, 1925–1933.* Series in Jewish Studies, no. 23. Leiden: Brill, 2002.

Rausch, David A. "Protofundamentalism's Attitudes Toward Zionism, 1878–1918." *Jewish Social Studies* (Spring 1981).

———. *Zionism Within Early American Fundamentalism, 1878–1918: A Convergence of Two Traditions.* Vol. 4 of *Texts and Studies in Religion.* New York: Edwin Mellen Press, 1979.

Ravitsky, Aviezer. *Messianism, Zionism, and Jewish Religious Radicalism.* Chicago: University of Chicago Press, 1996.

Reilly, James. "The Peasantry of Late Ottoman Palestine." *Journal of Palestine Studies* 10 (Summer 1981): 82–97.

Reinharz, Jehuda. *Chaim Weizman: The Making of a Statesman.* New York: Oxford University Press, 1993.

Rifkin, Ira. "Theology of the Land." *Sightings,* 4 November 2004.

———. "Wrong Turn of the Century." *Jewish Week,* 21 January 2005.

Roberts, Beth E. "W. H. Auden and the Jews." *Journal of Modern Literature* 28 (Winter 2005): 87–108.

Robinson, A., ed. *The Ten Commandments: Ten Short Novels of Hitler's War Against the Moral Code.* New York: Simon & Schuster, 1944.

Robinson, Edward, and Eli Smith. *Biblical Researches in Palestine, Mt. Sinai and Arabia Petraea. A Journal of Travel in the Year 1838.* Boston: Crocker & Brewster, 1841.

Rogel, Nakdimon. *The Imber File: In the Footsteps of N. H. Imber in Eretz Israel.* Jerusalem: Mossad Bialik, 1997. In Hebrew.

Röhl, J. "Herzl and Kaiser Wilhelm II." In *Theodore Herzl and the Origins of Zionism,* edited by R. Robertson and E. Timms, 27–38. Edinburgh: Edinburgh University Press, 1997.

Rokach, Livia. *The Catholic Church and the Question of Palestine.* London: Saqi Books, 1987.

Rose, Jacqueline. "Zionism as Psychoanalysis." *BookForum* 2 (February / March 2005): 34.

Rosen. " 'Nostra Aetate,' Forty Years After Vatican II, Present and Future Perspectives," <http://www.vatican.va/roman_curia/pontifical_councils/chrstuni/relations-jews-docs/rc_pc_chrstuni_doc_20051027_rabbi-rosen_en.html>.

Rosenberg, Alfred. *Immorality in the Talmud.* London: Friends of Europe, 1937.

Rossner, Rena. "A Sea of Oil?" *Jerusalem Report,* 19 April 2004, 30.

Royal, Robert, ed. *Jacques Maritain and the Jews.* Notre Dame: University of Notre Dame Press, 1994.

Rozenak, A. *Harav Kook*. Jerusalem: The Zalman Shazar Center, 2006. In Hebrew.

Rubenstein, D. *On The Lord's Side*. Tel Aviv: Hakibbutz Hameuchad, 1982. In Hebrew.

Rubinstein, Amnon. *The Zionist Dream Revisited: From Herzl to Gush Emunim and Back*. New York: Schocken Books, 1984.

Rubinstein, Danny. "The State of Judea." *Ha'aretz*, <http://www.haaretz.com/hasen/spages/816079.html>. 22 January 2007.

Ruzer, Serve. "David Flusser: Between the Study of Christianity and the Study of Judaism." *Mahanaim: A Review for Jewish Thought and Culture* 15 (2003): 125–32.

Rynne, Xavier. *The Second Session: The Debates and Decrees of Vatican Council II*. New York: Farrar, Straus, and Giroux, 1964.

———. *The Fourth Session: The Debates and Decrees of Vatican Council II*. New York: Farrar, Straus, and Giroux, 1966.

Saddington, James A. "Prophecy and Politics: A History of Christian Zionism in the Anglo-American Experience, 1800–1948." Ph.D. diss., Bowling Green State University, 1996.

Salmon, Yosef. *Religion and Zionism: First Encounters*. Jerusalem: The Hebrew University Magnes Press, 2002.

Schapiro, I. "Imber, Naphtali Herz." In *The Dictionary of American Biography*, 459–60.

Schiff, Stacy. *Vera (Mrs. Vladimir Nabokov)*. New York: Random House, 1999.

Schleifer, Yigal. "Sharon or Bush?" *Jerusalem Report*, 6 May 2002, 16–17.

Schoffman, Gershon. "Herbert Danby." *Hadoar*, 19 November 1926.

Scholch, Alexander. "Britain in Palestine, 1832–1882: The Roots of the Balfour Policy." *Journal of Palestine Studies* 22 (Autumn 1992): 39–56.

Schulman, Samuel. "Chesterton's *The New Jerusalem* and His Jew Baiting." New York: Beth Israel Pulpit, 1921.

Schuman, Samuel. "Beautiful Gate: Vladimir Nabokov and Orthodox Iconography." *Religion and Literature* 32 (Spring 2000): 47–66.

Schwartz, Adi. "This City Is Cardinal to Him." *Ha'aretz*, 6 March 2005, <http://www.haaretz daily.com>. 10 April 2005.

Schwartz, Dov. *Challenge and Crisis in Rabbi Kook's Circle*. Tel Aviv: 'Am 'Oved, 2001.

———. *Faith at the Crossroads: A Theological Portrait of Religious Zionism*. Leiden: Brill, 2002.

Scott, E. F. "A Jewish Interpretation of Jesus." *Journal of Religion* 6 (Winter 1926): 91–95.

Segal, Haggai. *Dear Brothers*. Jerusalem: Keter, 1978.

Segev, Tom. "An Illuminating Gesture." *Ha'aretz*, 19 May 2005.

———. *1949: The First Israelis*. New York: Free Press, 1986.

Segre, Dan V. "The Pope's Millennium Visit to Israel." *Jerusalem Center for Public Affairs*, 1 June 2000, <http://www.jcpa.org/jl/jl431.htm>. 15 December 2006.

Seymour, Miranda. *Robert Graves: Life on the Edge*. New York: Henry Holt & Co., 1995.

Seymour-Smith, Martin. *Robert Graves: His Life and Work*. London: Bloomsbury Publishing, 1995.

Shadur, Joseph. *Young Travellers to Jerusalem*. Ramat Gan: Bar Ilan University, 1999.

Shamir, Milette. " 'Our Jerusalem': Americans in the Holy Land and Protestant Narratives of National Entitlement." *American Quarterly* 55 (Spring 2003): 29–60.

Shapira, Anita. "Ben Gurion and the Bible." *Middle Eastern Studies* 33, no. 4 (1997): 673–74.

———. "The Bible and Israeli Identity." *AJS Review* 28 (Spring 2004): 11–42.

Sharif, Regina. "Christians for Zion, 1600–1919." *Journal of Palestine Studies* 5 (Spring–Summer 1976): 123–41.

——. *Non-Jewish Zionism: Its Roots in Western History.* London: Zed Books, 1983.

Shepherd, Naomi. *Ploughing Sand: British Rule in Palestine, 1917–1948.* New Brunswick, N.J.: Rutgers University Press, 2000.

——. *The Zealous Intruders: The Western Rediscovery of Palestine.* San Francisco: Harper & Row, 1987.

Shilhav, Joseph, and Menachem Friedman. "Growth and Segregation: The Ultra Orthodox Community of Jerusalem." *The Jerusalem Institute for Israel Studies* 15 (1985): 1–21.

Shimoni, Gideon. *The Zionist Ideology.* Hanover, Mass.: Brandeis University Press, 1995.

Shimoni, G., and R. Wistrich, eds. *Theodor Herzl: Visionary of the Jewish State.* Jerusalem: Magnes Press, 1999.

Shimron, Yonat. "Controversial Muslim Converts Find New Platform for Book." *Religous News Service,* 3 July 2002.

Shindler, Colin. "Likud and the Christian Dispensationalists: A Symbiotic Relationship." *Israel Studies* 5 (Spring 2000): 153–82.

Shlaim, Avi. *The Iron Wall: Israel and the Arab World.* New York: W. W. Norton, 2000.

Shoham, R. *The Hard Way, Readings in the Poetry of Lebenson, Imber Bialik, Tchernihovsky and Shlonsky.* Tel Aviv: Papyrus Publishing House, 1990.

Shragai, Nadav. *The Temple Mount Conflict.* Jerusalem: Keter, 1995.

Shrayer, Maxim D. "Death, Immortality, and Nabokov's Jewish Theme." *The Nabokovian* 38 (Spring 1997): 17–25.

Siegel, Ben. *The Controversial Sholem Asch: An Introduction to His Fiction.* Bowling Green: Bowling Green State University Popular Press, 1976.

Siegel, Jennifer. "Cardinals Study With Orthodox Students." *Forward,* 31 March 2006.

Signer, Michael A. "John Paul II: Pilgrimage to the Holy Land." The Institute for Christian and Jewish Studies, <http://www.icjs.org/what/njsp/pilgrimage.htm>. 17 June 2007.

Silberschlag, Eisig. "Naphtali Herz Imber (1856–1909)." *Judaism* 5 (Spring 1956): 147–59.

Simon, Merrill. *Jerry Falwell and the Jews.* New York: Jonathan David Publishers, 1984.

Singer, David G. "American Catholic Attitudes toward the Zionist Movement and the Jewish State as Reflected in the Pages of *America, Commonweal,* and *The Catholic World,* 1945–1976." *Journal of Ecumenical Studies* 22 (Fall 1985): 715–40.

Sitwell, Edith. *English Eccentrics.* New York: Vanguard Press, 1957.

Sizer, Stephen R. *Christian Zionism: Road-Map to Armageddon?* Downers Grove: Inter-Varsity Press, 2005.

——. "Hal Lindsey: Father of Apocalyptic Christian Zionism," <http://www.virginia water.co.uk/christchurch/articles/hallindsey.HTM>.

Sloan, Rev. G. L. B. "Problems and Prospects of the Jewish Mission in Present Day Palestine." Tiberias: Archival Records, St. George's Cathedral.

Smith, Hannah Whitall. *Religious Fanaticism: Extracts from the Papers of Hanna Whithall Smith.* Edited by Ray Strachey. London: Faber and Gwyer, 1928.

Smith, Haskett. *For God and Humanity: A Romance of Mount Carmel.* Edinburgh: Blackwood, 1891.

Smith, Julie Ann. " 'My Lord's Native Land': Mapping the Christian Holy Land." *Church History* 76 (March 2007): 1–31.

Sokolow, N. *The History of Zionism, 1600–1918*. London: Longmans, Green and Co., 1919.

Sonaberg, Maria. *Ambivalent Friendship: Anglican Conflict Handling and Education for Peace in Jerusalem, 1920–1948*. Lund: Lund University, 2005.

Soulen, Kendall. "Michael Wyschogrod and God's First Love." *Christian Century*, 27 July 2004, 22–27.

Sprinzak, Ehud. *Brother Against Brother*. New York: Free Press, 1999.

Stanislawski, Michael. *Zionism and the Fin de Siècle: Cosmopolitanism and Nationalism from Nordau to Jabotinsky*. Berkeley: University of Californina Press, 2001.

Stavans, Ilan. "Borges's Zionist Bent: Newly Translated Poems." *Forward*, 2 January 2009.

———. "Why Borges Wished He Was an Israelite." *Forward*, 19 April 2004.

Stebbing, Henry. *The Christian in Palestine; or, Scenes of Sacred History, Historical and Descriptive*. London: George Virtue, 1847.

Stein, Joshua B. *Our Great Solicitor: Josiah C. Wedgwood and the Jews*. Selinsgrove: Susquehanna University Press, 1992.

Stein, Rebecca L., and Ted Swedenburg, eds. *Palestine, Israel, and the Politics of Popular Culture*. Durham: Duke University Press, 2005.

Steiner, George. *After Babel: Aspects of Language and Translation*. New York: Oxford University Press, 1975.

Sternberger, Ilse. *Princes Without a Home: Modern Zionism and the Strange Fate of Herzl's Children, 1900–1945*. San Francisco: International Scholarly Publishers, 1994.

Stewart, Desmond. "Herzl's Journeys in Palestine and Egypt." *Journal of Palestine Studies* 3, no. 3 (Spring 1974): 18–38.

Stransky, Thomas. "The Genesis of Nostra Aetate." *America, The National Catholic Weekly*, 24 October 2005.

———. "A Trouble Past and Present." *First Things* (March 2002): 57–60.

Sutherland, John. "Apocalypse Now." *London Review of Books*, 12 June 2003.

Sykes, Christopher. *Crossroads to Israel*. Bloomington: Indiana University Press, 1965.

———. *Two Studies in Virtue*. New York: Knopf, 1953.

Szold, Henrietta. *Recent Jewish Progress in Palestine*. America and the Holy Land. New York: Arno Press, 1977.

Taylor, Alan R. "Zionism and Jewish History." *Journal of Palestine Studies* 1 (Winter 1972): 35–51.

Taylor, Anne. *Laurence Oliphant, 1828–1888*. London: Oxford University Press, 1982.

Tessler, Mark. *A History of the Israeli-Palestinian Conflict*. Bloomington: Indiana University Press, 1994.

Toker, Leona. *Nabokov: The Mystery of Literary Structures*. Ithaca: Cornell University Press, 1989.

Tolson, Jay. "The New Old-Time Religion." *U.S. News and World Report*, 8 December 2003, 38–44.

Tuchman, Barbara. *Bible and Sword: England and Palestine from the Bronze Age to Balfour*. New York: New York University Press, 1956.

Turner, F. M. *John Henry Newman*. New Haven: Yale University Press, 2002.

Uriel: A Magazine of Cabbalistic Science. Boston, 1895. Edited by N. H. Imber.

Uris, Leon. *Exodus*. Garden City, N.Y.: Doubleday, 1958.

Vambrey, Arminius. *Arminius Vambrey: His Life and Adventures / Written by Himself; With Portrait and Illustrations*. 3rd ed. London: T. Fisher Unwin, 1884.

——. *The Story of My Stuggles*. London: Unwin, 1904.

Vereté, Mayir. "The Idea of the Restoration of the Jews." In *From Palmerston to Balfour: Collected Essays of Mayir Vereté*. London: Frank Cass Publishers, 1992.

Vester, Bertha Spafford. *Our Jerusalem: An American Family in the Holy City, 1881–1949*. America and the Holy Land. Garden City, N.Y.: Doubleday, 1950.

Vickery, John B. *Robert Graves and the White Goddess*. Lincoln: University of Nebraska Press, 1972.

Vital, David. *The Origins of Zionism*. Oxford: Clarendon Press, 1975.

Vogel, Lester Irwin. *To See a Promised Land: Americans and the Holy Land in the Nineteenth Century*. University Park: Pennsylvania State University Press, 1993.

Voss, Carl Hermann. *Rabbi and Minister: The Friendship of Stephen S. Wise and John Haynes Holmes*. Cleveland: World Publishing Company, 1964.

Wagner, Donald. "A Heavenly Match: Bush and the Christian Zionists." *Daily Star*, 11 October 2003.

——. "Bible and Sword: US Christian Zionists Discover Israel." *Daily Star*, 9 October 2003.

——. "Christians and Zion: British Stirrings." *Daily Star*, 7 October 2003.

——. "Christian Zionists, Israel and the 'Second Coming.'" *Daily Star*, 8 October 2003.

——. "The Interregnum: Christian Zionism in the Clinton Years." *Daily Star*, 10 October 2003.

——. "Short Fuse to Apocalypse?" *Sojourners Magazine*, July–August 2003.

Wallis, Jim. *God's Politics: Why the Right Gets It Wrong and the Left Doesn't Get It*. San Francisco: Harper, 2005.

Walsh, Andrew. "Two Cheers for the Pilgrimage." *Religion in the News* 3, no. 2 (Summer 2000), <http://www.trincoll.edu/depts/csrpl/RINVol3No2/pope_pilgrimage.htm>.

Walt, Stephen M., and John J. Mearsheimer. *The Israel Lobby and U.S. Foreign Policy*. London: Allen Lane, 2007.

Walvoord, John F. *Israel in Prophecy*. Grand Rapids: Zondervan Publishing House, 1962.

Wasserstein, Bernard. *Divided Jerusalem: The Struggle for the Holy City*. London: Profile Books, 2001.

Weaver, Alain Epp. "Israel: Demography of the Land." *Sightings*, <http://marty-center.uchicago.edu/sightings/archive_2004/1118.shtml>. 18 November 2004.

Webber, Sabra J. "Inventing Palestine: Review of Imagining the Holy Land: Maps, Models, and Fantasy Travels." *H-Net: Humanities & Social Sciences Online* (2004).

Weber, Timothy P. *On the Road to Armageddon: How Evangelicals Became Israel's Best Friend*. Grand Rapids: Baker Academic, 2005.

Wedgwood, Julia. *Nineteenth Century Teachers, and Other Essays*. London: Hodder and Stoughton, 1909.

Weiman, Racelle R. "From Recognition to Reconciliation: The Catholic Church and the Jewish State." Ph.D. diss., Temple University, 1996.

Weinberger, Moses, and Jonathan D. Sarna. *People Walk on Their Heads: Moses Weinberger's Jews and Judaism in New York*. New York: Holmes & Meier Publishers, 1982.

Weiss, Timothy. *Translating Orients: Between Ideology and Utopia*. Toronto: University of Toronto Press, 2004.

Weller, Robert. "Arrests Won't Deter Cult, Members' Relatives Warn." *Atlanta Journal-Constitution*, 4 January 1999.

Werblowsky, Z. "Jewish Messianism." *Encyclopedia of Religion*, 9:473.

Whale, John. "Tribulations." *Times Literary Supplement*, 4 February 2005, 9.

White, Gayle. "Christian Zionists Win Jews for GOP." *Atlanta Journal-Constitution*, 9 May 2004, A1, A5.

———. "Faith Rooted in the Past—and Prophecy." *Atlanta Journal-Constitution*, 2 January 1999, F4.

———. "Yes, Jesus Was Jewish." *Atlanta Journal-Constitution*, 2 January 1999, F4.

Whitley, H. C. *Blinded Eagle: An Introduction to the Life and Teaching of Edward Irving.* London: SCM Press, 1955.

Wicks, Ben. *Dawn of the Promised Land.* New York: Hyperion Books, 1997.

Wikipedia. "Tom Delay Wikipedia." BlinkBits (29 September 2005), <http://www.blinkbits .com/bits/viewtopic/tom_delay_wikipedia?t=617305>. 22 August 2007.

Wilk, G. H. "The Bohemian Who Wrote *Hatikvah*: The Career of Naphtali Herz Imber." *Commentary*, January 1951, 48–60.

Wilken, Robert Louis. *The Land Called Holy: Palestine in Christian History and Thought.* New Haven: Yale University Press, 1992.

Wilkinson, Paul Richard. *For Zion's Sake: Christian Zionism and the Role of John Nelson Darby.* Colorado Springs: Paternoster, 2007.

Williamson, Edwin. *Borges: A Life.* New York: Penguin, 2005.

Wise, Stephen. *Challenging Years: The Autobiography of Stephen Wise.* New York: Putnam's Sons, 1949.

Witt, Louise. "Onward, Christian Soldiers." *Salon*, <http://dir.salon.com/story/news/feature/2003/01/03/christian/index.html>. 3 January 2003.

Wohlberg, Steve. *End Time Delusions: The Rapture, the Antichrist, Israel, and the End of the World.* Shippensberg: Treasure House, 2004.

Wolf, Arnold J. "Israel as the False Messiah." *Conservative Judaism* 41, no. 3 (Spring 1988): 55–58.

Wolfe, A. "The Opening of the Evangelical Mind." *Atlantic Monthly*, October 2000, 55–76.

Wood, Michael. *The Magician's Doubts.* London: Chatto & Windus, 1994.

Woodall, James. *Borges: A Life.* New York: Basic Books, 1996.

Wurzburger, Walter S. "Theological Implications of the State of Israel: The Jewish View— Messianic Perspectives." In *Encyclopedia Judaica: Year Book 1974*, edited by Cecil Roth, 148–66. Jerusalem: Keter, 1974.

Yahuda, A. S. "Hechler." *Jewish Forum* 30, no. 3 (March 1947): 1–4.

Yardeni, Galia. "N. H. Imber and Laurence Oliphant." *Molad* 187–88 (1964): 41–50.

Yehezkel, Mordechai ben. "Vayehi Hayom." In *Bialik: Critical Essays on His Works*, edited by Gershom Shaked, 337–72. Tel Aviv: Mossad Bialik, 1974.

Yehoash (Solomon Baumgarten). *The Feet of the Messenger.* America and the Holy Land. New York: Arno Press, 1977.

Yellin, D. "Eliezer ben Yehuda." *Journal of the Palestinian Oriental Society* 15 (1935).

Yoffie, Eric, and Paul Menitoff. "Letter to the Presbyterian Leadership." *Central Conference of American Rabbis*, <http://ccarnet.org/Articles/index.cfm?id=48>.

Zangwill, Israel. *Children of the Ghetto: A Study of a Peculiar People.* Edited by M. Rochelson. Detroit: Wayne University Press, 1998.

——. "The Return to Palestine." *The New Liberal Review* 2 (December 1901): 615–34.

Zavylov-Leving, Yuri. "Phantom in Jerusalem, or the History of an Unrealized Visit." *The Nabokovian* 37 (Fall 1996): 31–43.

Ze'evi, Rehavam., ed. *L. Oliphant's Haifa*. Translated by Y. Burla. Jerusalem: Ben Zvi Institute, 1976. In Hebrew.

Zeldin, G. *Catholics and Protestants in Jerusalem and the Return of the Jews to Zion*. Ph.D. diss., The Hebrew University of Jerusalem, 1992.

Zohn, Harry. "Herzl, Hechler and the Grand Duke." *Herzl Year Book*. New York: Herzl Press, 1964.

Zoll, Rachel. "Opponents of Israel Policy Debate Divestment." *Atlanta Journal-Constitution*, 23 October 2004.

Index